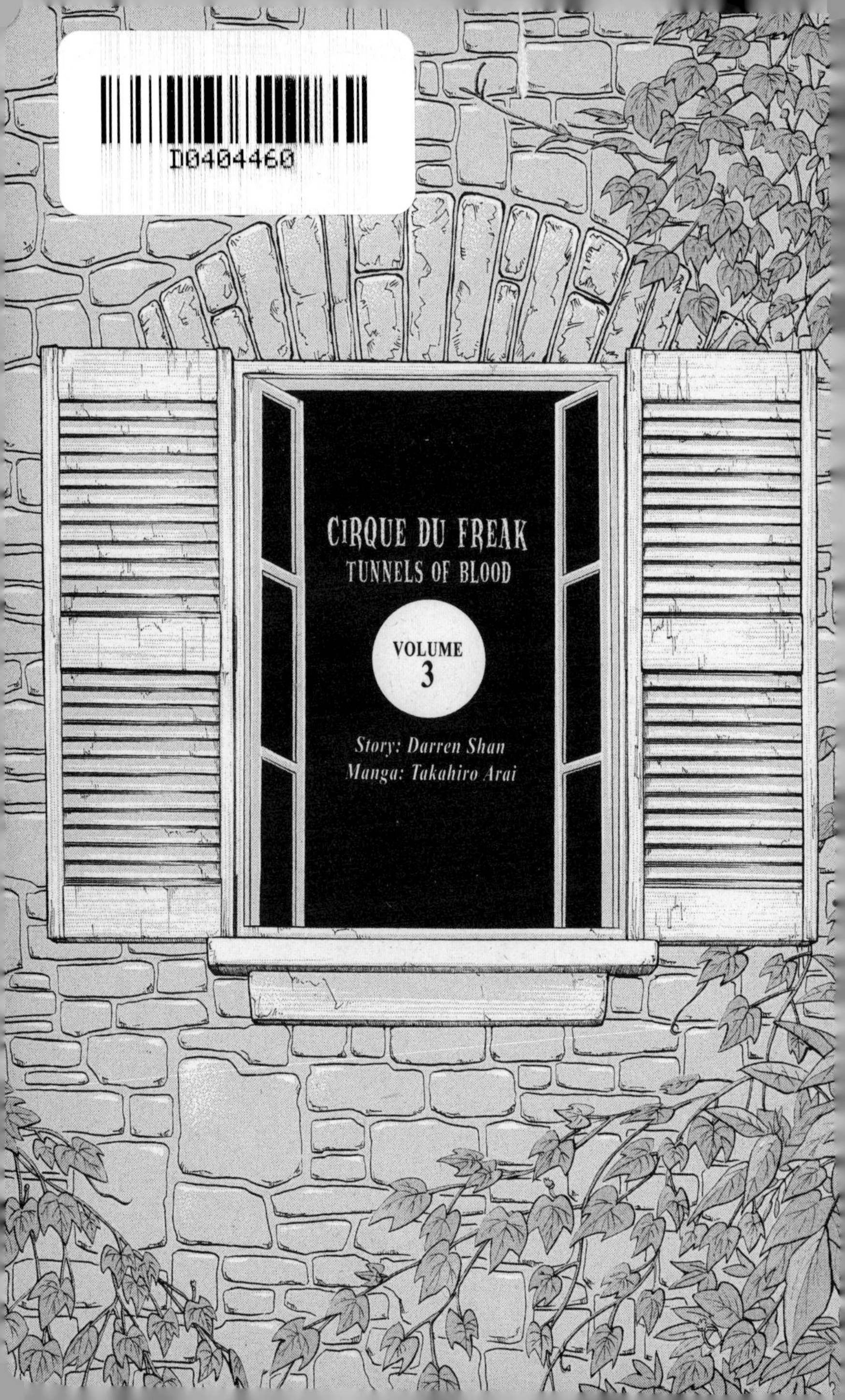
CIRQUE DU FREAK
TUNNELS OF BLOOD
VOLUME 3
Story: Darren Shan
Manga: Takahiro Arai

A SUMMARY OF THE VAMPIRE'S ASSISTANT:

DARREN SHAN IS TURNED INTO A HALF-VAMPIRE IN ORDER TO SAVE HIS BEST FRIEND'S LIFE. HIS PEACEFUL LIFE GONE, DARREN STARTS ANEW WITH HIS MASTER, MR. CREPSLEY, AS A MEMBER OF THE CIRQUE DU FREAK. THOUGH HE MAKES TWO NEW FRIENDS THERE IN EVRA VON, THE SNAKE-BOY, AND SAM GREST, HIS HAPPY NEW ARRANGEMENT IS SHATTERED WHEN THE CIRQUE'S CHAINED WOLF-MAN ESCAPES AND KILLS SAM. BURDENED WITH A TERRIBLE SADNESS, DARREN RETREATS INTO THE DARKNESS AGAIN...

CIRQUE DU FREAK 3
CONTENTS

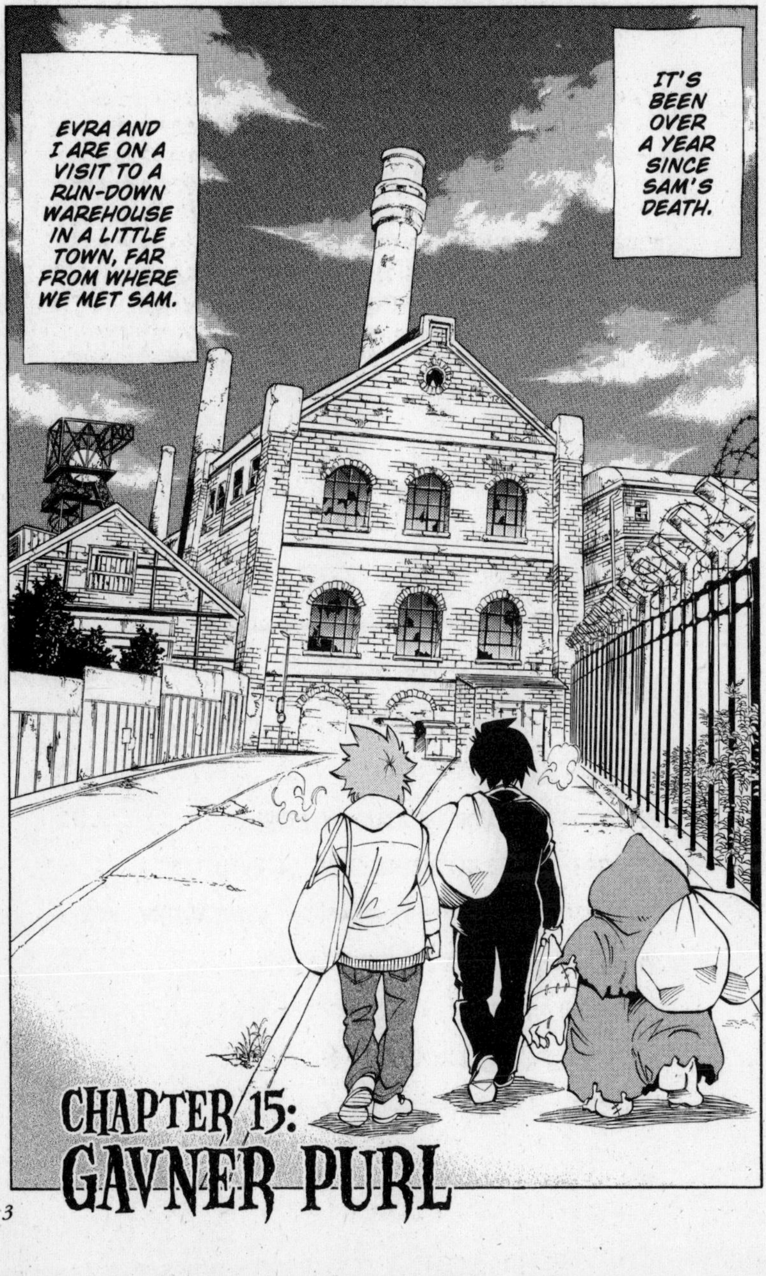
IT'S BEEN OVER A YEAR SINCE SAM'S DEATH.
EVRA AND I ARE ON A VISIT TO A RUN-DOWN WAREHOUSE IN A LITTLE TOWN, FAR FROM WHERE WE MET SAM.
CHAPTER 15: GAVNER PURL

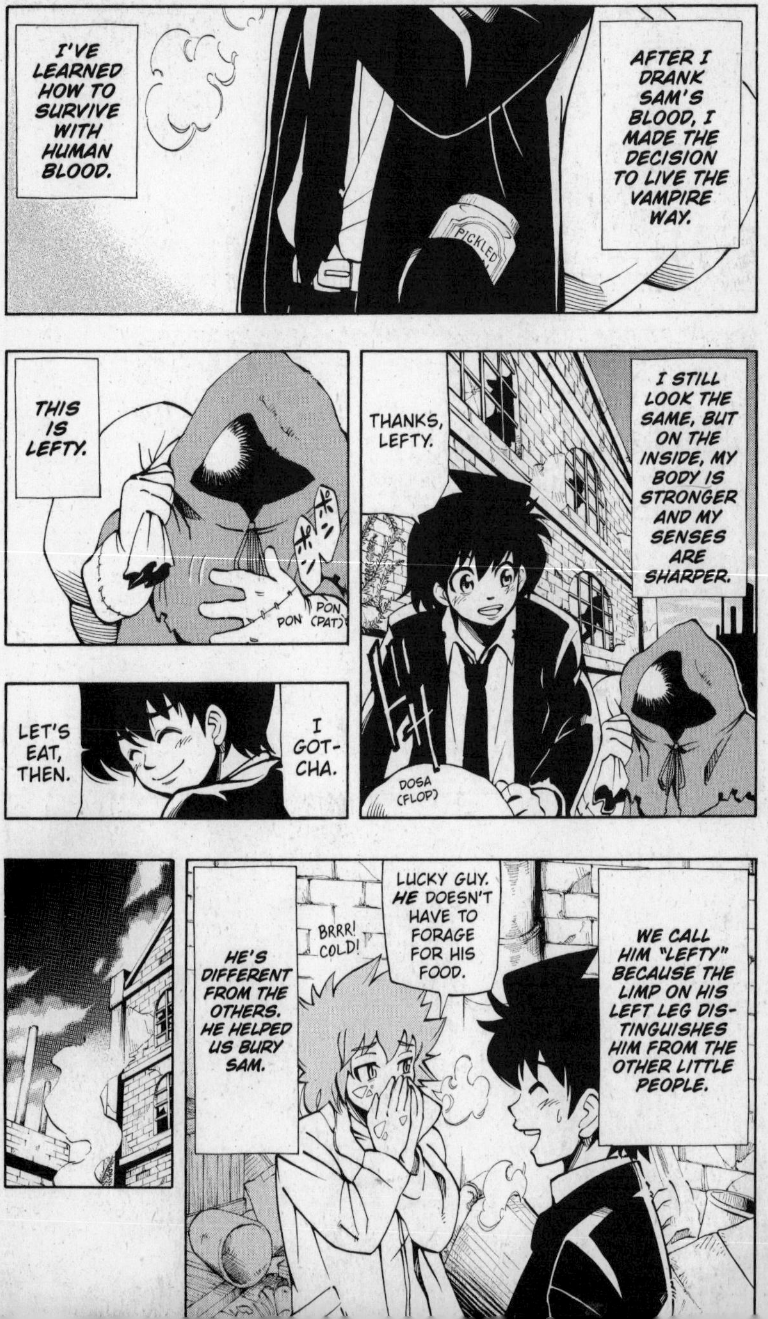
AFTER I DRANK SAM'S BLOOD, I MADE THE DECISION TO LIVE THE VAMPIRE WAY.
PICKLED
I'VE LEARNED HOW TO SURVIVE WITH HUMAN BLOOD.
I STILL LOOK THE SAME, BUT ON THE INSIDE, MY BODY IS STRONGER AND MY SENSES ARE SHARPER.
THANKS, LEFTY.
DOSA (FLOP)
THIS IS LEFTY.
PON PON (PAT)
I GOT-CHA.
LET'S EAT, THEN.
WE CALL HIM "LEFTY" BECAUSE THE LIMP ON HIS LEFT LEG DIS-TINGUISHES HIM FROM THE OTHER LITTLE PEOPLE.
LUCKY GUY. HE DOESN'T HAVE TO FORAGE FOR HIS FOOD.
BRRR! COLD!
HE'S DIFFERENT FROM THE OTHERS. HE HELPED US BURY SAM.

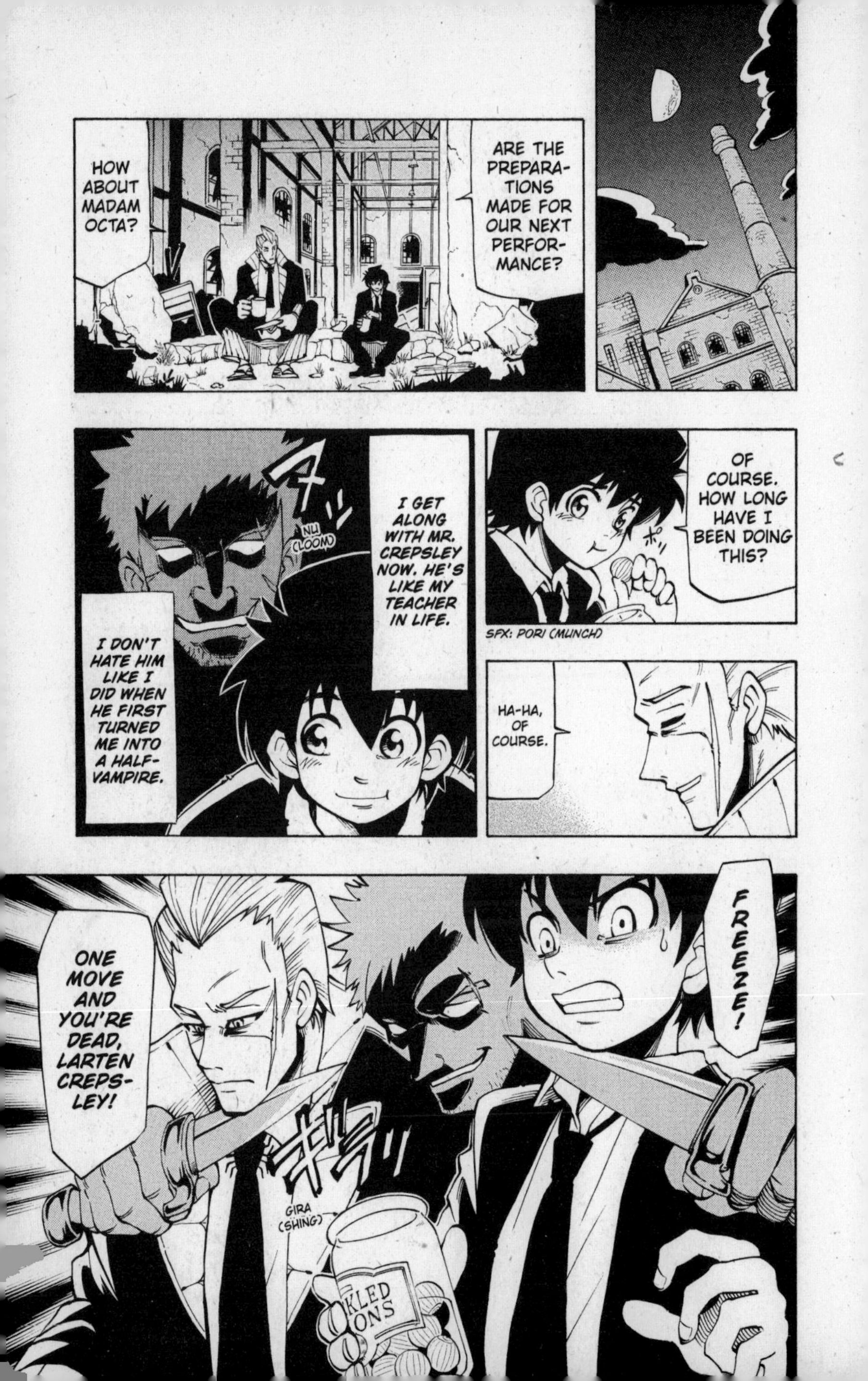
ARE THE PREPARATIONS MADE FOR OUR NEXT PERFORMANCE?
HOW ABOUT MADAM OCTA?
OF COURSE. HOW LONG HAVE I BEEN DOING THIS?
SFX: PORI (MUNCH)
HA-HA, OF COURSE.
I GET ALONG WITH MR. CREPSLEY NOW. HE'S LIKE MY TEACHER IN LIFE.
NU (LOOM)
I DON'T HATE HIM LIKE I DID WHEN HE FIRST TURNED ME INTO A HALF-VAMPIRE.
FREEZE!
ONE MOVE AND YOU'RE DEAD, LARTEN CREPSLEY!
GIRA (SHING)
KLED
ONS

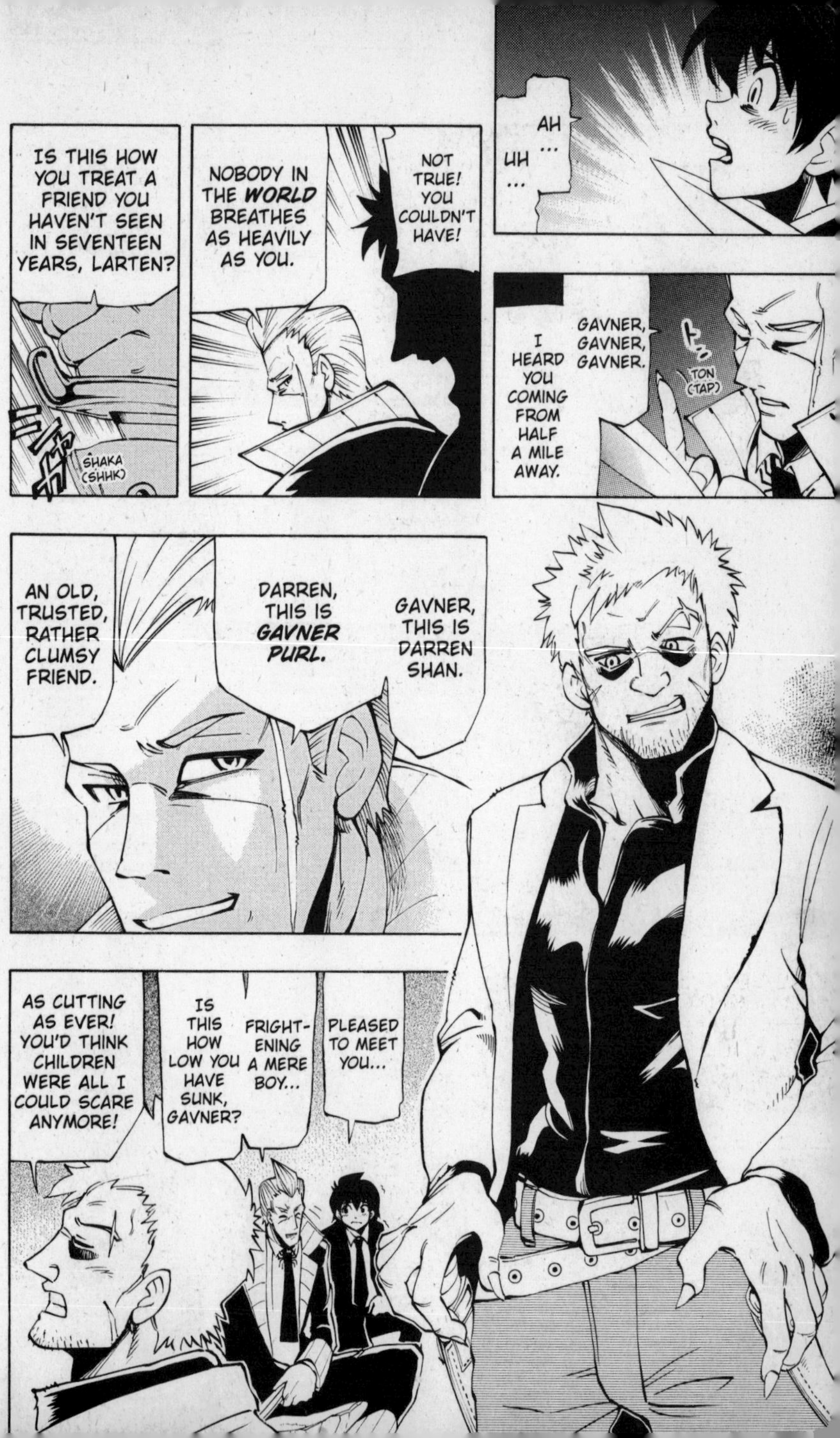
AH ... UH ...
GAVNER, GAVNER, GAVNER.
I HEARD YOU COMING FROM HALF A MILE AWAY.
TON (TAP)
NOT TRUE! YOU COULDN'T HAVE!
NOBODY IN THE WORLD BREATHES AS HEAVILY AS YOU.
IS THIS HOW YOU TREAT A FRIEND YOU HAVEN'T SEEN IN SEVENTEEN YEARS, LARTEN?
SHAKA (SHHK)
GAVNER, THIS IS DARREN SHAN.
DARREN, THIS IS GAVNER PURL.
AN OLD, TRUSTED, RATHER CLUMSY FRIEND.
PLEASED TO MEET YOU...
FRIGHT-ENING A MERE BOY...
IS THIS HOW LOW YOU HAVE SUNK, GAVNER?
AS CUTTING AS EVER! YOU'D THINK CHILDREN WERE ALL I COULD SCARE ANYMORE!

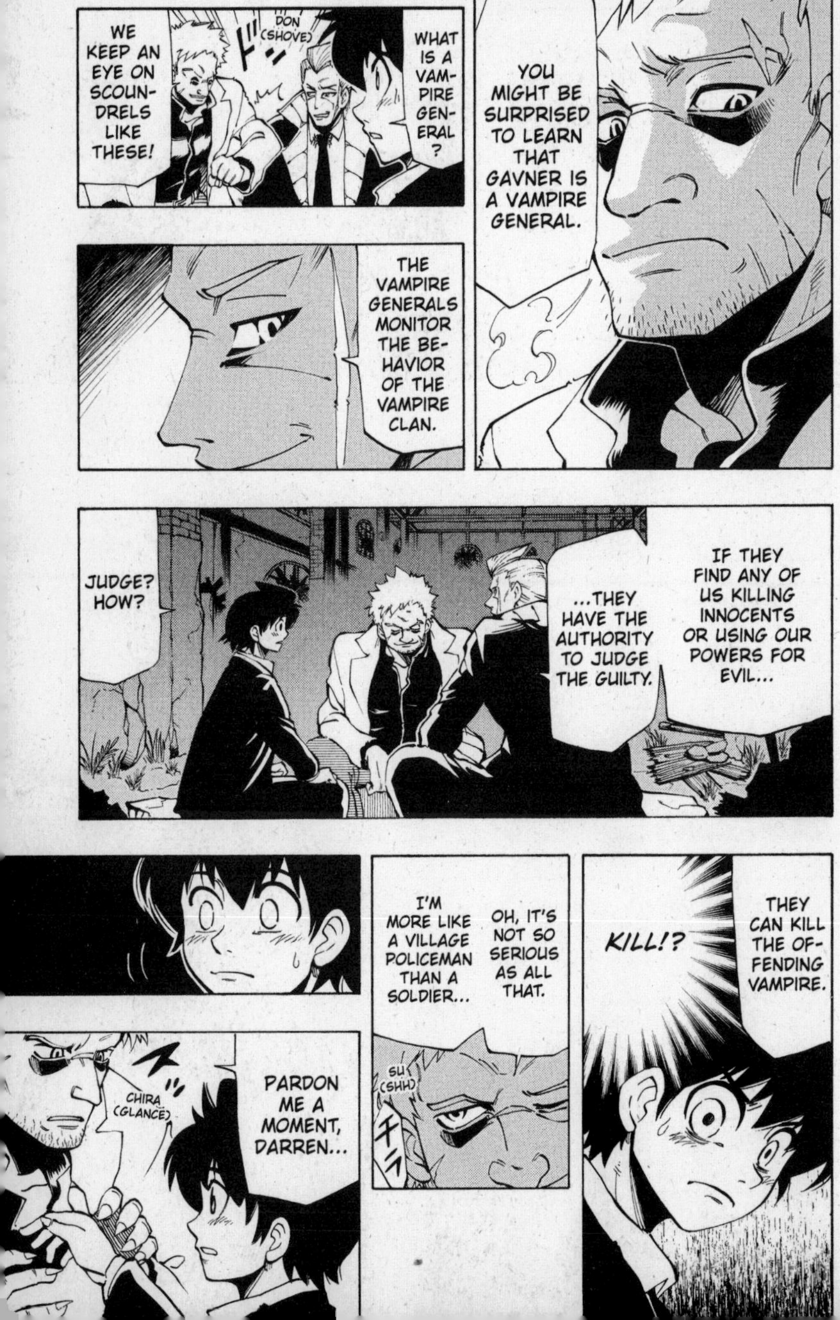
YOU MIGHT BE SURPRISED TO LEARN THAT GAVNER IS A VAMPIRE GENERAL.
WHAT IS A VAM-PIRE GEN-ERAL?
DON (SHOVE)
WE KEEP AN EYE ON SCOUN-DRELS LIKE THESE!
THE VAMPIRE GENERALS MONITOR THE BE-HAVIOR OF THE VAMPIRE CLAN.
IF THEY FIND ANY OF US KILLING INNOCENTS OR USING OUR POWERS FOR EVIL...
...THEY HAVE THE AUTHORITY TO JUDGE THE GUILTY.
JUDGE? HOW?
THEY CAN KILL THE OF-FENDING VAMPIRE.
KILL!?
OH, IT'S NOT SO SERIOUS AS ALL THAT.
I'M MORE LIKE A VILLAGE POLICEMAN THAN A SOLDIER...
SU (SHH)
PARDON ME A MOMENT, DARREN...
CHIRA (GLANCE)

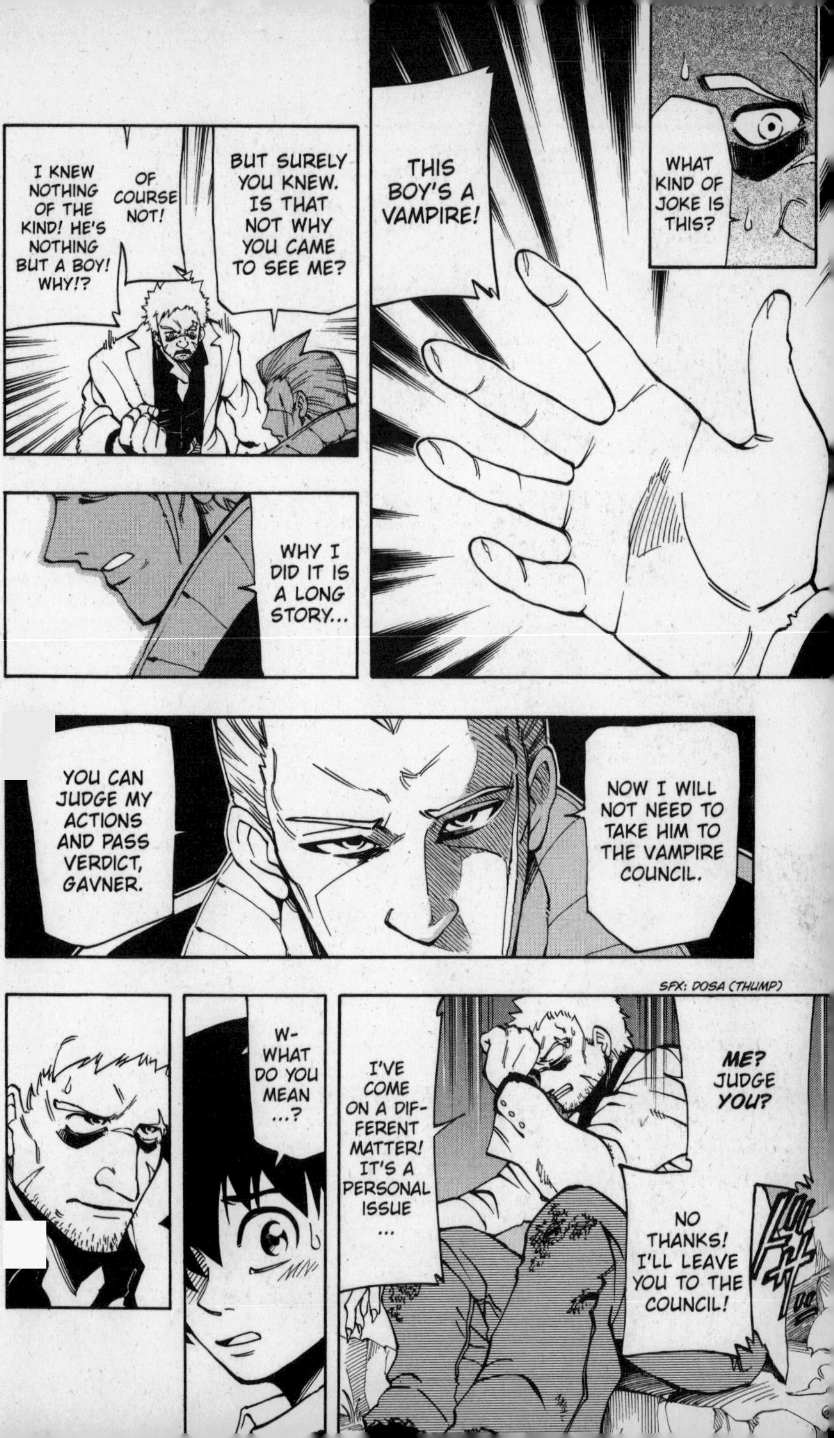
WHAT KIND OF JOKE IS THIS?
THIS BOY'S A VAMPIRE!
BUT SURELY YOU KNEW. IS THAT NOT WHY YOU CAME TO SEE ME?
OF COURSE NOT!
I KNEW NOTHING OF THE KIND! HE'S NOTHING BUT A BOY! WHY!?
WHY I DID IT IS A LONG STORY...
NOW I WILL NOT NEED TO TAKE HIM TO THE VAMPIRE COUNCIL.
YOU CAN JUDGE MY ACTIONS AND PASS VERDICT, GAVNER.
SFX: DOSA (THUMP)
ME? JUDGE YOU?
NO THANKS! I'LL LEAVE YOU TO THE COUNCIL!
I'VE COME ON A DIF-FERENT MATTER! IT'S A PERSONAL ISSUE ...
W-WHAT DO YOU MEAN ...?

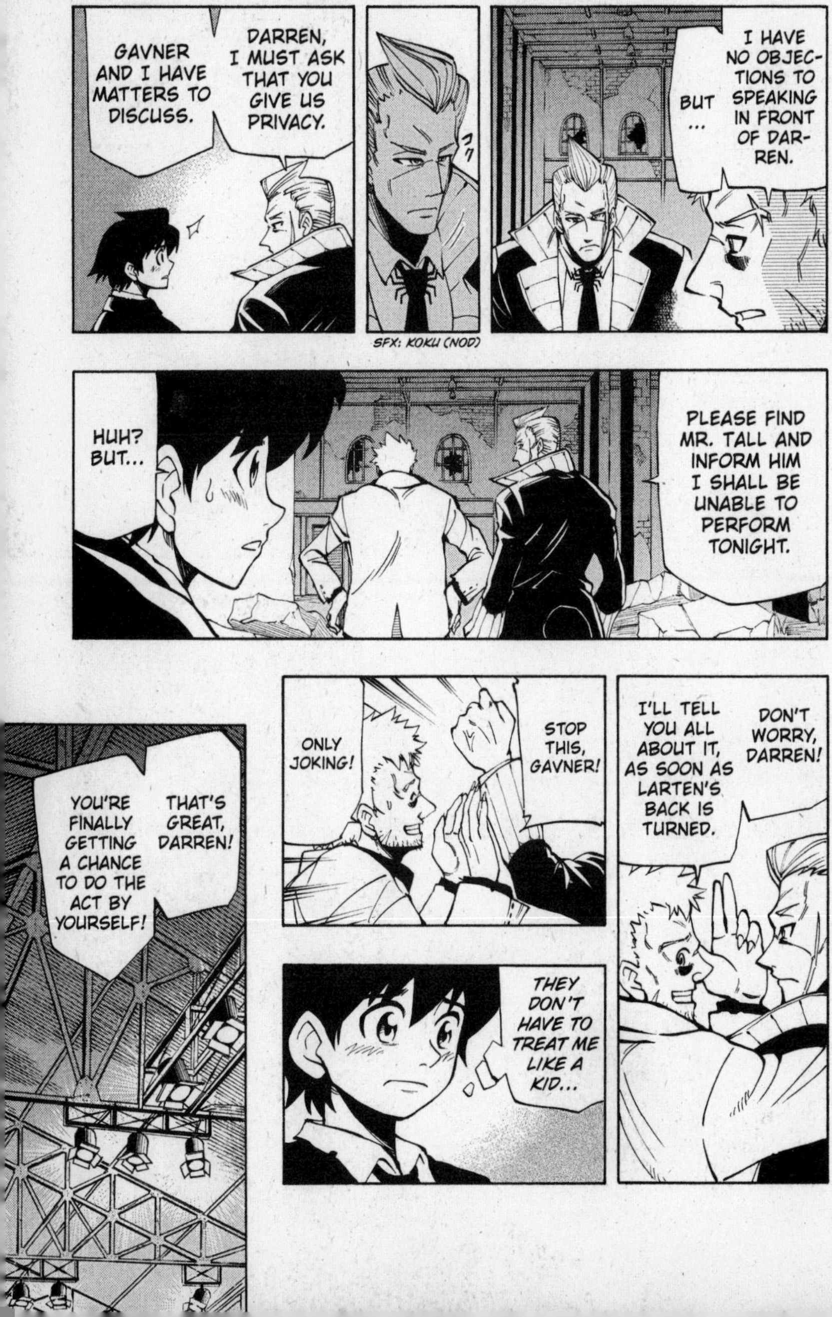
BUT ...
I HAVE NO OBJECTIONS TO SPEAKING IN FRONT OF DARREN.
SFX: KOKU (NOD)
DARREN, I MUST ASK THAT YOU GIVE US PRIVACY.
GAVNER AND I HAVE MATTERS TO DISCUSS.
PLEASE FIND MR. TALL AND INFORM HIM I SHALL BE UNABLE TO PERFORM TONIGHT.
HUH? BUT...
DON'T WORRY, DARREN!
I'LL TELL YOU ALL ABOUT IT, AS SOON AS LARTEN'S BACK IS TURNED.
STOP THIS, GAVNER!
ONLY JOKING!
THEY DON'T HAVE TO TREAT ME LIKE A KID...
THAT'S GREAT, DARREN!
YOU'RE FINALLY GETTING A CHANCE TO DO THE ACT BY YOURSELF!

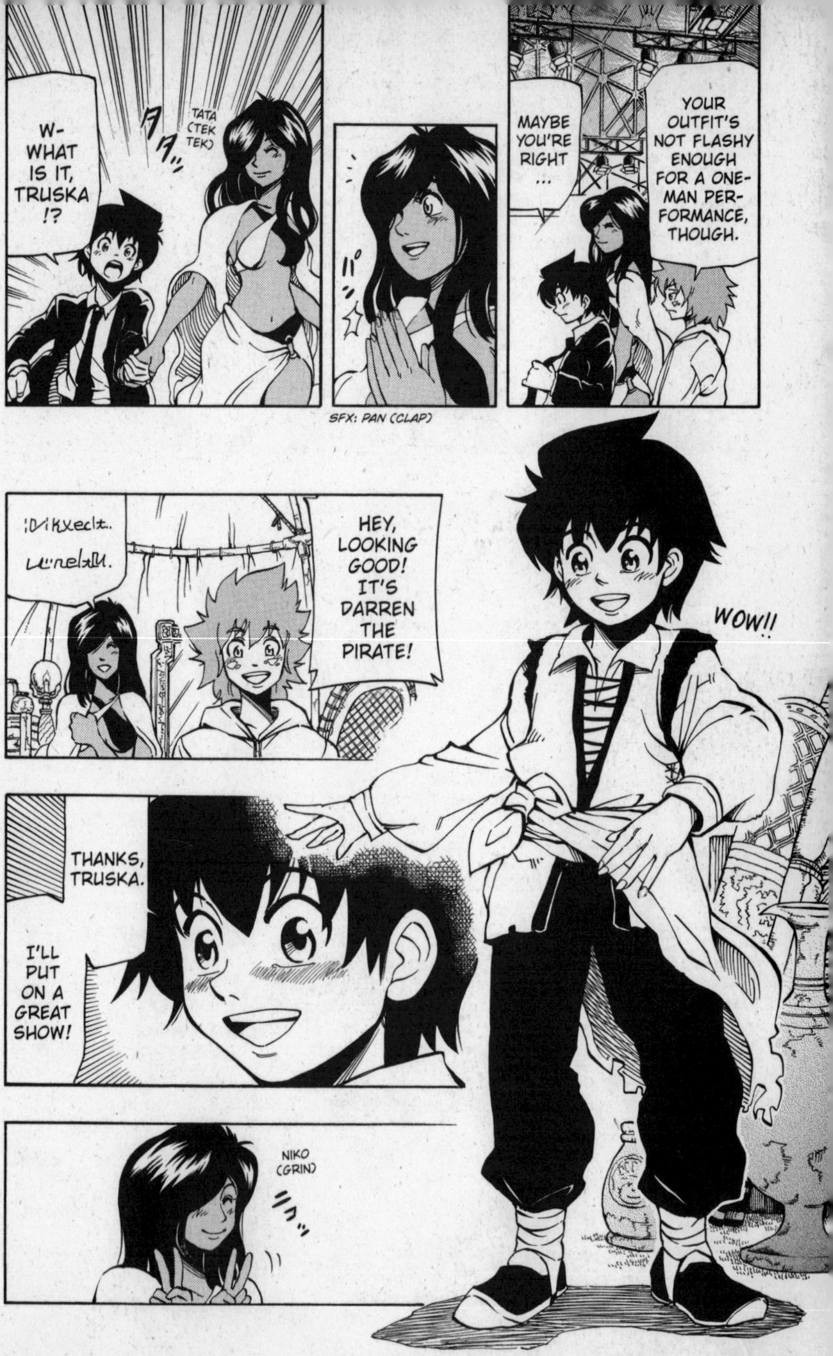
YOUR OUTFIT'S NOT FLASHY ENOUGH FOR A ONE-MAN PERFORMANCE, THOUGH.
MAYBE YOU'RE RIGHT ...
SFX: PAN (CLAP)
TATA (TEK TEK)
W-WHAT IS IT, TRUSKA!?
WOW!!
HEY, LOOKING GOOD! IT'S DARREN THE PIRATE!
THANKS, TRUSKA.
I'LL PUT ON A GREAT SHOW!
NIKO (GRIN)

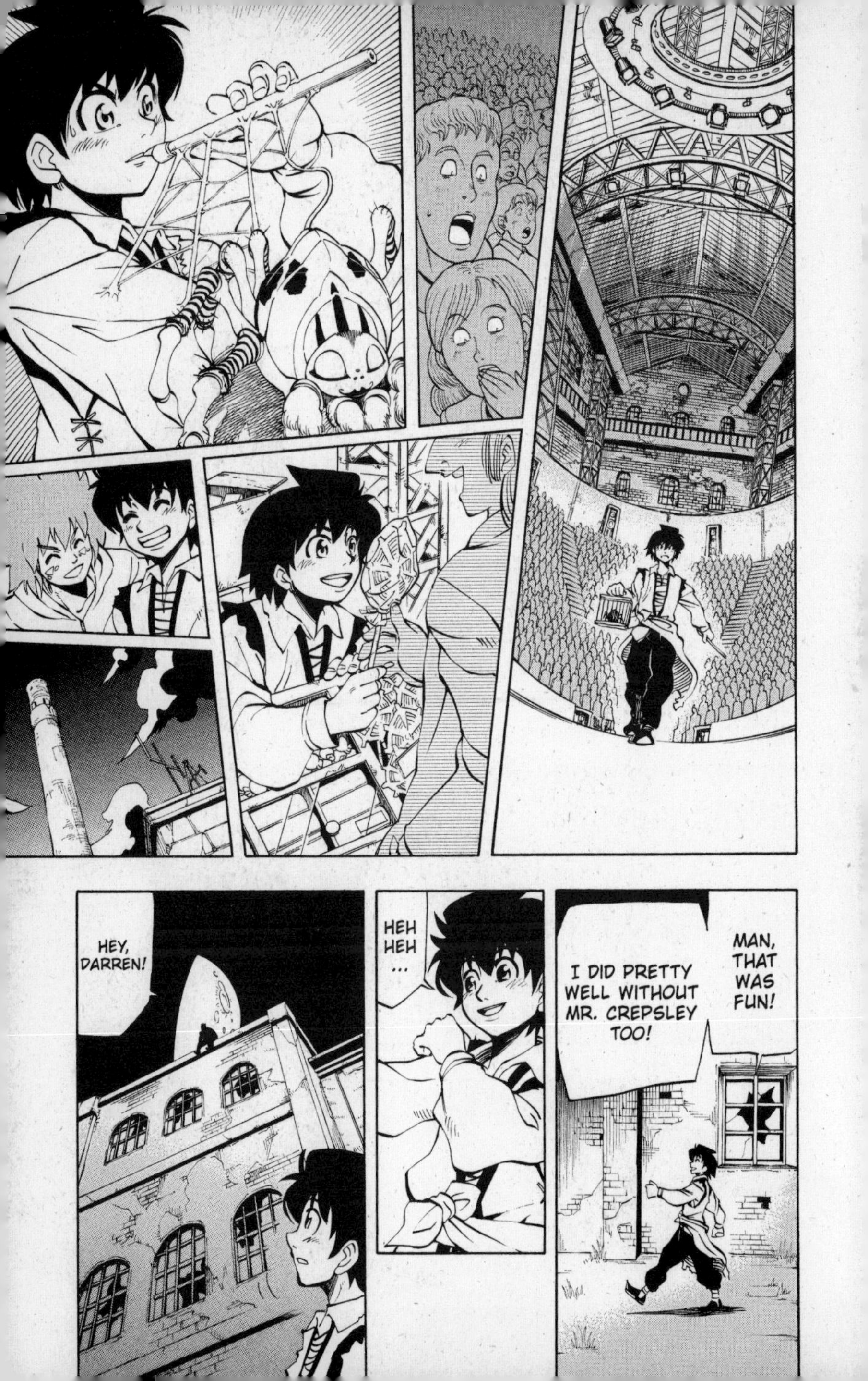
MAN, THAT WAS FUN!
I DID PRETTY WELL WITHOUT MR. CREPSLEY TOO!
HEH HEH ...
HEY, DARREN!

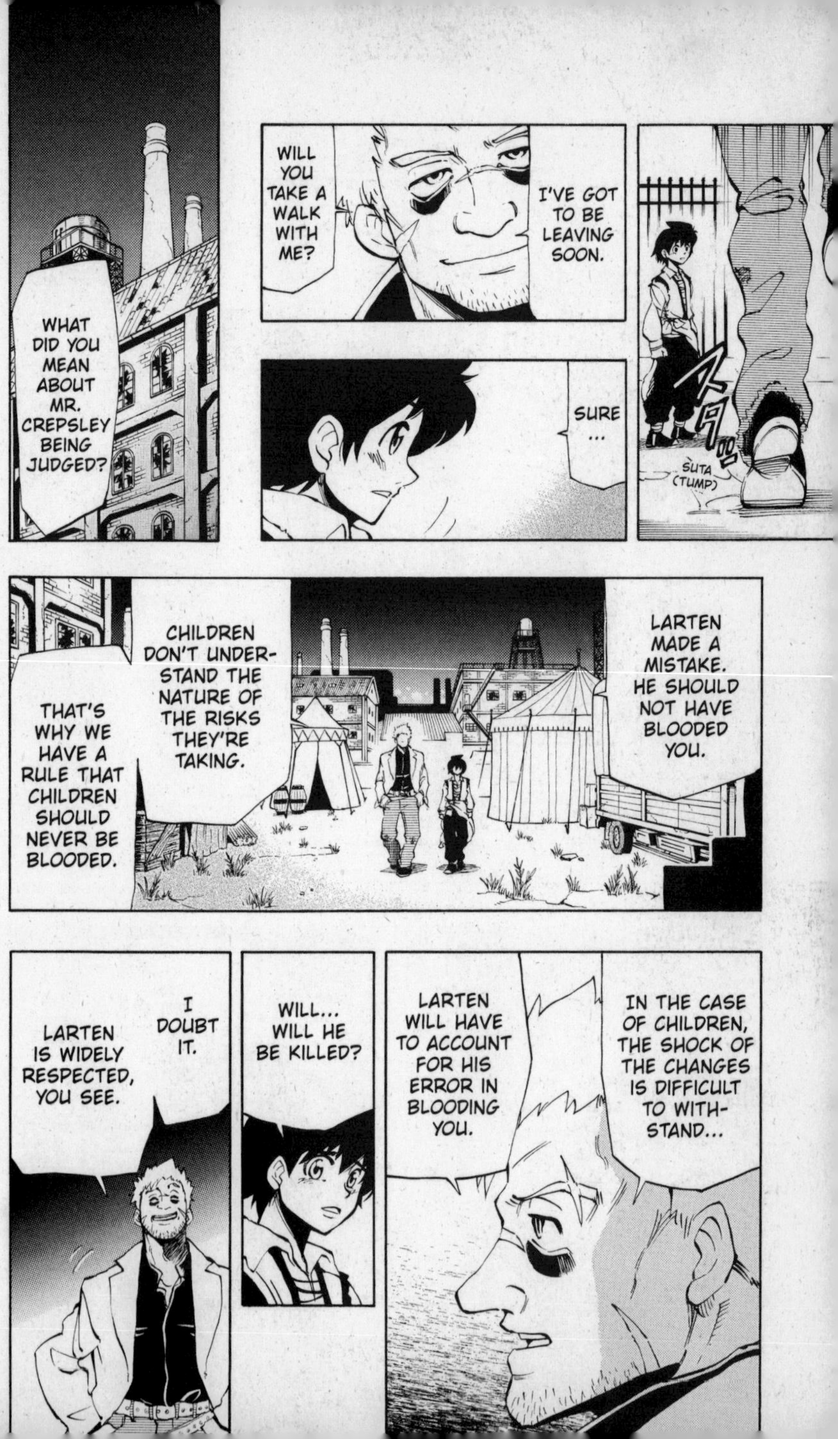
SUTA (TUMP)
I'VE GOT TO BE LEAVING SOON.
WILL YOU TAKE A WALK WITH ME?
SURE ...
WHAT DID YOU MEAN ABOUT MR. CREPSLEY BEING JUDGED?
LARTEN MADE A MISTAKE. HE SHOULD NOT HAVE BLOODED YOU.
CHILDREN DON'T UNDER-STAND THE NATURE OF THE RISKS THEY'RE TAKING.
THAT'S WHY WE HAVE A RULE THAT CHILDREN SHOULD NEVER BE BLOODED.
IN THE CASE OF CHILDREN, THE SHOCK OF THE CHANGES IS DIFFICULT TO WITH-STAND...
LARTEN WILL HAVE TO ACCOUNT FOR HIS ERROR IN BLOODING YOU.
WILL... WILL HE BE KILLED?
I DOUBT IT.
LARTEN IS WIDELY RESPECTED, YOU SEE.

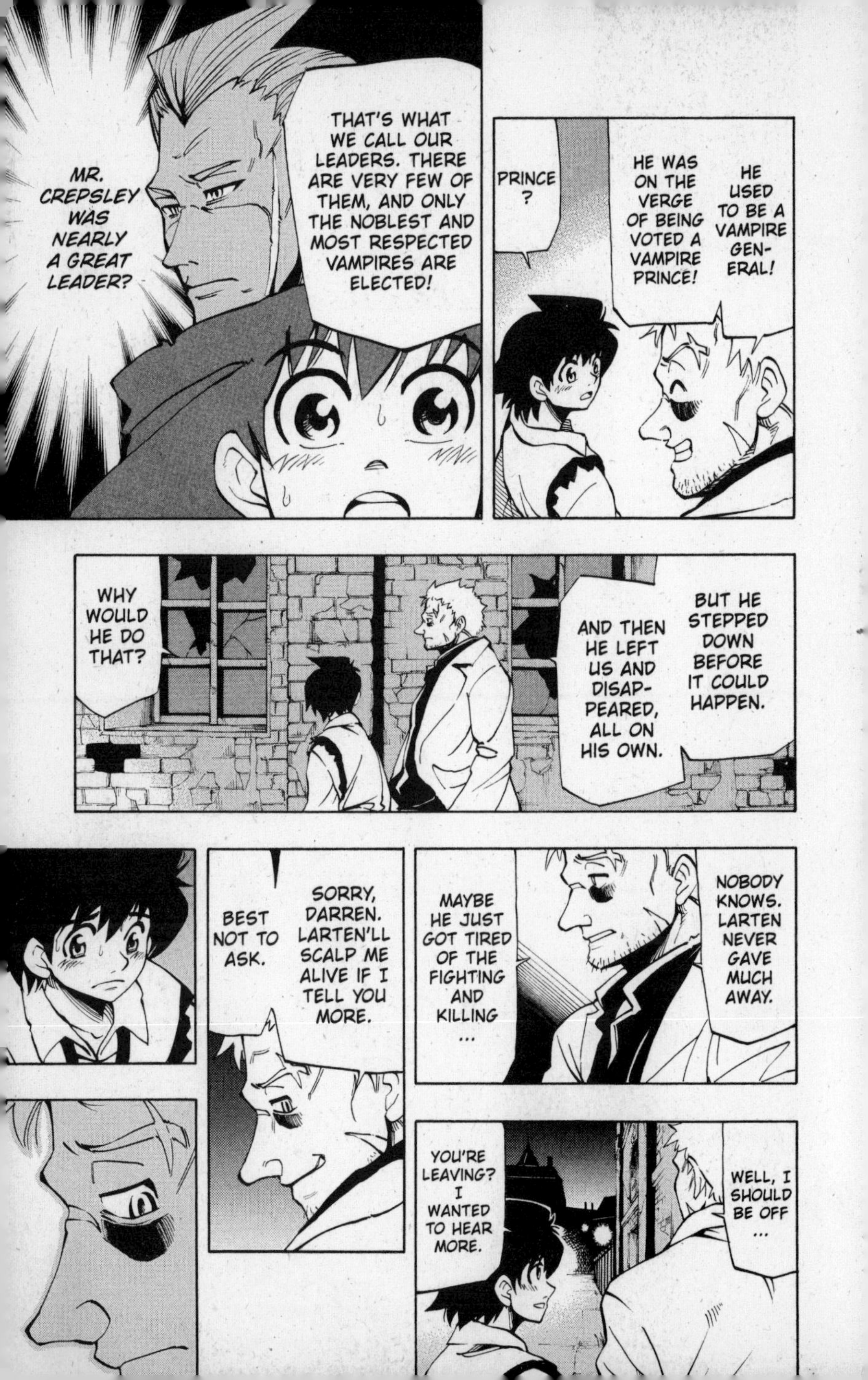
HE USED TO BE A VAMPIRE GENERAL!
HE WAS ON THE VERGE OF BEING VOTED A VAMPIRE PRINCE!
PRINCE?
THAT'S WHAT WE CALL OUR LEADERS. THERE ARE VERY FEW OF THEM, AND ONLY THE NOBLEST AND MOST RESPECTED VAMPIRES ARE ELECTED!
MR. CREPSLEY WAS NEARLY A GREAT LEADER?
BUT HE STEPPED DOWN BEFORE IT COULD HAPPEN.
AND THEN HE LEFT US AND DISAPPEARED, ALL ON HIS OWN.
WHY WOULD HE DO THAT?
NOBODY KNOWS. LARTEN NEVER GAVE MUCH AWAY.
MAYBE HE JUST GOT TIRED OF THE FIGHTING AND KILLING ...
WELL, I SHOULD BE OFF ...
YOU'RE LEAVING? I WANTED TO HEAR MORE.
SORRY, DARREN. LARTEN'LL SCALP ME ALIVE IF I TELL YOU MORE.
BEST NOT TO ASK.

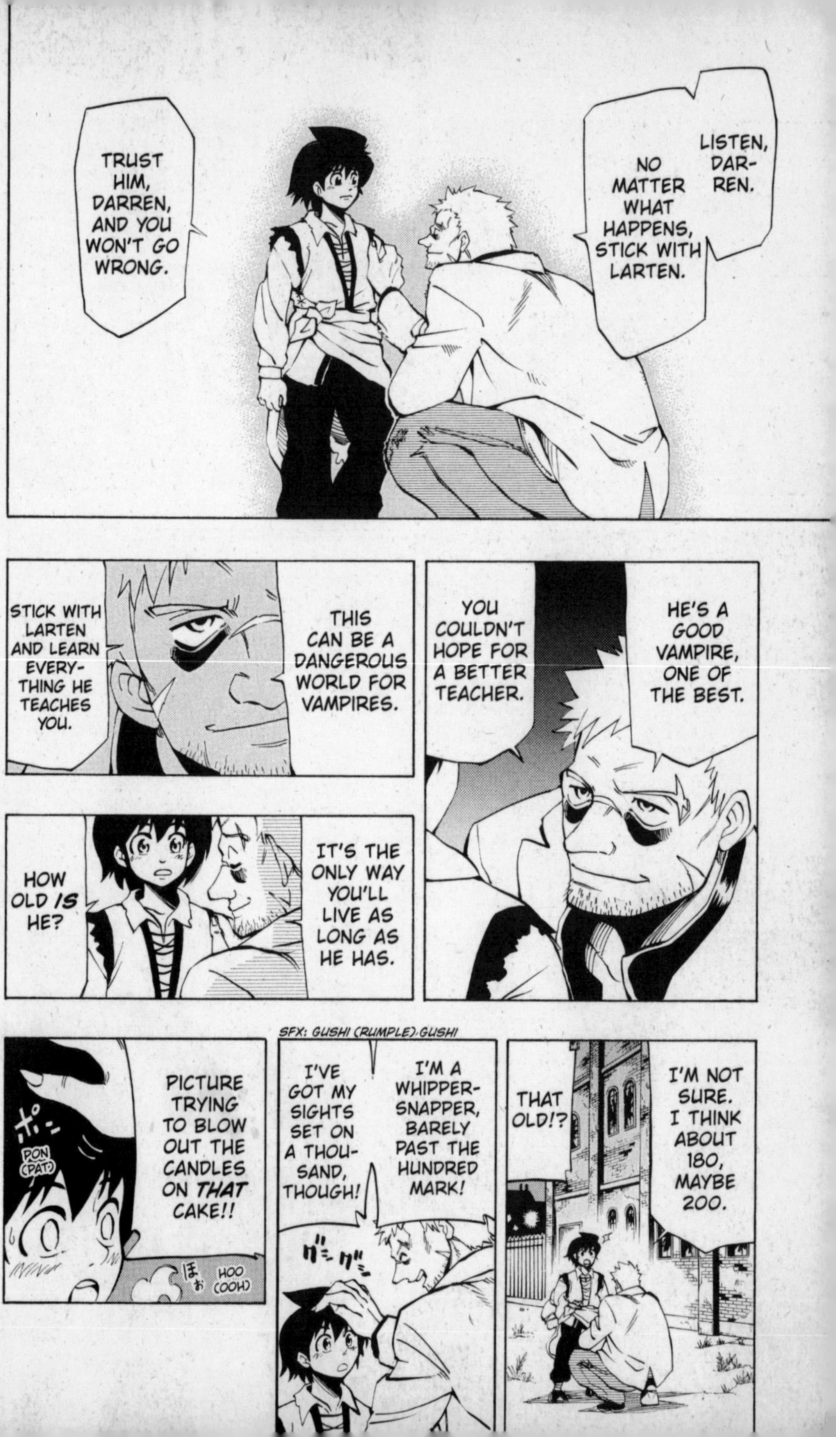
LISTEN, DARREN.
NO MATTER WHAT HAPPENS, STICK WITH LARTEN.
TRUST HIM, DARREN, AND YOU WON'T GO WRONG.
HE'S A GOOD VAMPIRE, ONE OF THE BEST.
YOU COULDN'T HOPE FOR A BETTER TEACHER.
THIS CAN BE A DANGEROUS WORLD FOR VAMPIRES.
STICK WITH LARTEN AND LEARN EVERY-THING HE TEACHES YOU.
IT'S THE ONLY WAY YOU'LL LIVE AS LONG AS HE HAS.
HOW OLD *IS* HE?
I'M NOT SURE. I THINK ABOUT 180, MAYBE 200.
THAT OLD!?
SFX: GUSHI (RUMPLE) GUSHI
I'M A WHIPPER-SNAPPER, BARELY PAST THE HUNDRED MARK!
I'VE GOT MY SIGHTS SET ON A THOU-SAND, THOUGH!
PICTURE TRYING TO BLOW OUT THE CANDLES ON *THAT* CAKE!!
PON (PAT)
HOO (OOH)

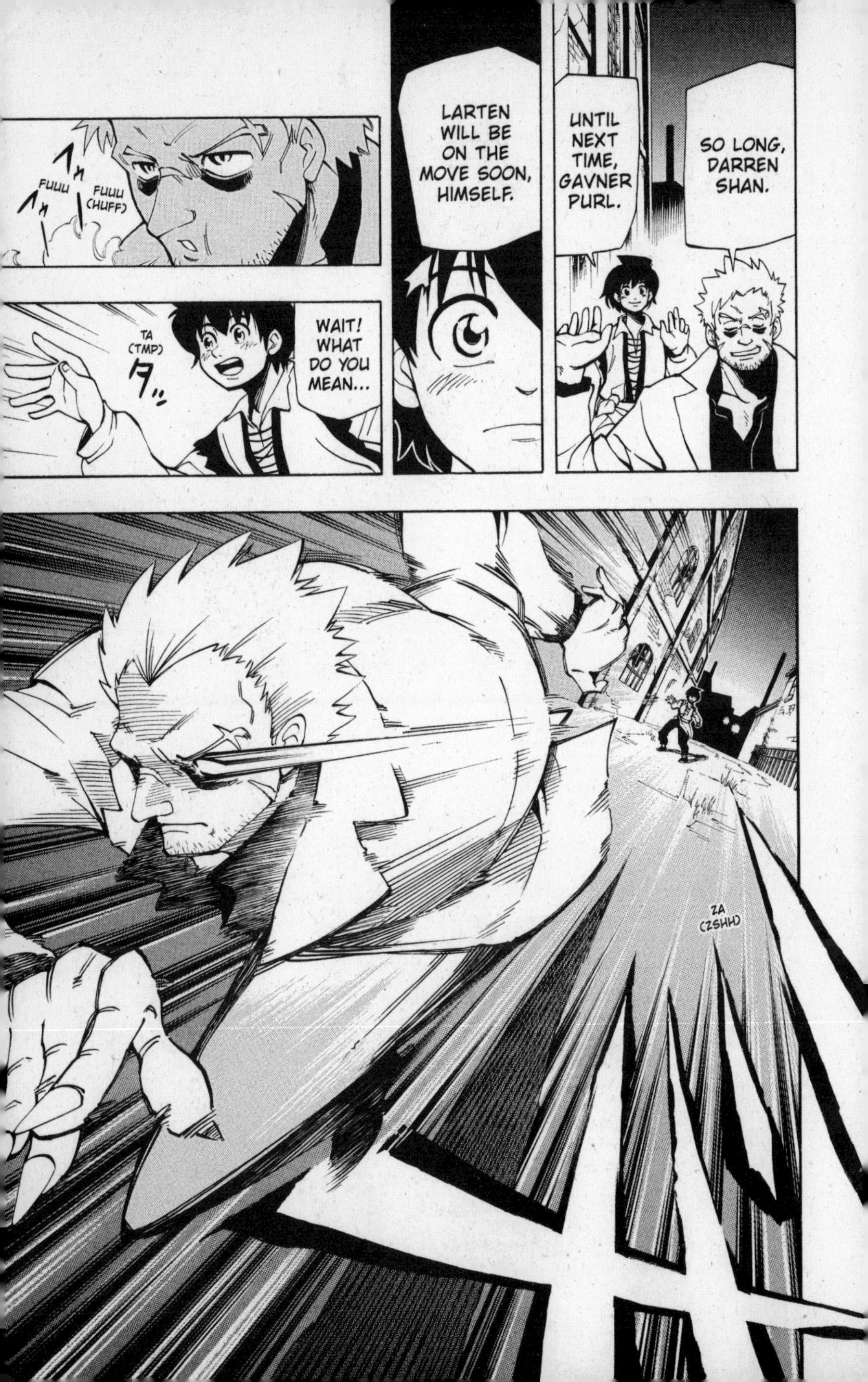
SO LONG, DARREN SHAN.
UNTIL NEXT TIME, GAVNER PURL.
LARTEN WILL BE ON THE MOVE SOON, HIMSELF.
FUUU
FUUU (CHUFF)
WAIT! WHAT DO YOU MEAN...
TA (TMP)
ZA (ZSHH)

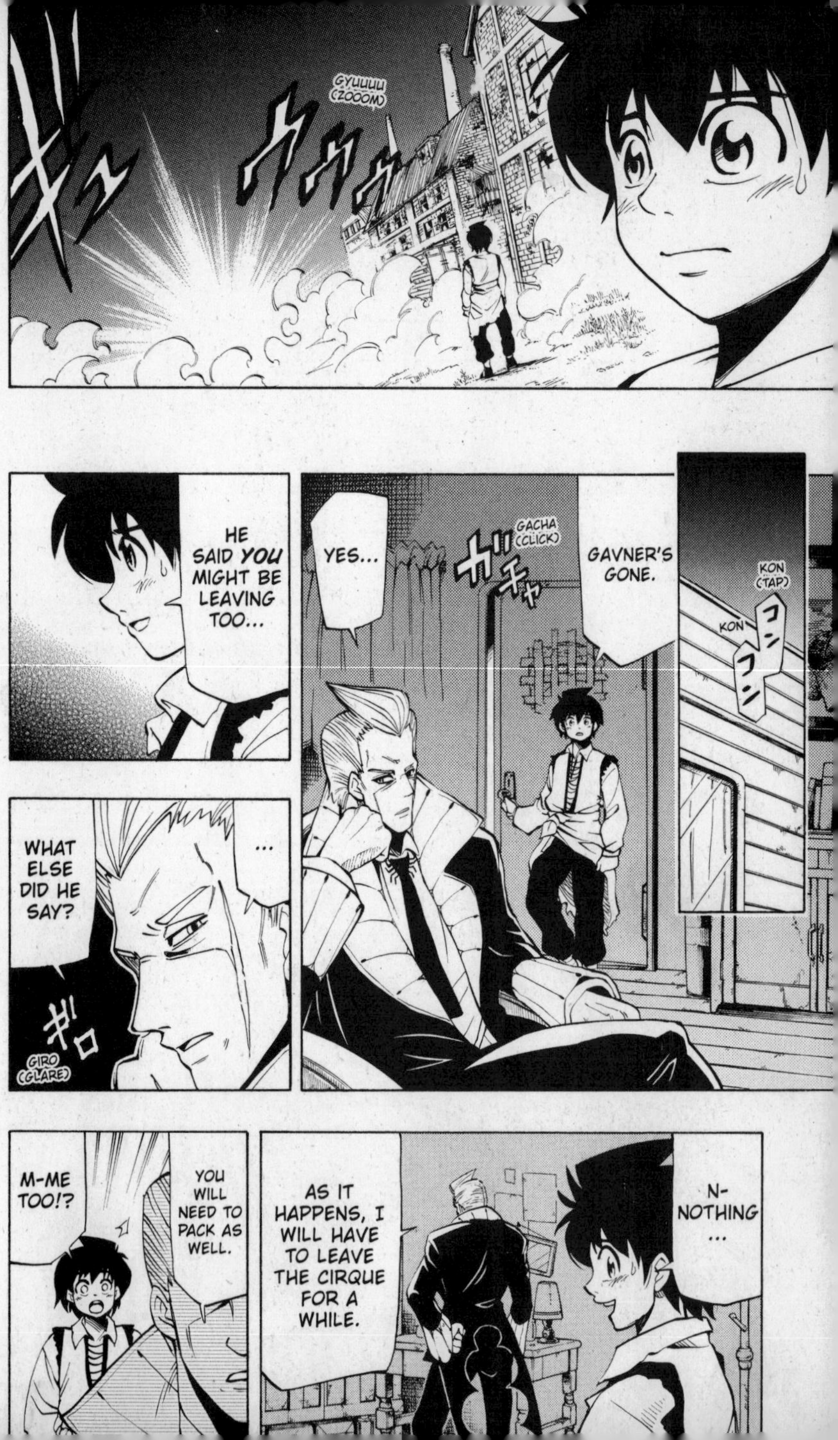
GYUUUU (ZOOOM)
KON (TAP)
KON
GAVNER'S GONE.
GACHA (CLICK)
YES...
HE SAID *YOU* MIGHT BE LEAVING TOO...
...
WHAT ELSE DID HE SAY?
GIRO (GLARE)
N-NOTHING...
AS IT HAPPENS, I WILL HAVE TO LEAVE THE CIRQUE FOR A WHILE.
YOU WILL NEED TO PACK AS WELL.
M-ME TOO!?

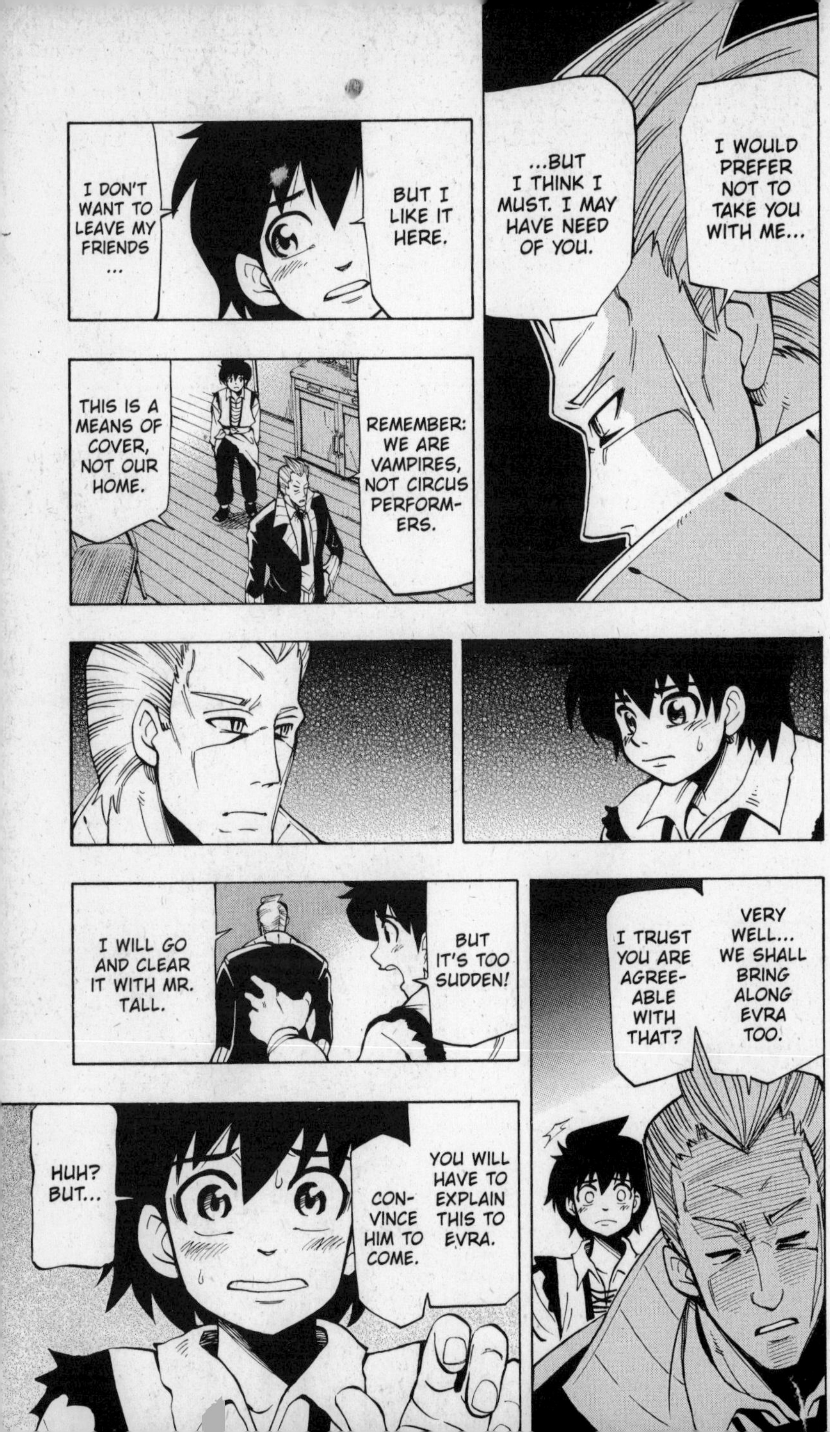
I WOULD PREFER NOT TO TAKE YOU WITH ME...
...BUT I THINK I MUST. I MAY HAVE NEED OF YOU.
BUT I LIKE IT HERE.
I DON'T WANT TO LEAVE MY FRIENDS ...
REMEMBER: WE ARE VAMPIRES, NOT CIRCUS PERFORM-ERS.
THIS IS A MEANS OF COVER, NOT OUR HOME.
VERY WELL... WE SHALL BRING ALONG EVRA TOO.
I TRUST YOU ARE AGREE-ABLE WITH THAT?
BUT IT'S TOO SUDDEN!
I WILL GO AND CLEAR IT WITH MR. TALL.
YOU WILL HAVE TO EXPLAIN THIS TO EVRA.
CON-VINCE HIM TO COME.
HUH? BUT...

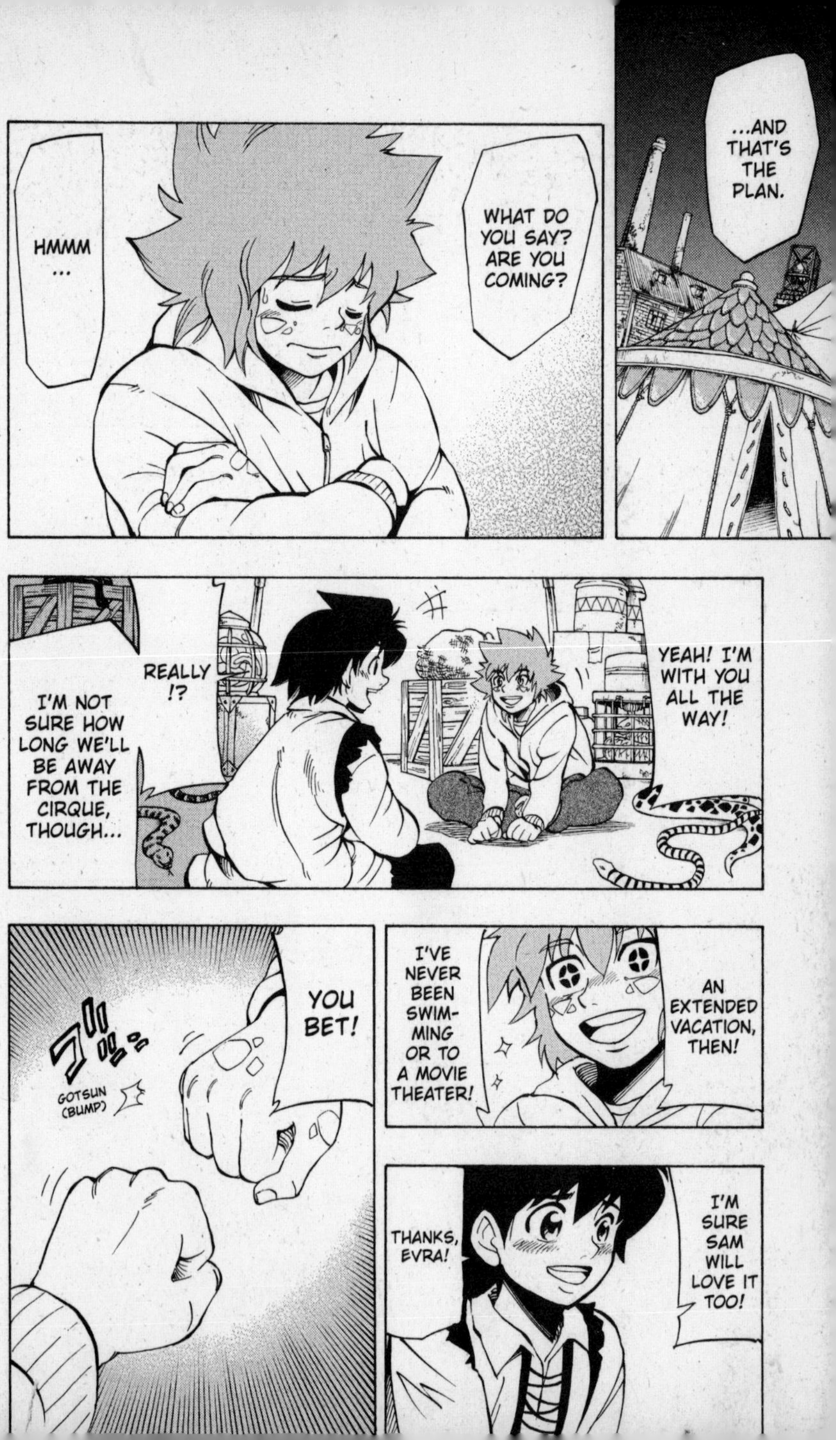
...AND THAT'S THE PLAN.
WHAT DO YOU SAY? ARE YOU COMING?
HMMM ...
YEAH! I'M WITH YOU ALL THE WAY!
REALLY !?
I'M NOT SURE HOW LONG WE'LL BE AWAY FROM THE CIRQUE, THOUGH...
AN EXTENDED VACATION, THEN!
I'VE NEVER BEEN SWIM-MING OR TO A MOVIE THEATER!
I'M SURE SAM WILL LOVE IT TOO!
THANKS, EVRA!
YOU BET!
GOTSUN (BUMP)

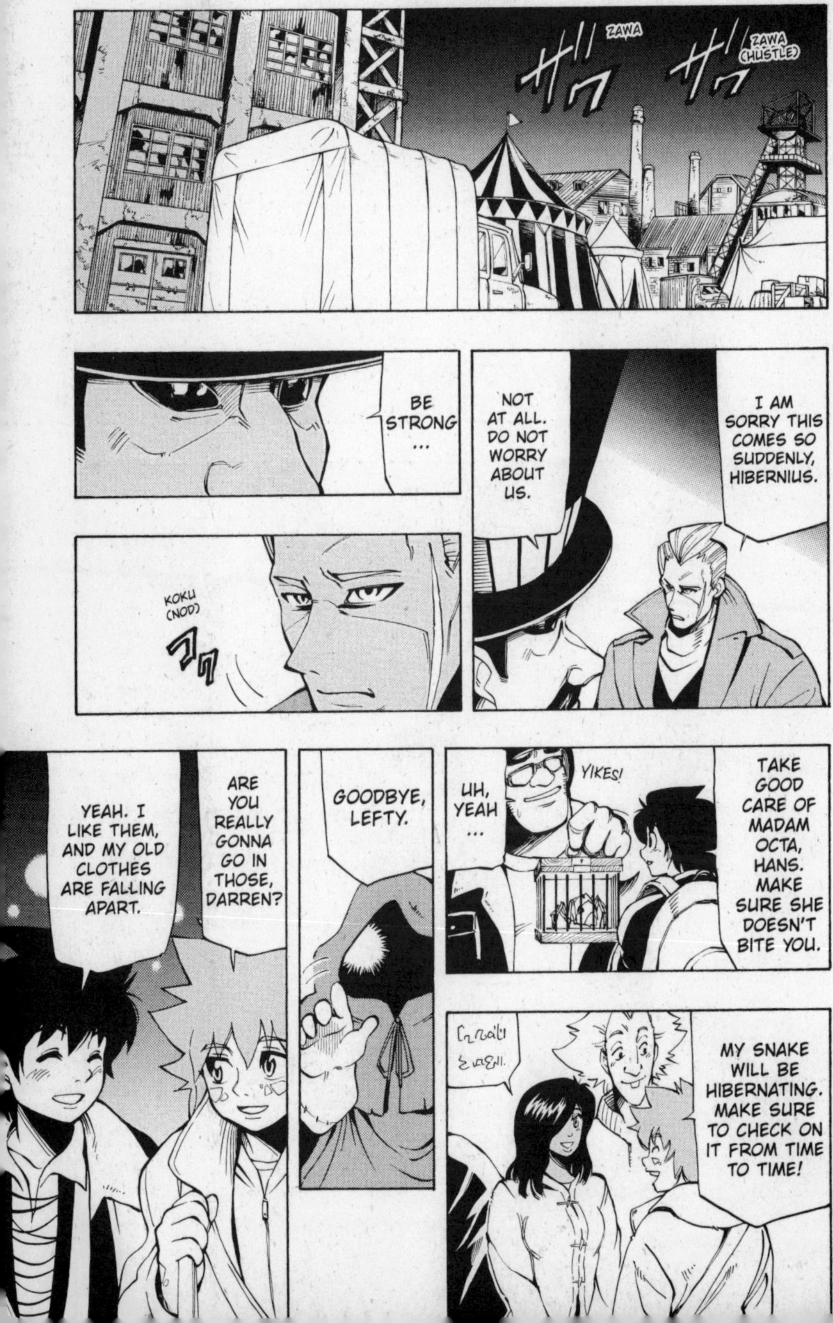
ZAWA (HUSTLE)
ZAWA
I AM SORRY THIS COMES SO SUDDENLY, HIBERNIUS.
NOT AT ALL. DO NOT WORRY ABOUT US.
BE STRONG...
KOKU (NOD)
TAKE GOOD CARE OF MADAM OCTA, HANS. MAKE SURE SHE DOESN'T BITE YOU.
YIKES!
UH, YEAH...
MY SNAKE WILL BE HIBERNATING. MAKE SURE TO CHECK ON IT FROM TIME TO TIME!
GOODBYE, LEFTY.
ARE YOU REALLY GONNA GO IN THOSE, DARREN?
YEAH. I LIKE THEM, AND MY OLD CLOTHES ARE FALLING APART.

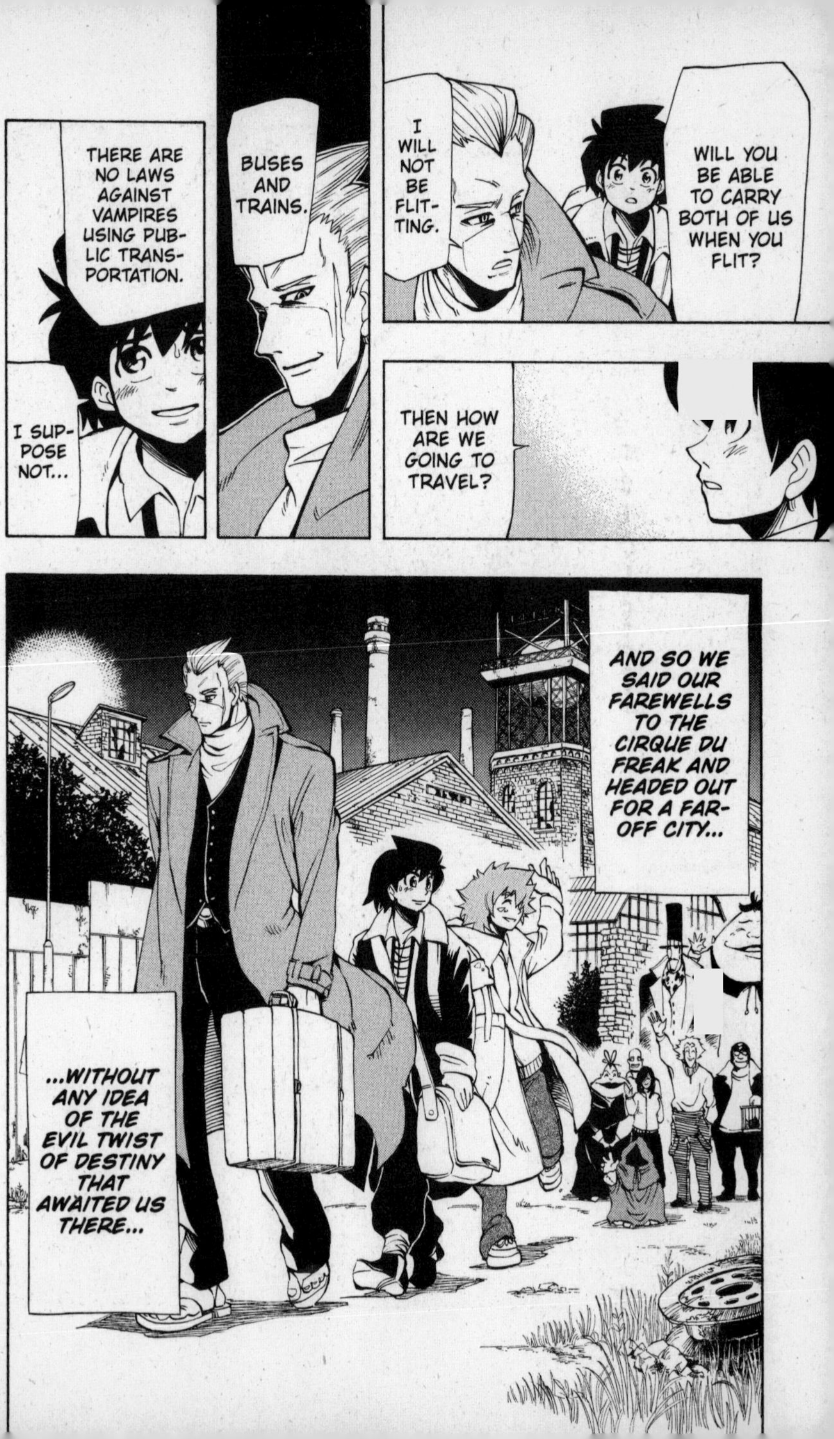
WILL YOU BE ABLE TO CARRY BOTH OF US WHEN YOU FLIT?
I WILL NOT BE FLIT-TING.
THEN HOW ARE WE GOING TO TRAVEL?
BUSES AND TRAINS.
THERE ARE NO LAWS AGAINST VAMPIRES USING PUB-LIC TRANS-PORTATION.
I SUP-POSE NOT...
AND SO WE SAID OUR FAREWELLS TO THE CIRQUE DU FREAK AND HEADED OUT FOR A FAR-OFF CITY...
...WITHOUT ANY IDEA OF THE EVIL TWIST OF DESTINY THAT AWAITED US THERE...

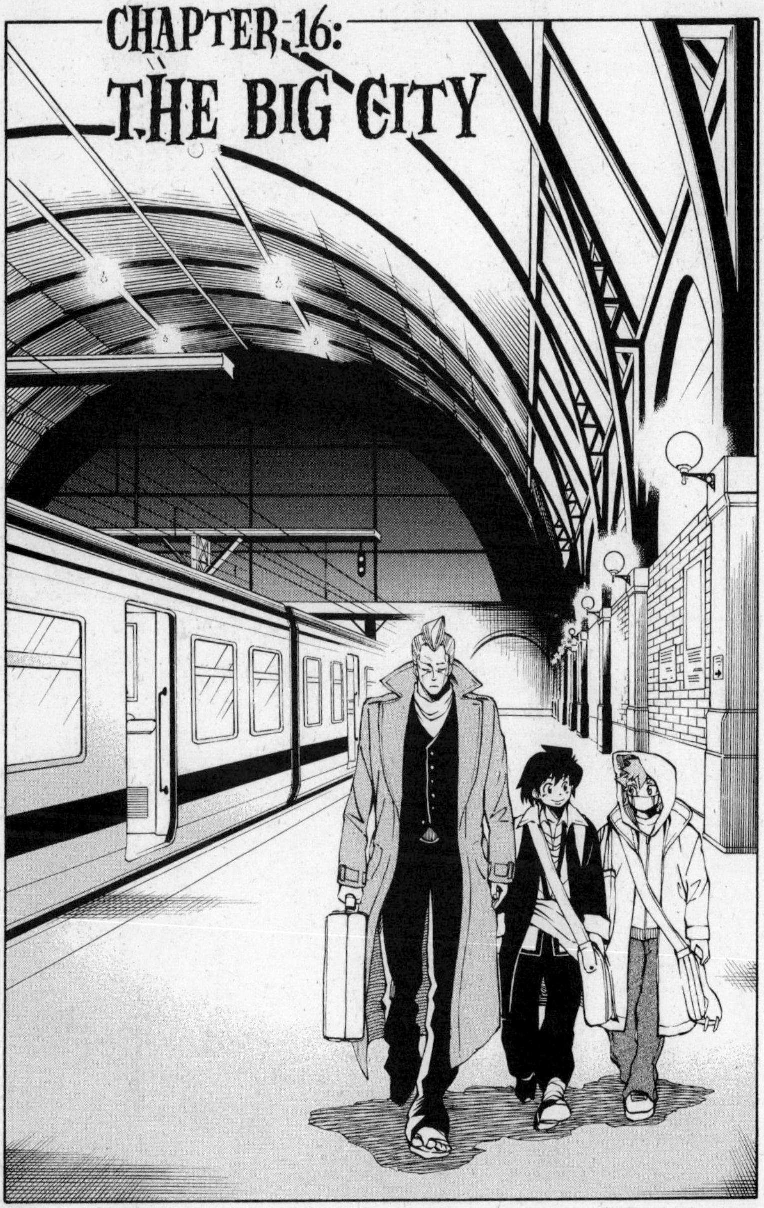
CHAPTER 16:
THE BIG CITY

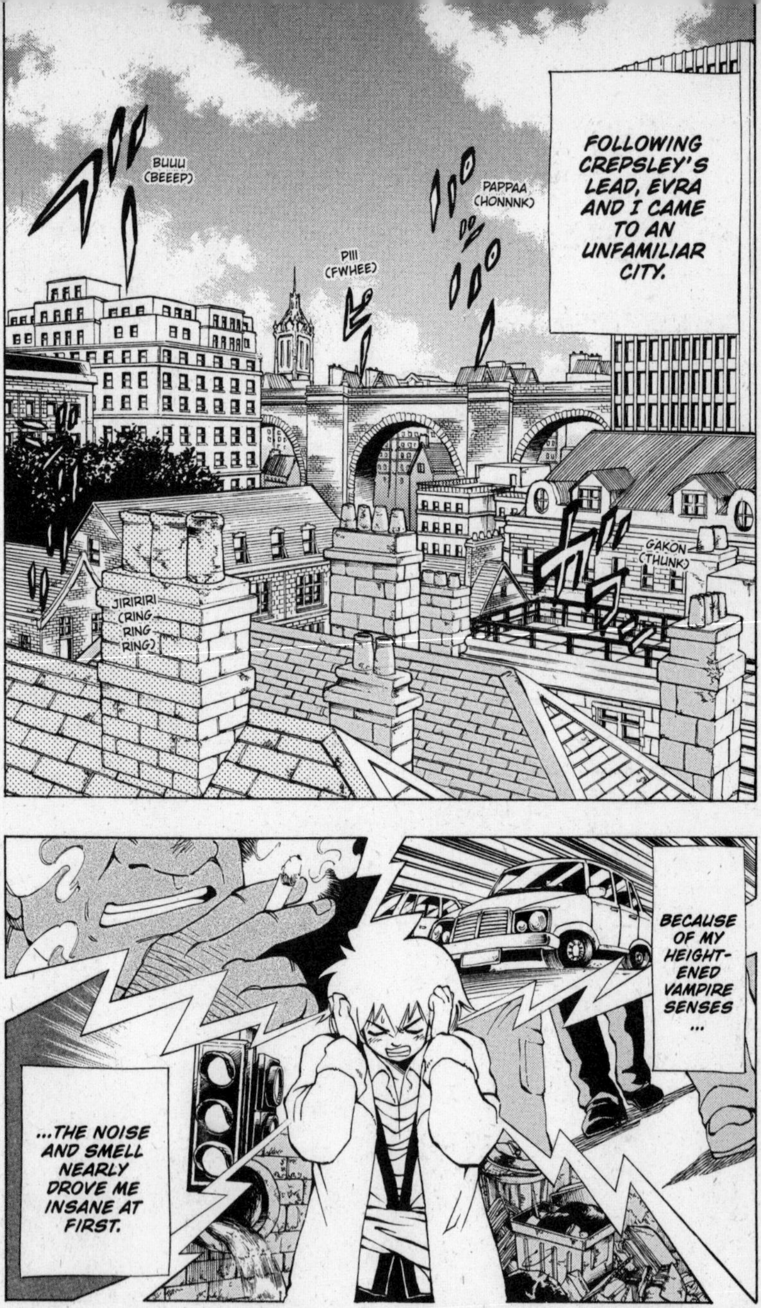
FOLLOWING CREPSLEY'S LEAD, EVRA AND I CAME TO AN UNFAMILIAR CITY.
PAPPAA (HONNNK)
PIII (FWHEE)
BUUU (BEEEP)
GAKON (THUNK)
JIRIRIRI (RING RING RING)
BECAUSE OF MY HEIGHT-ENED VAMPIRE SENSES ...
...THE NOISE AND SMELL NEARLY DROVE ME INSANE AT FIRST.

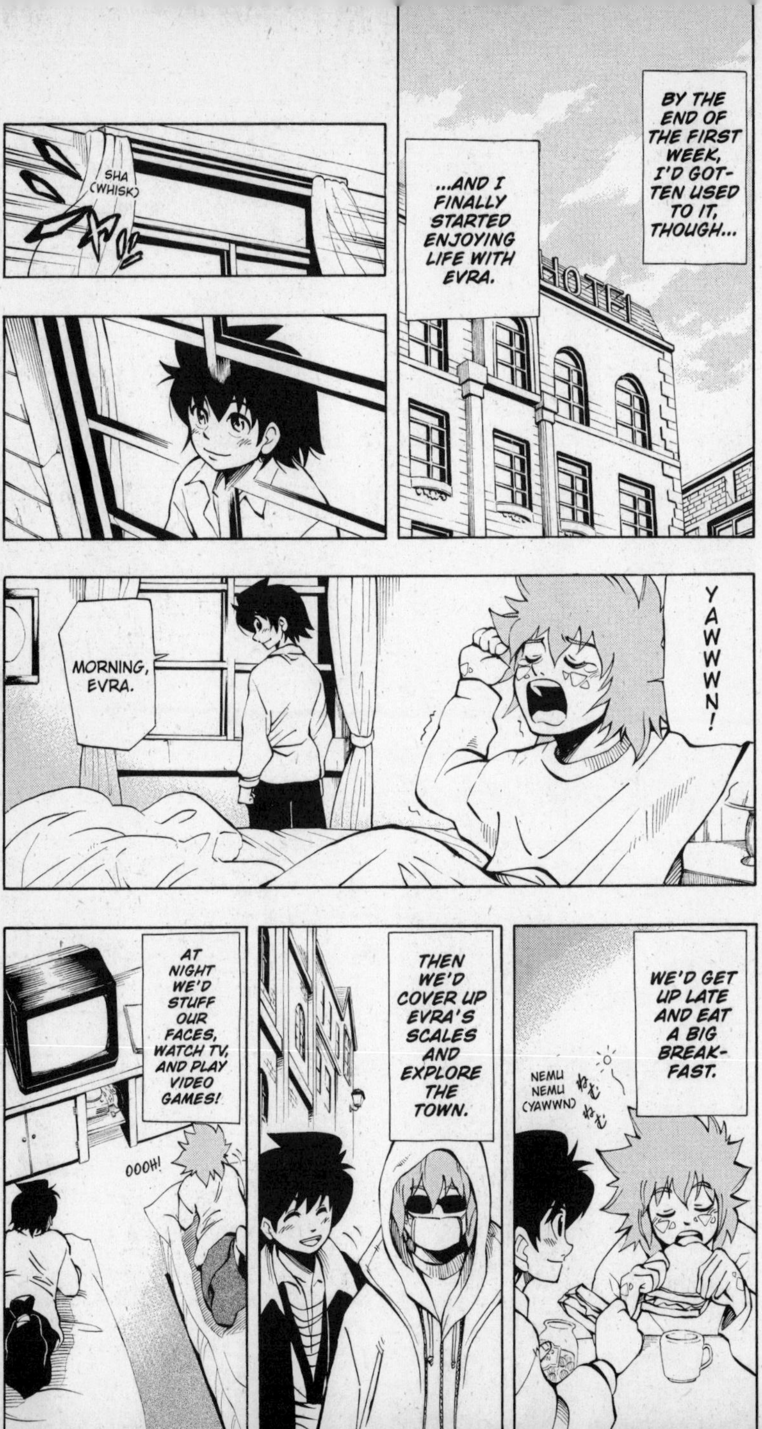
BY THE END OF THE FIRST WEEK, I'D GOTTEN USED TO IT, THOUGH...
...AND I FINALLY STARTED ENJOYING LIFE WITH EVRA.
HOTEL
SHA (WHISK)
YAWWWN!
MORNING, EVRA.
WE'D GET UP LATE AND EAT A BIG BREAKFAST.
NEMU NEMU (YAWWN)
THEN WE'D COVER UP EVRA'S SCALES AND EXPLORE THE TOWN.
AT NIGHT WE'D STUFF OUR FACES, WATCH TV, AND PLAY VIDEO GAMES!
OOOH!

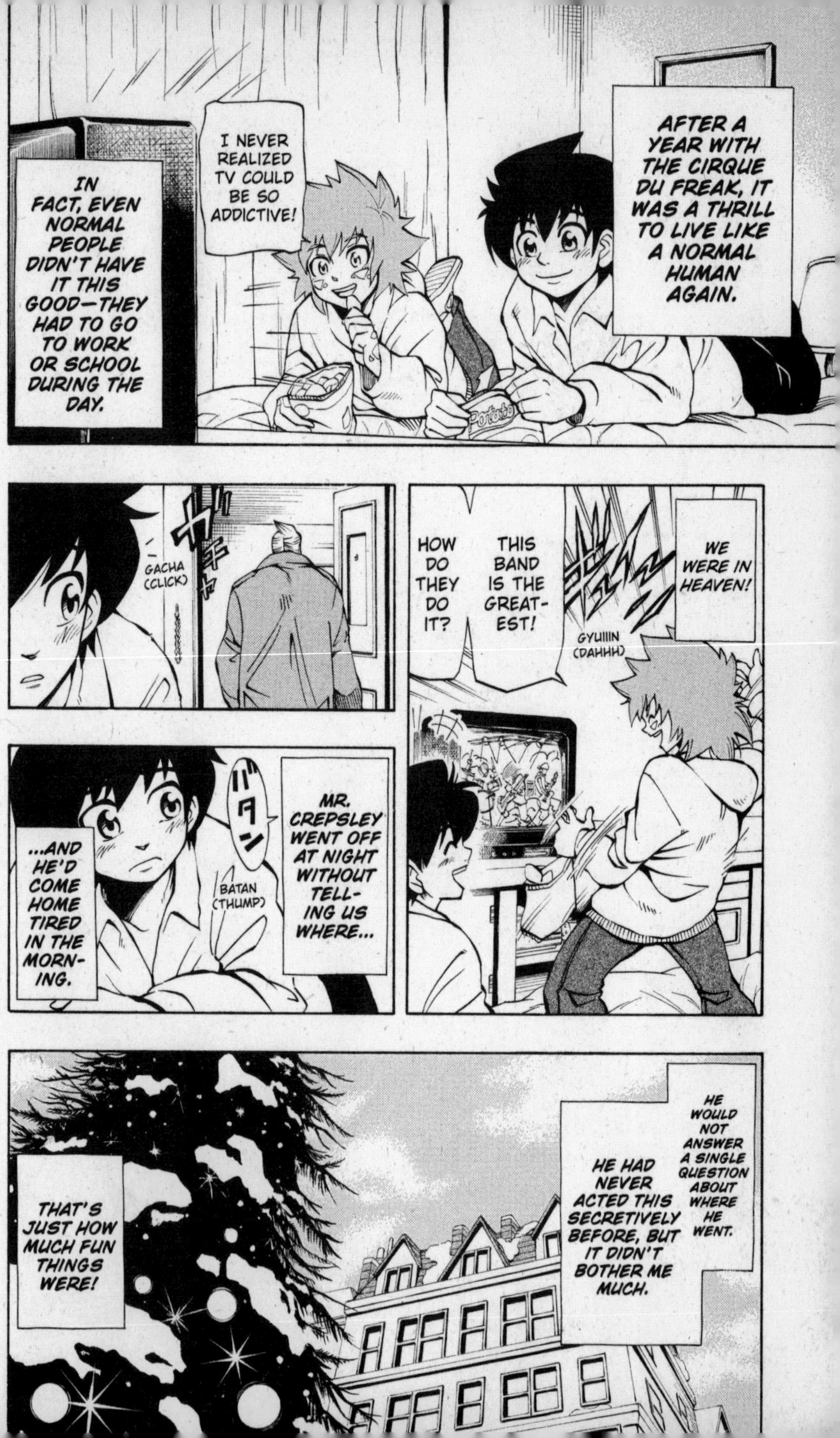
AFTER A YEAR WITH THE CIRQUE DU FREAK, IT WAS A THRILL TO LIVE LIKE A NORMAL HUMAN AGAIN.
I NEVER REALIZED TV COULD BE SO ADDICTIVE!
IN FACT, EVEN NORMAL PEOPLE DIDN'T HAVE IT THIS GOOD—THEY HAD TO GO TO WORK OR SCHOOL DURING THE DAY.
WE WERE IN HEAVEN!
GYUIIIN (DAHHH)
THIS BAND IS THE GREAT-EST!
HOW DO THEY DO IT?
GACHA (CLICK)
MR. CREPSLEY WENT OFF AT NIGHT WITHOUT TELL-ING US WHERE...
BATAN (THUMP)
...AND HE'D COME HOME TIRED IN THE MORN-ING.
HE WOULD NOT ANSWER A SINGLE QUESTION ABOUT WHERE HE WENT.
HE HAD NEVER ACTED THIS SECRETIVELY BEFORE, BUT IT DIDN'T BOTHER ME MUCH.
THAT'S JUST HOW MUCH FUN THINGS WERE!

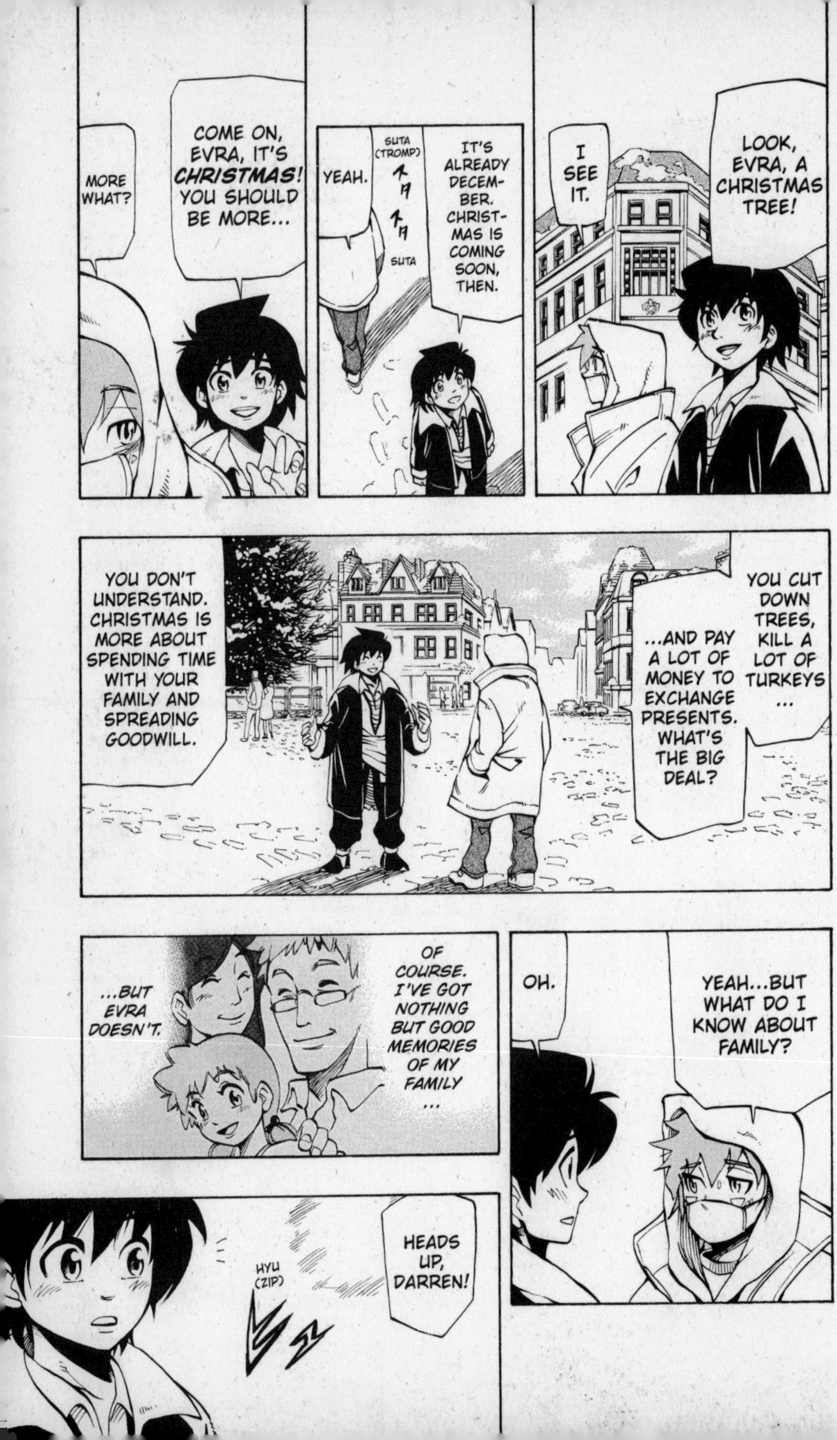
LOOK, EVRA, A CHRISTMAS TREE!
I SEE IT.
IT'S ALREADY DECEMBER. CHRISTMAS IS COMING SOON, THEN.
SUTA (TROMP)
SUTA
YEAH.
COME ON, EVRA, IT'S *CHRISTMAS*! YOU SHOULD BE MORE...
MORE WHAT?
YOU CUT DOWN TREES, KILL A LOT OF TURKEYS...
...AND PAY A LOT OF MONEY TO EXCHANGE PRESENTS. WHAT'S THE BIG DEAL?
YOU DON'T UNDERSTAND. CHRISTMAS IS MORE ABOUT SPENDING TIME WITH YOUR FAMILY AND SPREADING GOODWILL.
YEAH...BUT WHAT DO I KNOW ABOUT FAMILY?
OH.
OF COURSE. I'VE GOT NOTHING BUT GOOD MEMORIES OF MY FAMILY...
...BUT EVRA DOESN'T.
HEADS UP, DARREN!
HYU (ZIP)

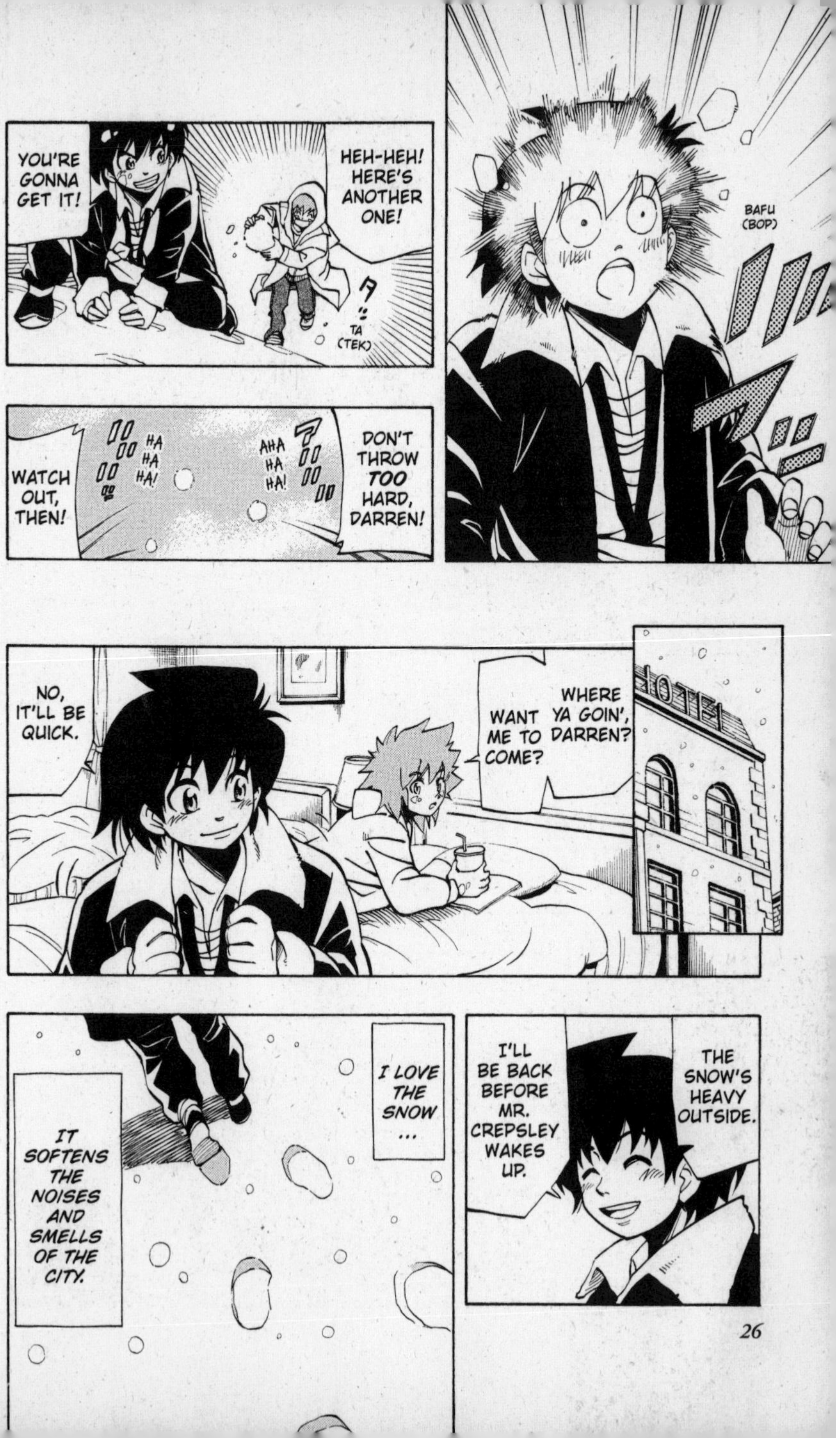
BAFU (BOP)
HEH-HEH! HERE'S ANOTHER ONE!
TA (TEK)
YOU'RE GONNA GET IT!
DON'T THROW *TOO* HARD, DARREN!
AHA HA HA!
HA HA HA!
WATCH OUT, THEN!
WHERE YA GOIN', DARREN?
WANT ME TO COME?
NO, IT'LL BE QUICK.
THE SNOW'S HEAVY OUTSIDE.
I'LL BE BACK BEFORE MR. CREPSLEY WAKES UP.
I LOVE THE SNOW ...
IT SOFTENS THE NOISES AND SMELLS OF THE CITY.

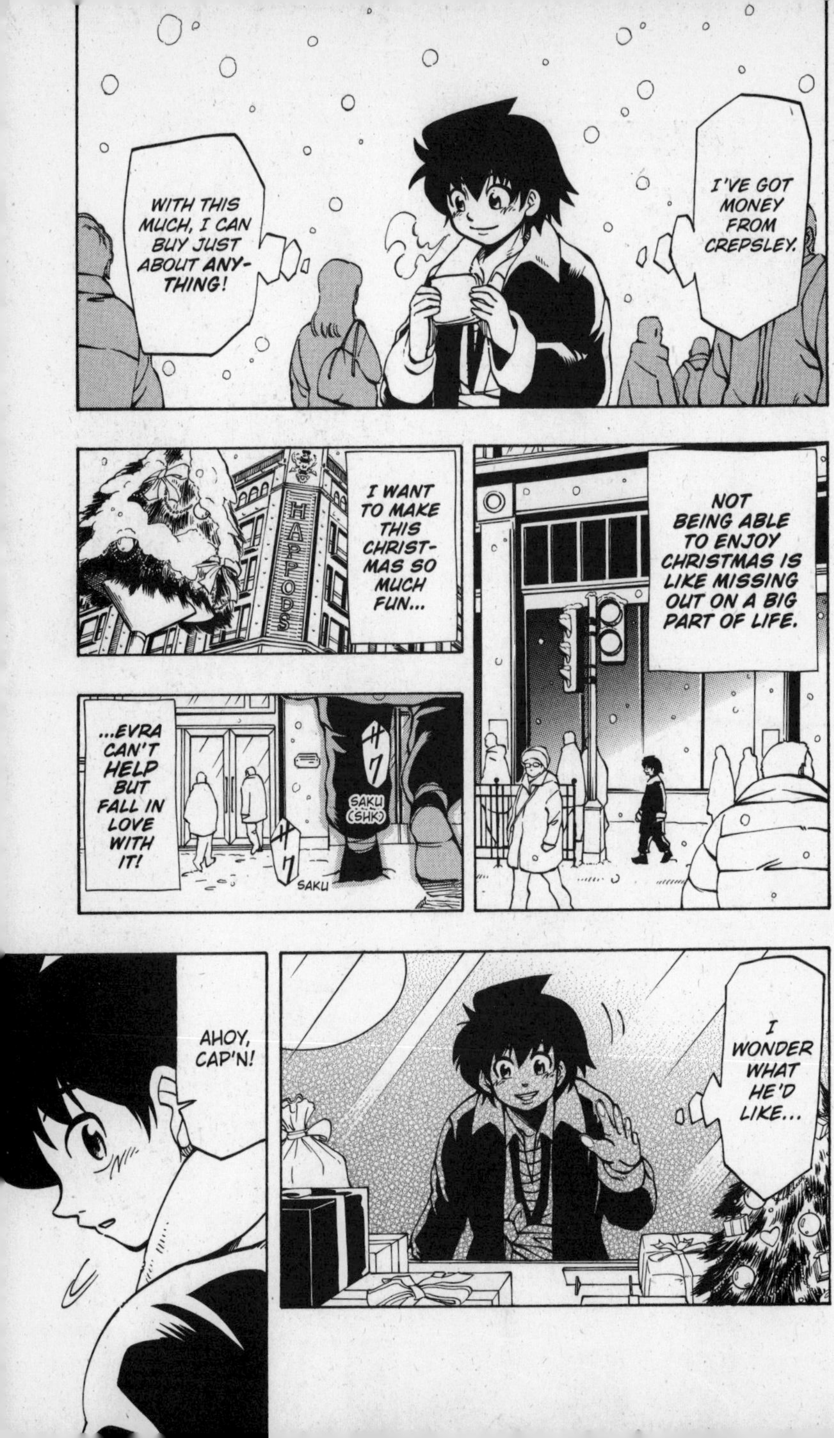
I'VE GOT MONEY FROM CREPSLEY.
WITH THIS MUCH, I CAN BUY JUST ABOUT ANYTHING!
NOT BEING ABLE TO ENJOY CHRISTMAS IS LIKE MISSING OUT ON A BIG PART OF LIFE.
HAPPODS
I WANT TO MAKE THIS CHRISTMAS SO MUCH FUN...
...EVRA CAN'T HELP BUT FALL IN LOVE WITH IT!
SAKU (SHK)
SAKU
I WONDER WHAT HE'D LIKE...
AHOY, CAP'N!

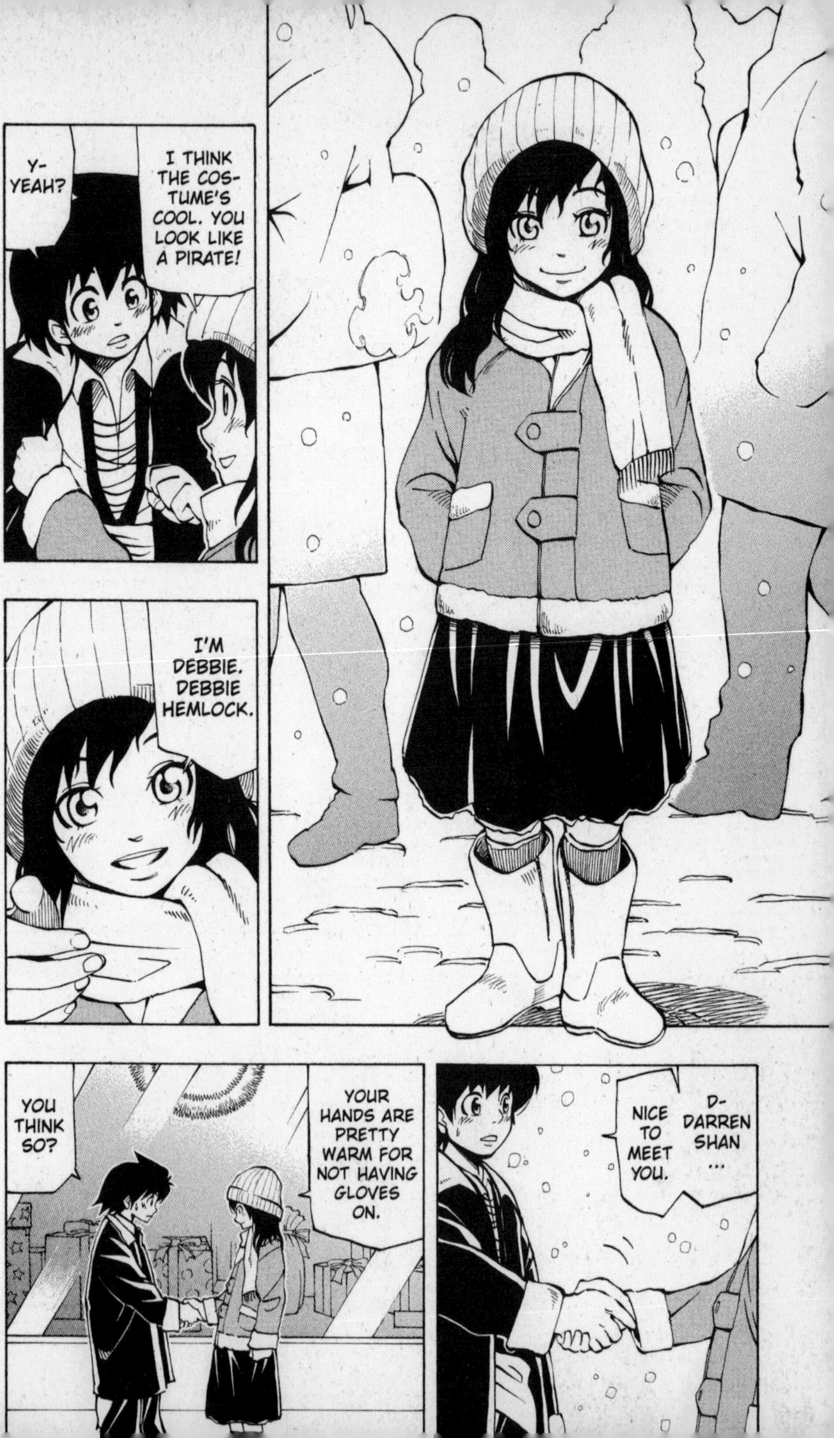
I THINK THE COS-TUME'S COOL. YOU LOOK LIKE A PIRATE!
Y-YEAH?
I'M DEBBIE. DEBBIE HEMLOCK.
D-DARREN SHAN...
NICE TO MEET YOU.
YOUR HANDS ARE PRETTY WARM FOR NOT HAVING GLOVES ON.
YOU THINK SO?

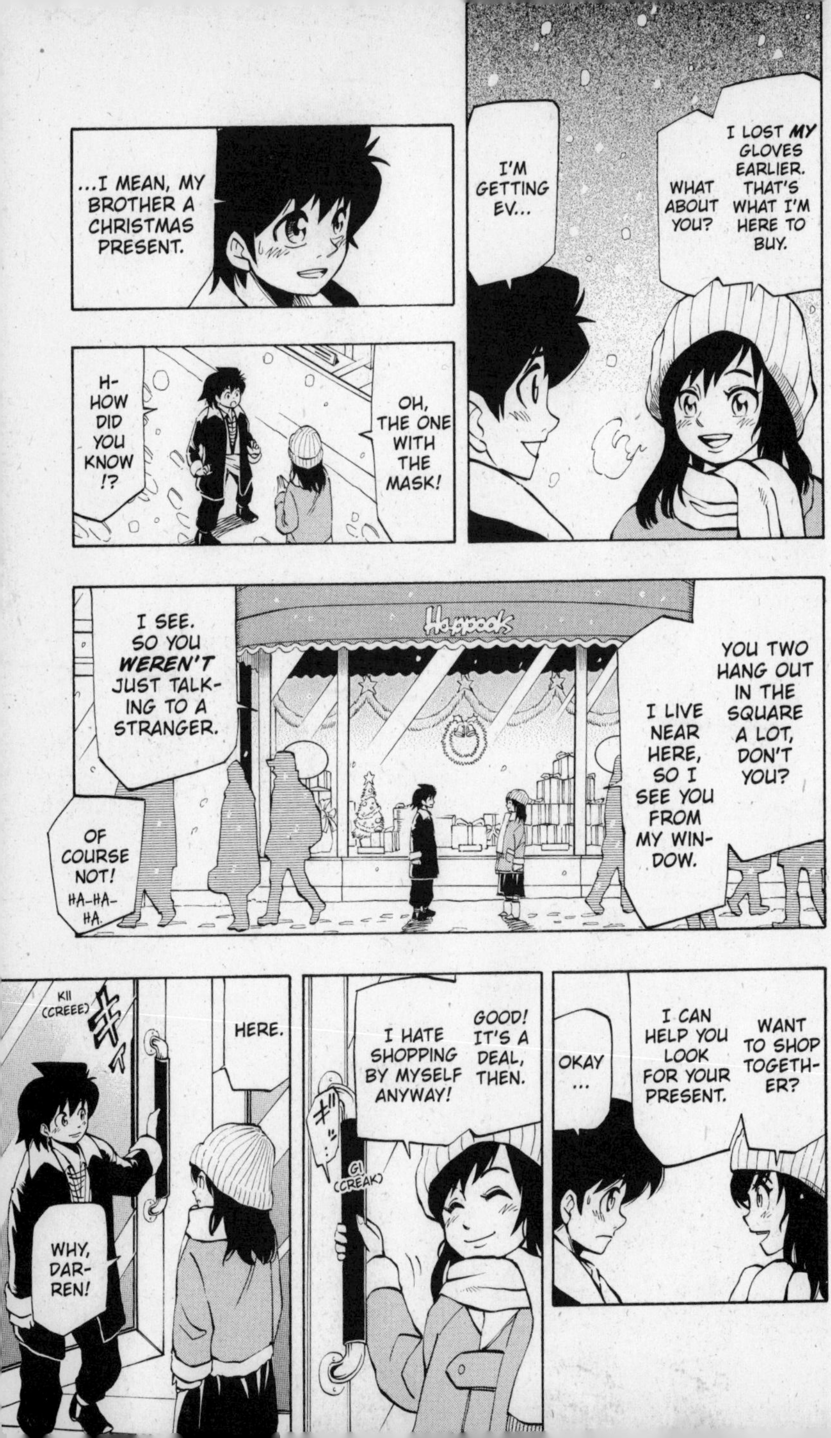
I LOST **MY** GLOVES EARLIER. THAT'S WHAT I'M HERE TO BUY.
WHAT ABOUT YOU?
I'M GETTING EV...
...I MEAN, MY BROTHER A CHRISTMAS PRESENT.
OH, THE ONE WITH THE MASK!
H-HOW DID YOU KNOW!?
YOU TWO HANG OUT IN THE SQUARE A LOT, DON'T YOU?
I LIVE NEAR HERE, SO I SEE YOU FROM MY WINDOW.
I SEE. SO YOU ***WEREN'T*** JUST TALKING TO A STRANGER.
OF COURSE NOT!
HA-HA-HA.
WANT TO SHOP TOGETHER?
I CAN HELP YOU LOOK FOR YOUR PRESENT.
OKAY...
GOOD! IT'S A DEAL, THEN.
I HATE SHOPPING BY MYSELF ANYWAY!
GI (CREAK)
HERE.
KII (CREEE)
WHY, DARREN!

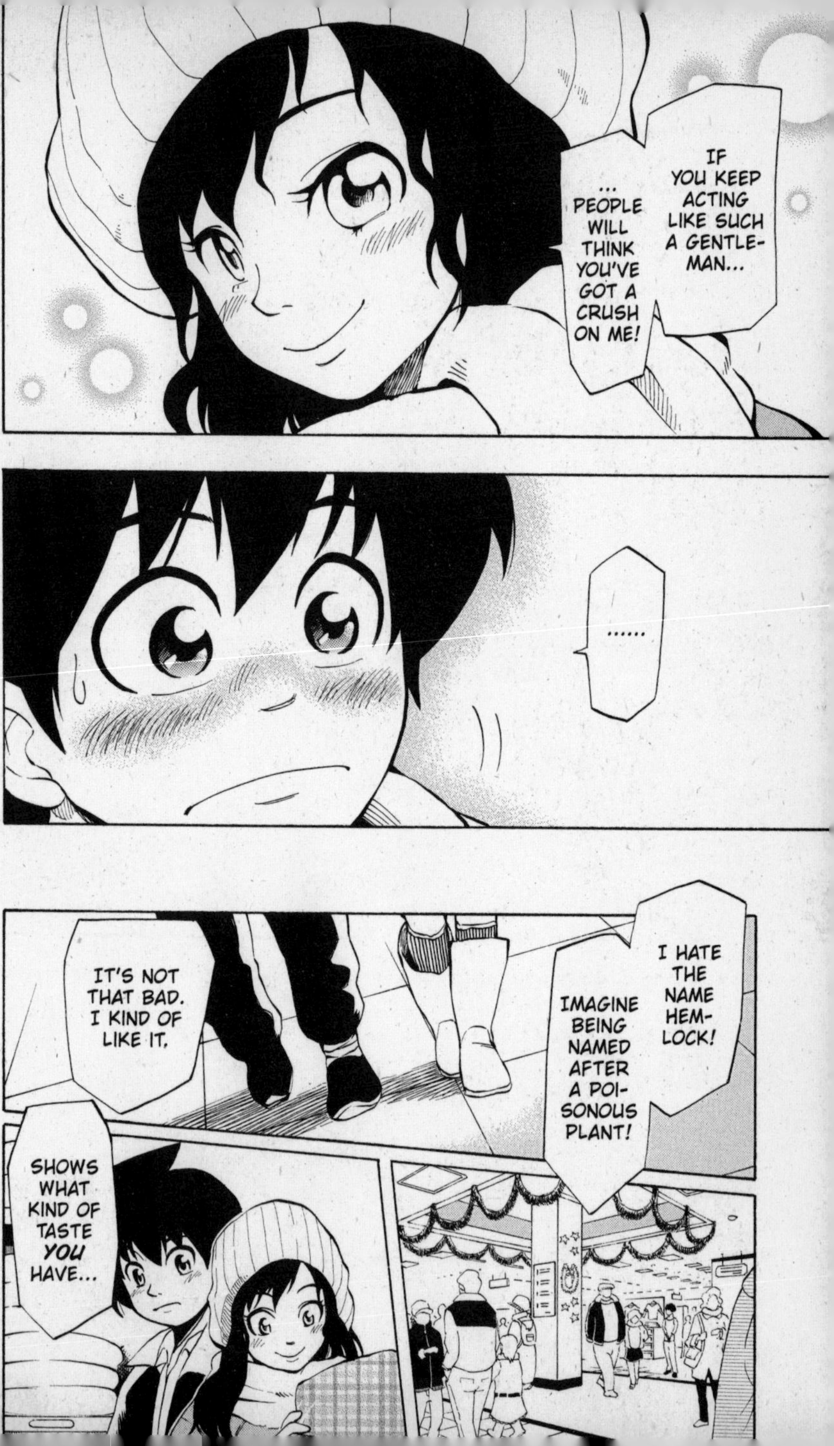
IF YOU KEEP ACTING LIKE SUCH A GENTLE-MAN...
...PEOPLE WILL THINK YOU'VE GOT A CRUSH ON ME!
......
I HATE THE NAME HEM-LOCK!
IMAGINE BEING NAMED AFTER A POI-SONOUS PLANT!
IT'S NOT THAT BAD. I KIND OF LIKE IT.
SHOWS WHAT KIND OF TASTE *YOU* HAVE...

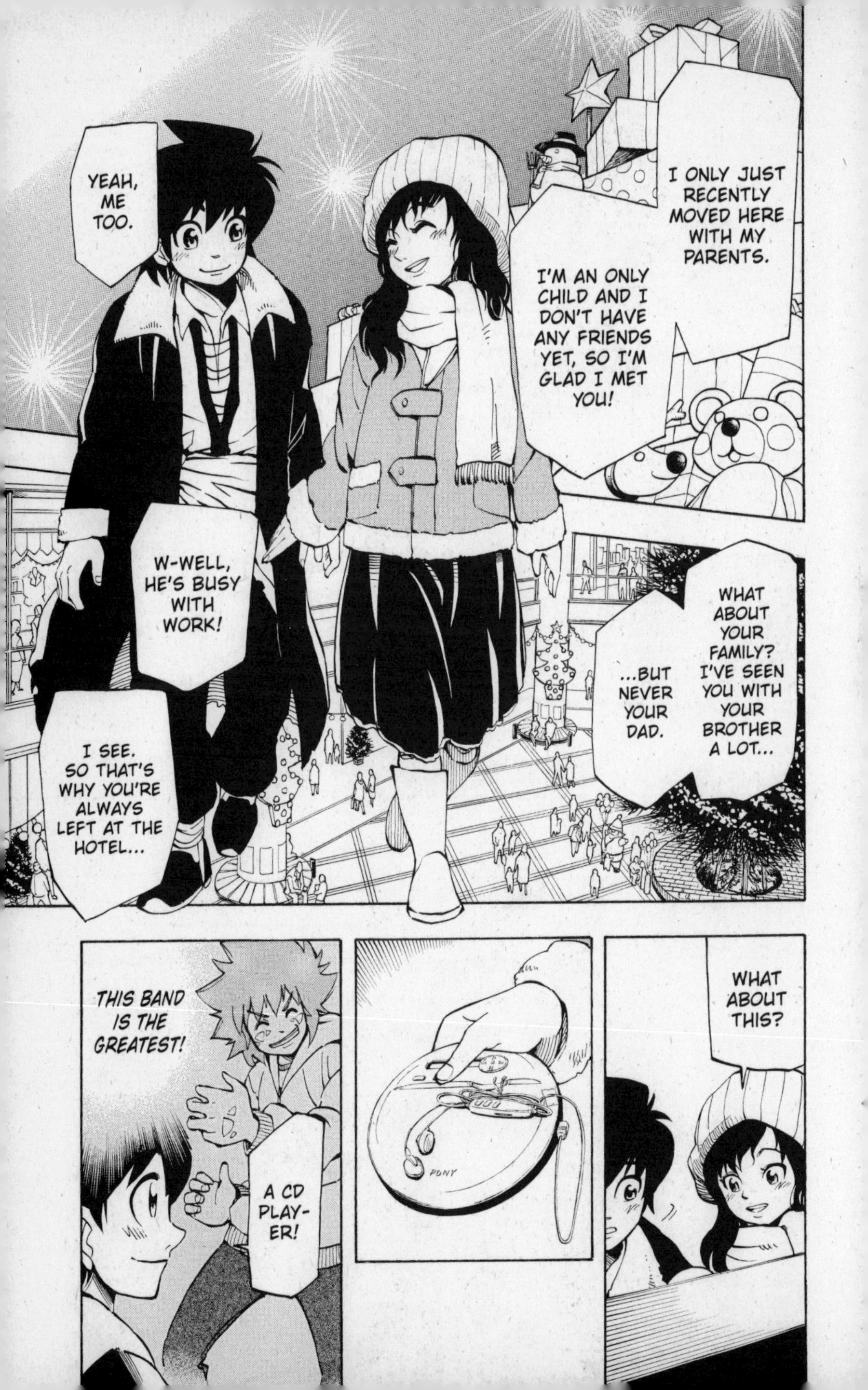
I ONLY JUST RECENTLY MOVED HERE WITH MY PARENTS.
I'M AN ONLY CHILD AND I DON'T HAVE ANY FRIENDS YET, SO I'M GLAD I MET YOU!
YEAH, ME TOO.
WHAT ABOUT YOUR FAMILY? I'VE SEEN YOU WITH YOUR BROTHER A LOT...
...BUT NEVER YOUR DAD.
W-WELL, HE'S BUSY WITH WORK!
I SEE. SO THAT'S WHY YOU'RE ALWAYS LEFT AT THE HOTEL...
WHAT ABOUT THIS?
PONY
THIS BAND IS THE GREATEST!
A CD PLAYER!

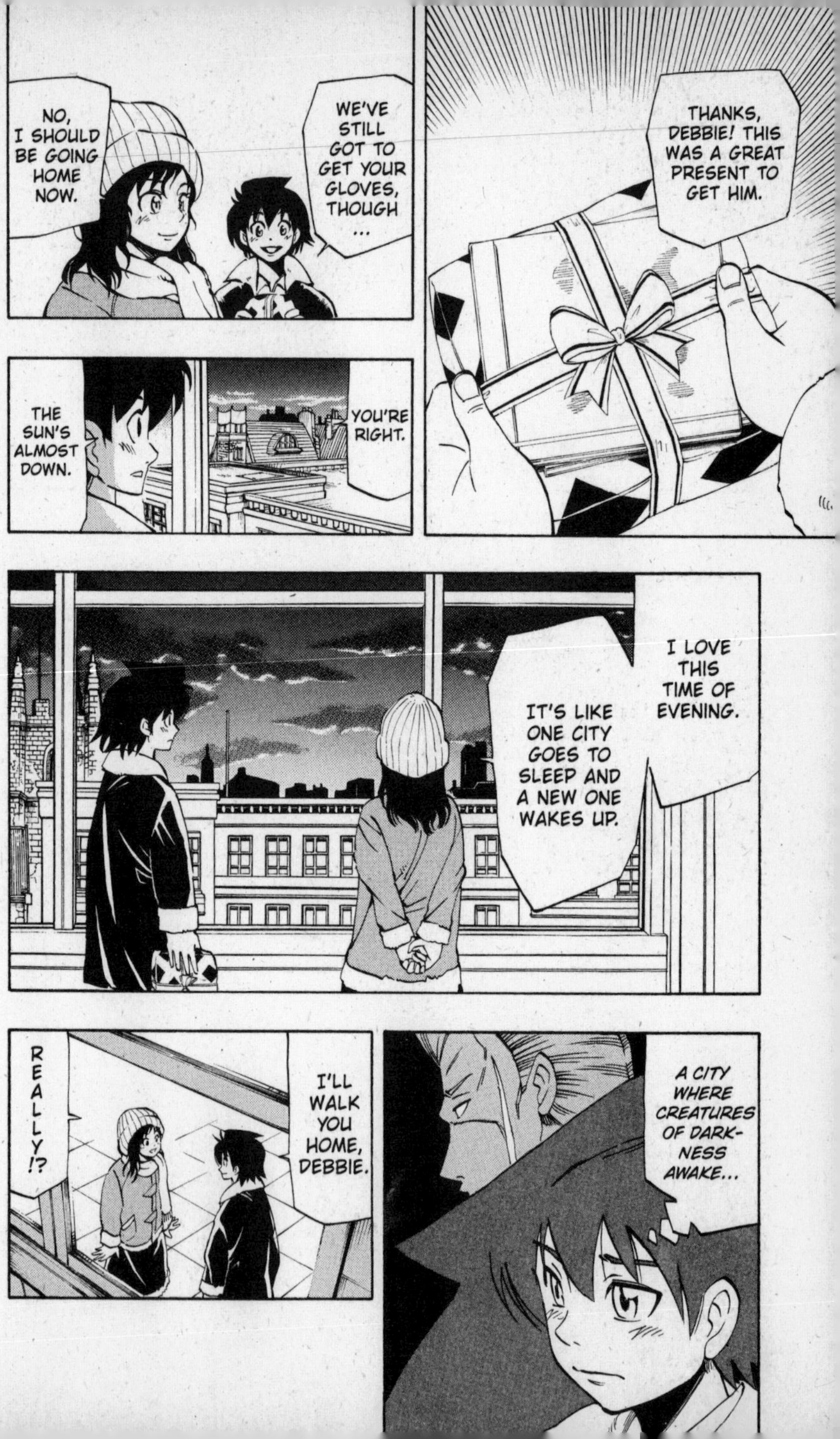
THANKS, DEBBIE! THIS WAS A GREAT PRESENT TO GET HIM.
WE'VE STILL GOT TO GET YOUR GLOVES, THOUGH ...
NO, I SHOULD BE GOING HOME NOW.
YOU'RE RIGHT.
THE SUN'S ALMOST DOWN.
I LOVE THIS TIME OF EVENING.
IT'S LIKE ONE CITY GOES TO SLEEP AND A NEW ONE WAKES UP.
A CITY WHERE CREATURES OF DARKNESS AWAKE...
I'LL WALK YOU HOME, DEBBIE.
REALLY!?

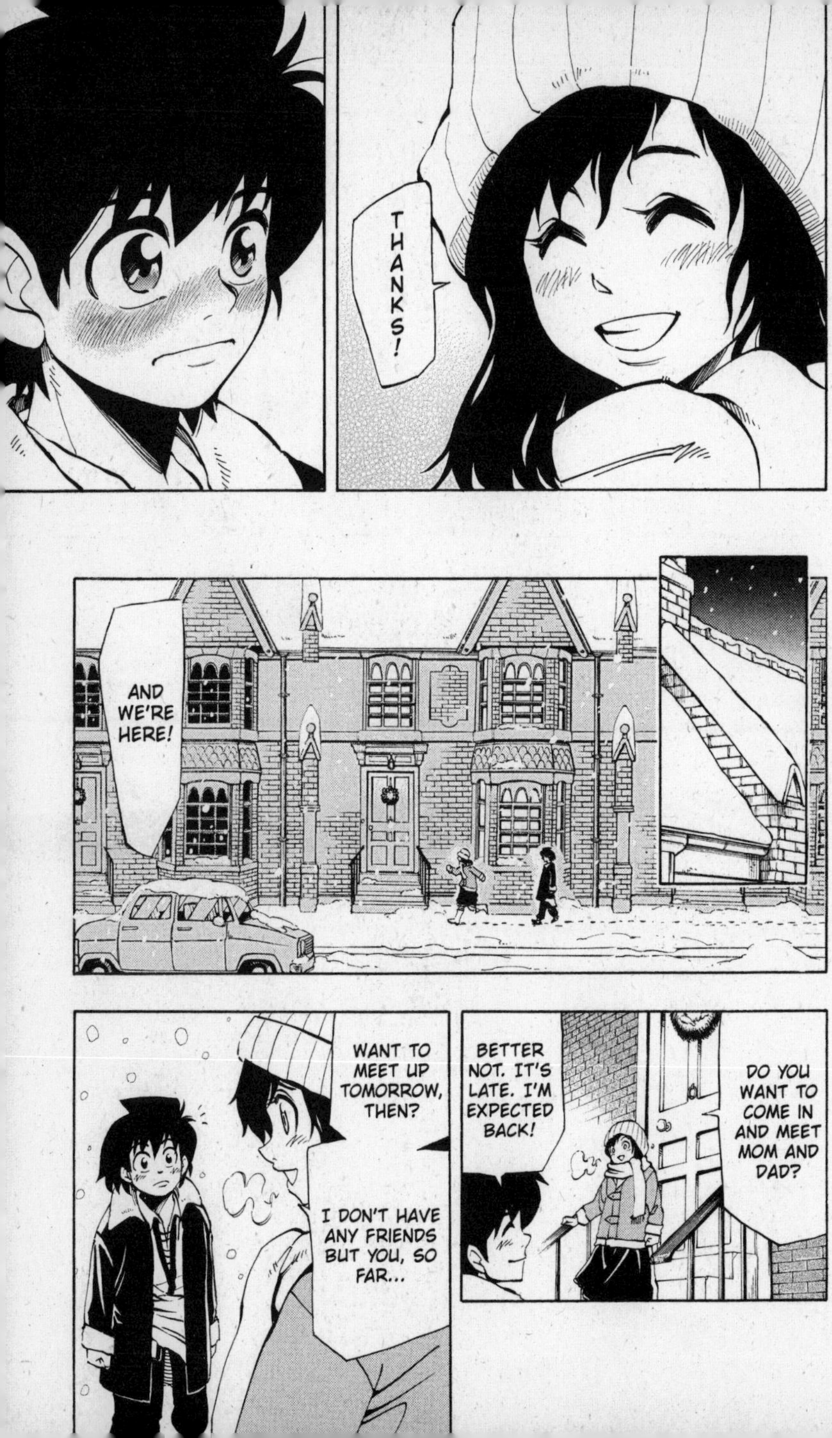
THANKS!
AND WE'RE HERE!
DO YOU WANT TO COME IN AND MEET MOM AND DAD?
BETTER NOT. IT'S LATE. I'M EXPECTED BACK!
WANT TO MEET UP TOMORROW, THEN?
I DON'T HAVE ANY FRIENDS BUT YOU, SO FAR...

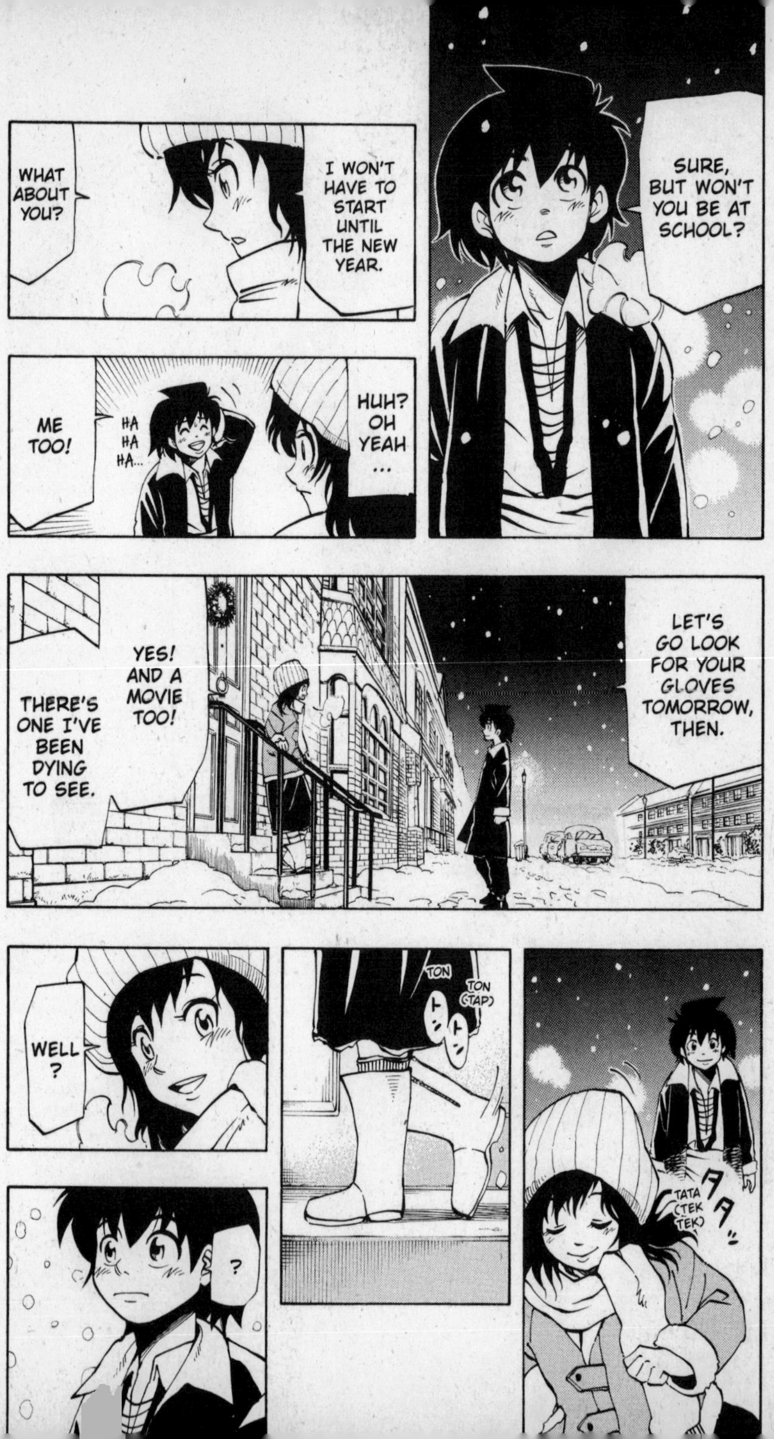
SURE, BUT WON'T YOU BE AT SCHOOL?
I WON'T HAVE TO START UNTIL THE NEW YEAR.
WHAT ABOUT YOU?
HUH? OH YEAH ...
HA HA HA...
ME TOO!
LET'S GO LOOK FOR YOUR GLOVES TOMORROW, THEN.
YES! AND A MOVIE TOO!
THERE'S ONE I'VE BEEN DYING TO SEE.
TATA (TEK TEK)
TON
TON (TAP)
WELL?
?

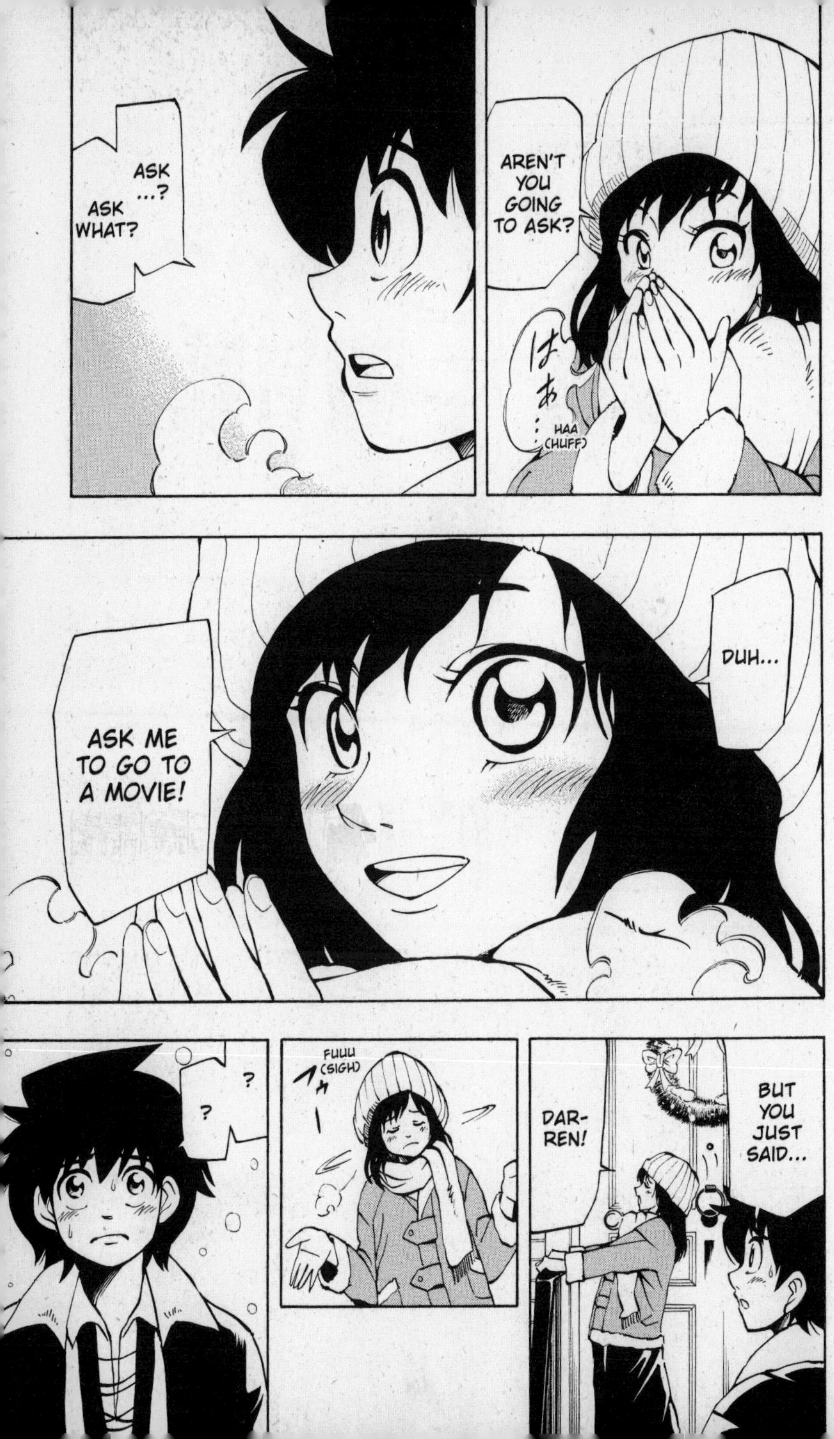
AREN'T YOU GOING TO ASK?
はあ…
HAA (HUFF)
ASK ...?
ASK WHAT?
DUH...
ASK ME TO GO TO A MOVIE!
BUT YOU JUST SAID...
DAR-REN!
FUUU (SIGH)
?
?

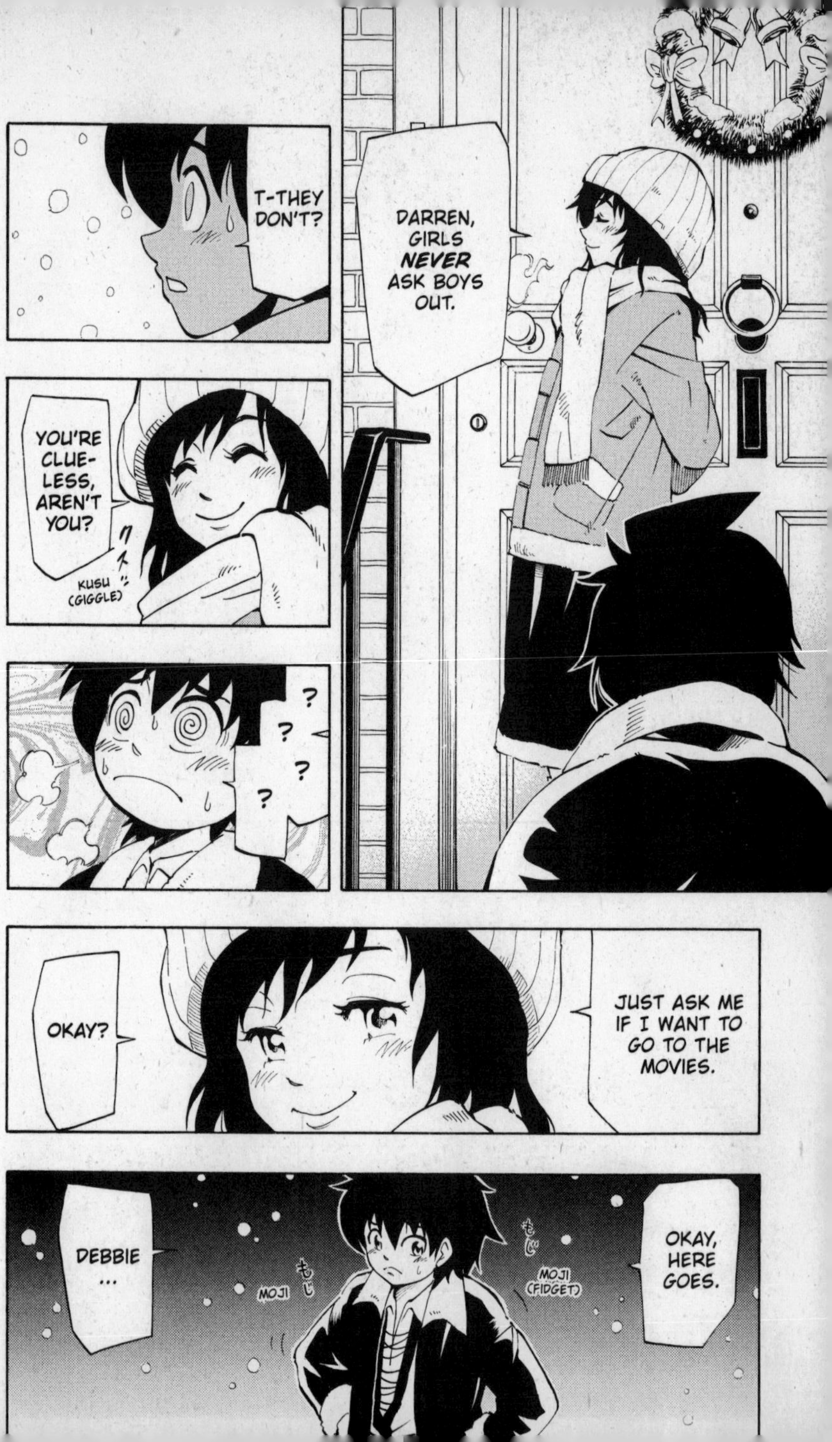
DARREN, GIRLS *NEVER* ASK BOYS OUT.
T-THEY DON'T?
YOU'RE CLUE-LESS, AREN'T YOU?
クス
KUSU (GIGGLE)
? ? ? ?
JUST ASK ME IF I WANT TO GO TO THE MOVIES.
OKAY?
OKAY, HERE GOES.
もじ
MOJI (FIDGET)
もじ
MOJI
DEBBIE ...

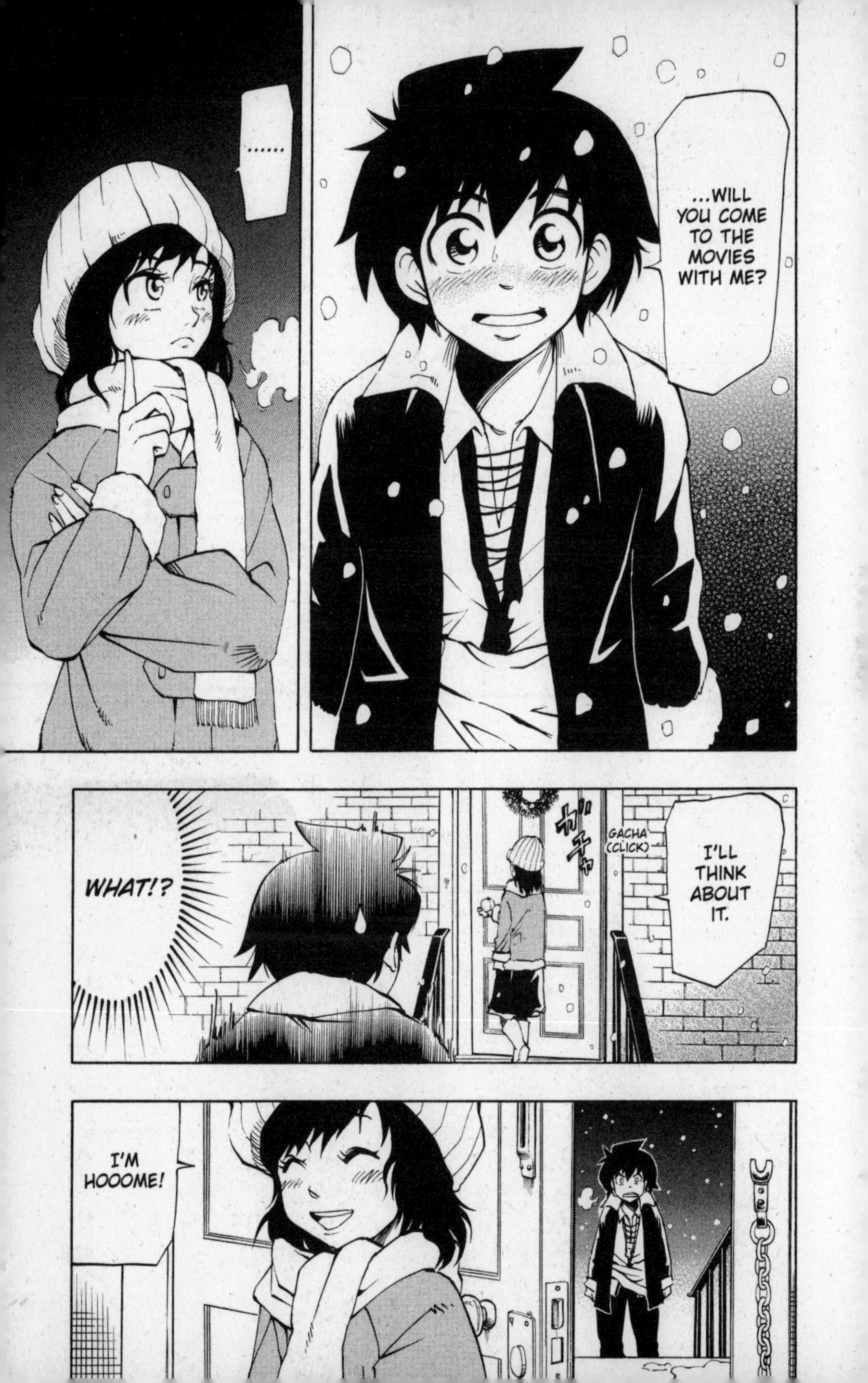
...WILL YOU COME TO THE MOVIES WITH ME?
......
I'LL THINK ABOUT IT.
GACHA (CLICK)
WHAT!?
I'M HOOOME!

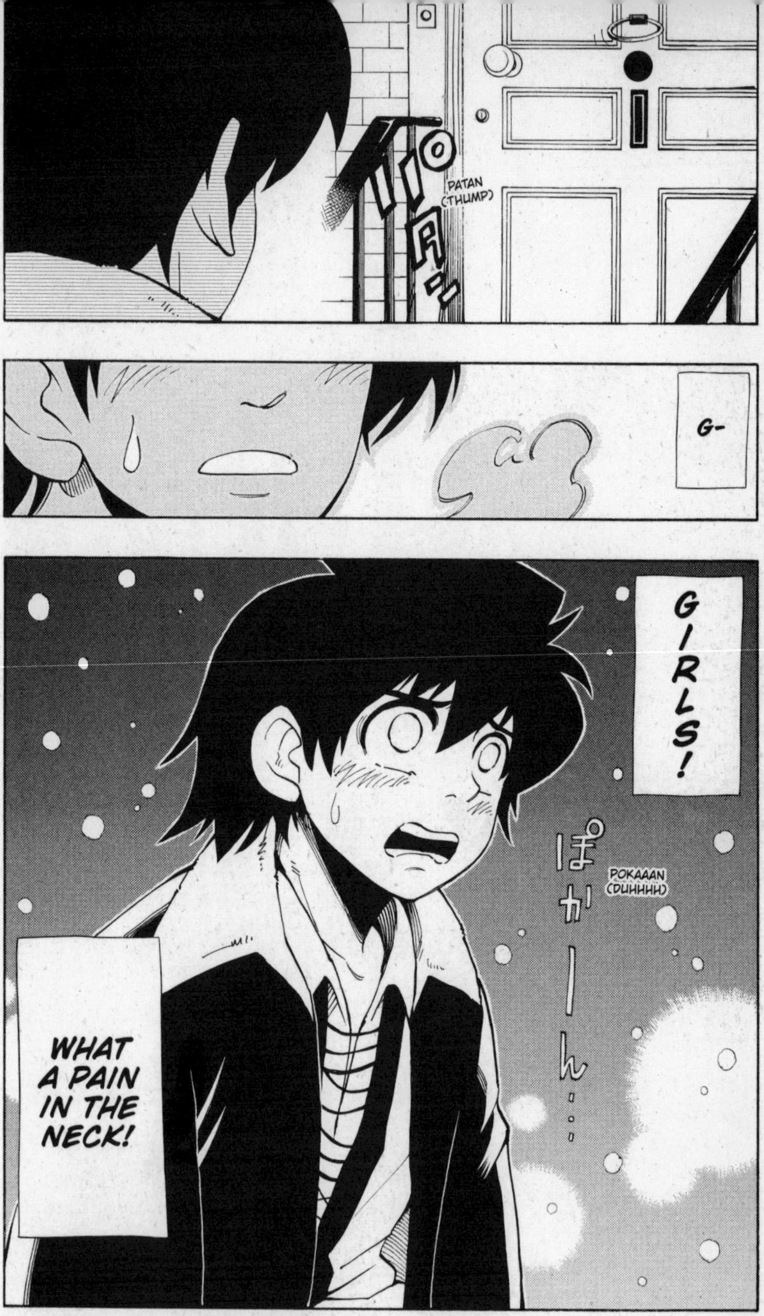
PATAN (THUMP)
G-
GIRLS!
ぽかーん…
POKAAAN (DUHHHH)
WHAT A PAIN IN THE NECK!

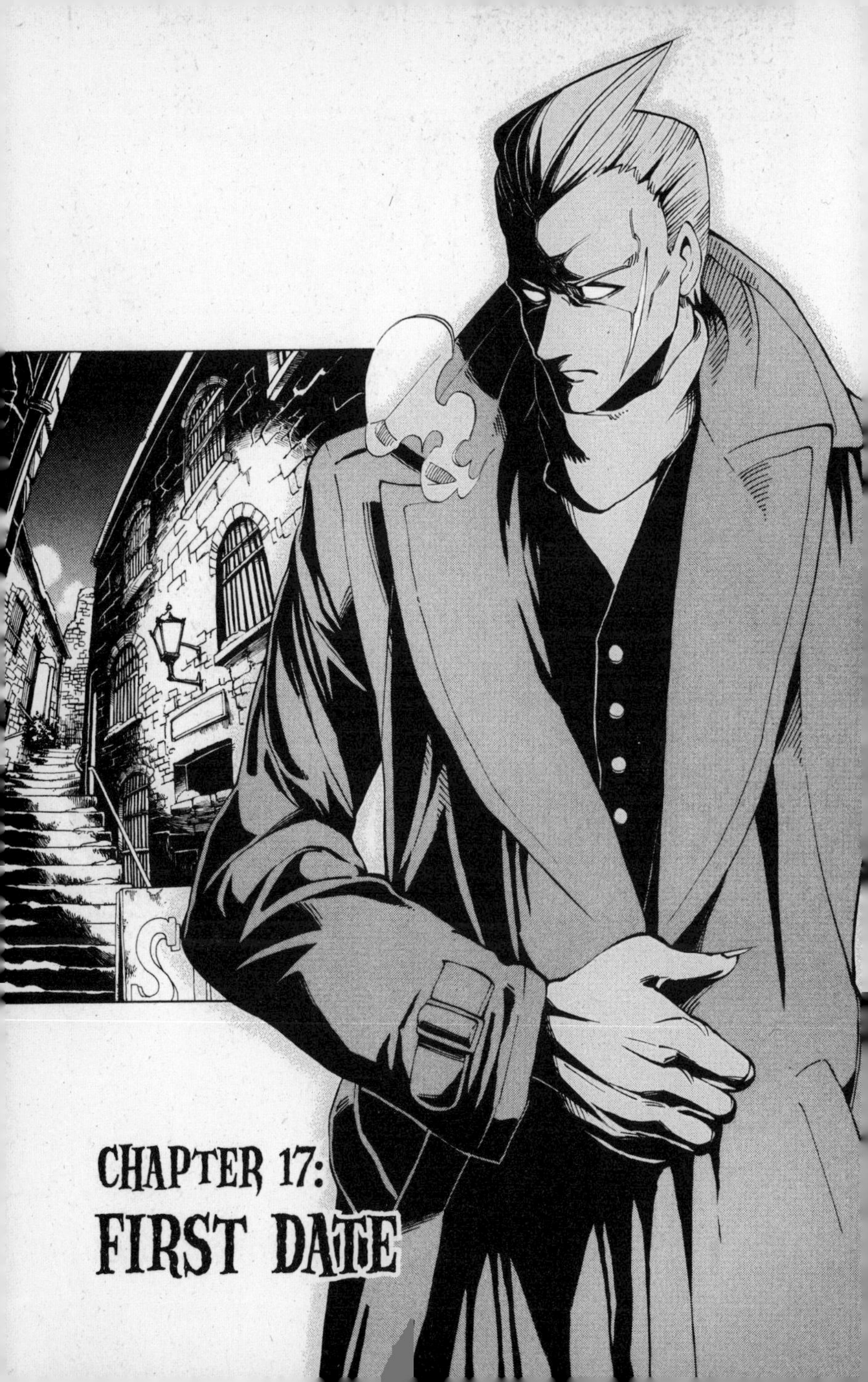
CHAPTER 17:
FIRST DATE

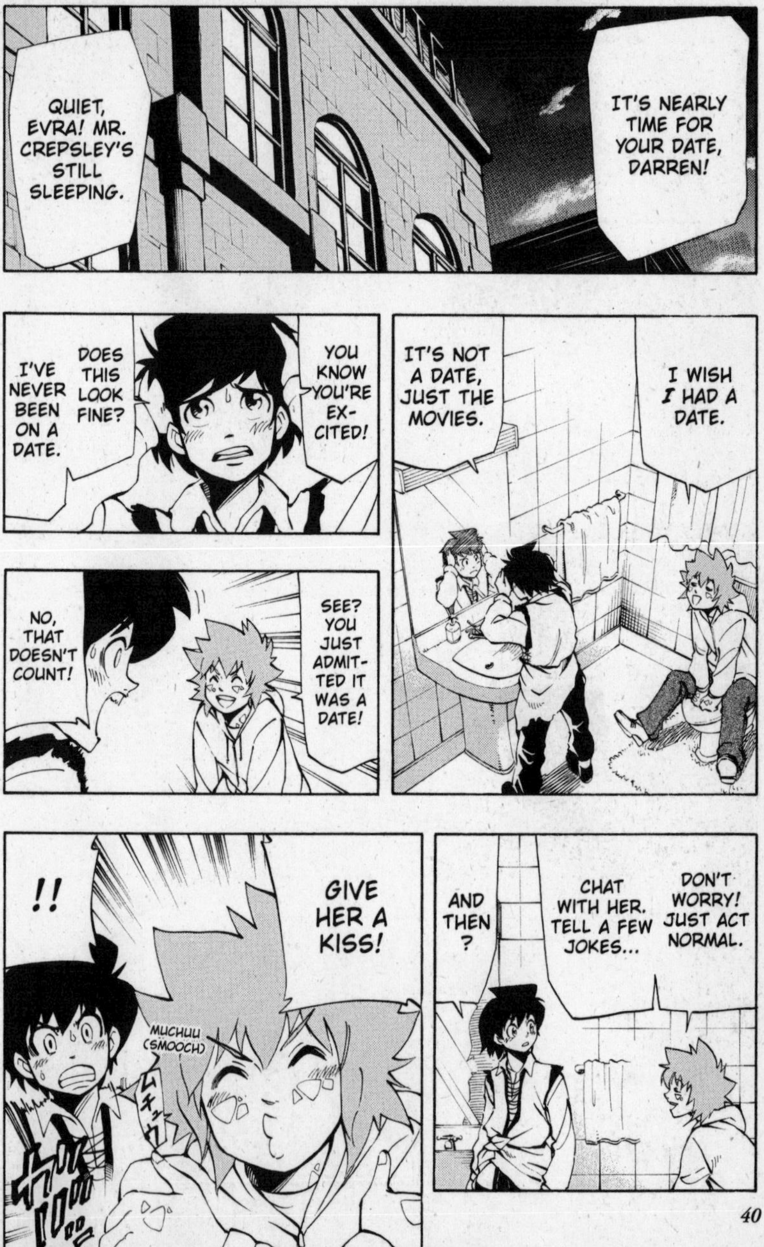
IT'S NEARLY TIME FOR YOUR DATE, DARREN!
QUIET, EVRA! MR. CREPSLEY'S STILL SLEEPING.
IT'S NOT A DATE, JUST THE MOVIES.
I WISH *I* HAD A DATE.
YOU KNOW YOU'RE EX-CITED!
DOES THIS LOOK FINE?
I'VE NEVER BEEN ON A DATE.
SEE? YOU JUST ADMIT-TED IT WAS A DATE!
NO, THAT DOESN'T COUNT!
DON'T WORRY! JUST ACT NORMAL.
CHAT WITH HER. TELL A FEW JOKES...
AND THEN?
GIVE HER A KISS!
!!
MUCHUU (SMOOCH)
GABA (GRAB)

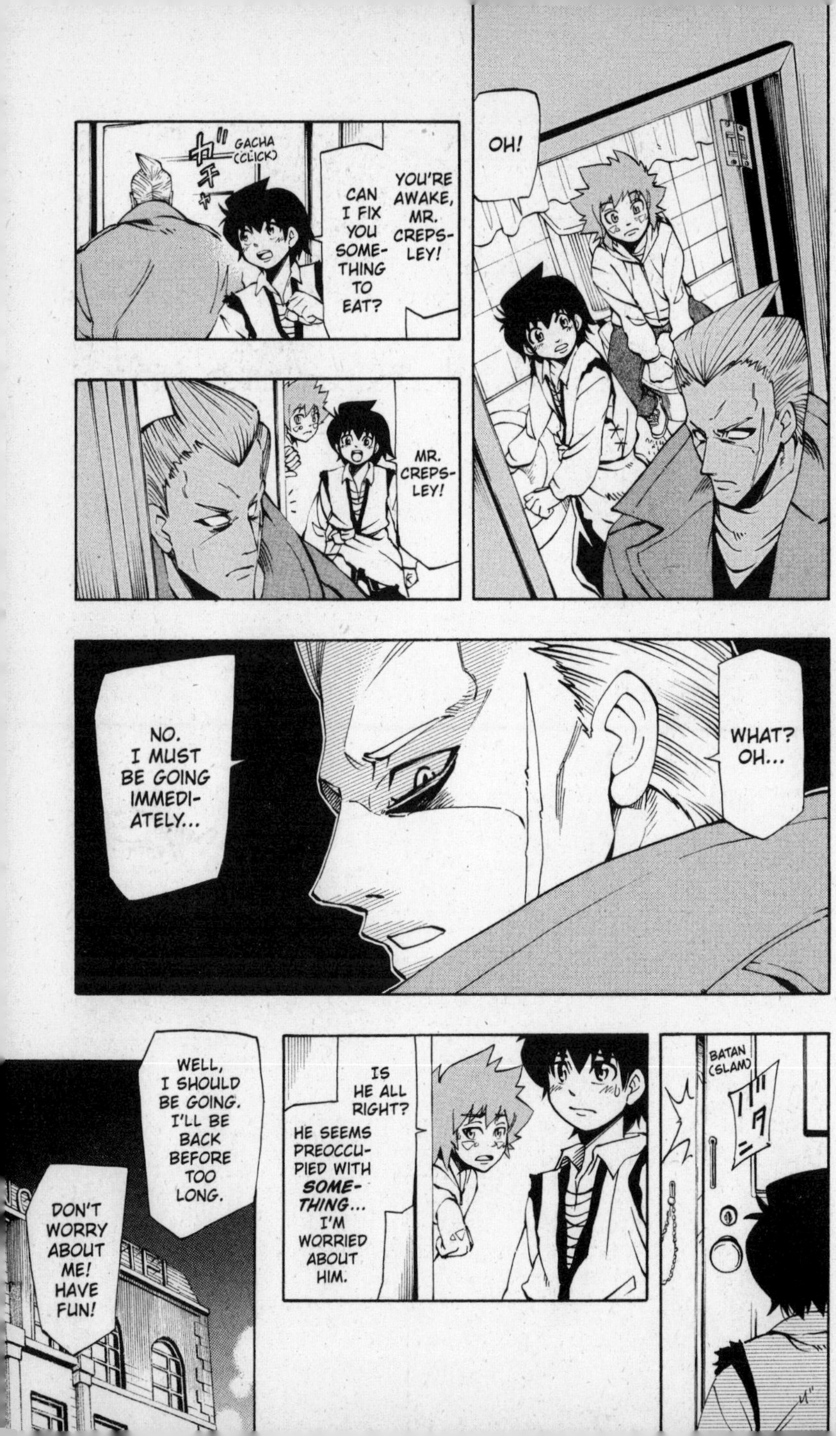
OH!
GACHA (CLICK)
YOU'RE AWAKE, MR. CREPSLEY!
CAN I FIX YOU SOMETHING TO EAT?
MR. CREPSLEY!
WHAT? OH...
NO. I MUST BE GOING IMMEDIATELY...
BATAN (SLAM)
IS HE ALL RIGHT?
HE SEEMS PREOCCUPIED WITH *SOMETHING*... I'M WORRIED ABOUT HIM.
WELL, I SHOULD BE GOING. I'LL BE BACK BEFORE TOO LONG.
DON'T WORRY ABOUT ME! HAVE FUN!

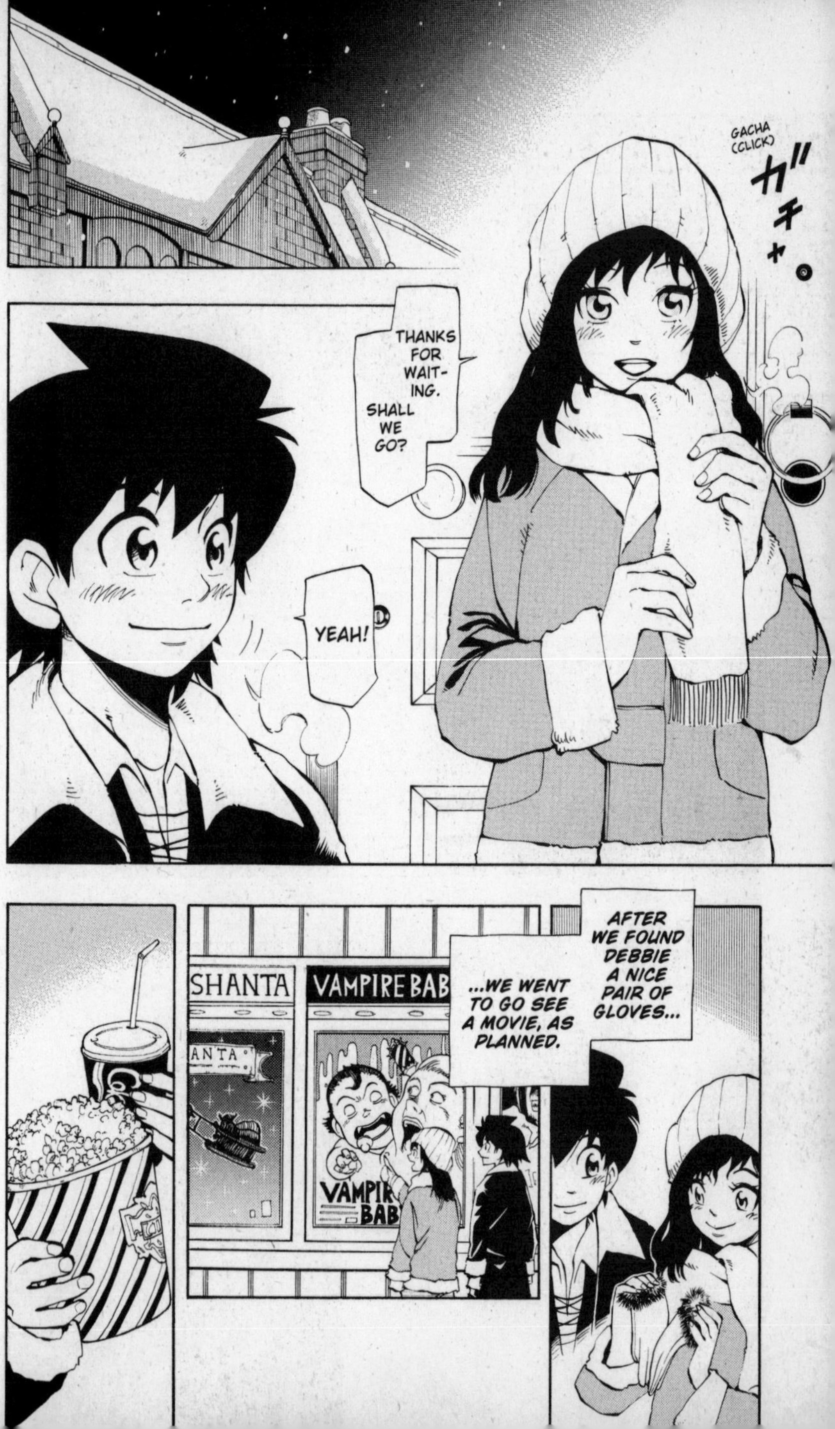
GACHA (CLICK)
ガチャ
THANKS FOR WAIT-ING. SHALL WE GO?
YEAH!
AFTER WE FOUND DEBBIE A NICE PAIR OF GLOVES...
...WE WENT TO GO SEE A MOVIE, AS PLANNED.
SHANTA
VAMPIRE BAB
ANTA
VAMPIR BAB

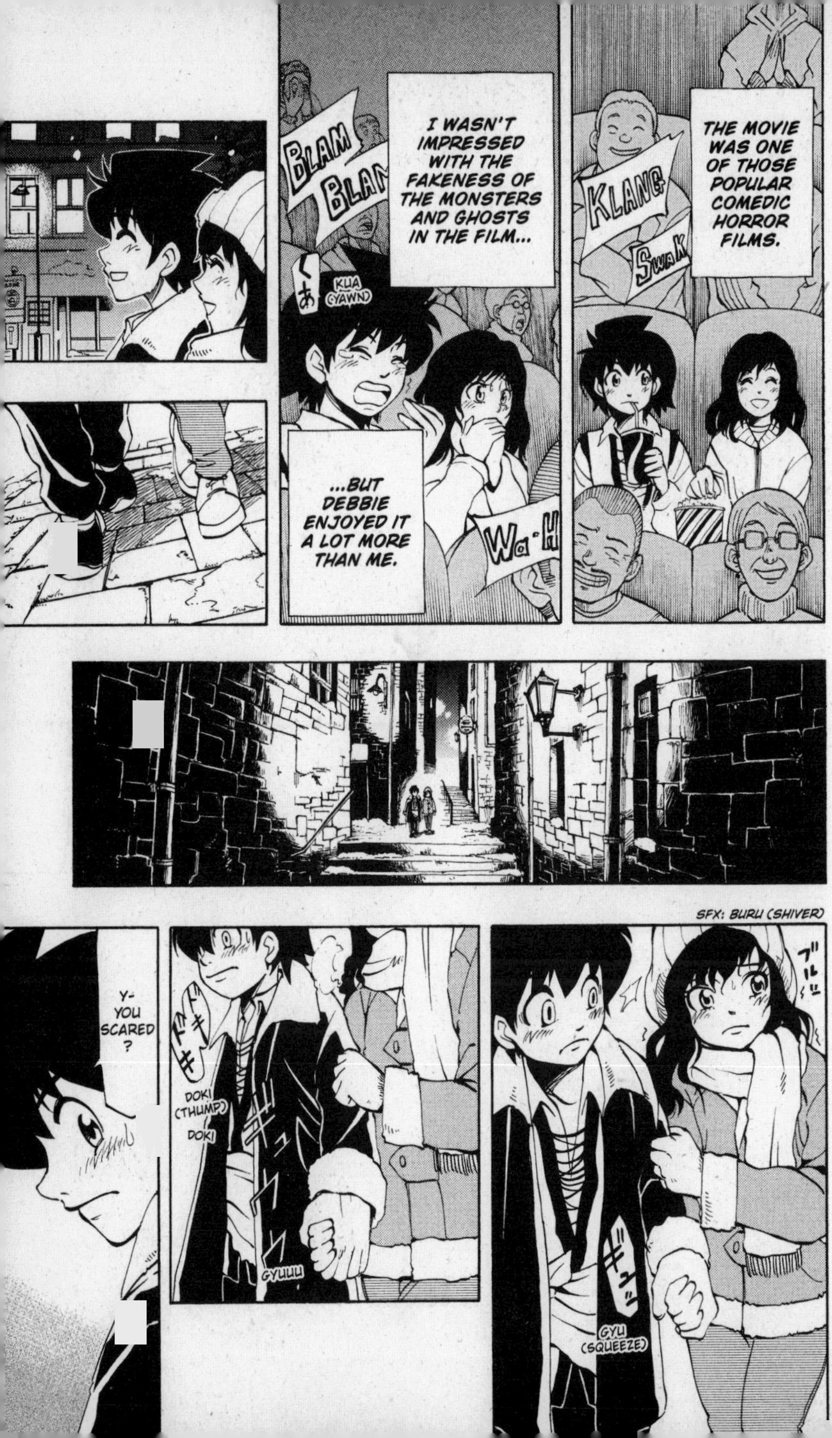
THE MOVIE WAS ONE OF THOSE POPULAR COMEDIC HORROR FILMS.
KLANG
SWAK
I WASN'T IMPRESSED WITH THE FAKENESS OF THE MONSTERS AND GHOSTS IN THE FILM...
BLAM BLAM
KUA (YAWN)
...BUT DEBBIE ENJOYED IT A LOT MORE THAN ME.
WA-H
SFX: BURU (SHIVER)
GYU (SQUEEZE)
DOKI (THUMP) DOKI
GYUUU
Y-YOU SCARED?

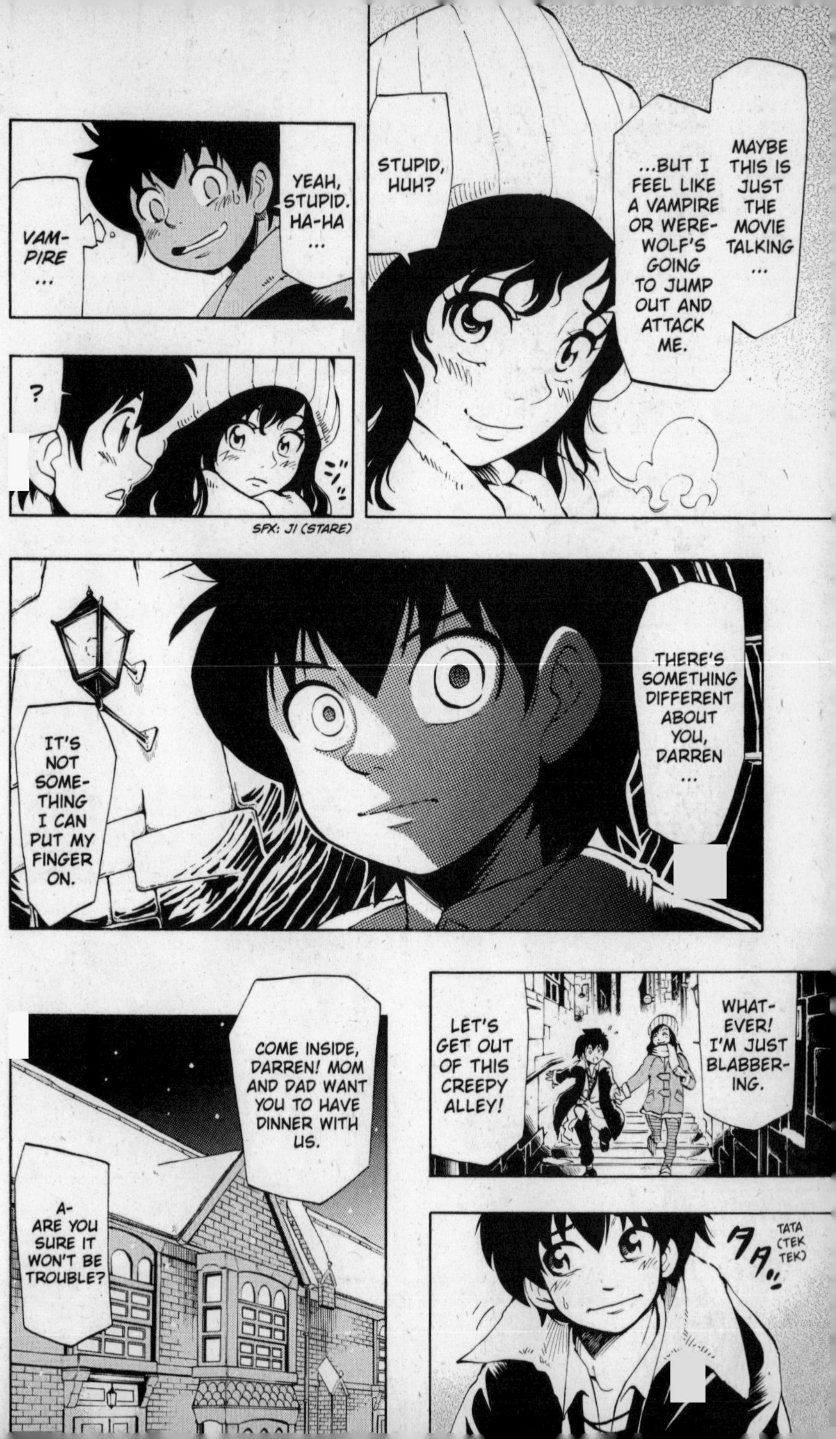
STUPID, HUH?
MAYBE THIS IS JUST THE MOVIE TALKING ...
...BUT I FEEL LIKE A VAMPIRE OR WERE-WOLF'S GOING TO JUMP OUT AND ATTACK ME.
YEAH, STUPID. HA-HA ...
VAM-PIRE ...
?
SFX: JI (STARE)
THERE'S SOMETHING DIFFERENT ABOUT YOU, DARREN ...
IT'S NOT SOME-THING I CAN PUT MY FINGER ON.
WHAT-EVER! I'M JUST BLABBER-ING.
LET'S GET OUT OF THIS CREEPY ALLEY!
TATA (TEK TEK)
COME INSIDE, DARREN! MOM AND DAD WANT YOU TO HAVE DINNER WITH US.
A- ARE YOU SURE IT WON'T BE TROUBLE?

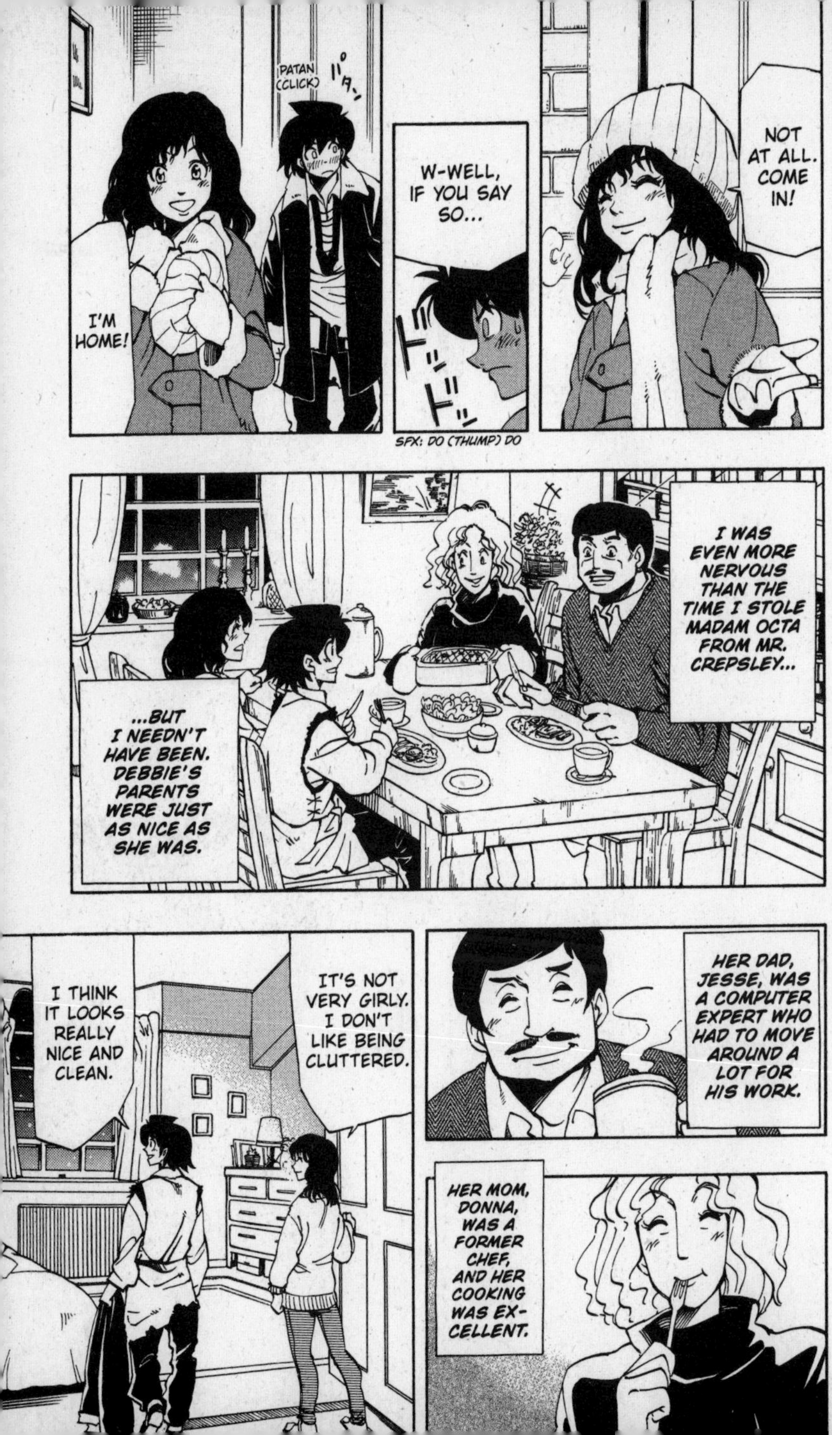
NOT AT ALL. COME IN!
W-WELL, IF YOU SAY SO...
SFX: DO (THUMP) DO
PATAN (CLICK)
I'M HOME!
I WAS EVEN MORE NERVOUS THAN THE TIME I STOLE MADAM OCTA FROM MR. CREPSLEY...
...BUT I NEEDN'T HAVE BEEN. DEBBIE'S PARENTS WERE JUST AS NICE AS SHE WAS.
HER DAD, JESSE, WAS A COMPUTER EXPERT WHO HAD TO MOVE AROUND A LOT FOR HIS WORK.
HER MOM, DONNA, WAS A FORMER CHEF, AND HER COOKING WAS EX-CELLENT.
IT'S NOT VERY GIRLY. I DON'T LIKE BEING CLUTTERED.
I THINK IT LOOKS REALLY NICE AND CLEAN.

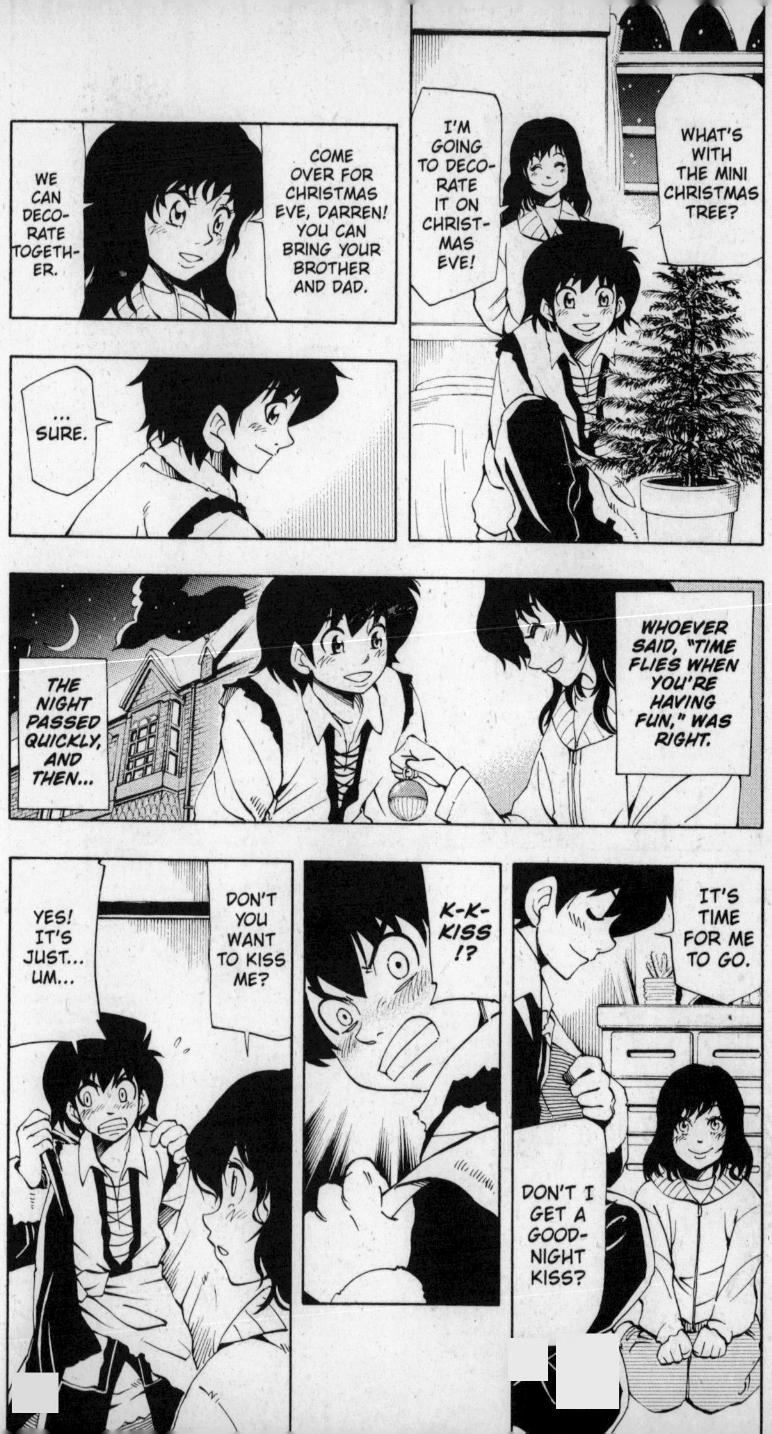
WHAT'S WITH THE MINI CHRISTMAS TREE?
I'M GOING TO DECORATE IT ON CHRISTMAS EVE!
COME OVER FOR CHRISTMAS EVE, DARREN! YOU CAN BRING YOUR BROTHER AND DAD.
WE CAN DECORATE TOGETHER.
... SURE.
WHOEVER SAID, "TIME FLIES WHEN YOU'RE HAVING FUN," WAS RIGHT.
THE NIGHT PASSED QUICKLY, AND THEN...
IT'S TIME FOR ME TO GO.
DON'T I GET A GOOD-NIGHT KISS?
K-K-KISS!?
DON'T YOU WANT TO KISS ME?
YES! IT'S JUST... UM...

C-CAN'T I SAY GOODBYE TO YOUR PARENTS?

I'LL SHOW YOU OUT.

TON (TEP)

TON

I... UH...

I DON'T CARE ONE WAY OR THE OTHER.

HEY, FORGET IT.

ガチャ...
GACHA (CLICK)

ONLY, BE A LITTLE BRAVER, OKAY?

OKAY, YOU CAN COME OVER TO-MORROW. I WANT YOU TO!

Y-YEAH... THAT'S IT.

......

SURE, IF YOU WANT TO.

CAN I COME OVER TOMOR-ROW?

SCARED?

LOOK, DEBBIE, I'M SORRY I DIDN'T KISS YOU. I'M JUST ...

クス (KUSU (GIGGLE)

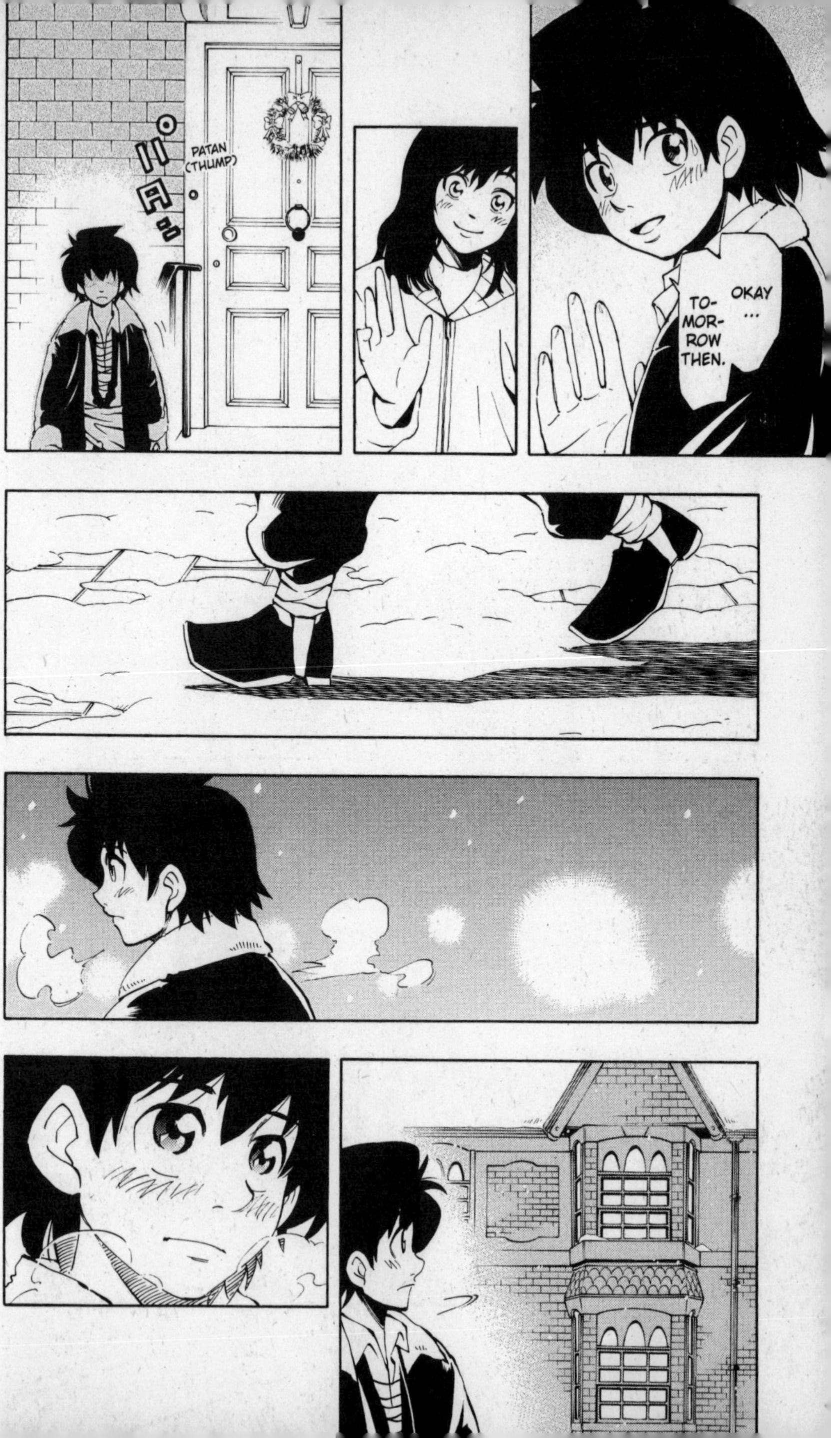
OKAY ...
TO-MORROW THEN.
パタン
PATAN (THUMP)

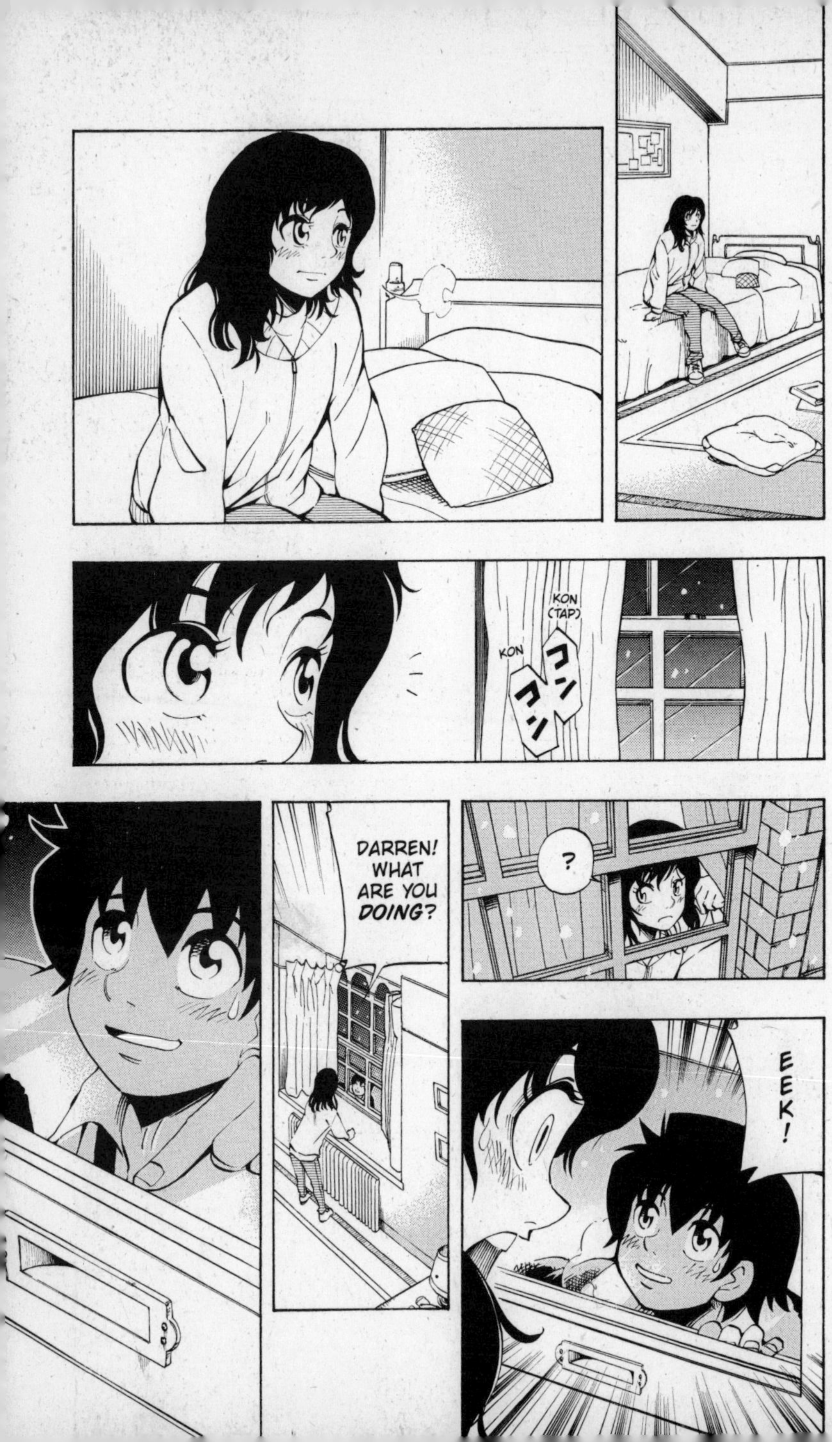
KON (TAP)
KON
コン
コン
?
DARREN! WHAT ARE YOU DOING?
EEK!

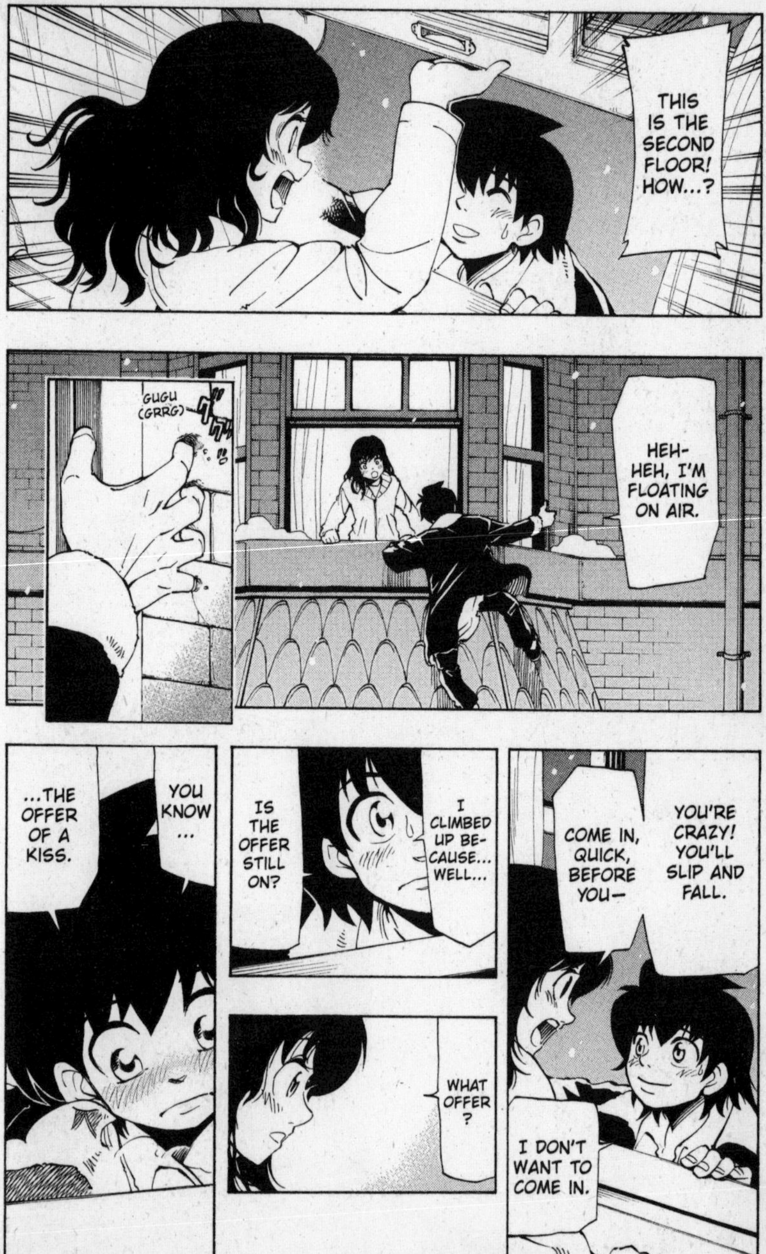
THIS IS THE SECOND FLOOR! HOW...?
HEH-HEH, I'M FLOATING ON AIR.
GUGU (GRRG)
YOU'RE CRAZY! YOU'LL SLIP AND FALL.
COME IN, QUICK, BEFORE YOU—
I DON'T WANT TO COME IN.
I CLIMBED UP BE-CAUSE... WELL...
IS THE OFFER STILL ON?
WHAT OFFER?
YOU KNOW...
...THE OFFER OF A KISS.

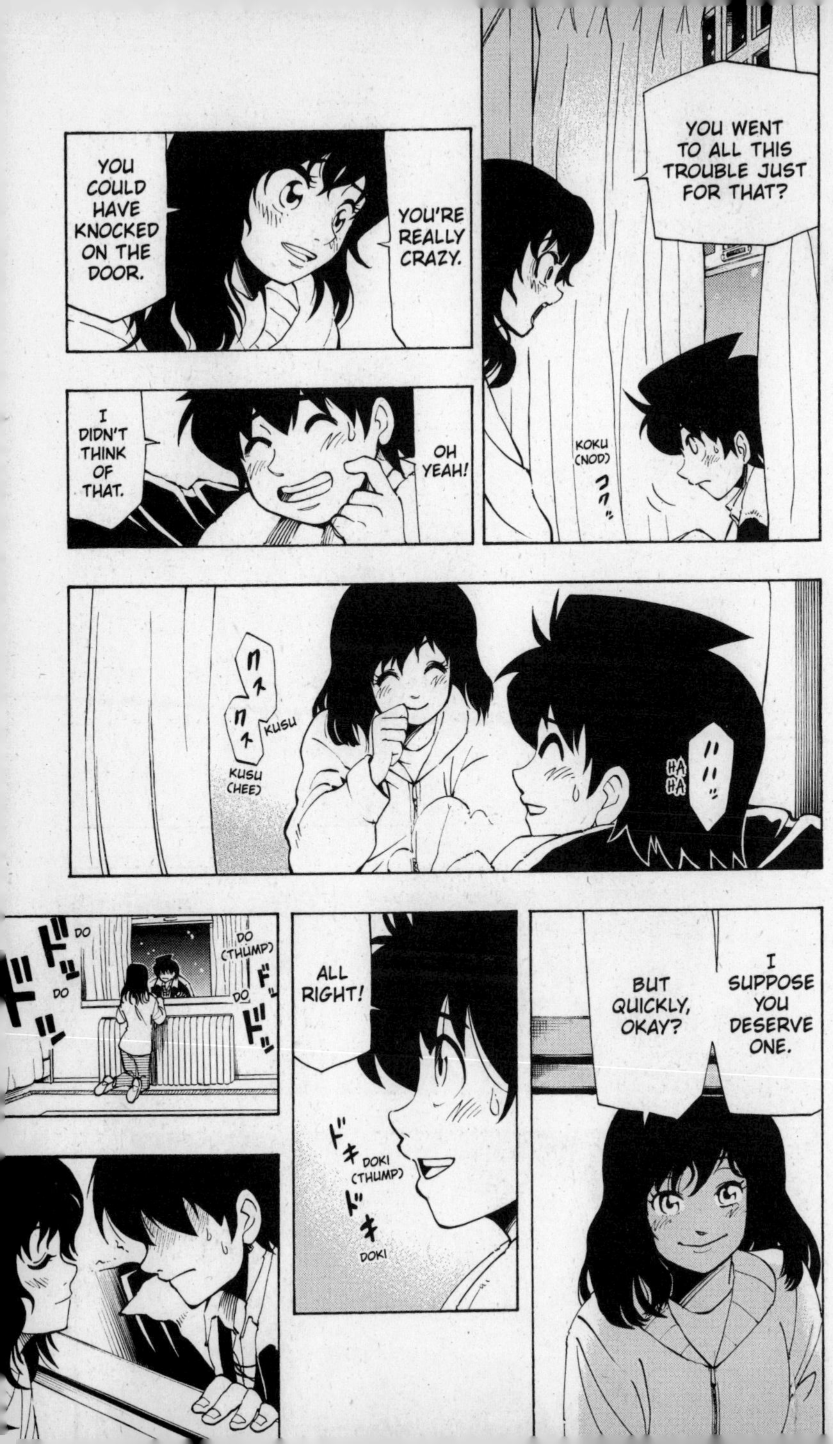
YOU WENT TO ALL THIS TROUBLE JUST FOR THAT?
コクッ
KOKU (NOD)
YOU'RE REALLY CRAZY.
YOU COULD HAVE KNOCKED ON THE DOOR.
OH YEAH!
I DIDN'T THINK OF THAT.
ハハ…
HA HA
クス
KUSU
クス
KUSU (HEE)
I SUPPOSE YOU DESERVE ONE.
BUT QUICKLY, OKAY?
ALL RIGHT!
ドキ
DOKI (THUMP)
ドキ
DOKI
ドッ
DO (THUMP)
ドッ
DO
ドッ
DO
ドッ
DO

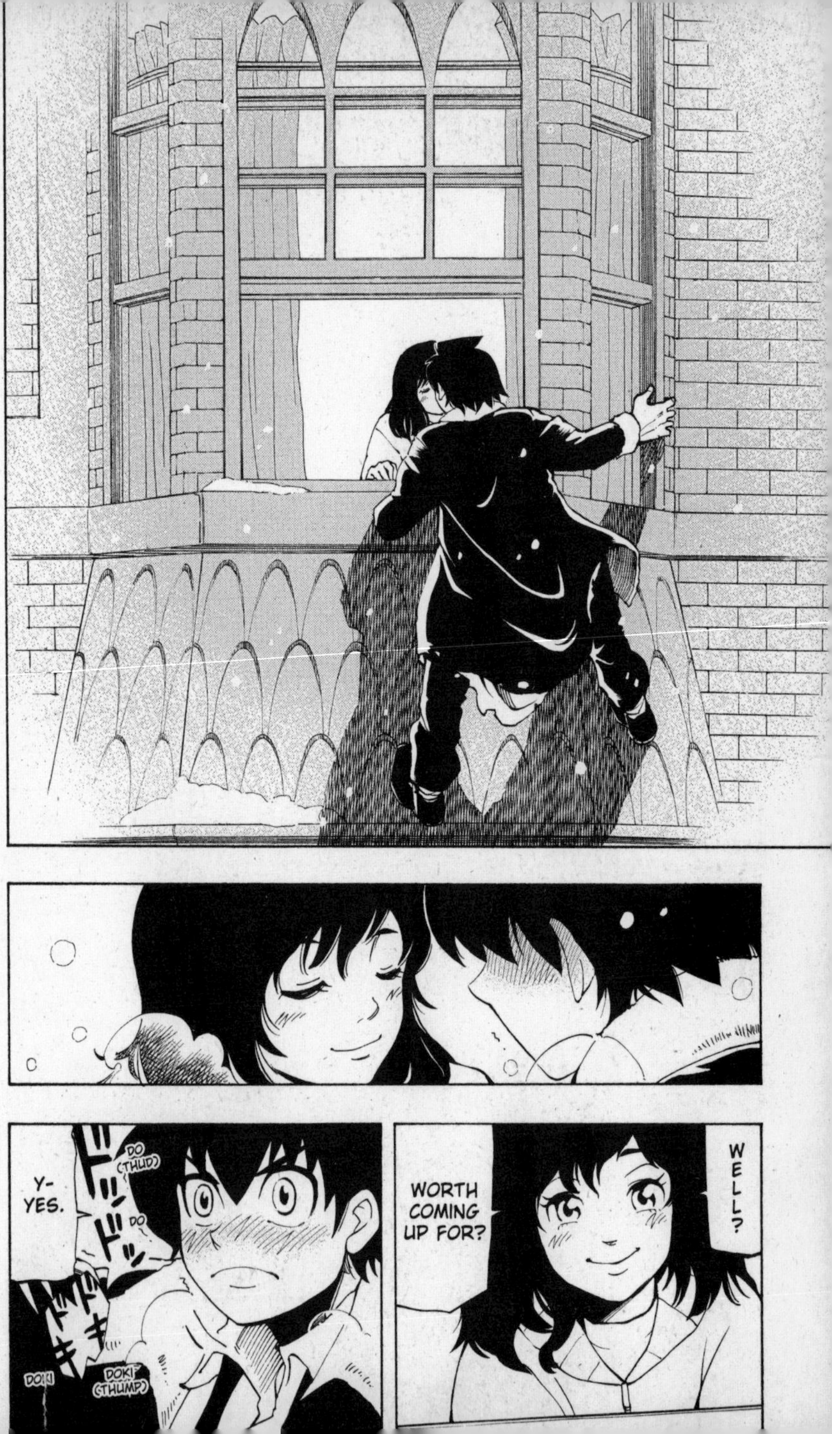
WELL?
WORTH COMING UP FOR?
Y- YES.
DO (THUD)
DO
DOKI
DOKI (THUMP)

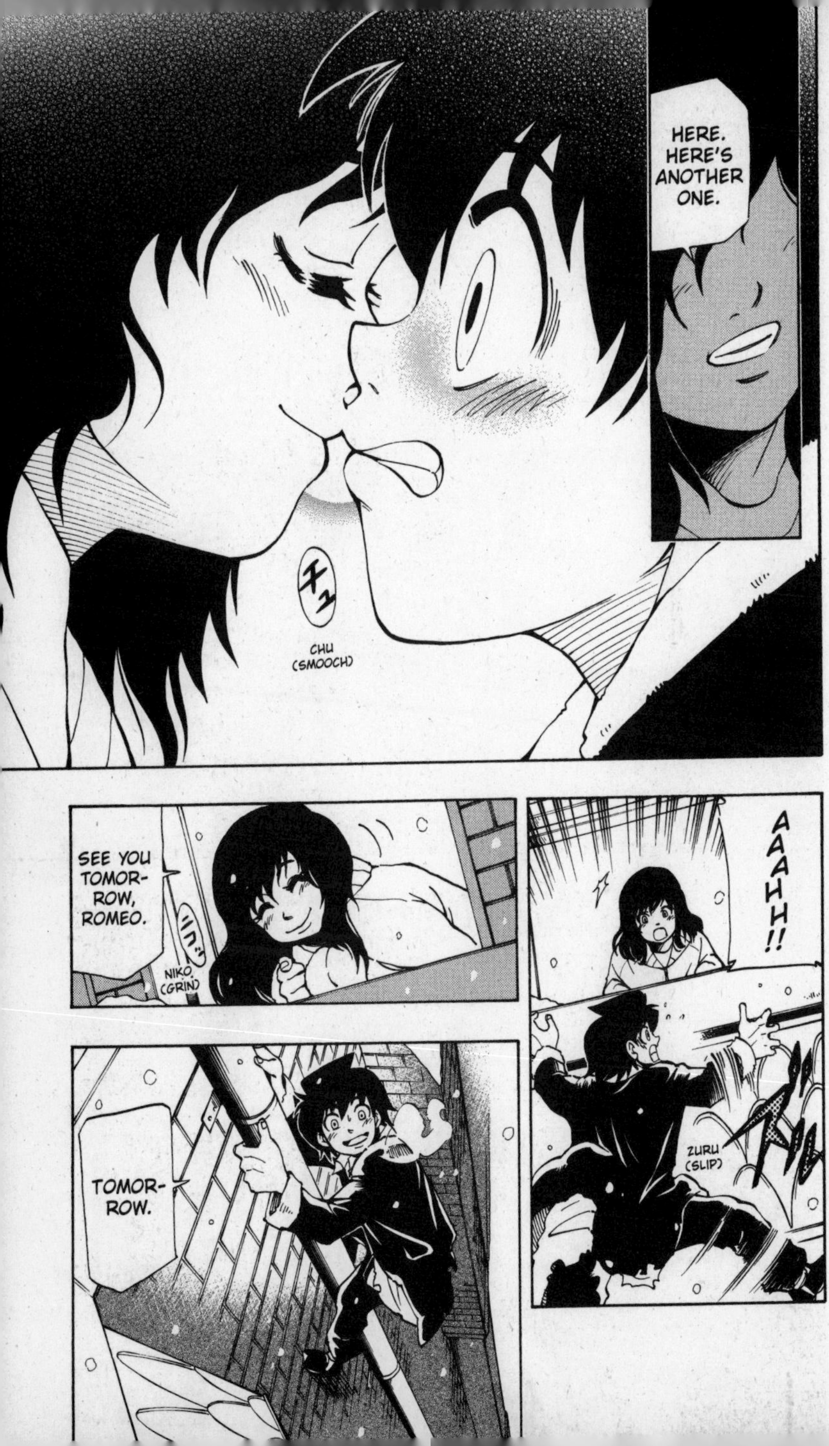
HERE. HERE'S ANOTHER ONE.
チュ
CHU (SMOOCH)
AAAHH!!
SEE YOU TOMOR-ROW, ROMEO.
NIKO (GRIN)
ZURU (SLIP)
TOMOR-ROW.

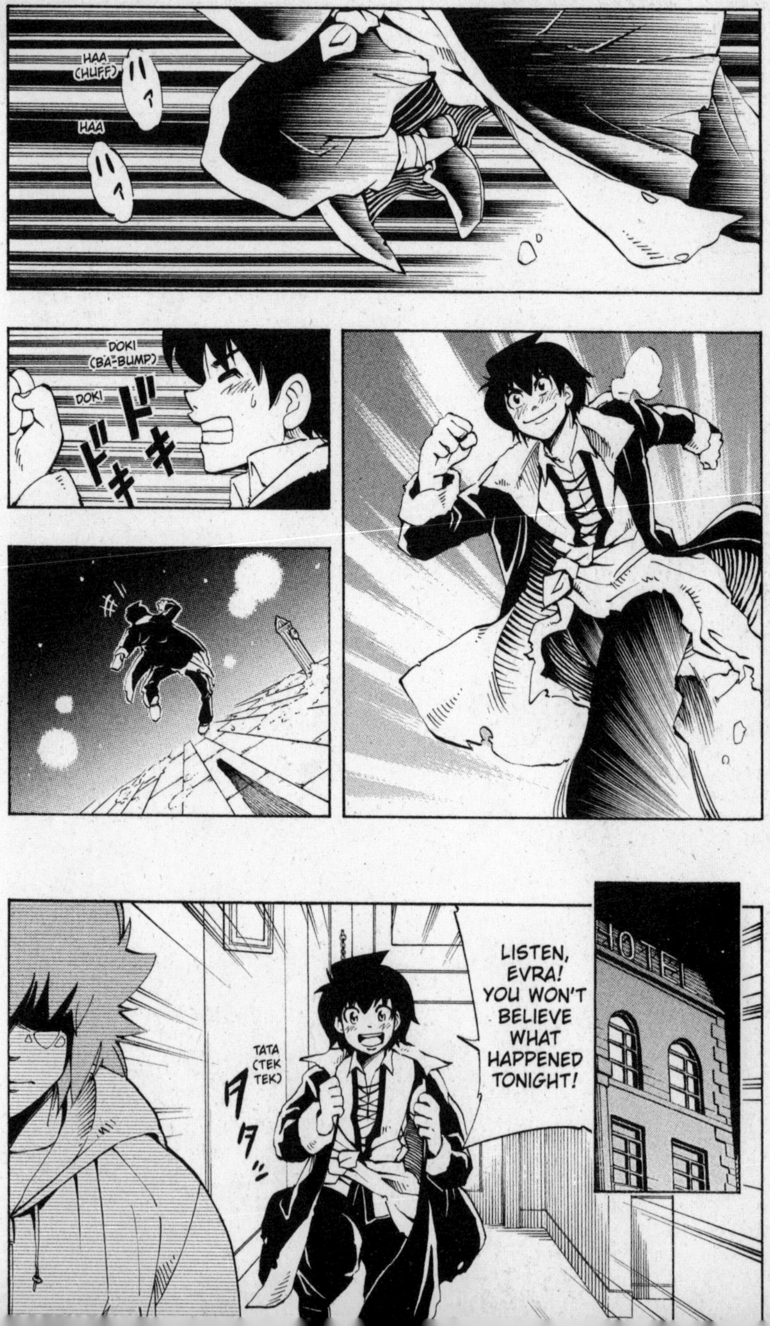
HAA (HUFF)
HAA
DOKI (BA-BUMP)
DOKI
ドキドキ
LISTEN, EVRA! YOU WON'T BELIEVE WHAT HAPPENED TONIGHT!
TATA (TEK TEK)
タタッ

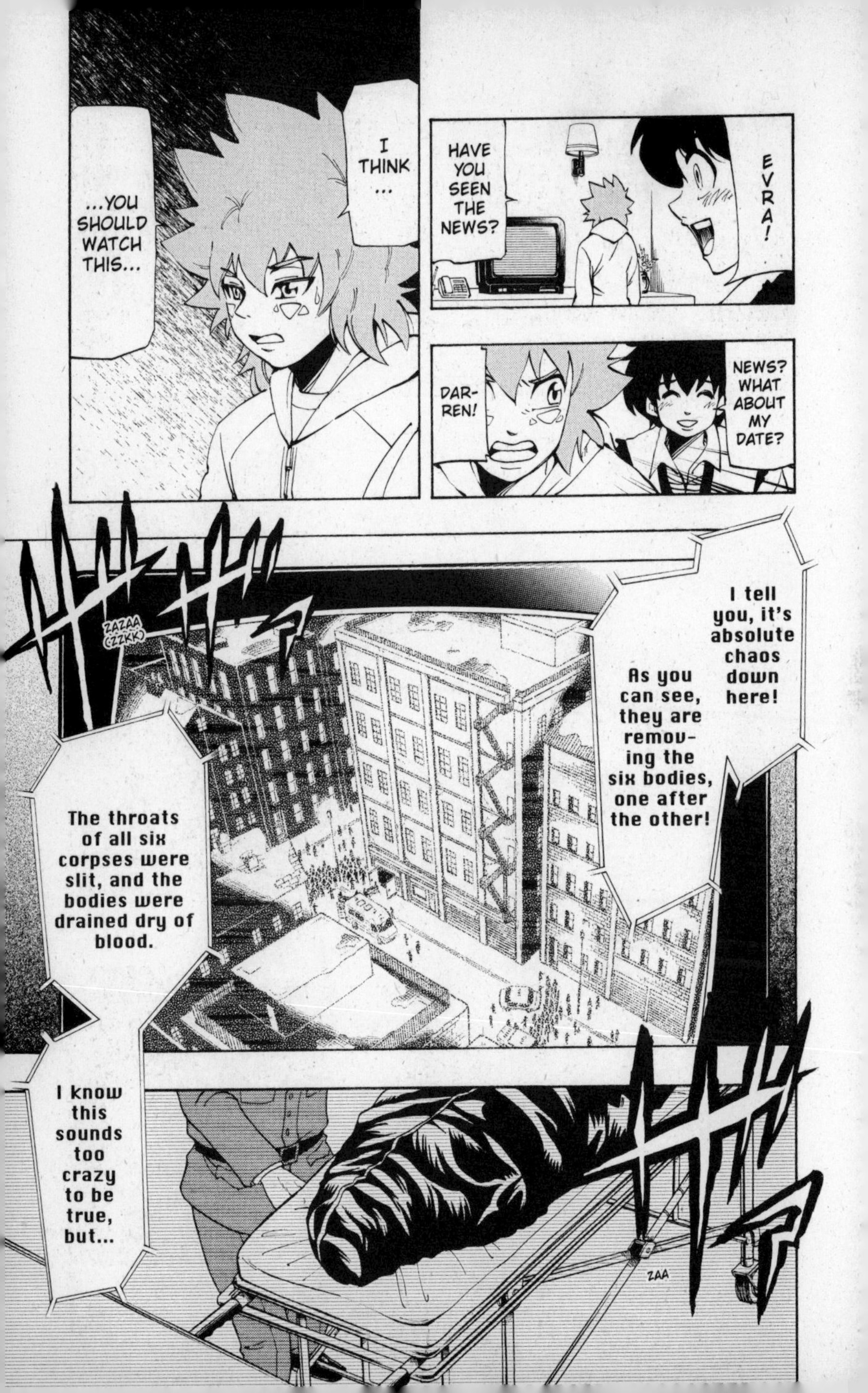
EVRA!
HAVE YOU SEEN THE NEWS?
NEWS? WHAT ABOUT MY DATE?
DAR-REN!
I THINK...
...YOU SHOULD WATCH THIS...
I tell you, it's absolute chaos down here!
As you can see, they are removing the six bodies, one after the other!
ZAZAA (ZZKK)
The throats of all six corpses were slit, and the bodies were drained dry of blood.
ZAA
I know this sounds too crazy to be true, but...

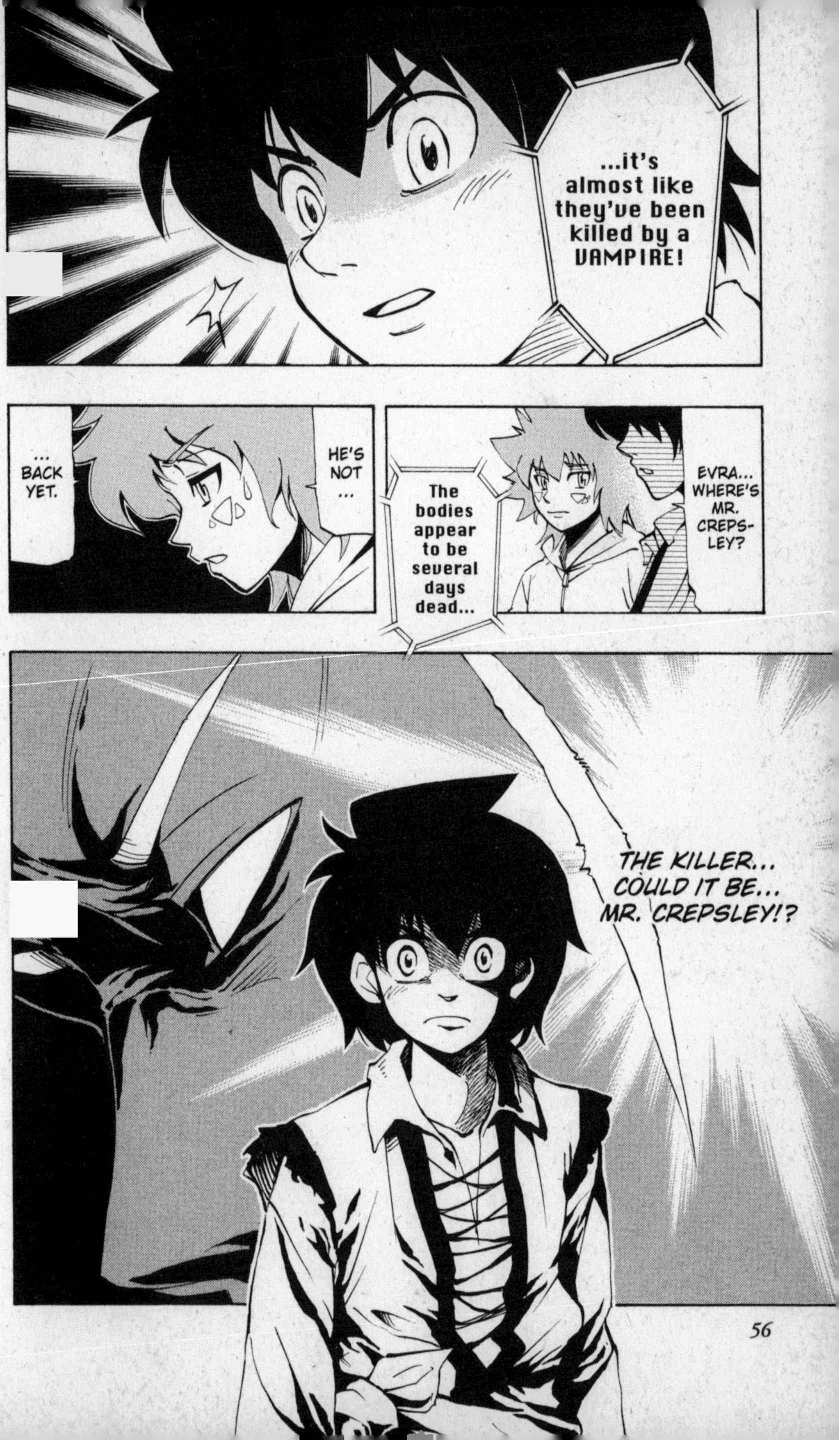
...it's almost like they've been killed by a VAMPIRE!
EVRA... WHERE'S MR. CREPSLEY?
The bodies appear to be several days dead...
HE'S NOT ...
... BACK YET.
THE KILLER... COULD IT BE... MR. CREPSLEY!?

CHAPTER 18:
SUSPICIOUS MINDS

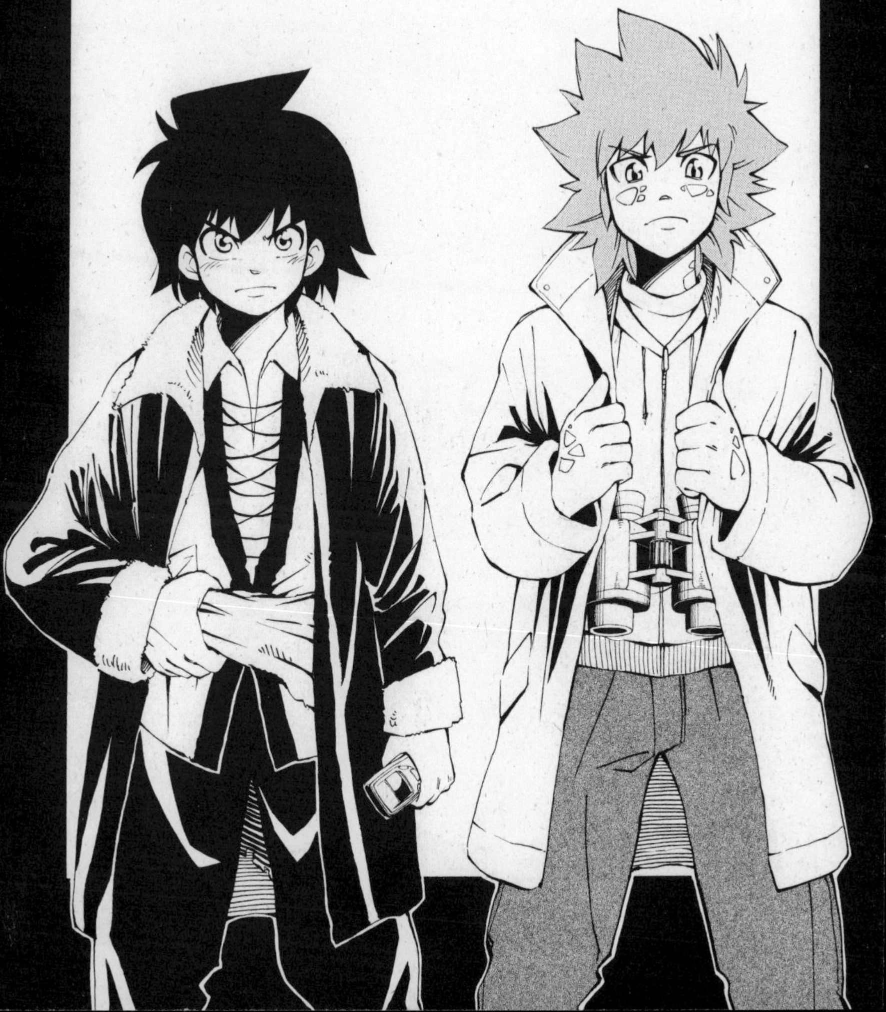

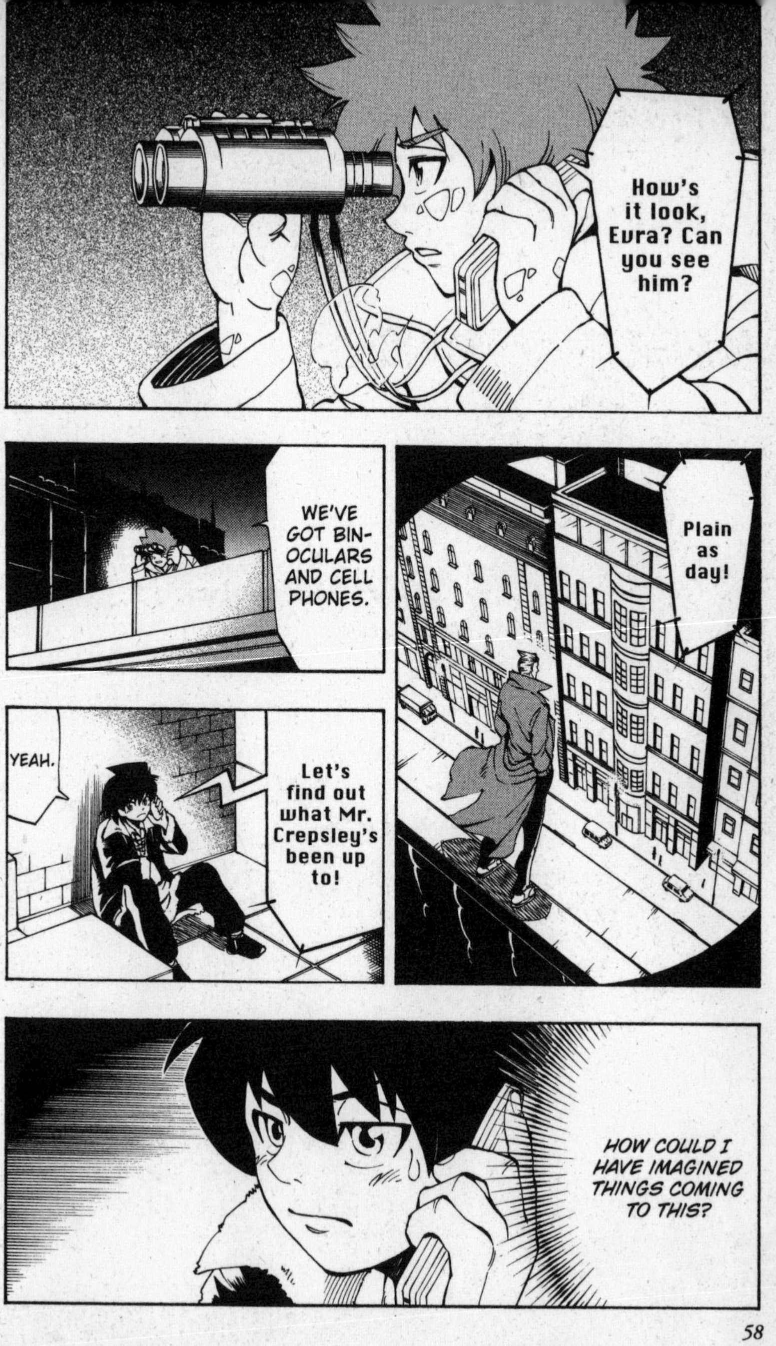
How's it look, Evra? Can you see him?
Plain as day!
WE'VE GOT BIN-OCULARS AND CELL PHONES.
Let's find out what Mr. Crepsley's been up to!
YEAH.
HOW COULD I HAVE IMAGINED THINGS COMING TO THIS?

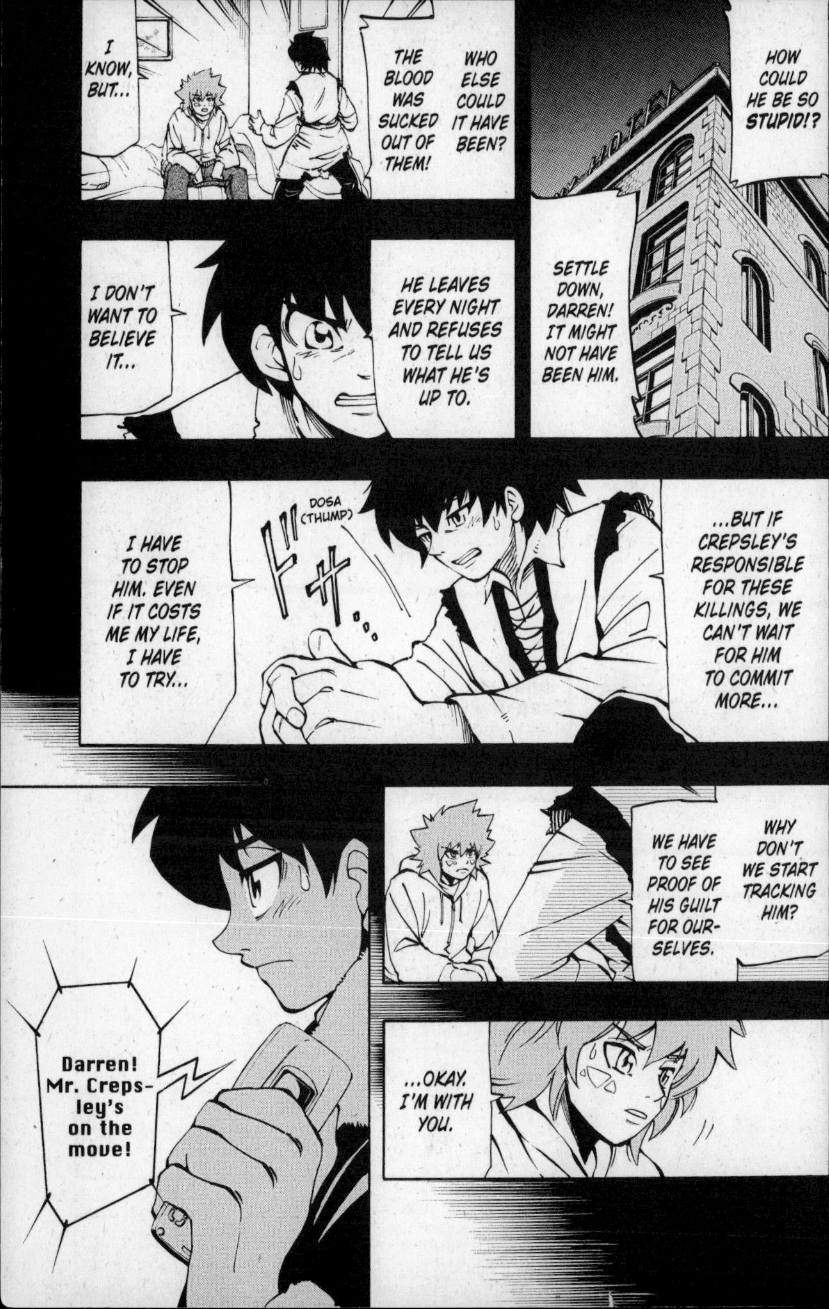
HOW COULD HE BE SO STUPID!?
SETTLE DOWN, DARREN! IT MIGHT NOT HAVE BEEN HIM.
WHO ELSE COULD IT HAVE BEEN?
THE BLOOD WAS SUCKED OUT OF THEM!
I KNOW, BUT...
HE LEAVES EVERY NIGHT AND REFUSES TO TELL US WHAT HE'S UP TO.
I DON'T WANT TO BELIEVE IT...
...BUT IF CREPSLEY'S RESPONSIBLE FOR THESE KILLINGS, WE CAN'T WAIT FOR HIM TO COMMIT MORE...
DOSA (THUMP)
I HAVE TO STOP HIM. EVEN IF IT COSTS ME MY LIFE, I HAVE TO TRY...
WHY DON'T WE START TRACKING HIM?
WE HAVE TO SEE PROOF OF HIS GUILT FOR OUR-SELVES.
...OKAY. I'M WITH YOU.
Darren! Mr. Creps-ley's on the move!

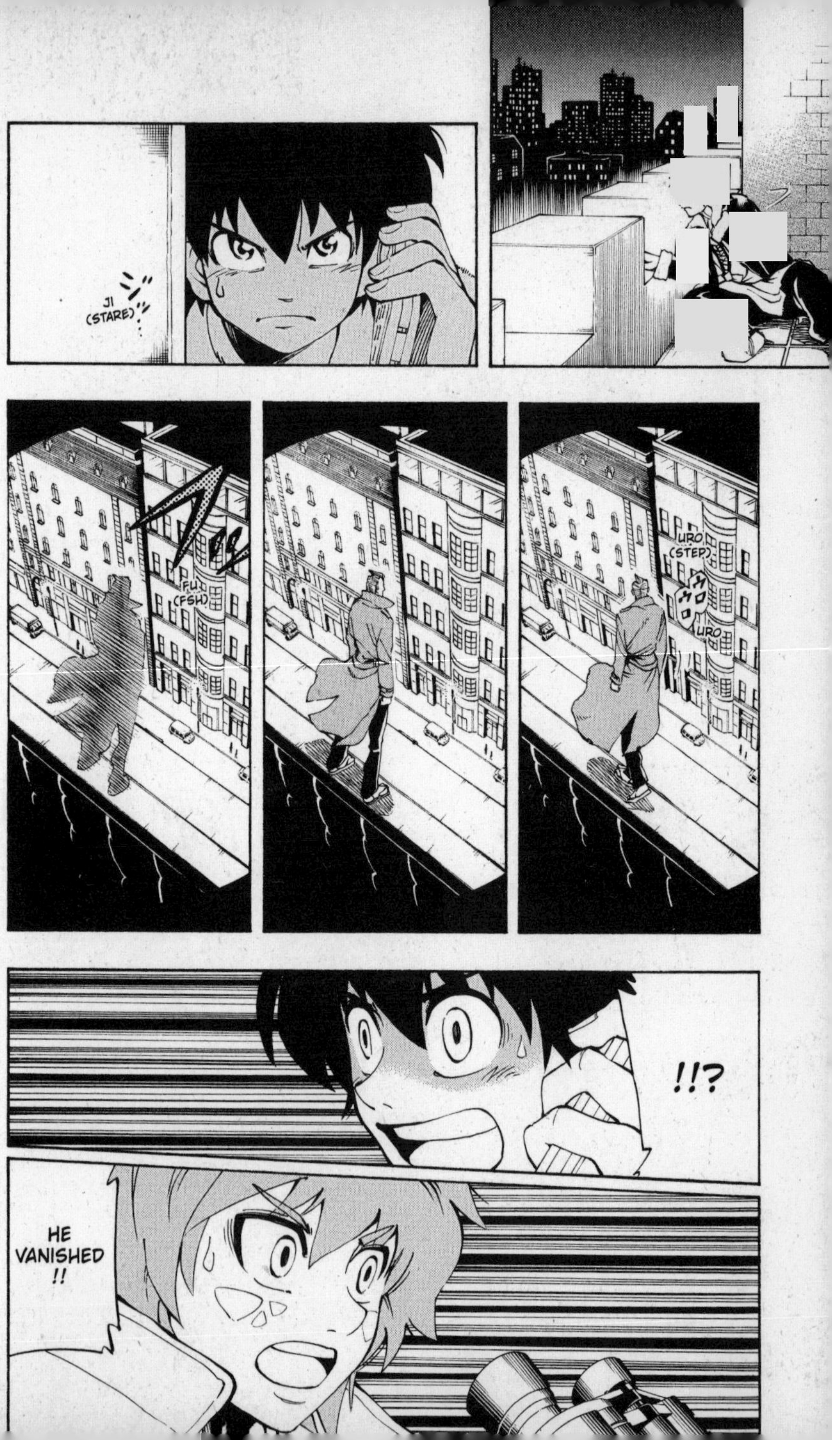
JI (STARE)
URO (STEP)
URO
FU (FSH)
!!?
HE VANISHED !!

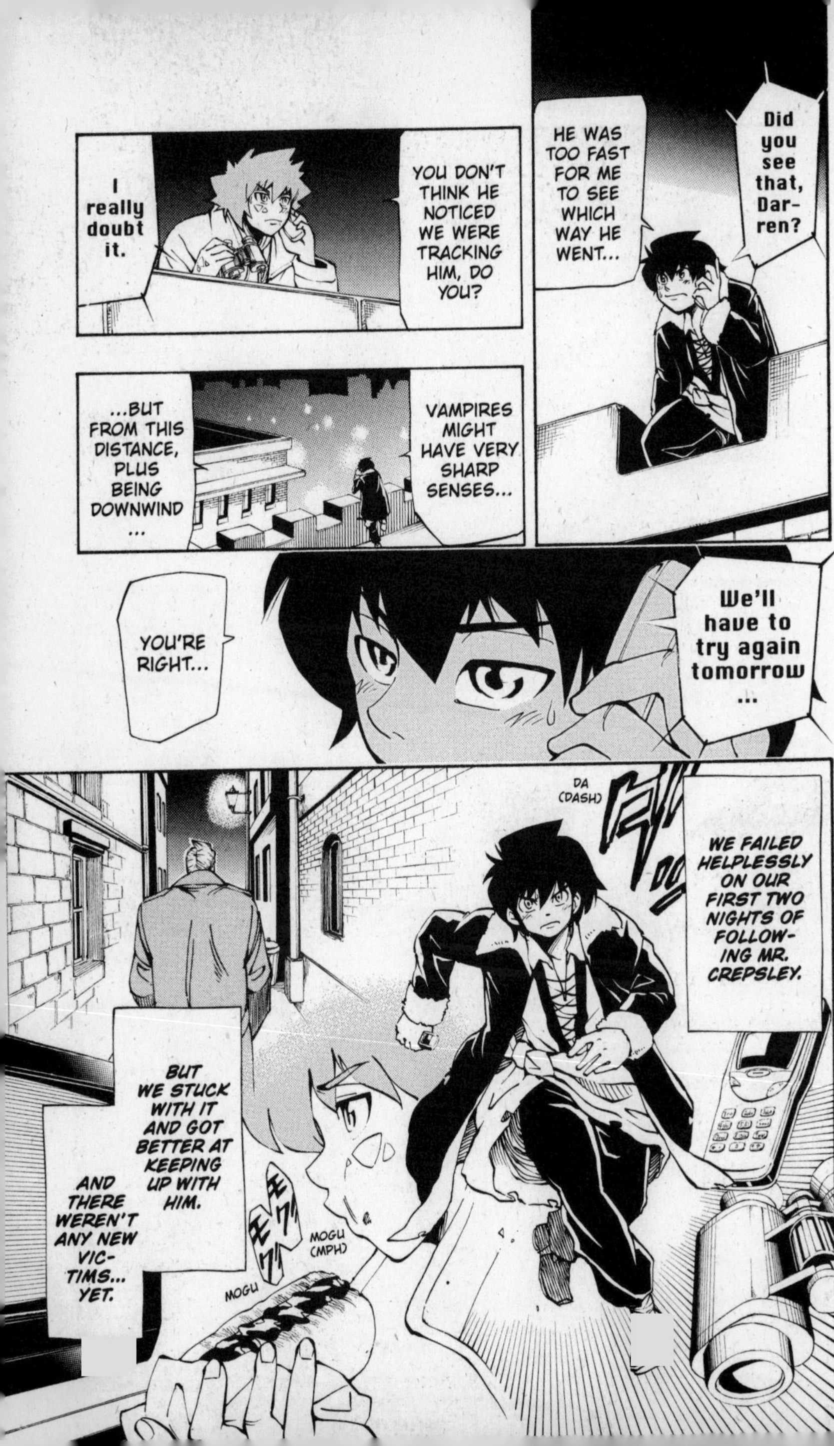

Did you see that, Dar-ren?
HE WAS TOO FAST FOR ME TO SEE WHICH WAY HE WENT...
YOU DON'T THINK HE NOTICED WE WERE TRACKING HIM, DO YOU?
I really doubt it.
VAMPIRES MIGHT HAVE VERY SHARP SENSES...
...BUT FROM THIS DISTANCE, PLUS BEING DOWNWIND...
We'll have to try again tomorrow...
YOU'RE RIGHT...
WE FAILED HELPLESSLY ON OUR FIRST TWO NIGHTS OF FOLLOW-ING MR. CREPSLEY.
DA (DASH)
BUT WE STUCK WITH IT AND GOT BETTER AT KEEPING UP WITH HIM.
AND THERE WEREN'T ANY NEW VIC-TIMS... YET.
MOGU (MPH)
MOGU

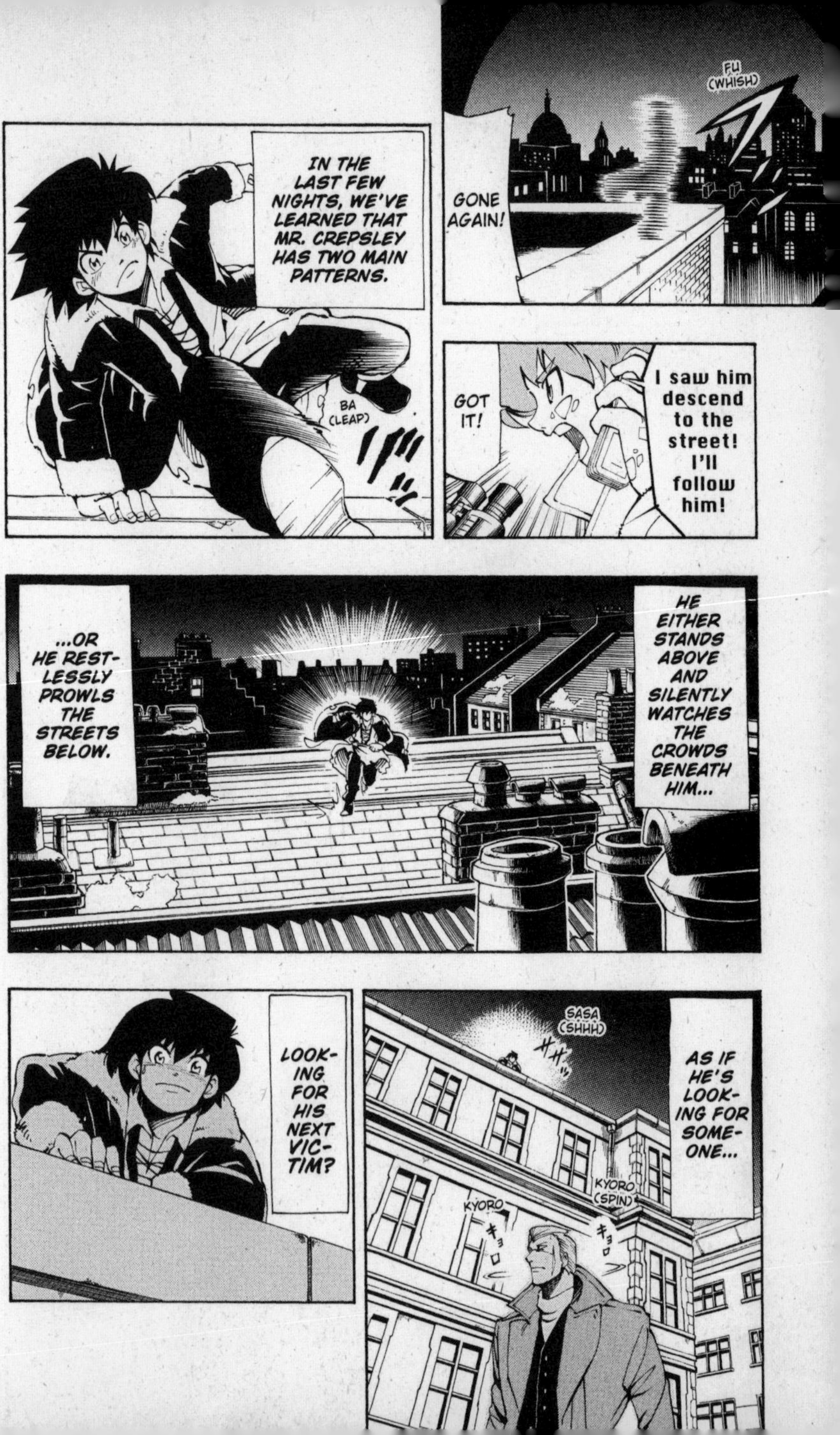
FU (WHISH)
GONE AGAIN!
I saw him descend to the street! I'll follow him!
GOT IT!
IN THE LAST FEW NIGHTS, WE'VE LEARNED THAT MR. CREPSLEY HAS TWO MAIN PATTERNS.
BA (LEAP)
HE EITHER STANDS ABOVE AND SILENTLY WATCHES THE CROWDS BENEATH HIM...
...OR HE RESTLESSLY PROWLS THE STREETS BELOW.
SASA (SHHH)
AS IF HE'S LOOKING FOR SOMEONE...
KYORO (SPIN)
キョロ
KYORO
キョロ
LOOKING FOR HIS NEXT VICTIM?

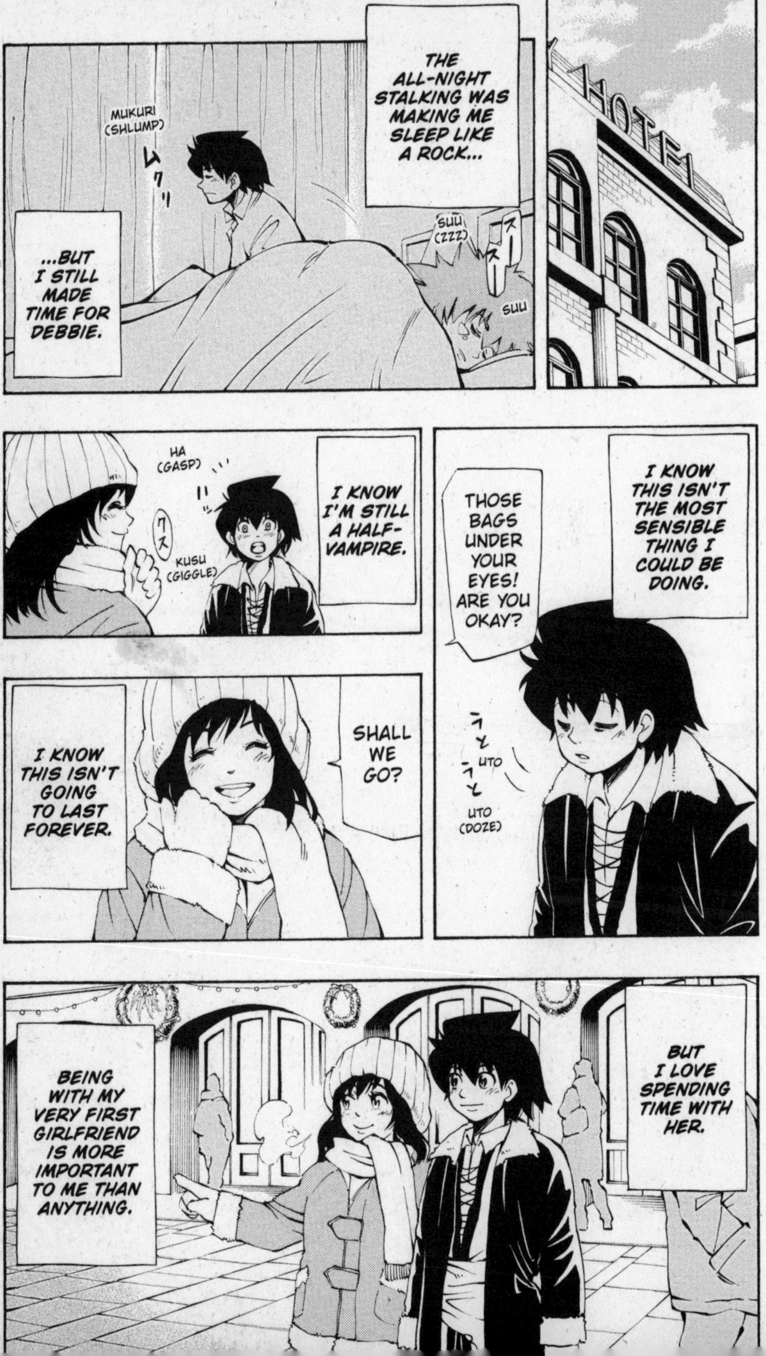
THE ALL-NIGHT STALKING WAS MAKING ME SLEEP LIKE A ROCK...
スース
SUU (ZZZ)
SUU
ムクリ
MUKURI (SHLUMP)
...BUT I STILL MADE TIME FOR DEBBIE.
I KNOW THIS ISN'T THE MOST SENSIBLE THING I COULD BE DOING.
THOSE BAGS UNDER YOUR EYES! ARE YOU OKAY?
ウト
UTO
ウト
UTO (DOZE)
I KNOW I'M STILL A HALF-VAMPIRE.
HA (GASP)
クス
KUSU (GIGGLE)
SHALL WE GO?
I KNOW THIS ISN'T GOING TO LAST FOREVER.
BUT I LOVE SPENDING TIME WITH HER.
BEING WITH MY VERY FIRST GIRLFRIEND IS MORE IMPORTANT TO ME THAN ANYTHING.

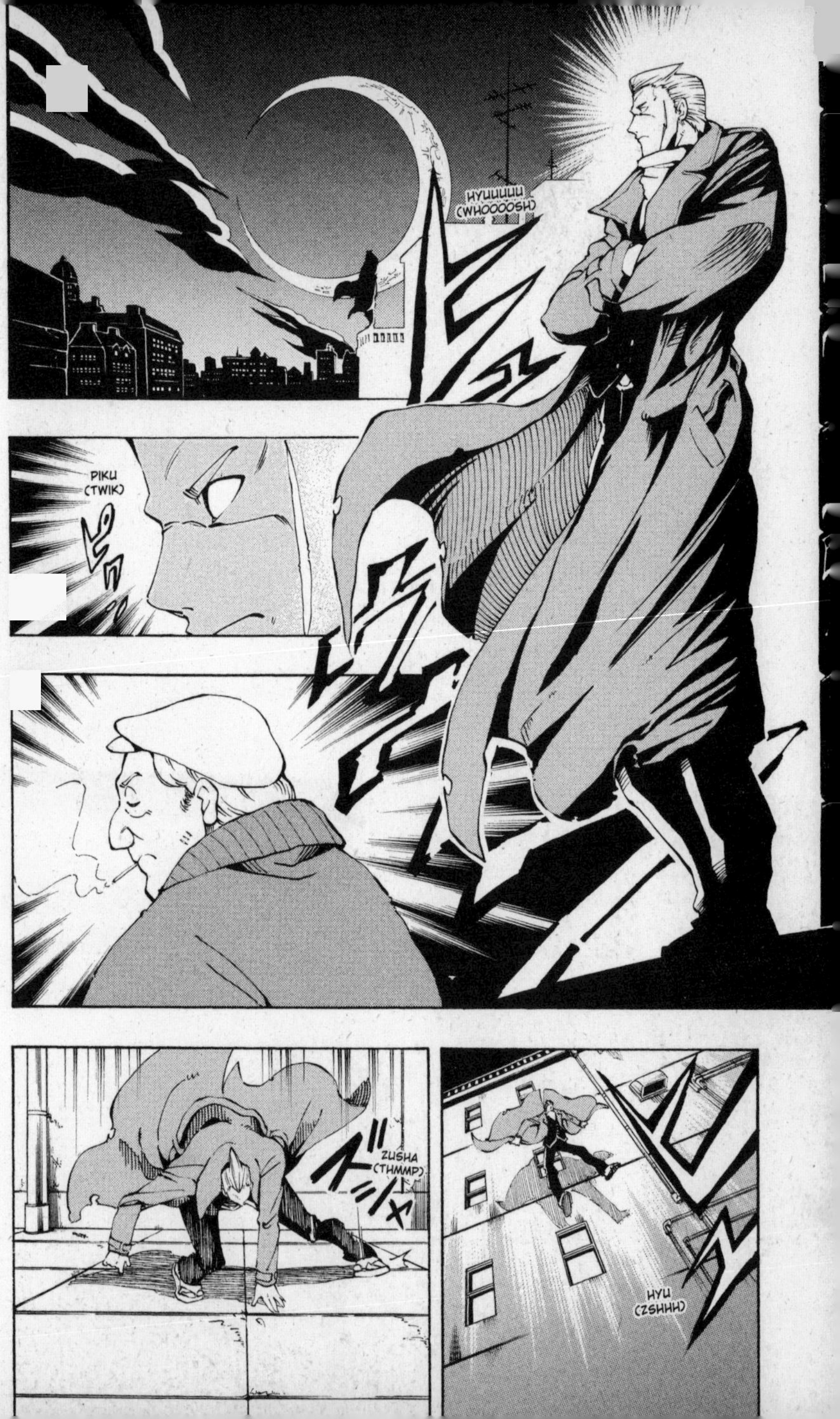
HYUUUUU (WHOOOOSH)
PIKU (TWIK)
HYU (ZSHHH)
ZUSHA (THMMP)

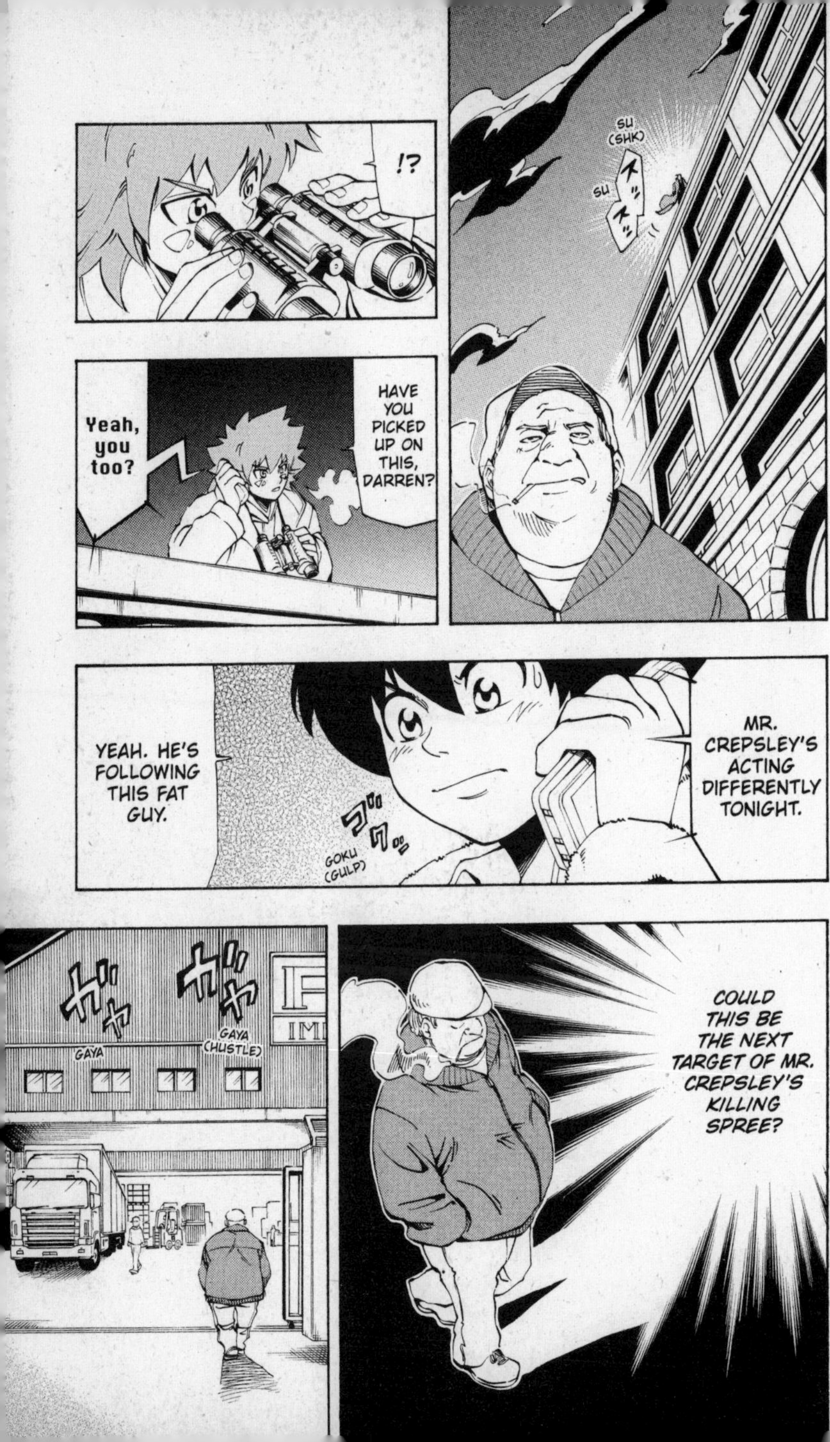
SU (SHK)
SU
!?
HAVE YOU PICKED UP ON THIS, DARREN?
Yeah, you too?
MR. CREPSLEY'S ACTING DIFFERENTLY TONIGHT.
GOKU (GULP)
YEAH. HE'S FOLLOWING THIS FAT GUY.
COULD THIS BE THE NEXT TARGET OF MR. CREPSLEY'S KILLING SPREE?
GAYA (HUSTLE)
GAYA

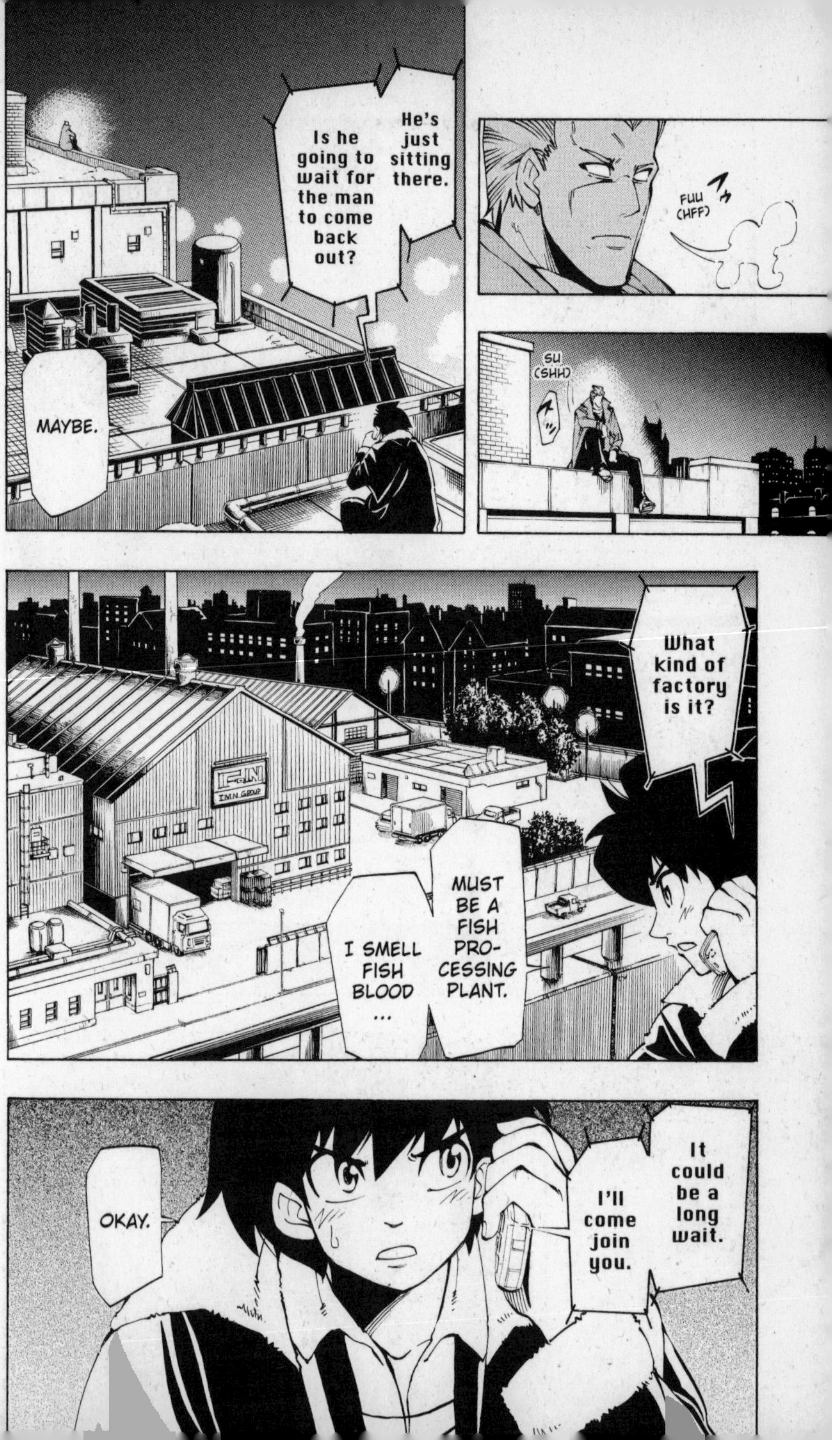
FUU (HFF)
SU (SHH)
He's just sitting there.
Is he going to wait for the man to come back out?
MAYBE.
What kind of factory is it?
IMN GROUP
MUST BE A FISH PROCESSING PLANT.
I SMELL FISH BLOOD ...
It could be a long wait.
I'll come join you.
OKAY.

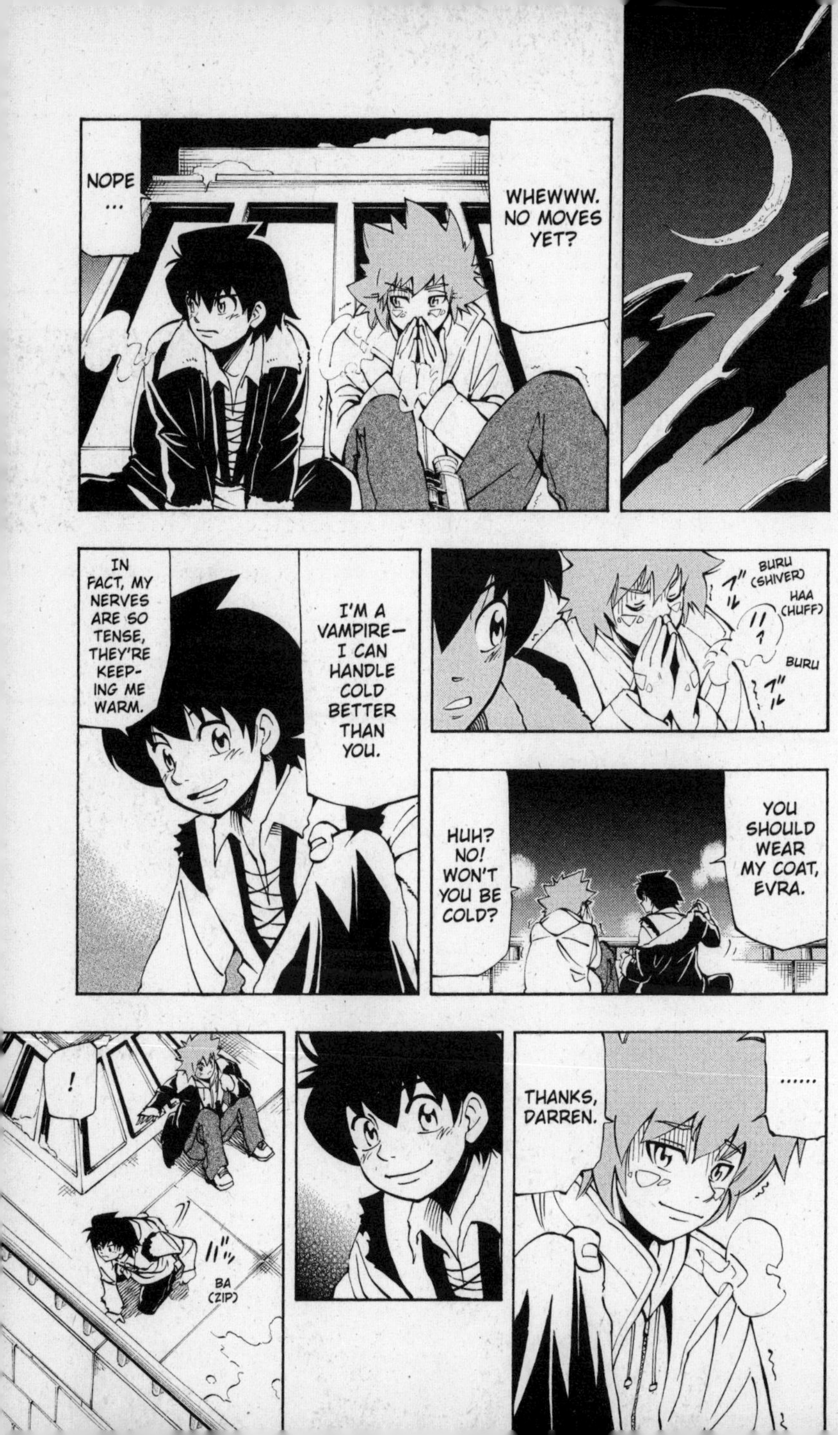
WHEWWW. NO MOVES YET?
NOPE ...
BURU (SHIVER)
HAA (HUFF)
BURU
I'M A VAMPIRE— I CAN HANDLE COLD BETTER THAN YOU.
IN FACT, MY NERVES ARE SO TENSE, THEY'RE KEEP-ING ME WARM.
YOU SHOULD WEAR MY COAT, EVRA.
HUH? NO! WON'T YOU BE COLD?
......
THANKS, DARREN.
!
BA (ZIP)

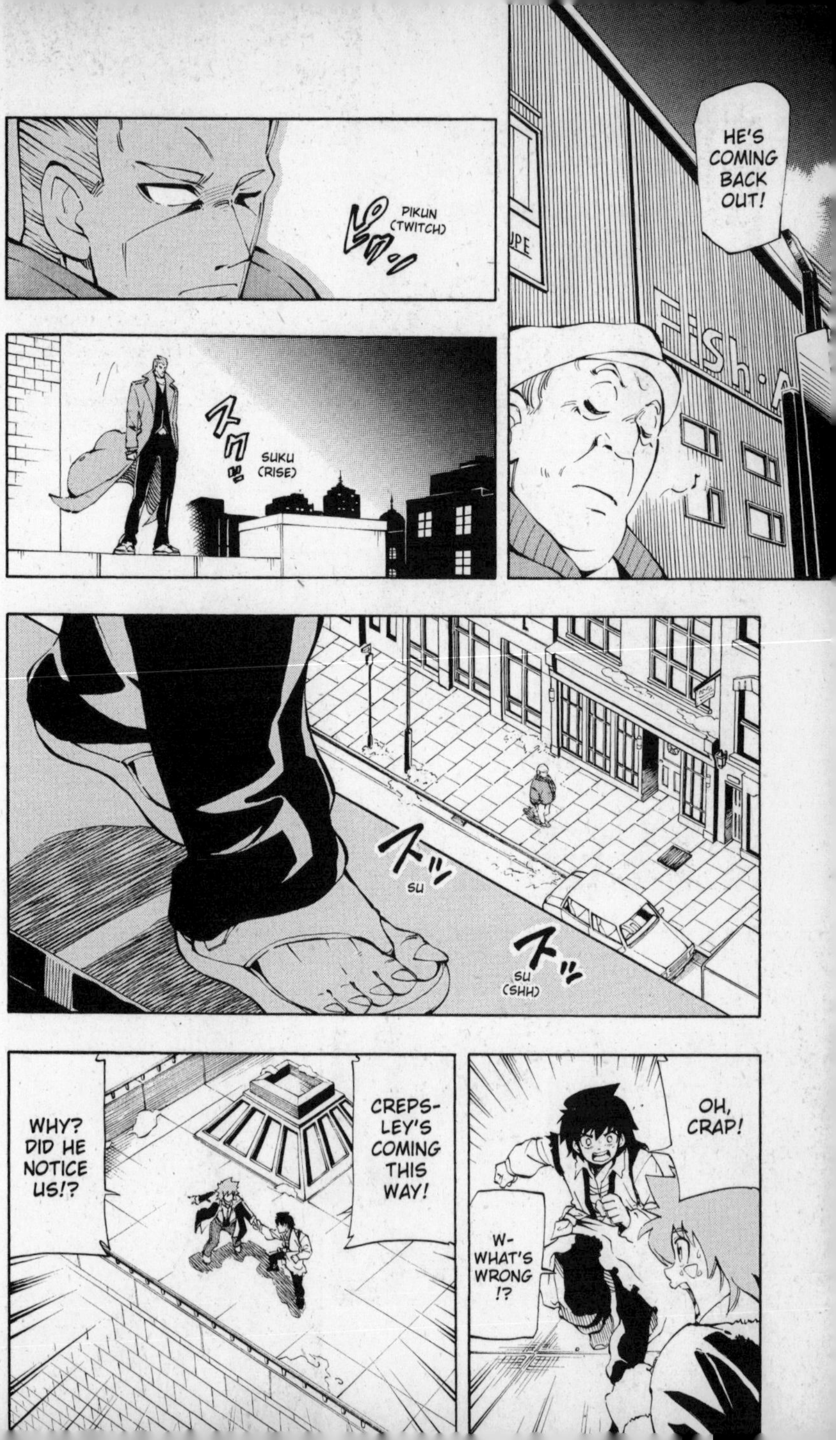
HE'S COMING BACK OUT!
PIKUN (TWITCH)
SUKU (RISE)
SU
SU (SHH)
OH, CRAP!
W-WHAT'S WRONG!?
CREPS-LEY'S COMING THIS WAY!
WHY? DID HE NOTICE US!?

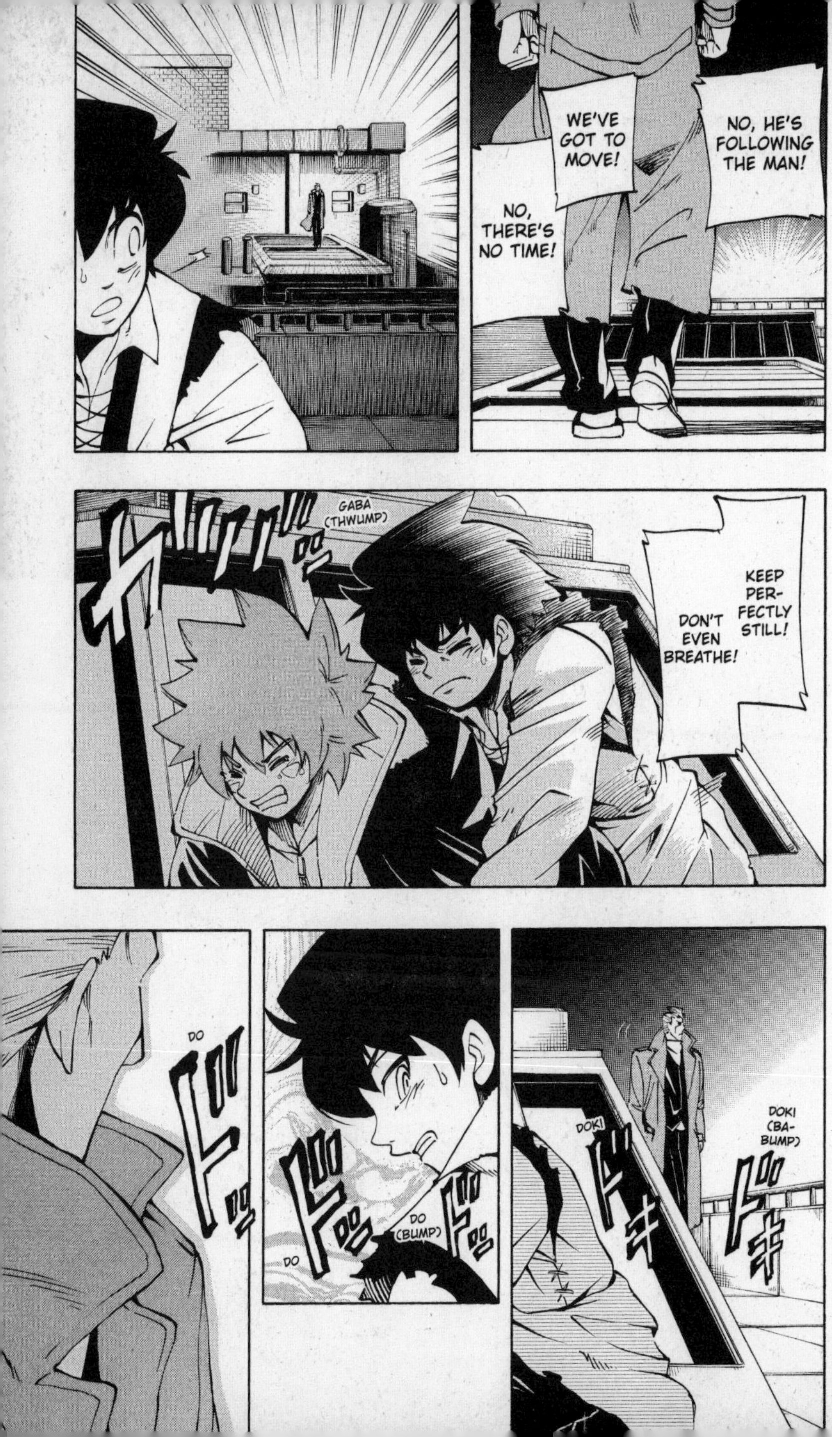
NO, HE'S FOLLOWING THE MAN!
WE'VE GOT TO MOVE!
NO, THERE'S NO TIME!
KEEP PER-FECTLY STILL!
DON'T EVEN BREATHE!
GABA (THWUMP)
DOKI (BA-BUMP)
DOKI
DO (BUMP)
DO
DO

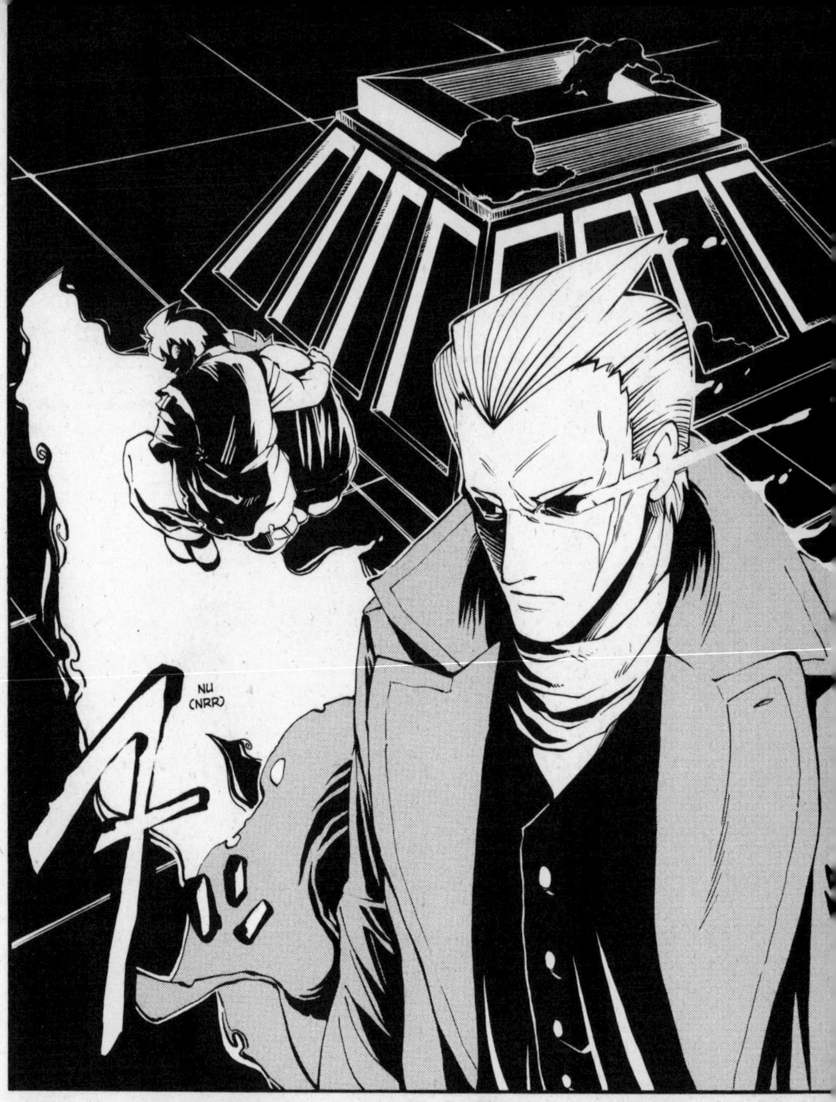
NU
(NRR)
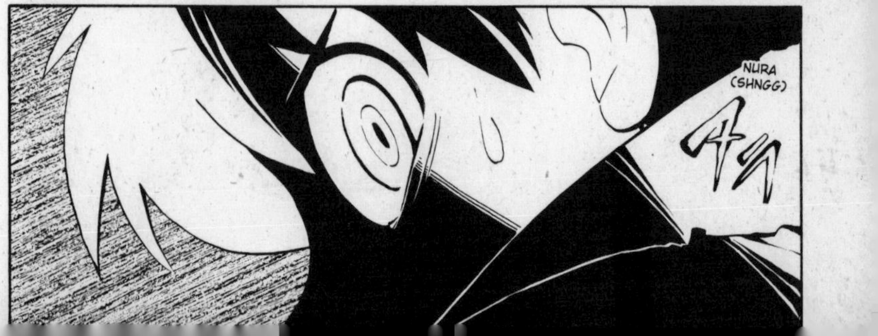
NURA
(SHNGG)

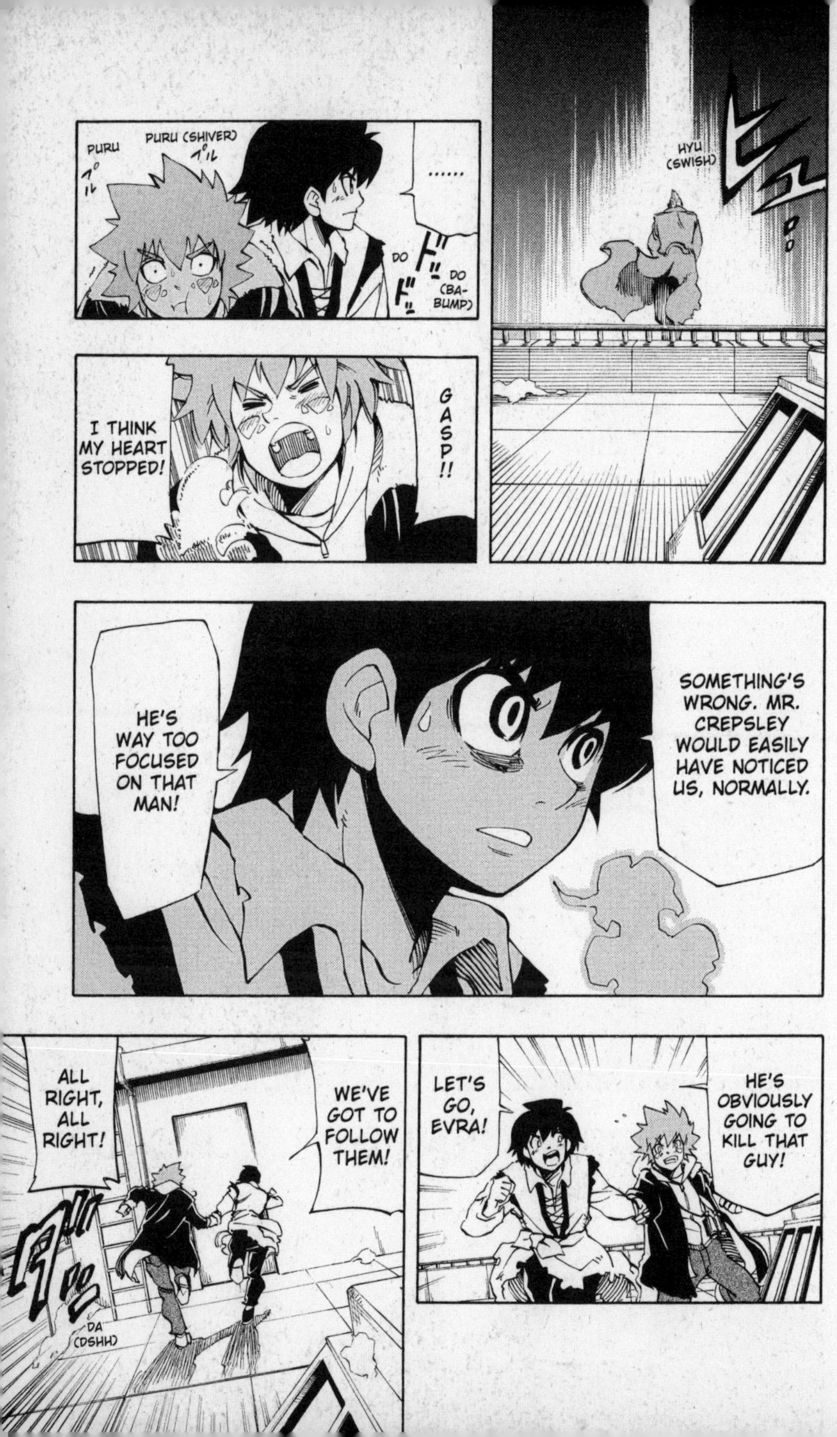

HYU (SWISH)
PURU (SHIVER)
PURU
......
DO
DO (BA-BUMP)
GASP!!
I THINK MY HEART STOPPED!
SOMETHING'S WRONG. MR. CREPSLEY WOULD EASILY HAVE NOTICED US, NORMALLY.
HE'S WAY TOO FOCUSED ON THAT MAN!
HE'S OBVIOUSLY GOING TO KILL THAT GUY!
LET'S GO, EVRA!
WE'VE GOT TO FOLLOW THEM!
ALL RIGHT, ALL RIGHT!
DA (DSHH)

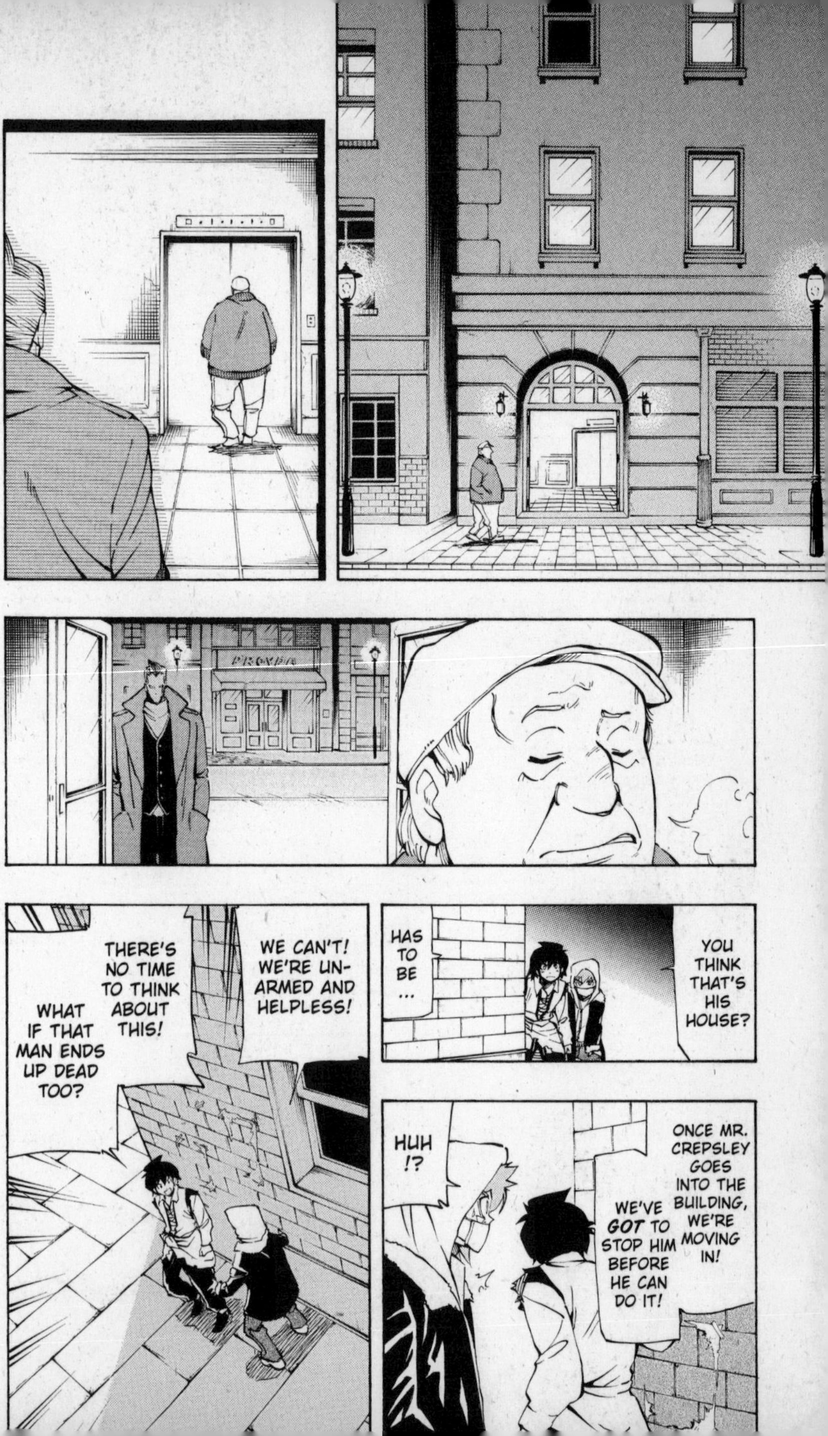
YOU THINK THAT'S HIS HOUSE?
HAS TO BE ...
ONCE MR. CREPSLEY GOES INTO THE BUILDING, WE'RE MOVING IN!
WE'VE GOT TO STOP HIM BEFORE HE CAN DO IT!
HUH !?
WE CAN'T! WE'RE UN-ARMED AND HELPLESS!
THERE'S NO TIME TO THINK ABOUT THIS!
WHAT IF THAT MAN ENDS UP DEAD TOO?

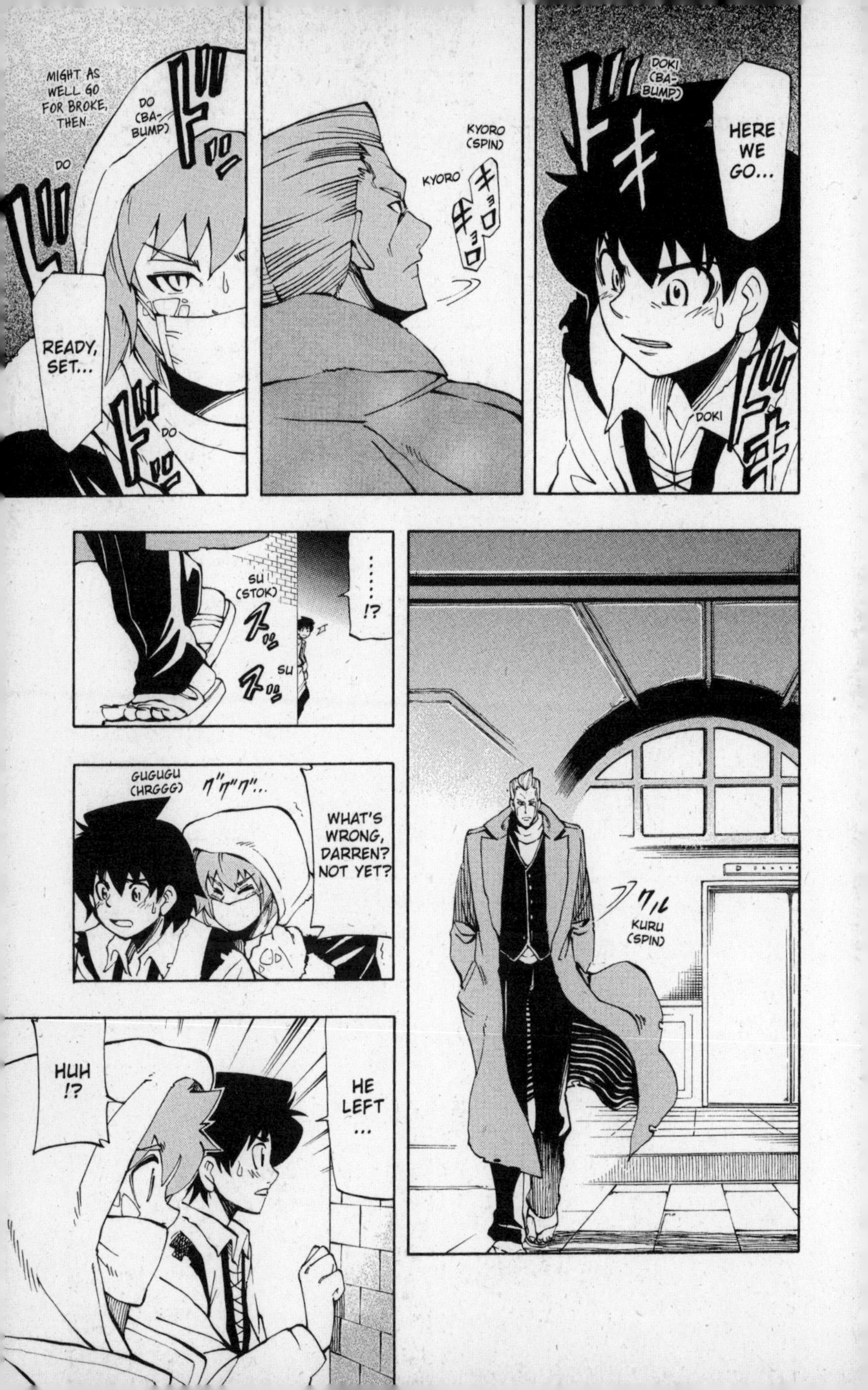
DOKI (BA-BUMP)
HERE WE GO...
DOKI
KYORO (SPIN)
KYORO
MIGHT AS WELL GO FOR BROKE, THEN...
DO (BA-BUMP)
DO
READY, SET...
DO
KURU (SPIN)
......!?
SU (STOK)
SU
WHAT'S WRONG, DARREN? NOT YET?
GUGUGU (HRGGG)
HE LEFT ...
HUH !?

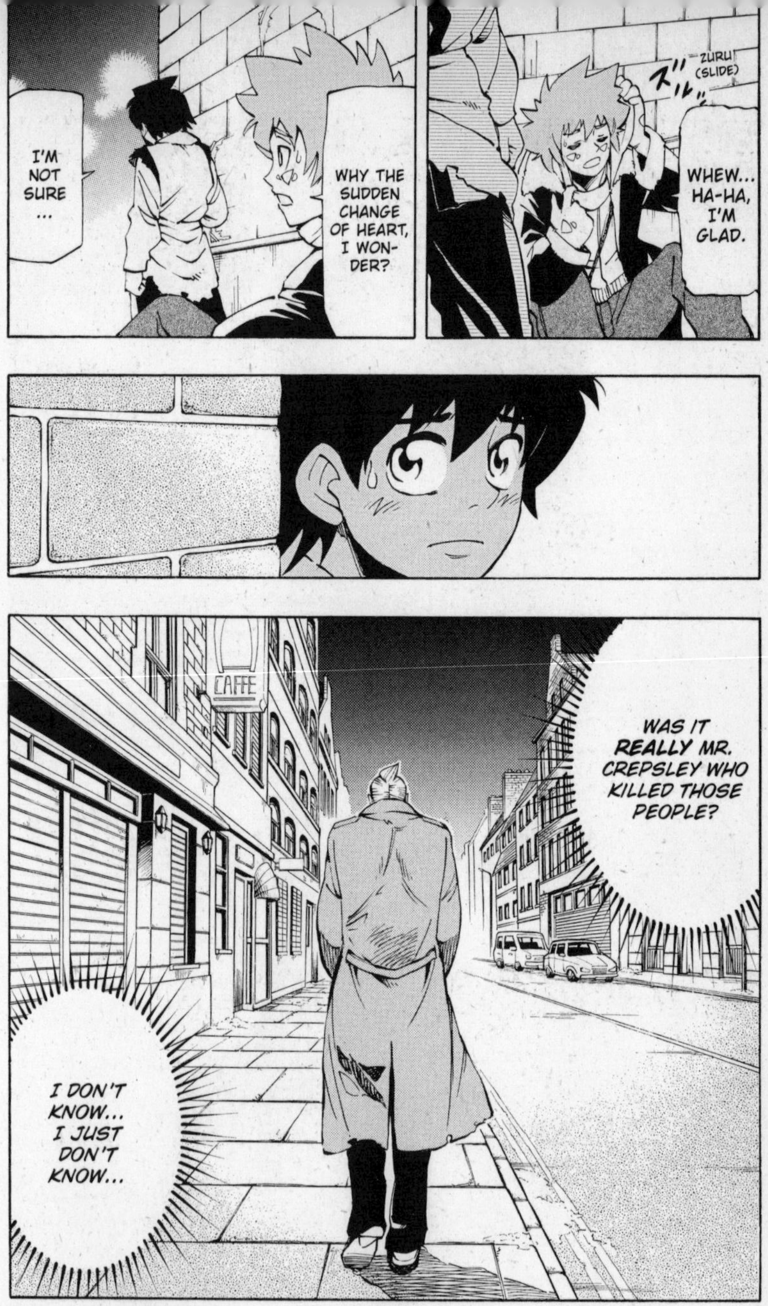
ZURU (SLIDE)
WHEW... HA-HA, I'M GLAD.
WHY THE SUDDEN CHANGE OF HEART, I WONDER?
I'M NOT SURE...
WAS IT REALLY MR. CREPSLEY WHO KILLED THOSE PEOPLE?
I DON'T KNOW... I JUST DON'T KNOW...
CAFFE

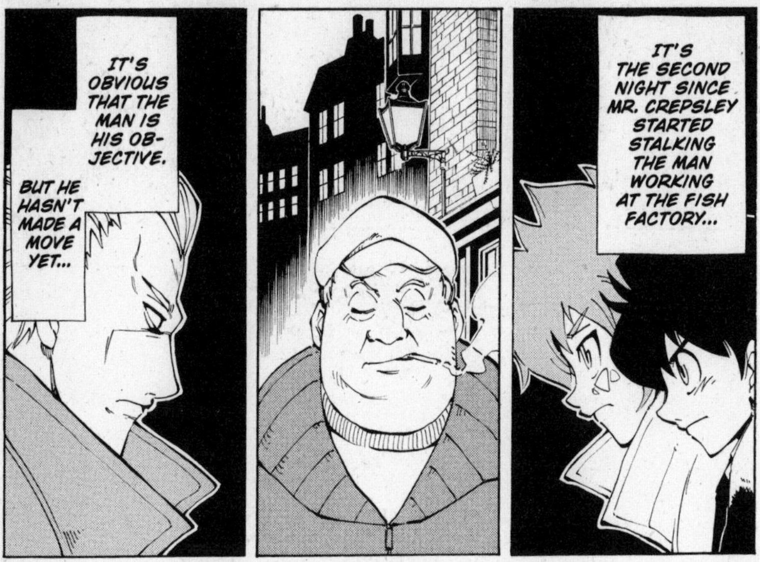
IT'S THE SECOND NIGHT SINCE MR. CREPSLEY STARTED STALKING THE MAN WORKING AT THE FISH FACTORY...
IT'S OBVIOUS THAT THE MAN IS HIS OBJECTIVE.
BUT HE HASN'T MADE A MOVE YET...

CHAPTER 19:
A MYSTERIOUS CREATURE

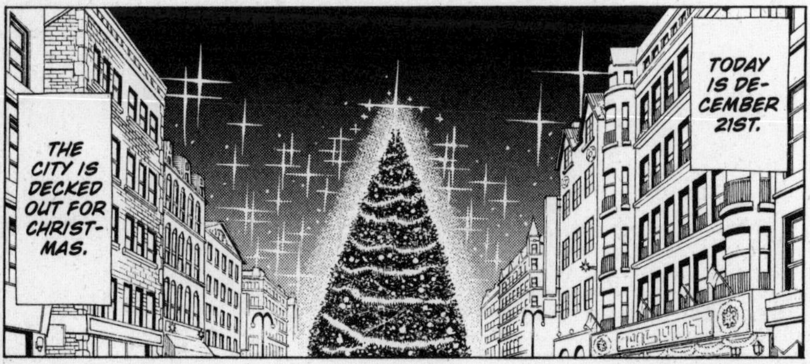
TODAY IS DECEMBER 21ST.
THE CITY IS DECKED OUT FOR CHRISTMAS.

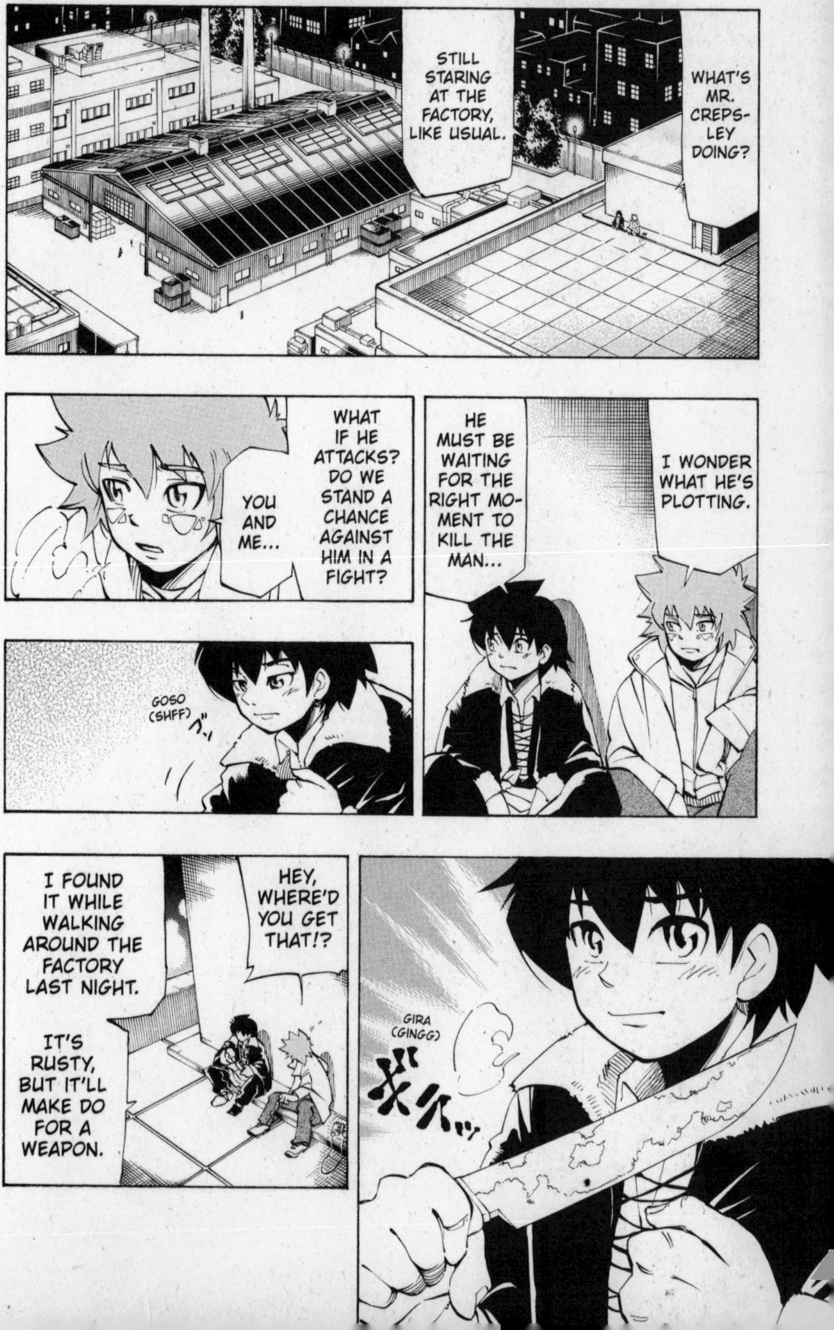
WHAT'S MR. CREPS-LEY DOING?
STILL STARING AT THE FACTORY, LIKE USUAL.
I WONDER WHAT HE'S PLOTTING.
HE MUST BE WAITING FOR THE RIGHT MO-MENT TO KILL THE MAN...
WHAT IF HE ATTACKS? DO WE STAND A CHANCE AGAINST HIM IN A FIGHT?
YOU AND ME...
GOSO (SHFF)
GIRA (GINGG)
HEY, WHERE'D YOU GET THAT!?
I FOUND IT WHILE WALKING AROUND THE FACTORY LAST NIGHT.
IT'S RUSTY, BUT IT'LL MAKE DO FOR A WEAPON.

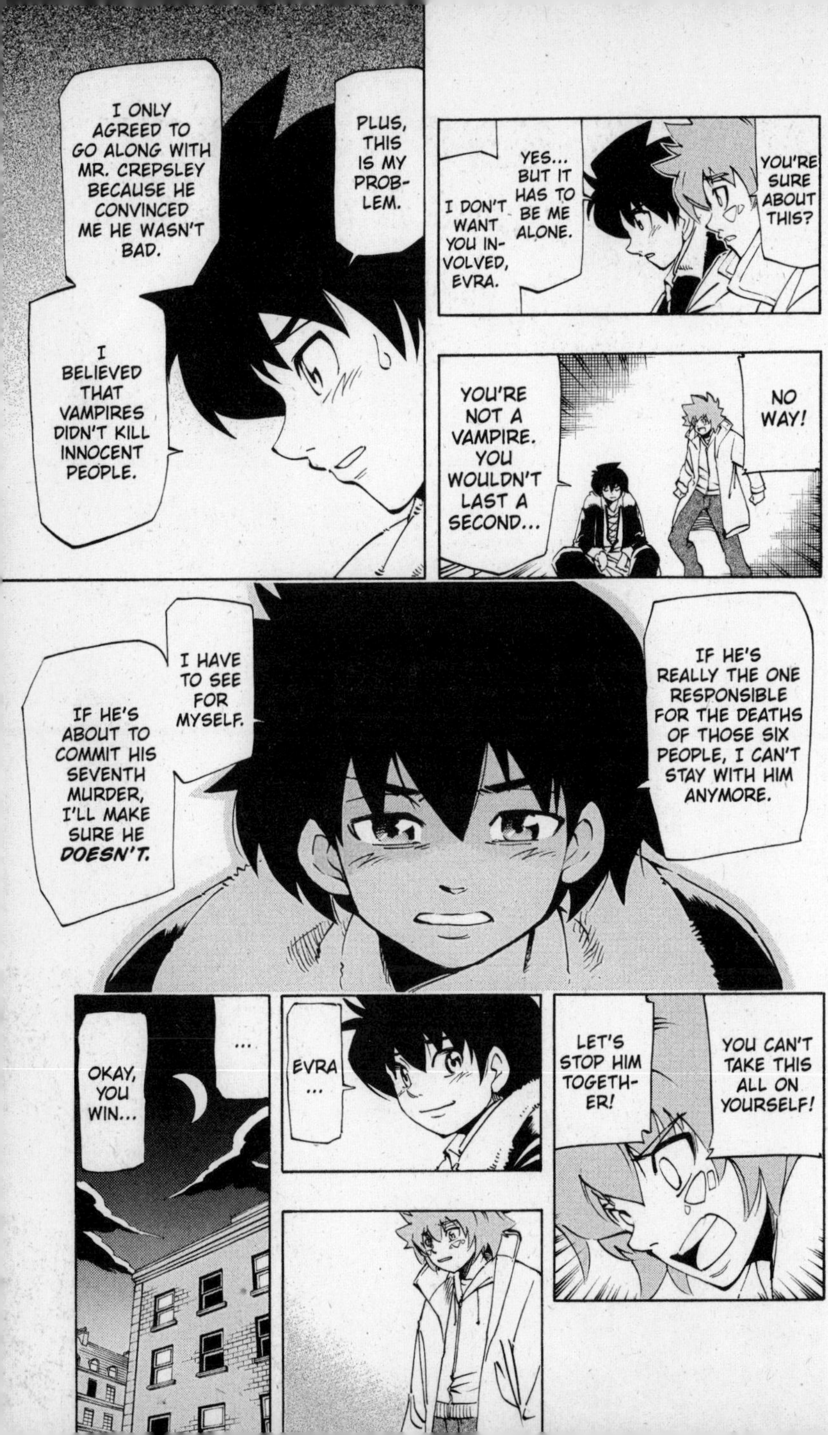
YOU'RE SURE ABOUT THIS?
YES... BUT IT HAS TO BE ME ALONE.
I DON'T WANT YOU INVOLVED, EVRA.
NO WAY!
YOU'RE NOT A VAMPIRE. YOU WOULDN'T LAST A SECOND...
PLUS, THIS IS MY PROBLEM.
I ONLY AGREED TO GO ALONG WITH MR. CREPSLEY BECAUSE HE CONVINCED ME HE WASN'T BAD.
I BELIEVED THAT VAMPIRES DIDN'T KILL INNOCENT PEOPLE.
IF HE'S REALLY THE ONE RESPONSIBLE FOR THE DEATHS OF THOSE SIX PEOPLE, I CAN'T STAY WITH HIM ANYMORE.
I HAVE TO SEE FOR MYSELF.
IF HE'S ABOUT TO COMMIT HIS SEVENTH MURDER, I'LL MAKE SURE HE ***DOESN'T.***
YOU CAN'T TAKE THIS ALL ON YOURSELF!
LET'S STOP HIM TOGETHER!
EVRA...
...
OKAY, YOU WIN...

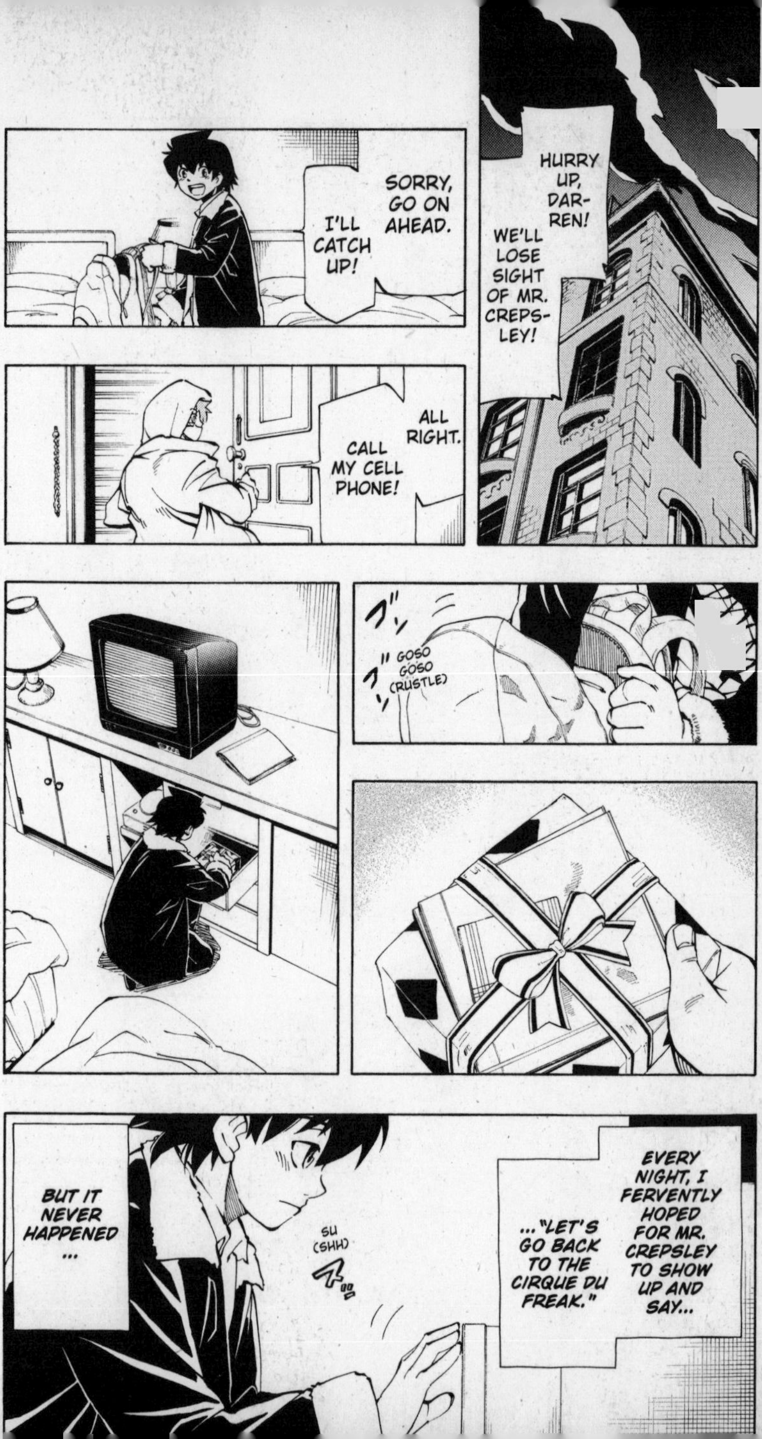
HURRY UP, DAR-REN!
WE'LL LOSE SIGHT OF MR. CREPS-LEY!
SORRY, GO ON AHEAD.
I'LL CATCH UP!
ALL RIGHT.
CALL MY CELL PHONE!
GOSO GOSO (RUSTLE)
EVERY NIGHT, I FERVENTLY HOPED FOR MR. CREPSLEY TO SHOW UP AND SAY...
..."LET'S GO BACK TO THE CIRQUE DU FREAK."
SU (SHH)
BUT IT NEVER HAPPENED...

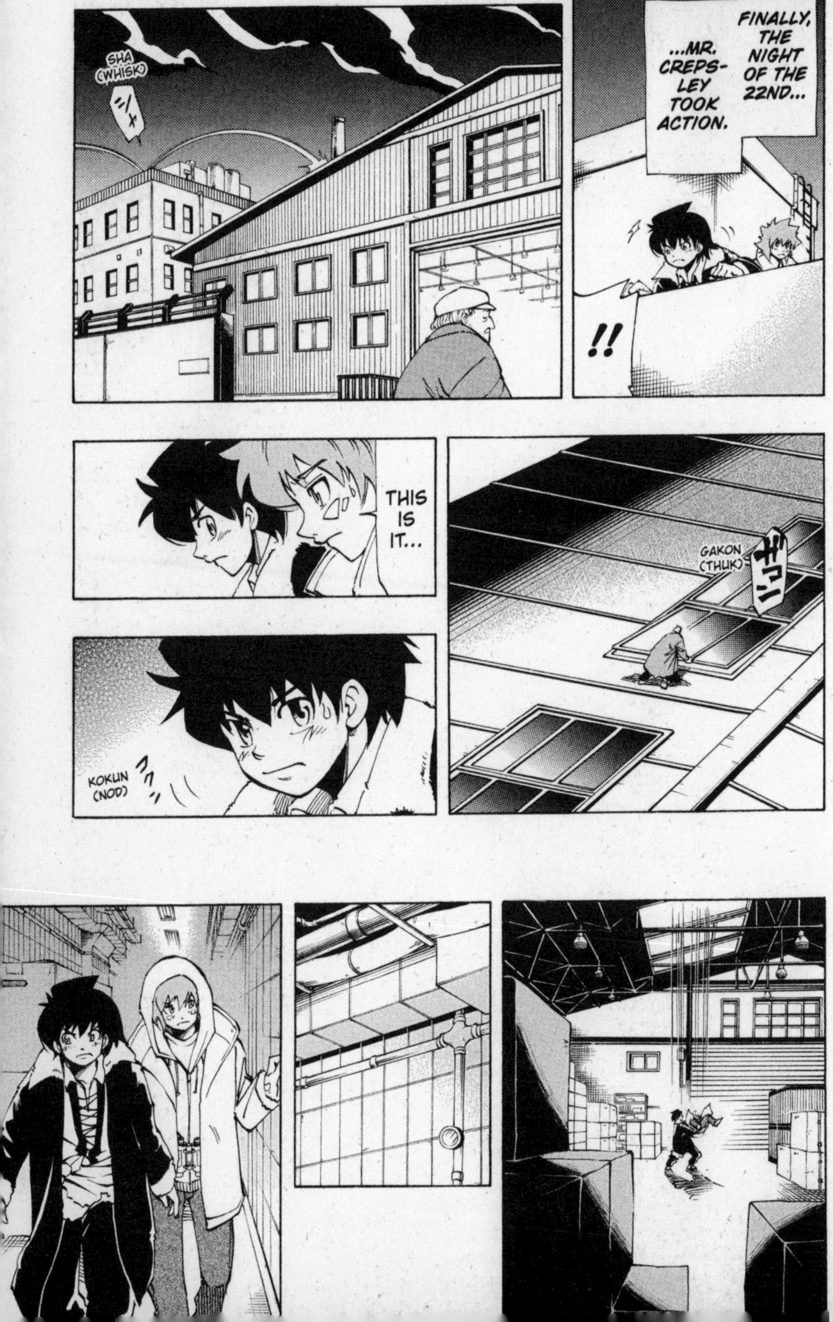
FINALLY, THE NIGHT OF THE 22ND...
...MR. CREPSLEY TOOK ACTION.
!!
SHA (WHISK)
GAKON (THUK)
ガコン
THIS IS IT...
KOKUN (NOD)

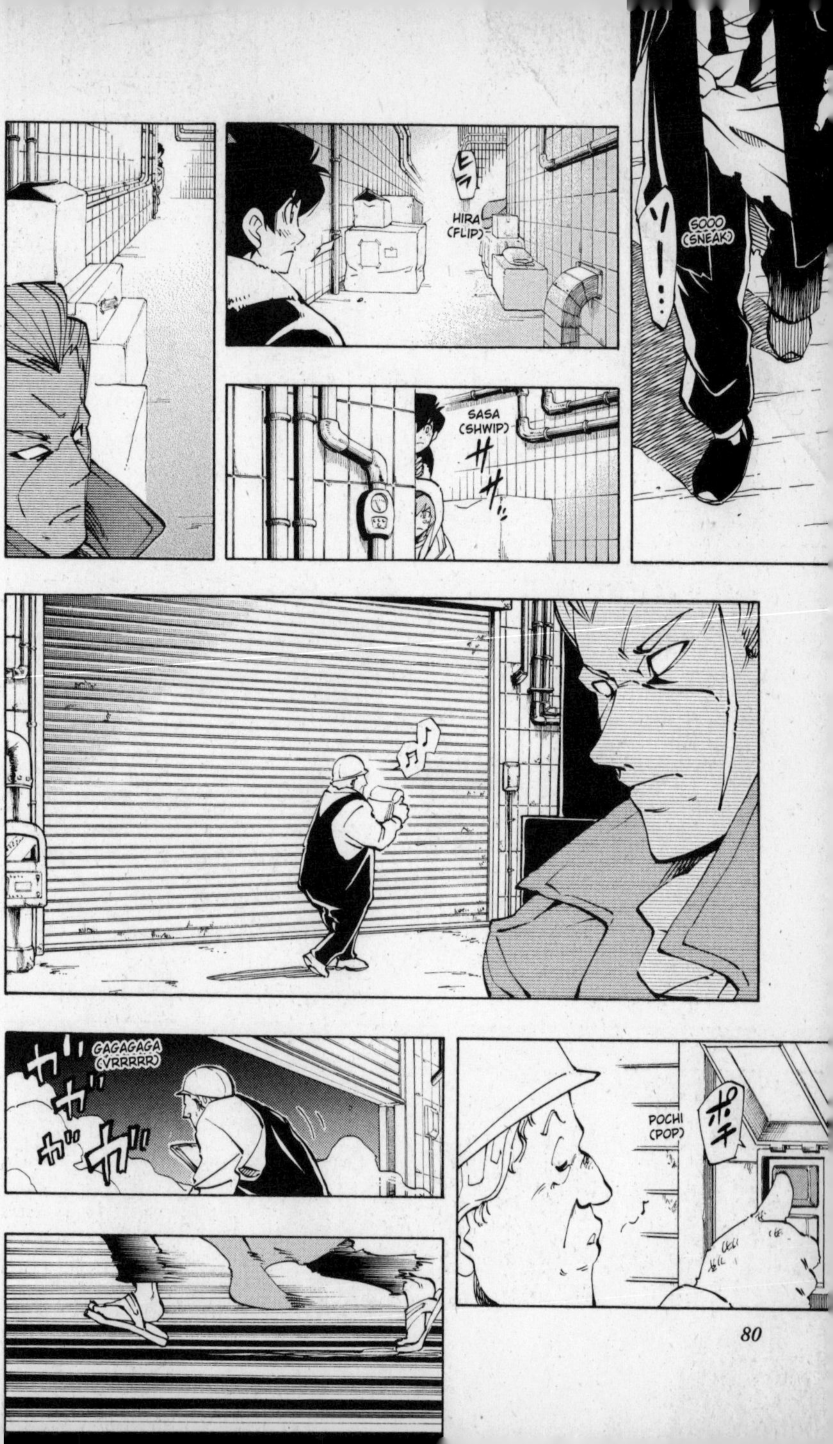
SOOO (SNEAK)
HIRA (FLIP)
SASA (SHWIP)
POCHI (POP)
GAGAGAGA (VRRRRR)

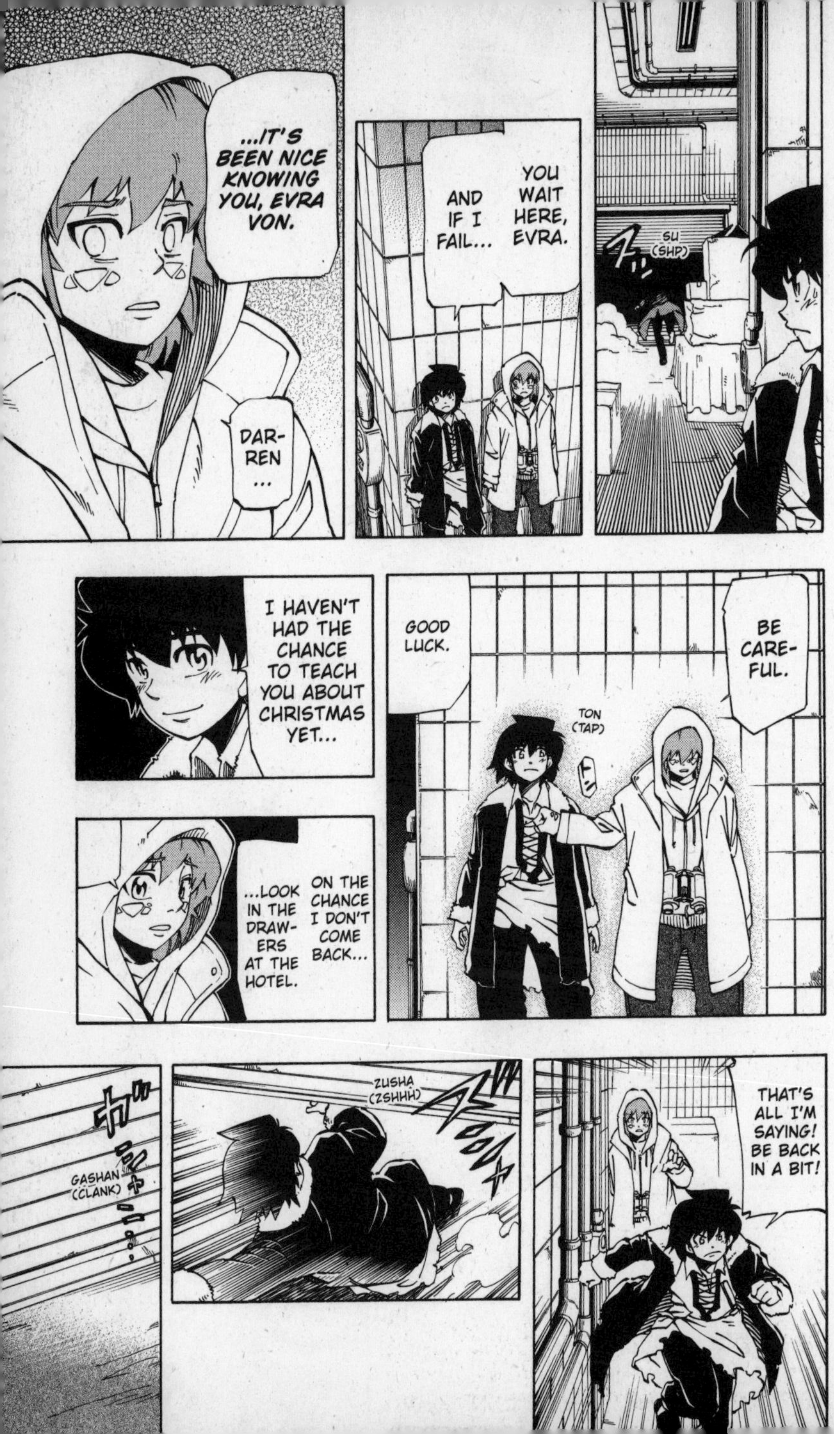
SU (SHP)
YOU WAIT HERE, EVRA.
AND IF I FAIL...
...IT'S BEEN NICE KNOWING YOU, EVRA VON.
DAR-REN...
BE CARE-FUL.
GOOD LUCK.
TON (TAP)
I HAVEN'T HAD THE CHANCE TO TEACH YOU ABOUT CHRISTMAS YET...
ON THE CHANCE I DON'T COME BACK...
...LOOK IN THE DRAW-ERS AT THE HOTEL.
THAT'S ALL I'M SAYING! BE BACK IN A BIT!
ZUSHA (ZSHHH)
GASHAN (CLANK)

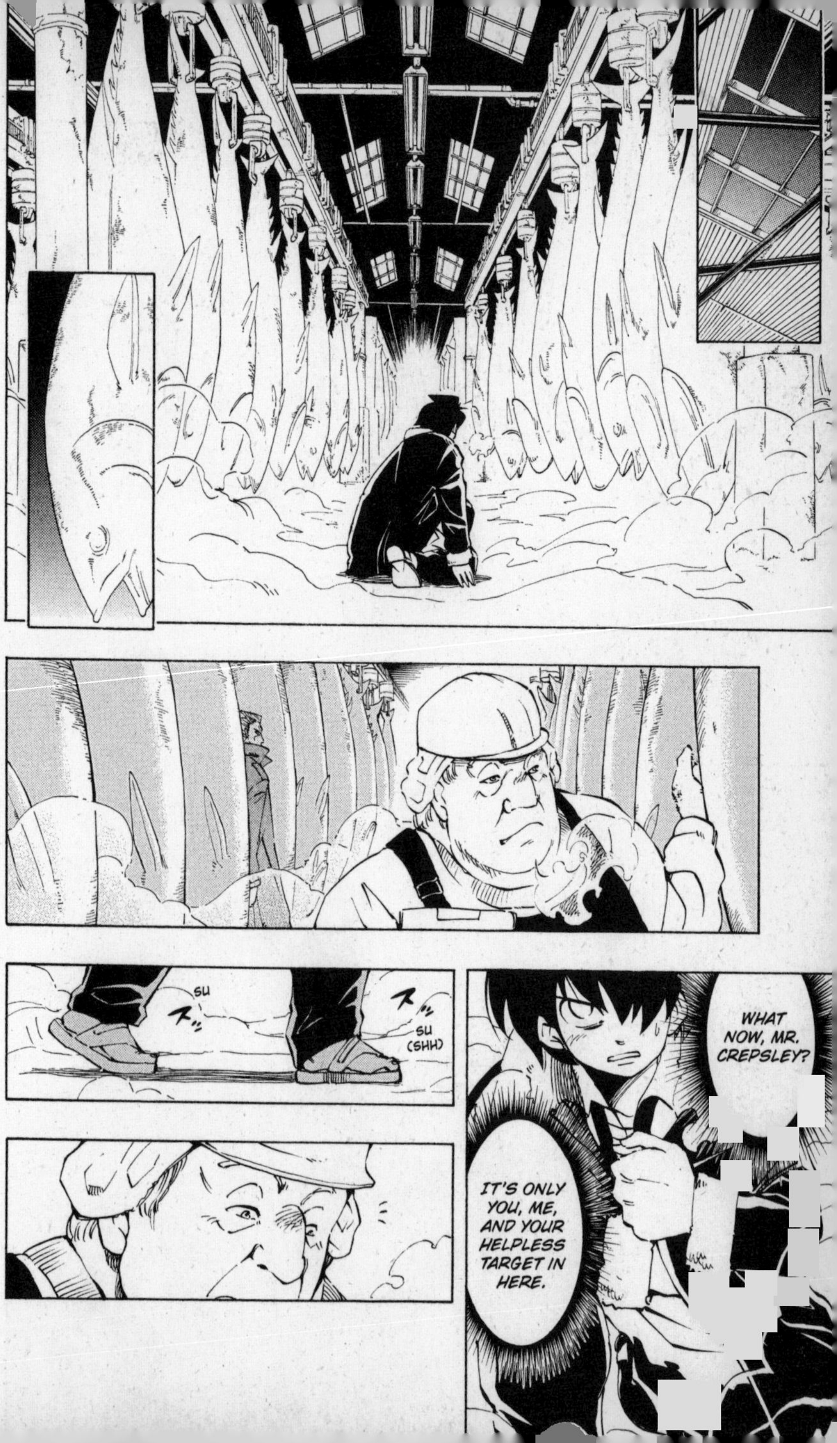
WHAT NOW, MR. CREPSLEY?
IT'S ONLY YOU, ME, AND YOUR HELPLESS TARGET IN HERE.
ス SU (SHH)
ス SU

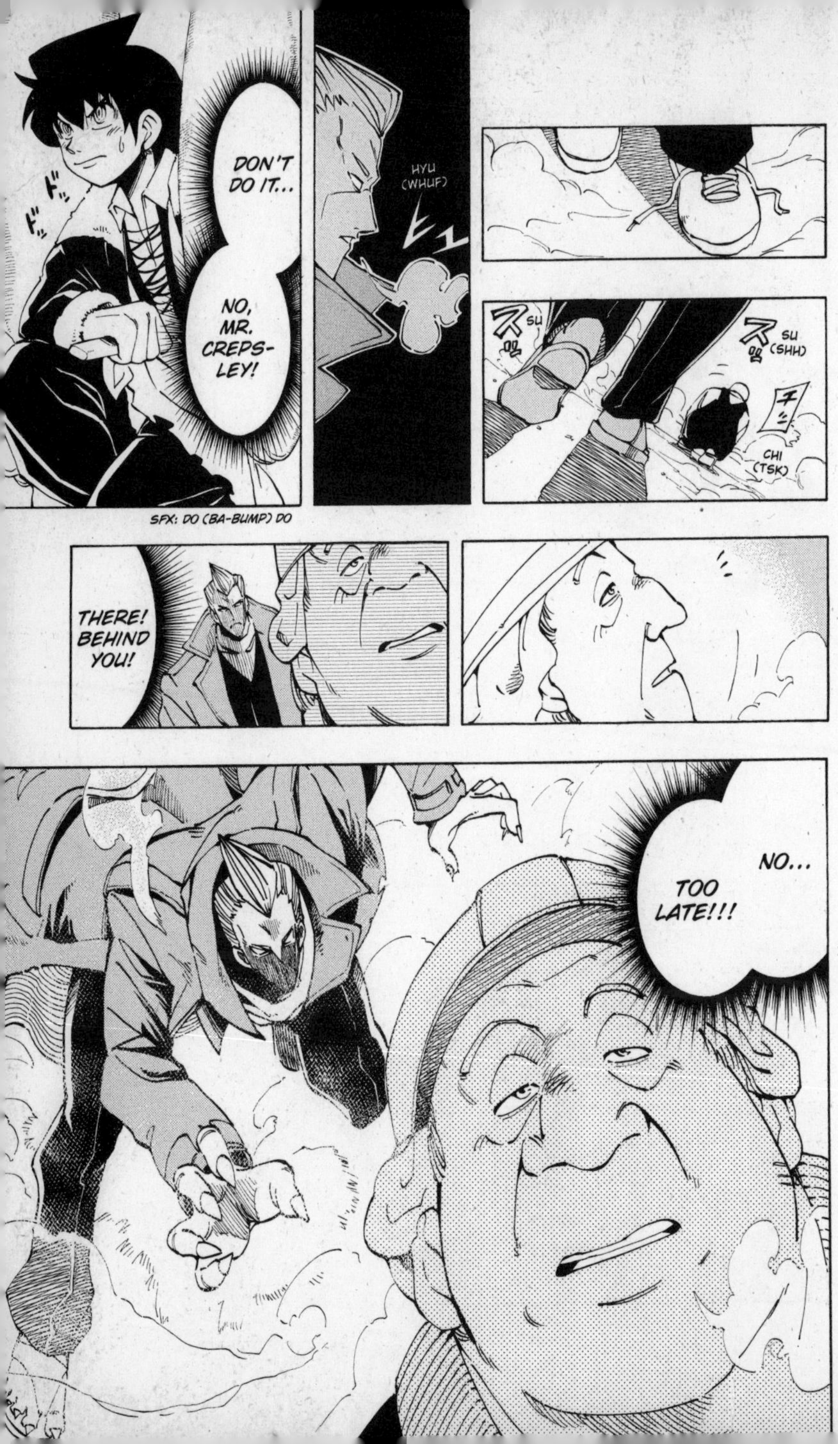
SU
SU (SHH)
CHI (TSK)
HYU (WHUF)
DON'T DO IT...
NO, MR. CREPSLEY!
SFX: DO (BA-BUMP) DO
THERE! BEHIND YOU!
NO... TOO LATE!!!

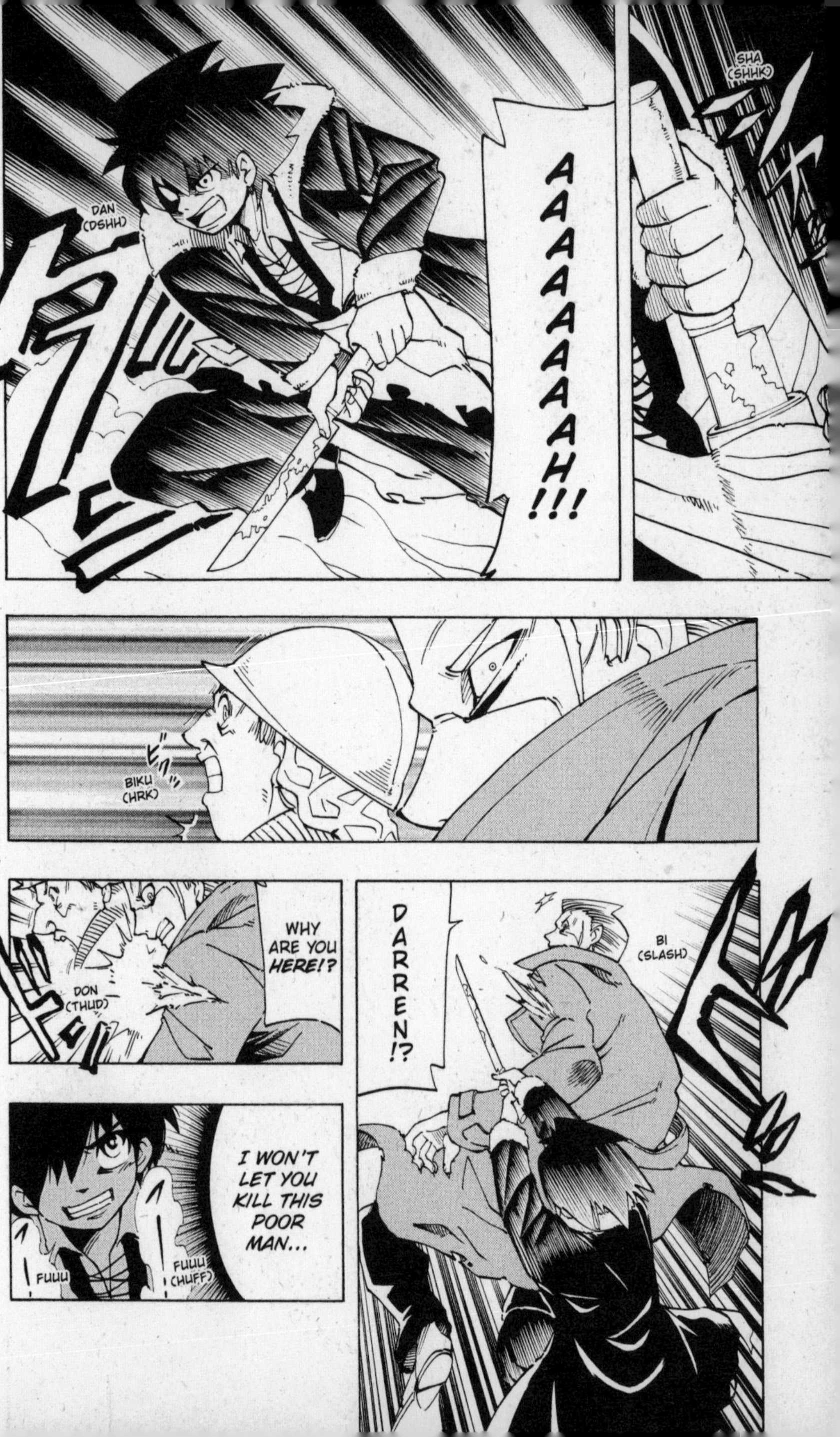
SHA
(SHHK)
AAAAAAAAH!!!
DAN
(DSHH)
BIKU
(HRK)
DARREN!?
BI
(SLASH)
WHY ARE YOU HERE!?
DON
(THUD)
I WON'T LET YOU KILL THIS POOR MAN...
FUUU
(CHUFF)
FUUU

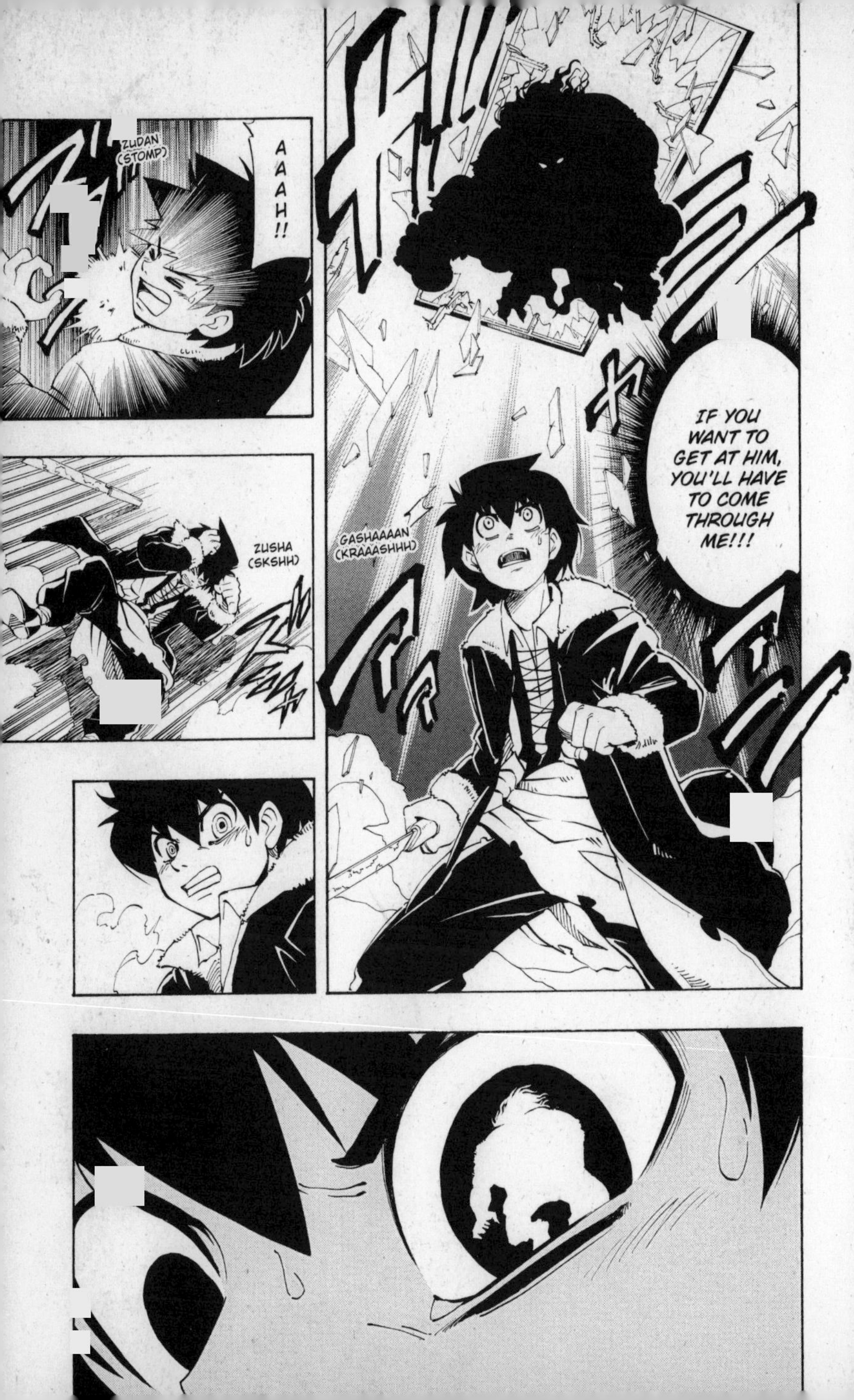
IF YOU WANT TO GET AT HIM, YOU'LL HAVE TO COME THROUGH ME!!!
GASHAAAAN (KRAAASHHH)
ZUDAN (STOMP)
AAAAH!!
ZUSHA (SKSHH)

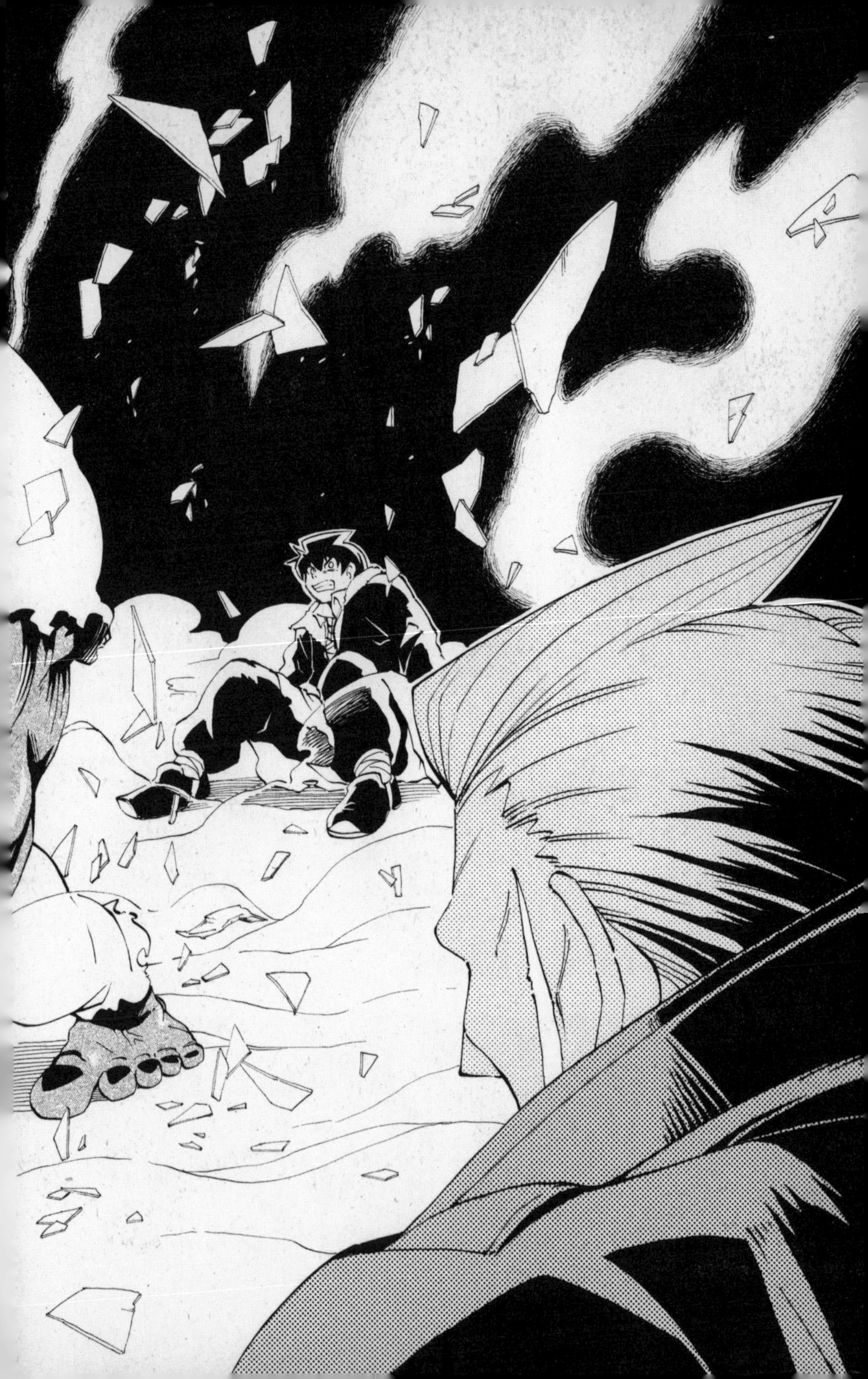

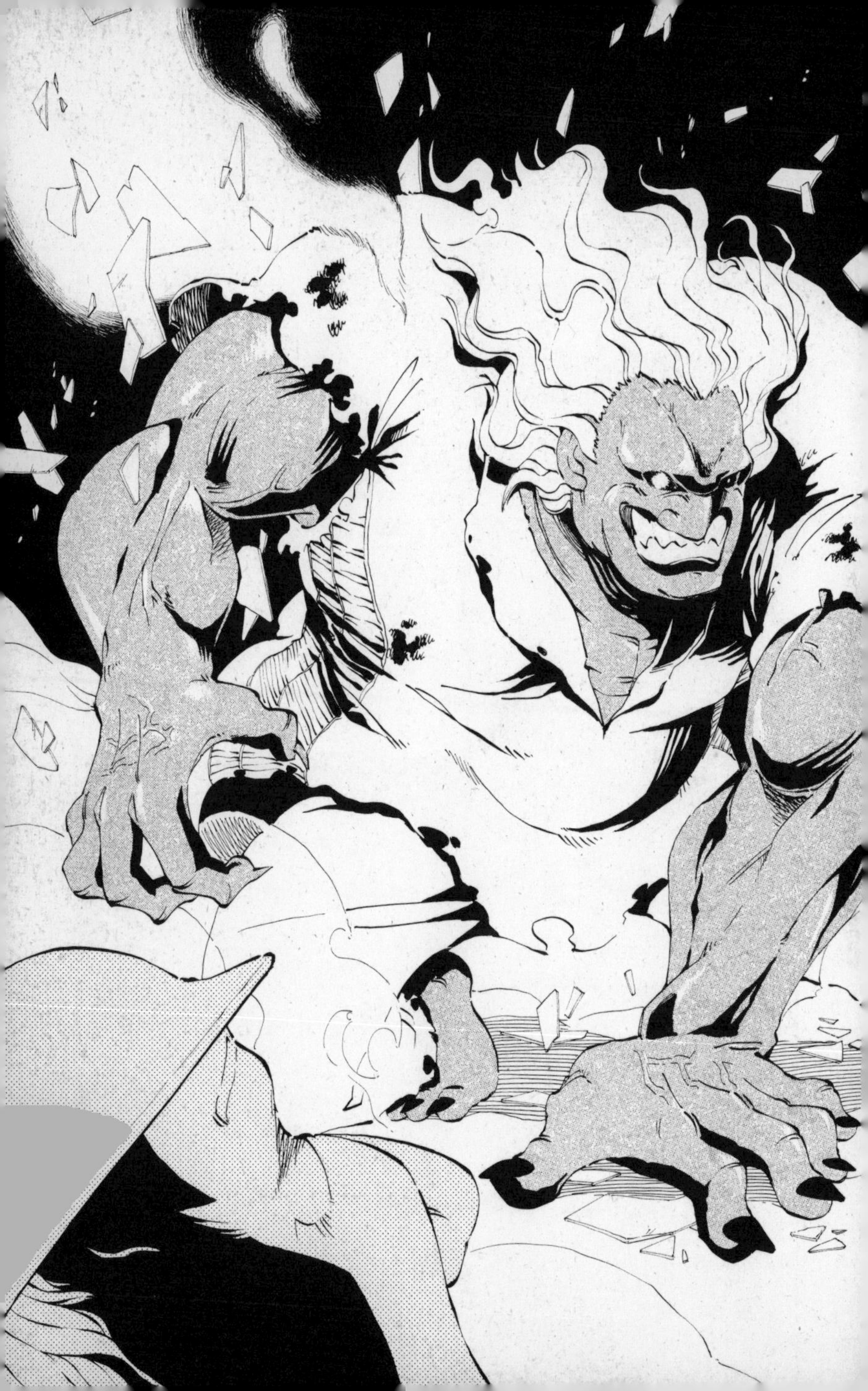

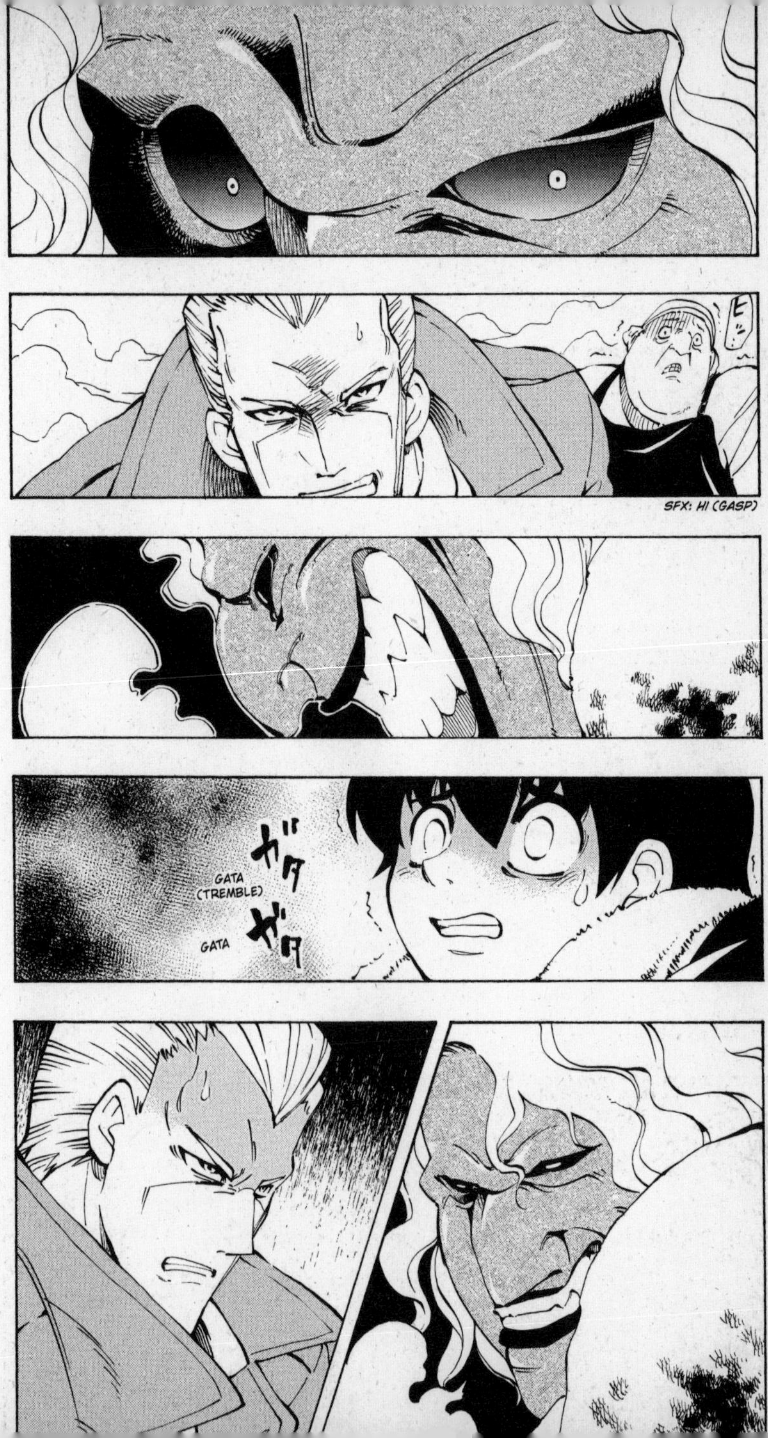
SFX: HI (GASP)
ガタ ガタ
GATA (TREMBLE)
GATA

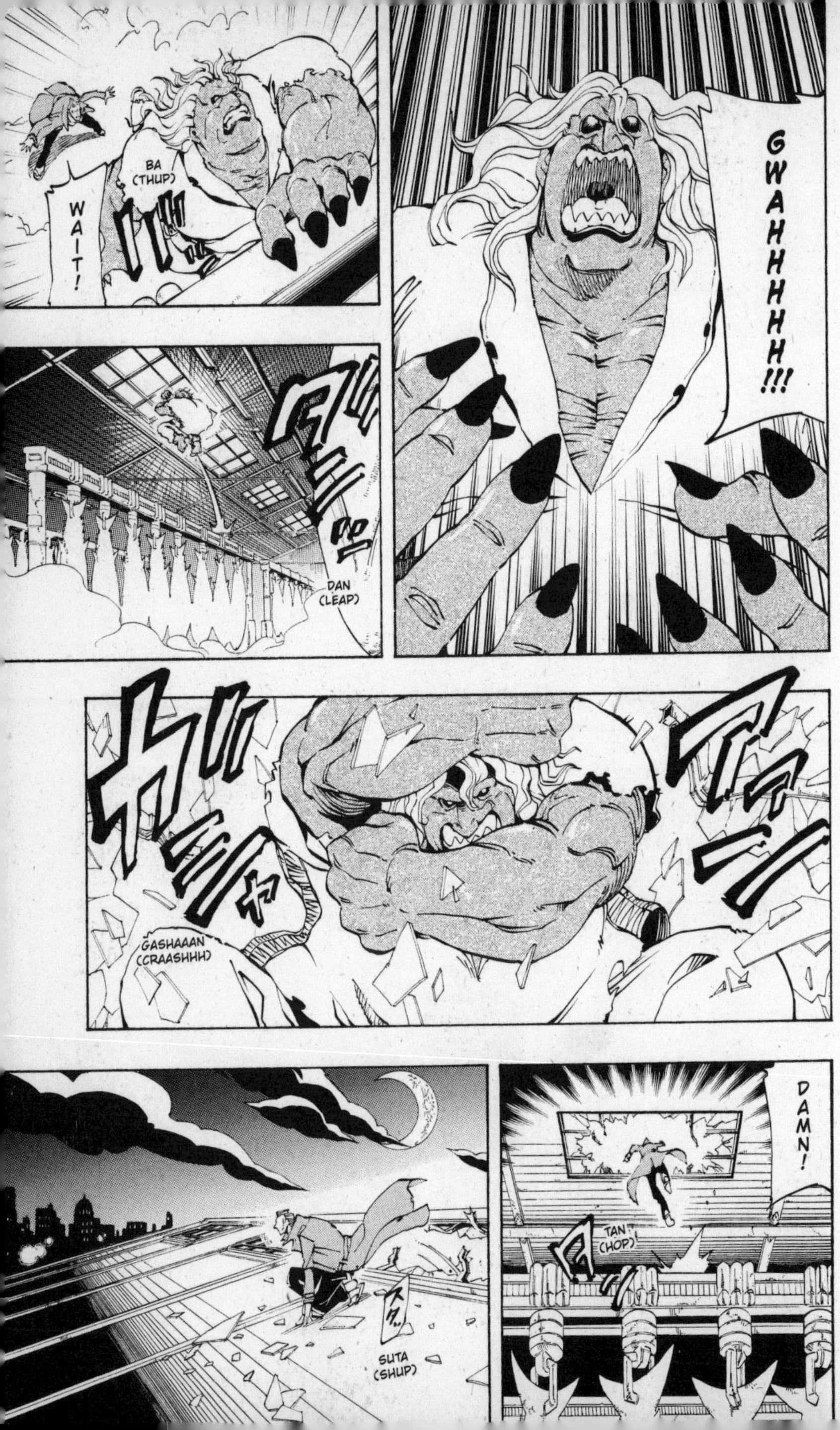
GWAHHHHHH!!!
WAIT!
BA (THUP)
DAN (LEAP)
GASHAAAN (CRAASHHH)
DAMN!
TAN (HOP)
SUTA (SHUP)

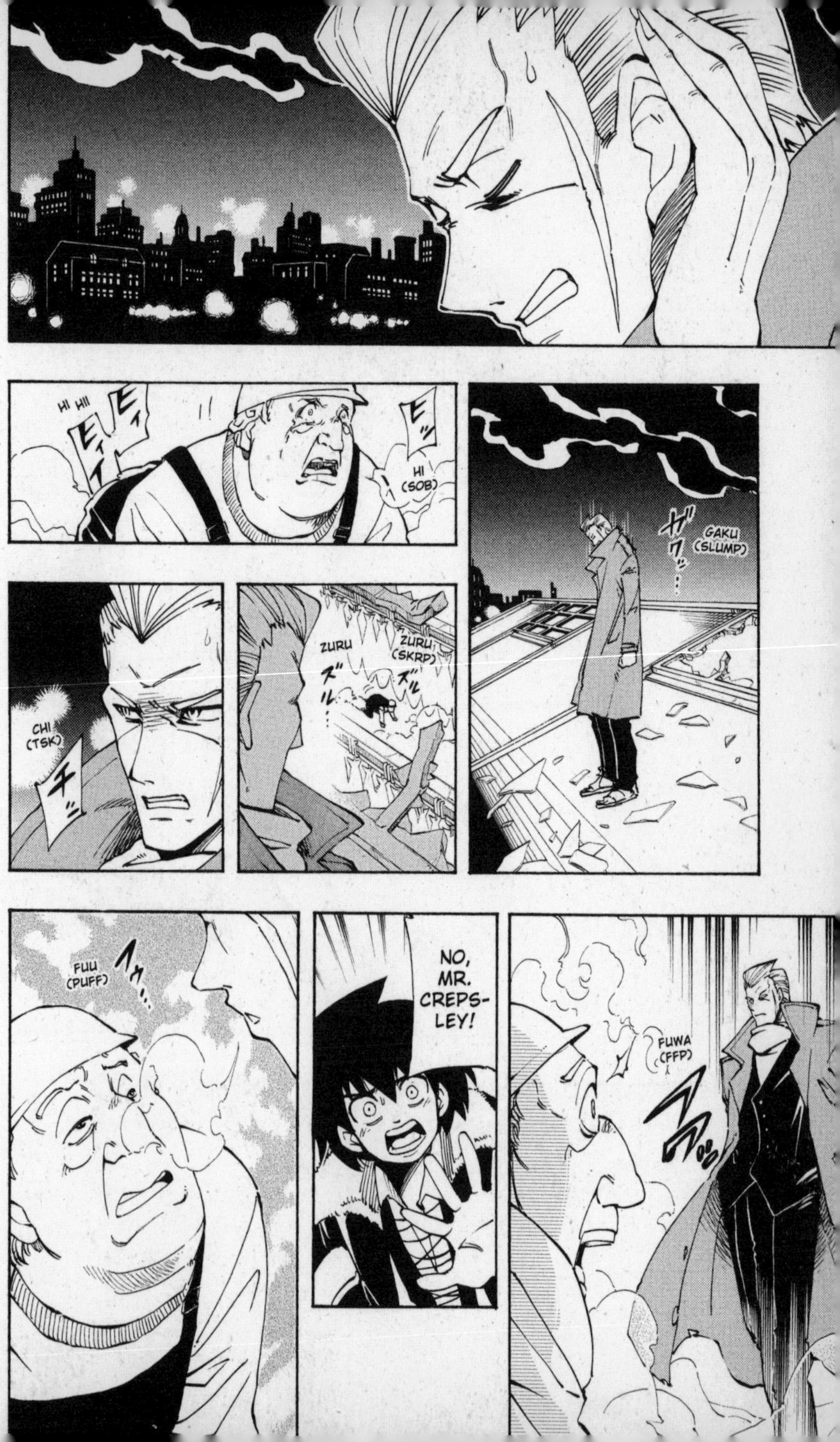
GAKU (SLUMP)
HI (SOB)
HI HII
ZURU
ZURU (SKRP)
CHI (TSK)
FUWA (FFP)
NO, MR. CREPS-LEY!
FUU (PUFF)

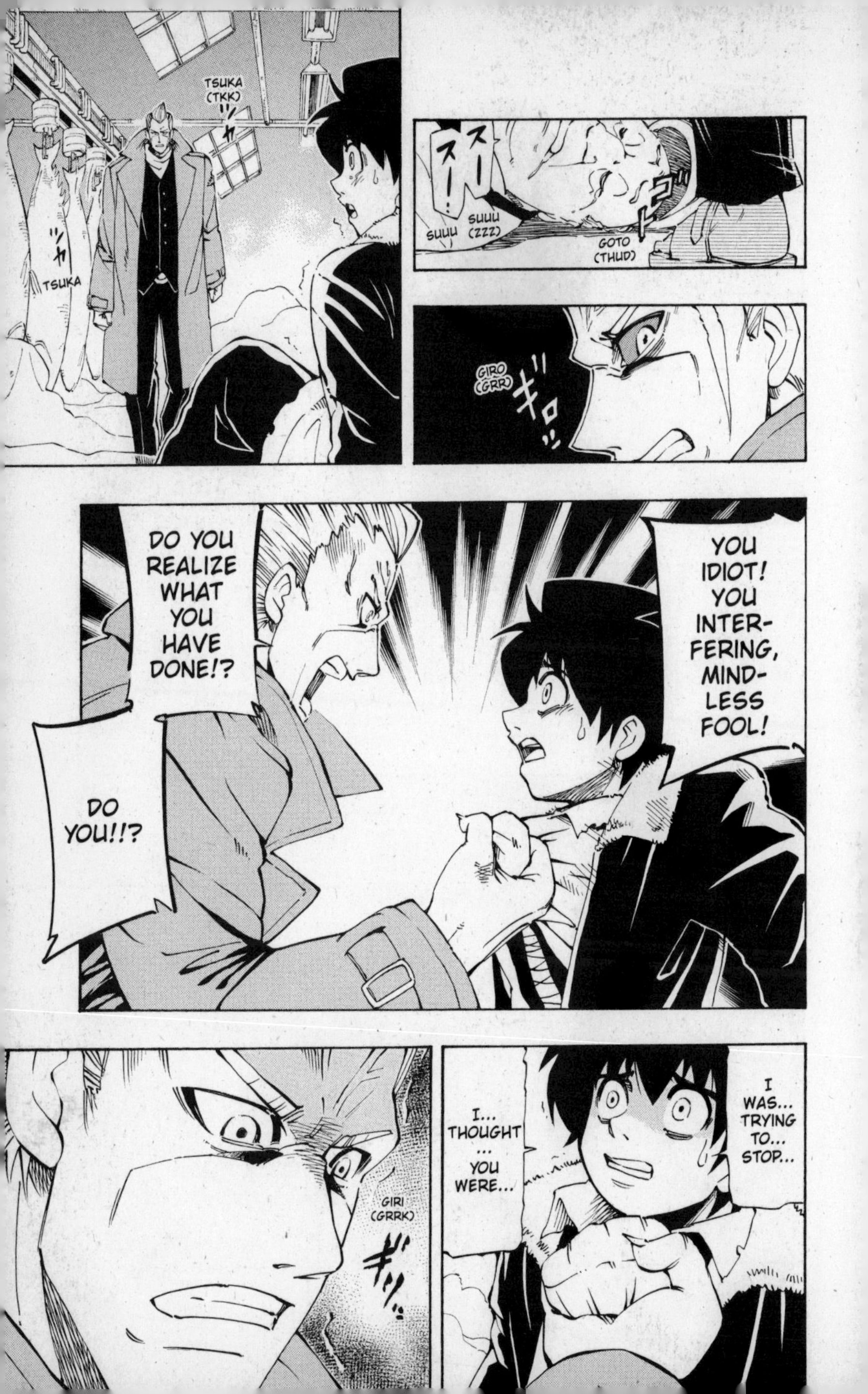

SUUU
SUUU (ZZZ)
GOTO (THUD)
GIRO (GRR)
TSUKA (TKK)
TSUKA
YOU IDIOT! YOU INTER-FERING, MIND-LESS FOOL!
DO YOU REALIZE WHAT YOU HAVE DONE!?
DO YOU!!?
I WAS... TRYING TO... STOP...
I... THOUGHT ... YOU WERE...
GIRI (GRRK)

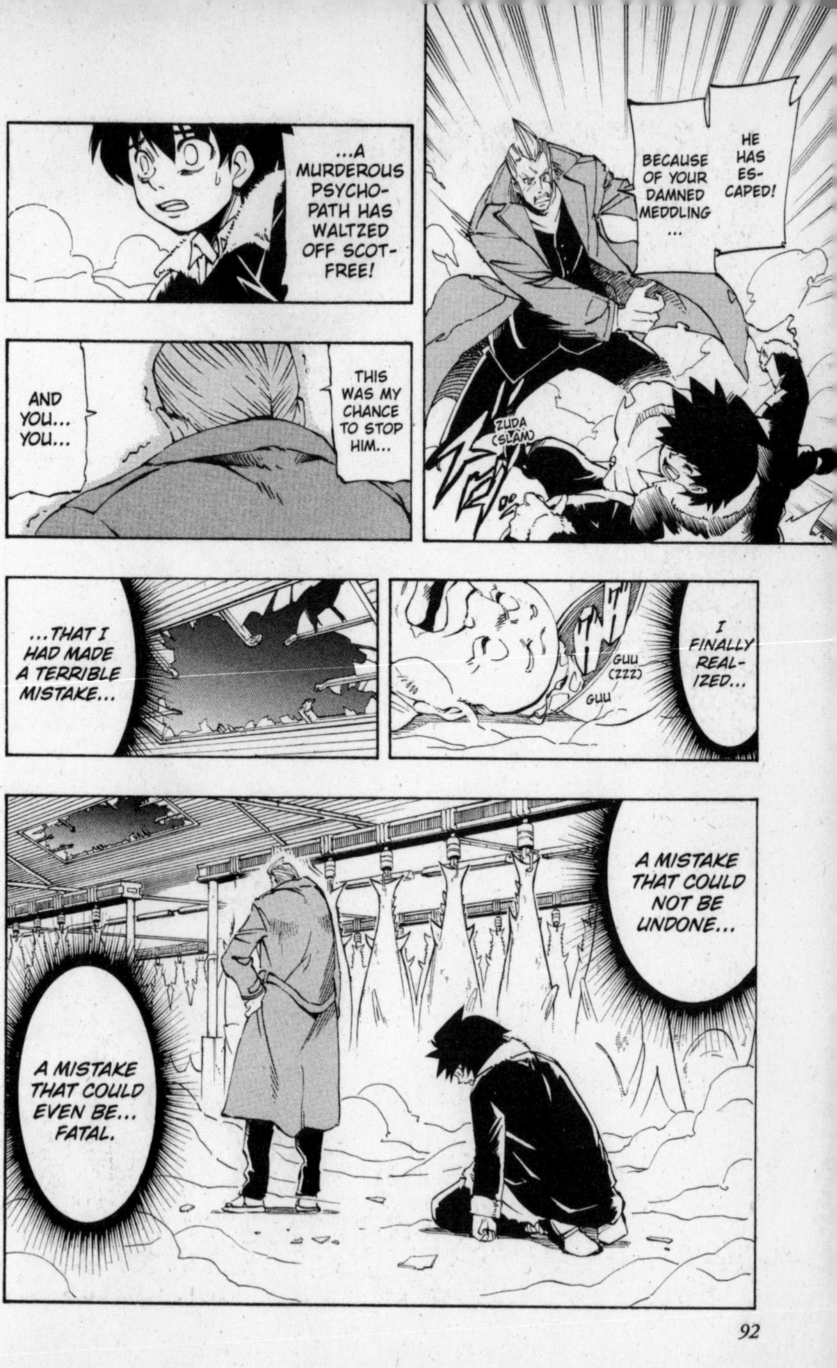
HE HAS ES-CAPED!
BECAUSE OF YOUR DAMNED MEDDLING ...
ZUDA (SLAM)
...A MURDEROUS PSYCHO-PATH HAS WALTZED OFF SCOT-FREE!
THIS WAS MY CHANCE TO STOP HIM...
AND YOU... YOU...
I FINALLY REAL-IZED...
GUU (ZZZ)
GUU
...THAT I HAD MADE A TERRIBLE MISTAKE...
A MISTAKE THAT COULD NOT BE UNDONE...
A MISTAKE THAT COULD EVEN BE... FATAL.

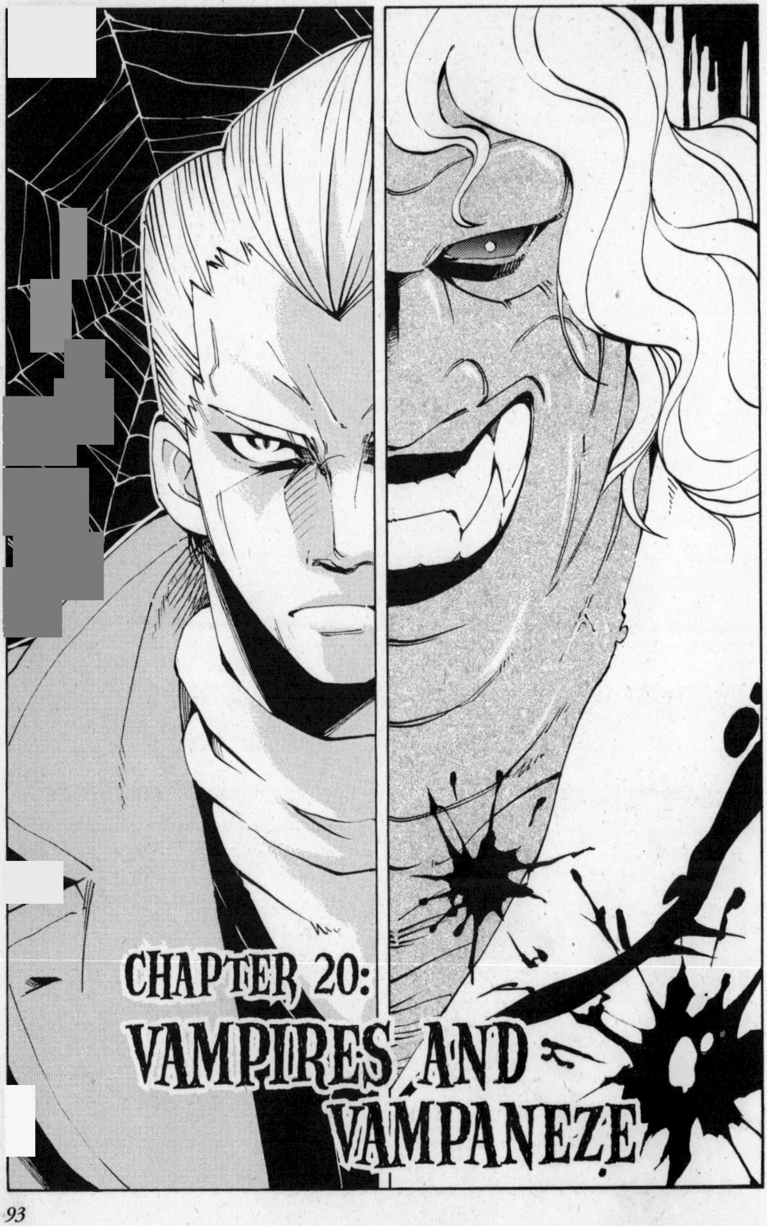
CHAPTER 20:
VAMPIRES AND VAMPANEZE

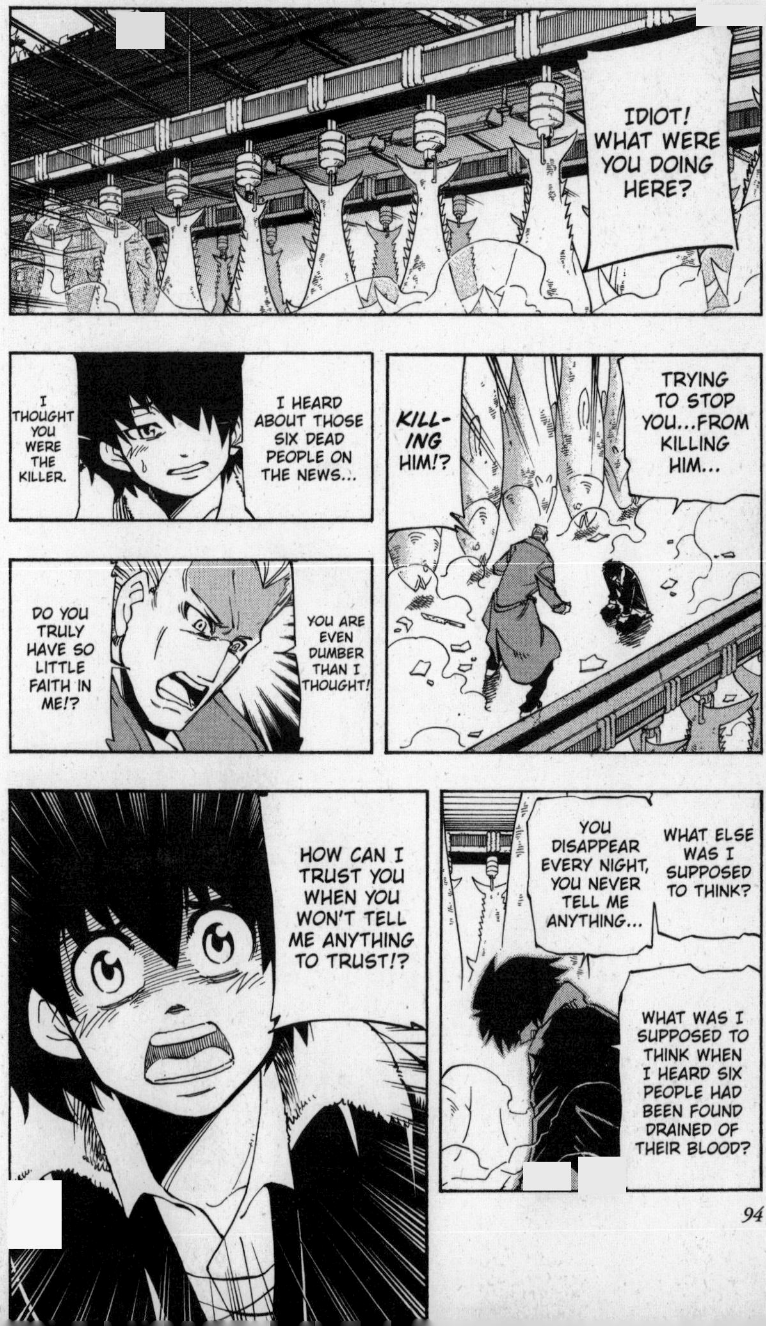

IDIOT! WHAT WERE YOU DOING HERE?
TRYING TO STOP YOU...FROM KILLING HIM...
KILLING HIM!?
I HEARD ABOUT THOSE SIX DEAD PEOPLE ON THE NEWS...
I THOUGHT YOU WERE THE KILLER.
YOU ARE EVEN DUMBER THAN I THOUGHT!
DO YOU TRULY HAVE SO LITTLE FAITH IN ME!?
WHAT ELSE WAS I SUPPOSED TO THINK?
YOU DISAPPEAR EVERY NIGHT, YOU NEVER TELL ME ANYTHING...
WHAT WAS I SUPPOSED TO THINK WHEN I HEARD SIX PEOPLE HAD BEEN FOUND DRAINED OF THEIR BLOOD?
HOW CAN I TRUST YOU WHEN YOU WON'T TELL ME ANYTHING TO TRUST!?

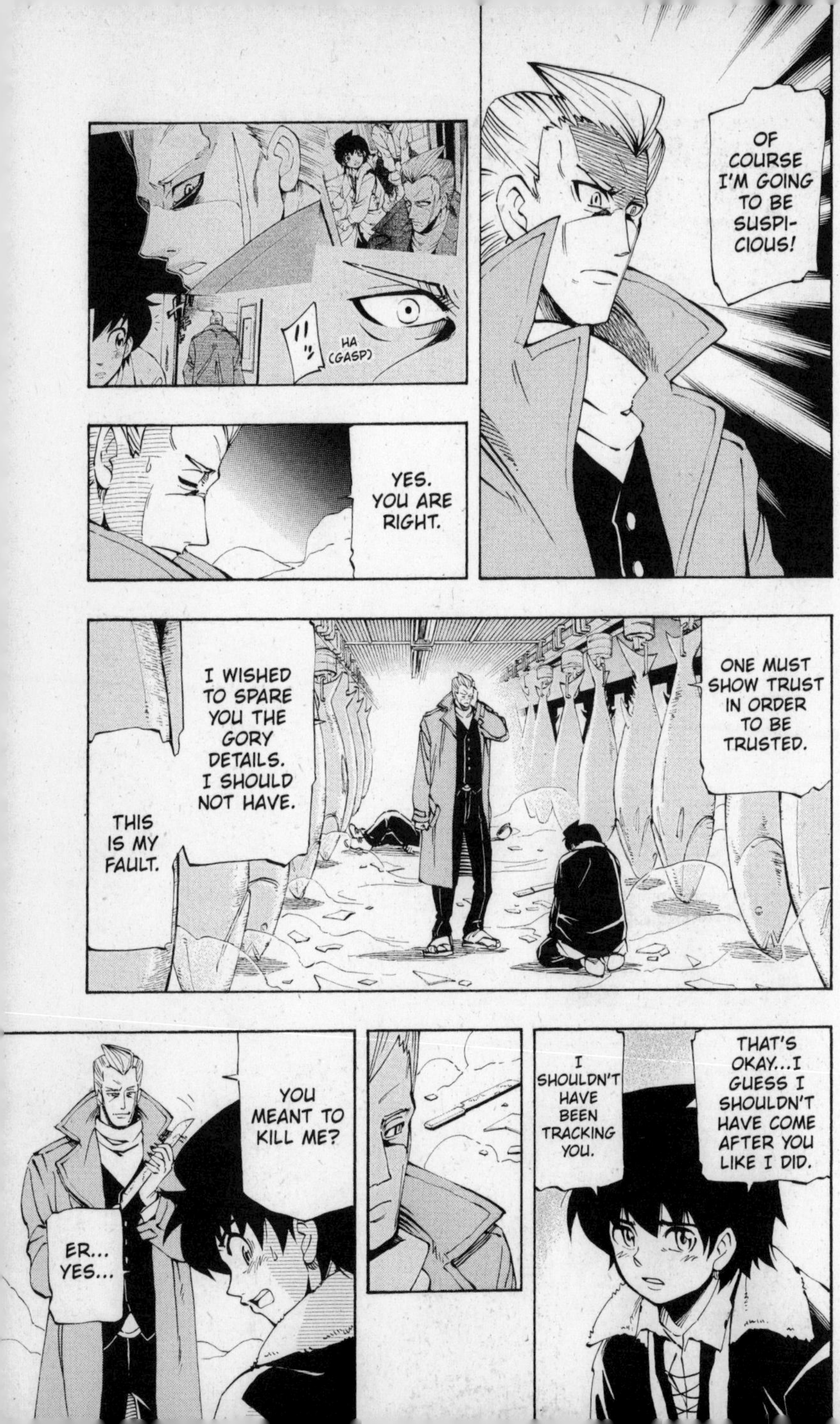
OF COURSE I'M GOING TO BE SUSPICIOUS!
!!
HA (GASP)
YES. YOU ARE RIGHT.
ONE MUST SHOW TRUST IN ORDER TO BE TRUSTED.
I WISHED TO SPARE YOU THE GORY DETAILS. I SHOULD NOT HAVE.
THIS IS MY FAULT.
THAT'S OKAY...I GUESS I SHOULDN'T HAVE COME AFTER YOU LIKE I DID.
I SHOULDN'T HAVE BEEN TRACKING YOU.
YOU MEANT TO KILL ME?
ER... YES...

BUT I KNEW THAT WHEN I TOOK YOU ON AS MY ASSISTANT.

YOU ARE A RECKLESS YOUNG MAN, MASTER SHAN.

NIYA (SMIRK)

IN A WORST-CASE SCENARIO, I GUESS...

I WILL LIVE. A SHAME ABOUT MY COAT, HOW-EVER.

HA-HA.

WILL YOU BE OKAY?

I'M SORRY...

ZO (SHIVER)

WHO *WAS* HE...?

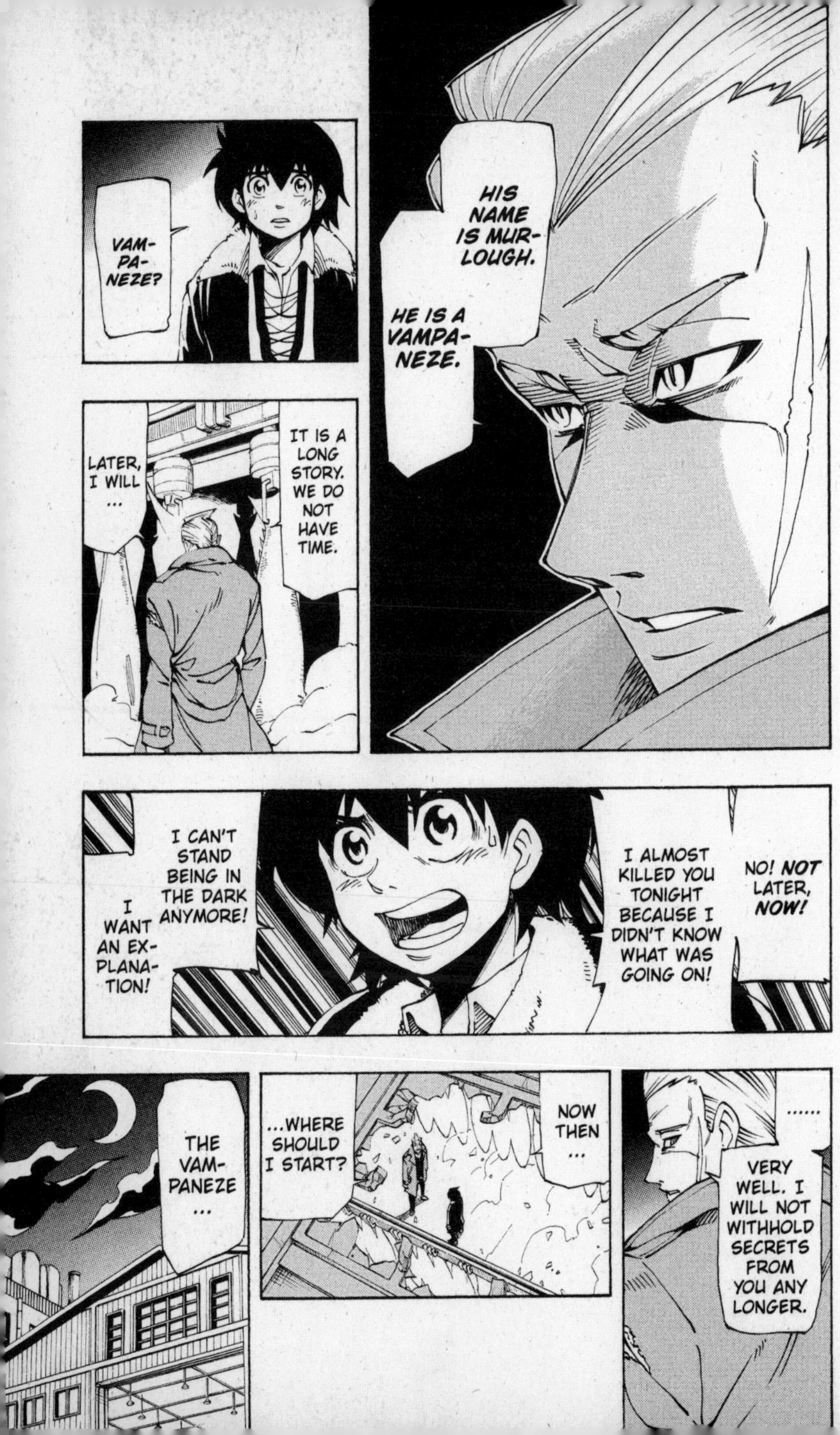
HIS NAME IS MURLOUGH.
HE IS A VAMPANEZE.
VAMPANEZE?
IT IS A LONG STORY. WE DO NOT HAVE TIME.
LATER, I WILL ...
NO! NOT LATER, NOW!
I ALMOST KILLED YOU TONIGHT BECAUSE I DIDN'T KNOW WHAT WAS GOING ON!
I CAN'T STAND BEING IN THE DARK ANYMORE!
I WANT AN EXPLANATION!
......
VERY WELL. I WILL NOT WITHHOLD SECRETS FROM YOU ANY LONGER.
NOW THEN ...
...WHERE SHOULD I START?
THE VAMPANEZE ...

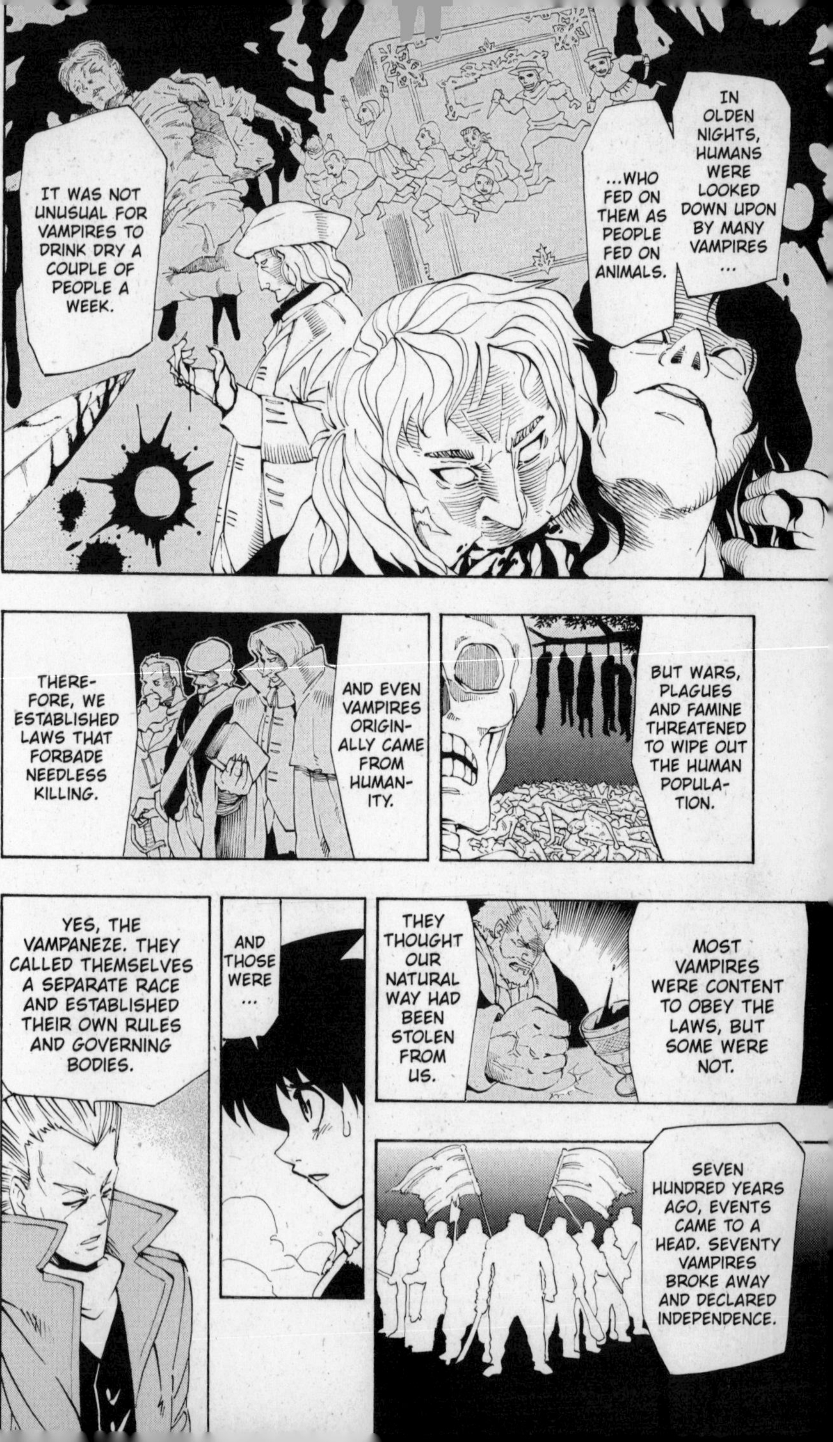
IN OLDEN NIGHTS, HUMANS WERE LOOKED DOWN UPON BY MANY VAMPIRES ...
...WHO FED ON THEM AS PEOPLE FED ON ANIMALS.
IT WAS NOT UNUSUAL FOR VAMPIRES TO DRINK DRY A COUPLE OF PEOPLE A WEEK.
BUT WARS, PLAGUES AND FAMINE THREATENED TO WIPE OUT THE HUMAN POPULATION.
AND EVEN VAMPIRES ORIGINALLY CAME FROM HUMANITY.
THEREFORE, WE ESTABLISHED LAWS THAT FORBADE NEEDLESS KILLING.
MOST VAMPIRES WERE CONTENT TO OBEY THE LAWS, BUT SOME WERE NOT.
THEY THOUGHT OUR NATURAL WAY HAD BEEN STOLEN FROM US.
SEVEN HUNDRED YEARS AGO, EVENTS CAME TO A HEAD. SEVENTY VAMPIRES BROKE AWAY AND DECLARED INDEPENDENCE.
AND THOSE WERE ...
YES, THE VAMPANEZE. THEY CALLED THEMSELVES A SEPARATE RACE AND ESTABLISHED THEIR OWN RULES AND GOVERNING BODIES.

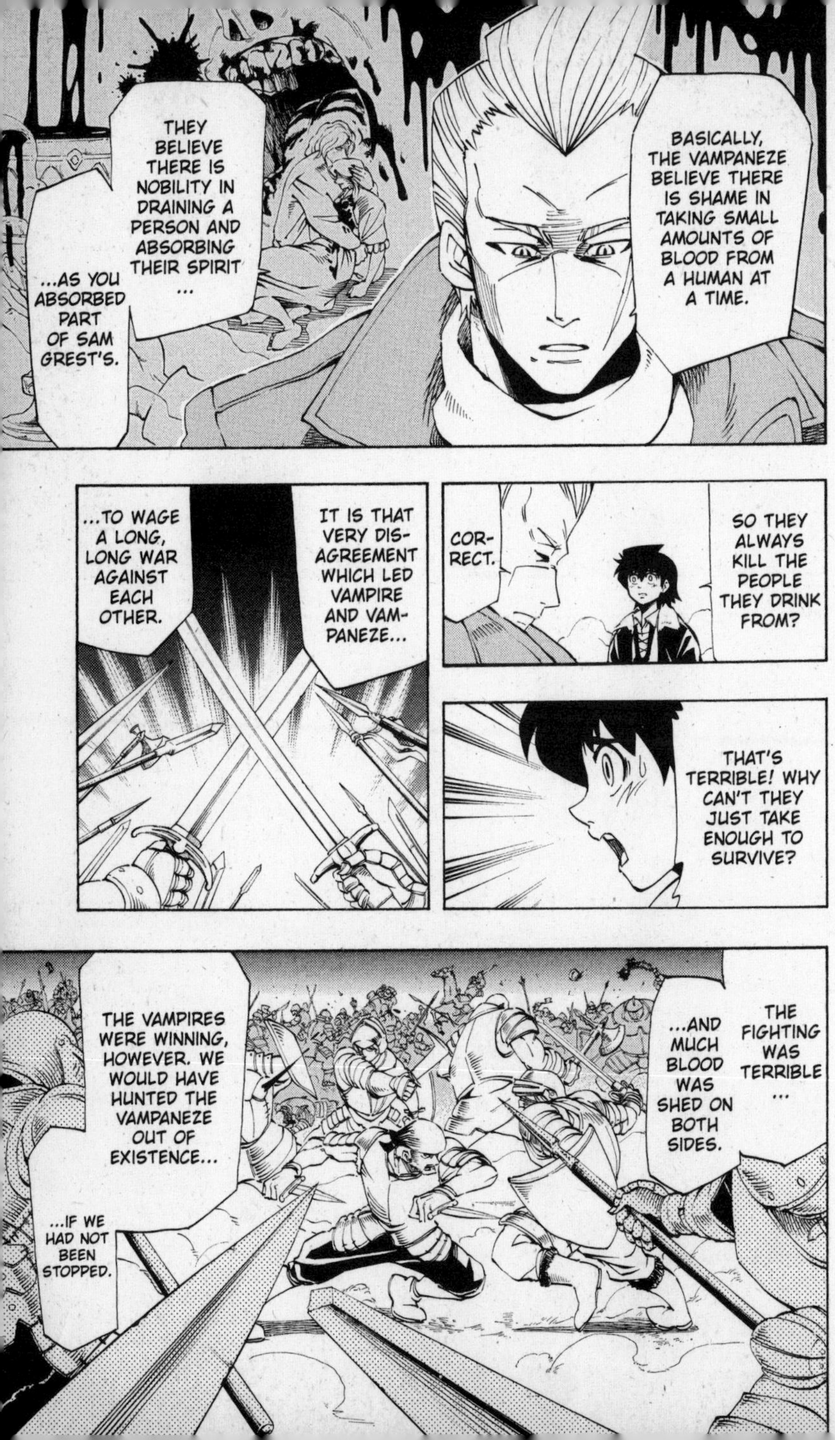
BASICALLY, THE VAMPANEZE BELIEVE THERE IS SHAME IN TAKING SMALL AMOUNTS OF BLOOD FROM A HUMAN AT A TIME.
THEY BELIEVE THERE IS NOBILITY IN DRAINING A PERSON AND ABSORBING THEIR SPIRIT ...
...AS YOU ABSORBED PART OF SAM GREST'S.
SO THEY ALWAYS KILL THE PEOPLE THEY DRINK FROM?
COR-RECT.
THAT'S TERRIBLE! WHY CAN'T THEY JUST TAKE ENOUGH TO SURVIVE?
IT IS THAT VERY DIS-AGREEMENT WHICH LED VAMPIRE AND VAM-PANEZE...
...TO WAGE A LONG, LONG WAR AGAINST EACH OTHER.
THE FIGHTING WAS TERRIBLE ...
...AND MUCH BLOOD WAS SHED ON BOTH SIDES.
THE VAMPIRES WERE WINNING, HOWEVER. WE WOULD HAVE HUNTED THE VAMPANEZE OUT OF EXISTENCE...
...IF WE HAD NOT BEEN STOPPED.

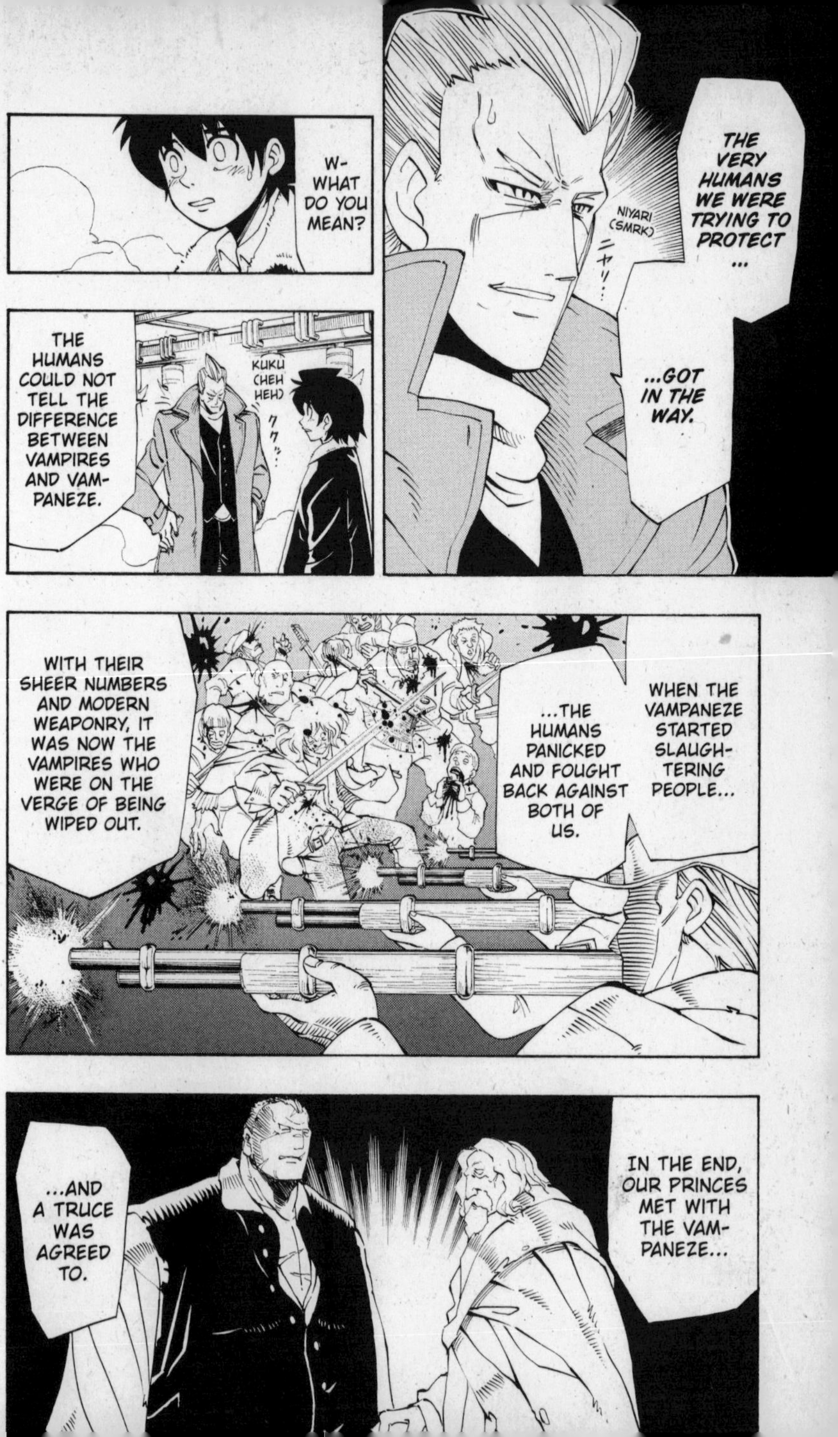
THE VERY HUMANS WE WERE TRYING TO PROTECT...
NIYARI (SMRK)
...GOT IN THE WAY.
W-WHAT DO YOU MEAN?
THE HUMANS COULD NOT TELL THE DIFFERENCE BETWEEN VAMPIRES AND VAMPANEZE.
KUKU (HEH HEH)
WHEN THE VAMPANEZE STARTED SLAUGHTERING PEOPLE...
...THE HUMANS PANICKED AND FOUGHT BACK AGAINST BOTH OF US.
WITH THEIR SHEER NUMBERS AND MODERN WEAPONRY, IT WAS NOW THE VAMPIRES WHO WERE ON THE VERGE OF BEING WIPED OUT.
IN THE END, OUR PRINCES MET WITH THE VAMPANEZE...
...AND A TRUCE WAS AGREED TO.

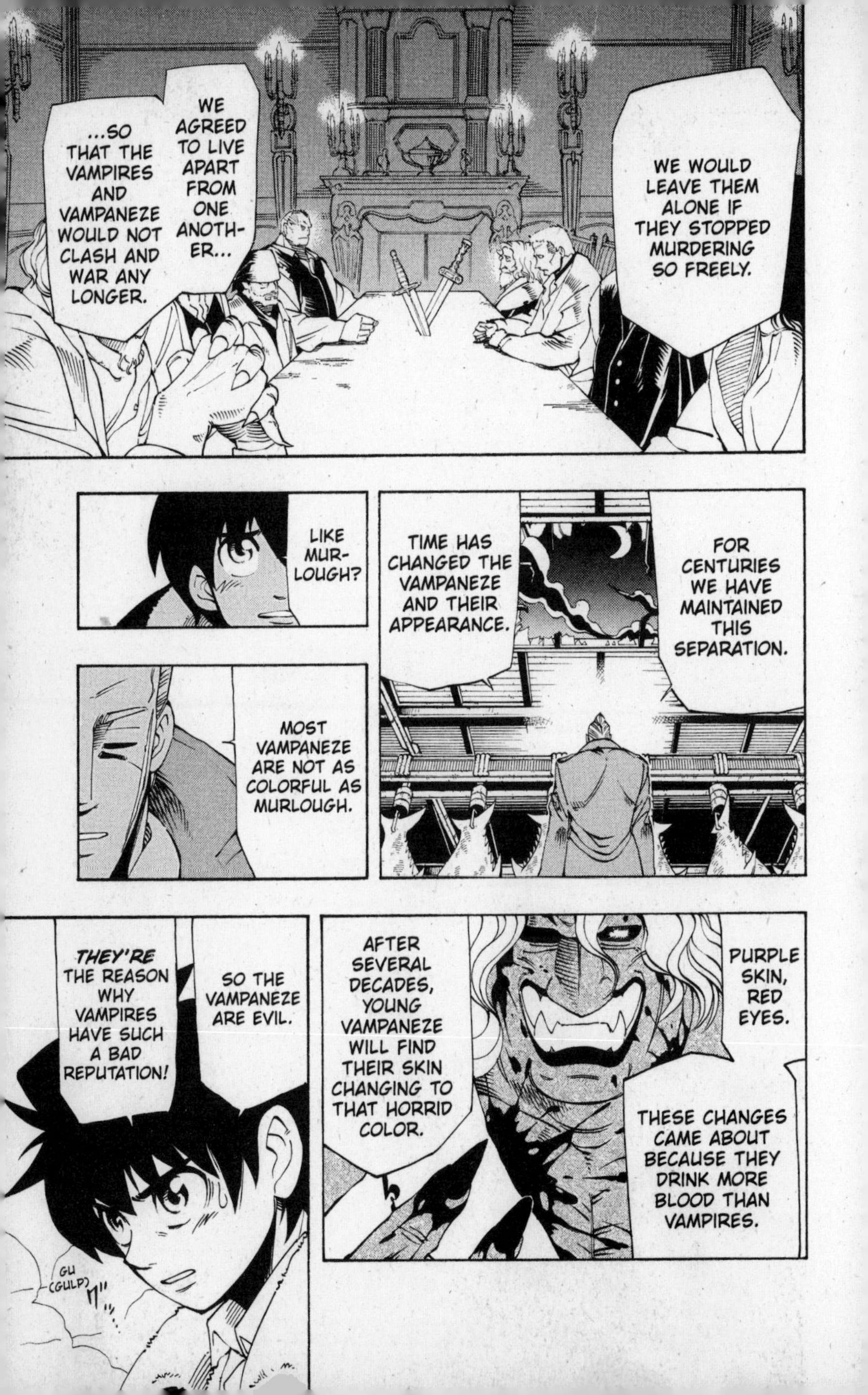
WE WOULD LEAVE THEM ALONE IF THEY STOPPED MURDERING SO FREELY.
WE AGREED TO LIVE APART FROM ONE ANOTHER...
...SO THAT THE VAMPIRES AND VAMPANEZE WOULD NOT CLASH AND WAR ANY LONGER.
FOR CENTURIES WE HAVE MAINTAINED THIS SEPARATION.
TIME HAS CHANGED THE VAMPANEZE AND THEIR APPEARANCE.
LIKE MURLOUGH?
MOST VAMPANEZE ARE NOT AS COLORFUL AS MURLOUGH.
PURPLE SKIN, RED EYES.
AFTER SEVERAL DECADES, YOUNG VAMPANEZE WILL FIND THEIR SKIN CHANGING TO THAT HORRID COLOR.
THESE CHANGES CAME ABOUT BECAUSE THEY DRINK MORE BLOOD THAN VAMPIRES.
SO THE VAMPANEZE ARE EVIL.
THEY'RE THE REASON WHY VAMPIRES HAVE SUCH A BAD REPUTATION!
GU (GULP)

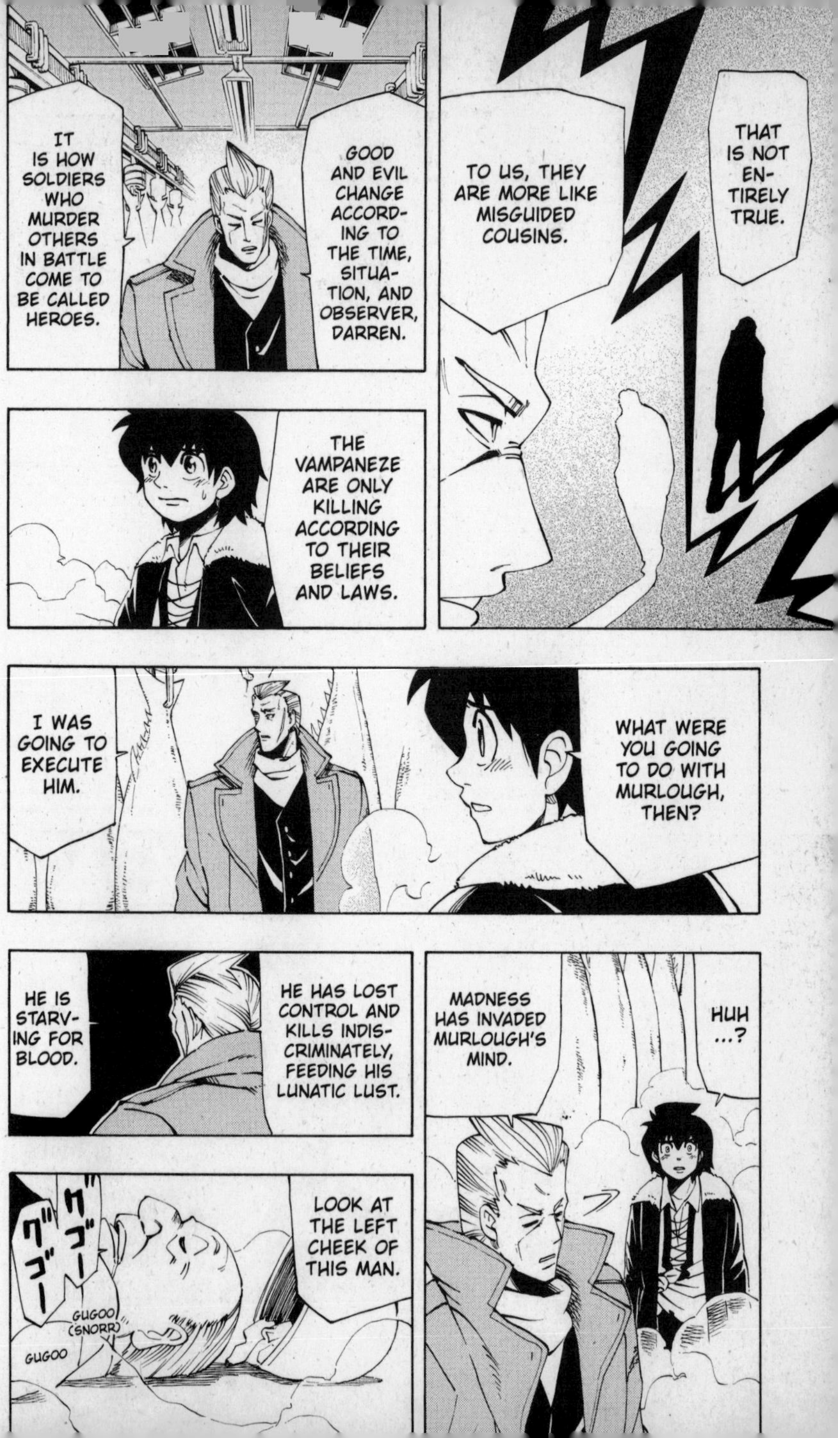

THAT IS NOT ENTIRELY TRUE.
TO US, THEY ARE MORE LIKE MISGUIDED COUSINS.
GOOD AND EVIL CHANGE ACCORDING TO THE TIME, SITUATION, AND OBSERVER, DARREN.
IT IS HOW SOLDIERS WHO MURDER OTHERS IN BATTLE COME TO BE CALLED HEROES.
THE VAMPANEZE ARE ONLY KILLING ACCORDING TO THEIR BELIEFS AND LAWS.
WHAT WERE YOU GOING TO DO WITH MURLOUGH, THEN?
I WAS GOING TO EXECUTE HIM.
HUH ...?
MADNESS HAS INVADED MURLOUGH'S MIND.
HE HAS LOST CONTROL AND KILLS INDISCRIMINATELY, FEEDING HIS LUNATIC LUST.
HE IS STARVING FOR BLOOD.
LOOK AT THE LEFT CHEEK OF THIS MAN.
グゴー
グゴー
GUGOO (SNORR)
GUGOO

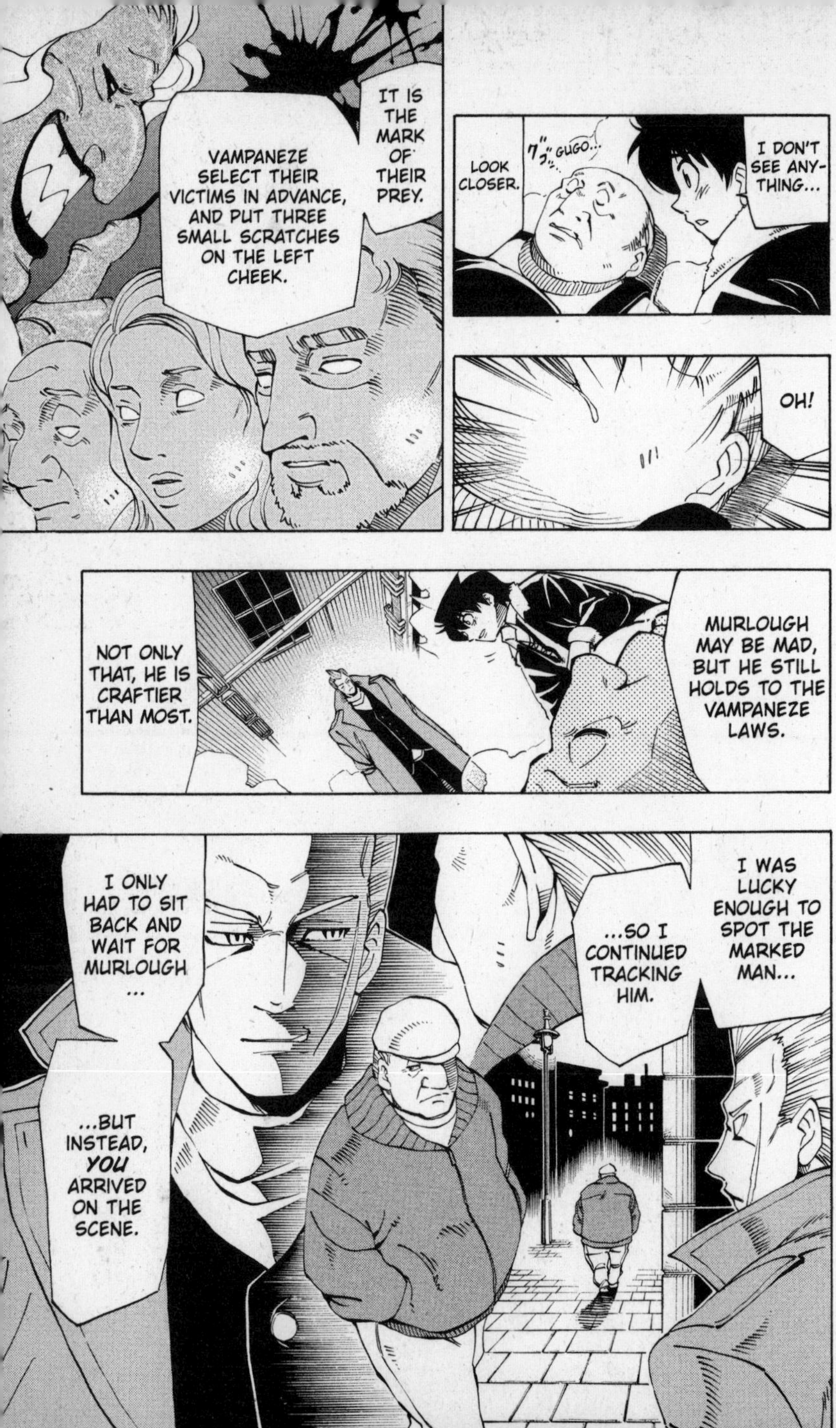
I DON'T SEE ANYTHING...
GUGO...
LOOK CLOSER.
OH!
IT IS THE MARK OF THEIR PREY.
VAMPANEZE SELECT THEIR VICTIMS IN ADVANCE, AND PUT THREE SMALL SCRATCHES ON THE LEFT CHEEK.
MURLOUGH MAY BE MAD, BUT HE STILL HOLDS TO THE VAMPANEZE LAWS.
NOT ONLY THAT, HE IS CRAFTIER THAN MOST.
I WAS LUCKY ENOUGH TO SPOT THE MARKED MAN...
...SO I CONTINUED TRACKING HIM.
I ONLY HAD TO SIT BACK AND WAIT FOR MURLOUGH...
...BUT INSTEAD, *YOU* ARRIVED ON THE SCENE.

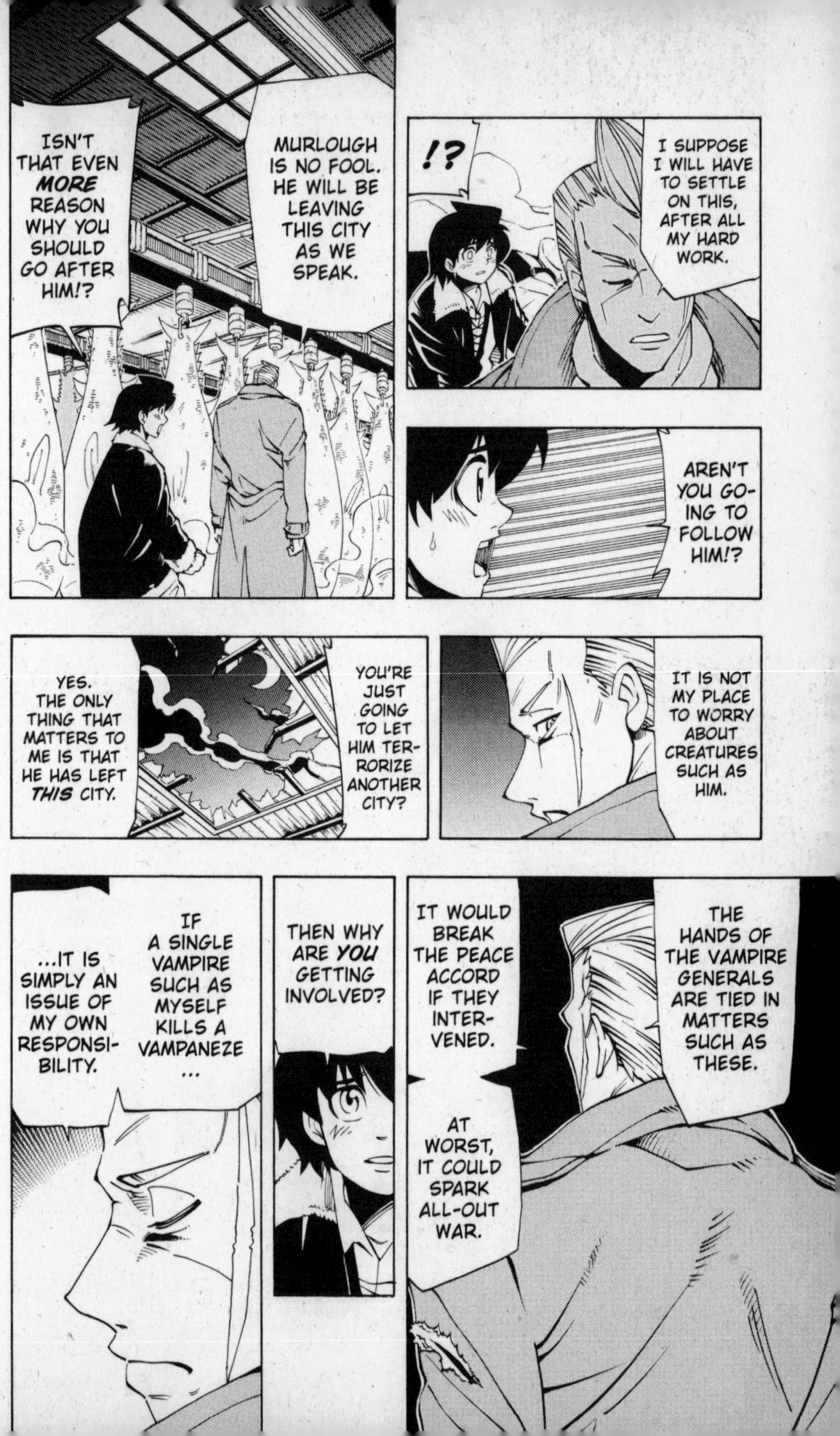
I SUPPOSE I WILL HAVE TO SETTLE ON THIS, AFTER ALL MY HARD WORK.
!?
AREN'T YOU GO-ING TO FOLLOW HIM!?
MURLOUGH IS NO FOOL. HE WILL BE LEAVING THIS CITY AS WE SPEAK.
ISN'T THAT EVEN *MORE* REASON WHY YOU SHOULD GO AFTER HIM!?
IT IS NOT MY PLACE TO WORRY ABOUT CREATURES SUCH AS HIM.
YOU'RE JUST GOING TO LET HIM TER-RORIZE ANOTHER CITY?
YES. THE ONLY THING THAT MATTERS TO ME IS THAT HE HAS LEFT *THIS* CITY.
THE HANDS OF THE VAMPIRE GENERALS ARE TIED IN MATTERS SUCH AS THESE.
IT WOULD BREAK THE PEACE ACCORD IF THEY INTER-VENED.
AT WORST, IT COULD SPARK ALL-OUT WAR.
THEN WHY ARE *YOU* GETTING INVOLVED?
IF A SINGLE VAMPIRE SUCH AS MYSELF KILLS A VAMPANEZE ...
...IT IS SIMPLY AN ISSUE OF MY OWN RESPONSI-BILITY.

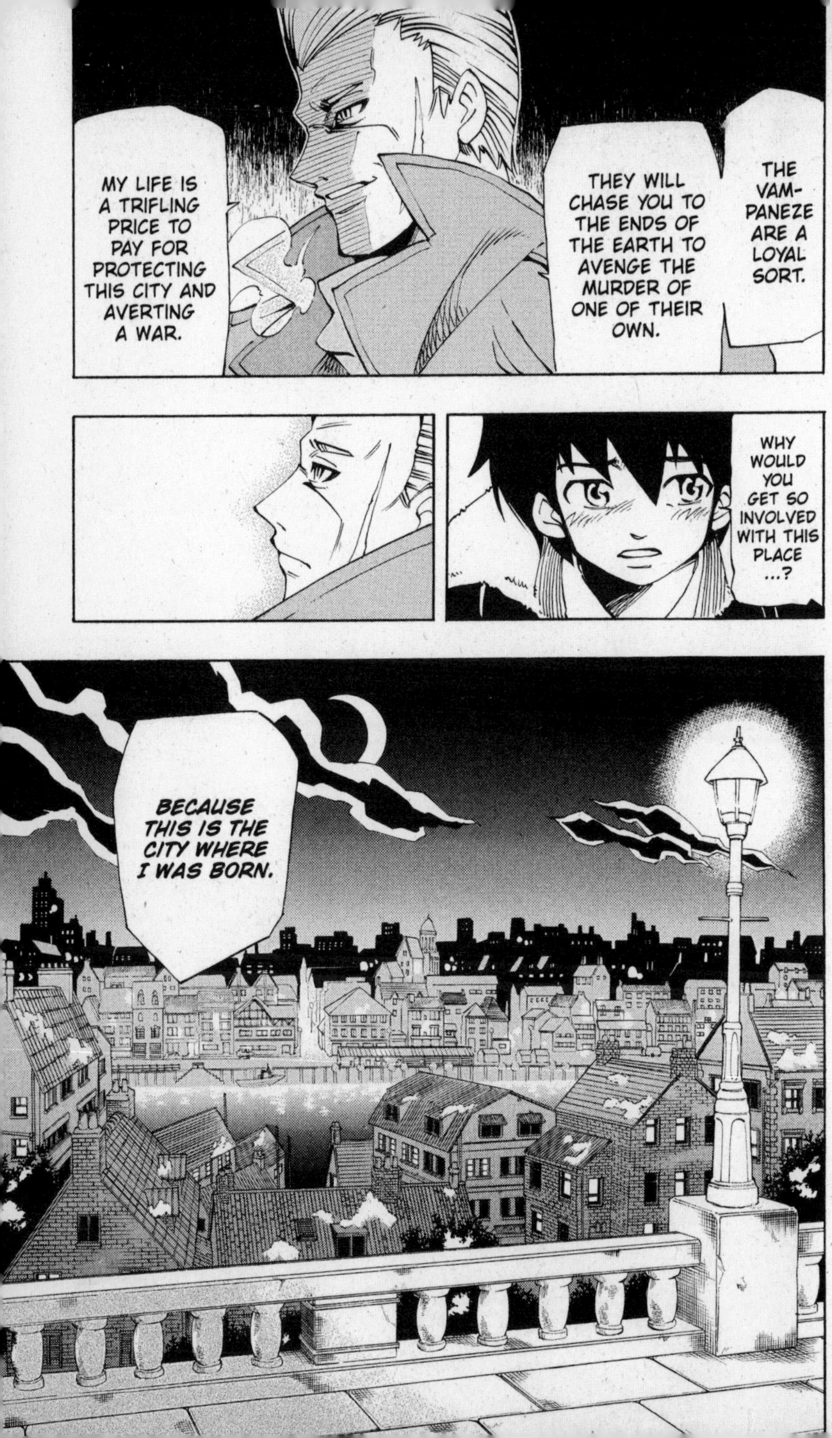
THE VAM-PANEZE ARE A LOYAL SORT.
THEY WILL CHASE YOU TO THE ENDS OF THE EARTH TO AVENGE THE MURDER OF ONE OF THEIR OWN.
MY LIFE IS A TRIFLING PRICE TO PAY FOR PROTECTING THIS CITY AND AVERTING A WAR.
WHY WOULD YOU GET SO INVOLVED WITH THIS PLACE ...?
BECAUSE THIS IS THE CITY WHERE I WAS BORN.

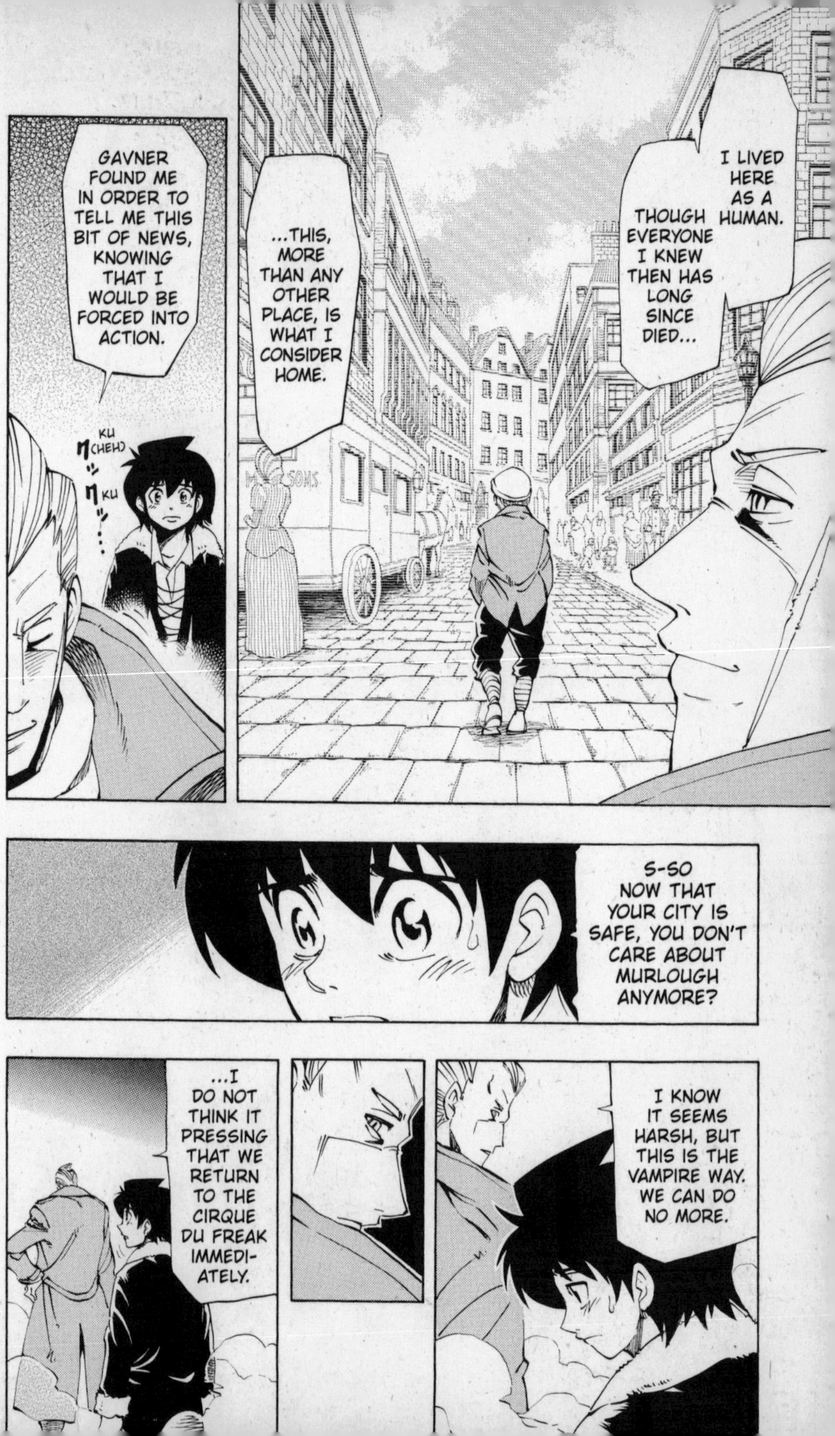
I LIVED HERE AS A HUMAN.
THOUGH EVERYONE I KNEW THEN HAS LONG SINCE DIED...
...THIS, MORE THAN ANY OTHER PLACE, IS WHAT I CONSIDER HOME.
GAVNER FOUND ME IN ORDER TO TELL ME THIS BIT OF NEWS, KNOWING THAT I WOULD BE FORCED INTO ACTION.
クッ KU (HEH)
クッ KU
...
S-SO NOW THAT YOUR CITY IS SAFE, YOU DON'T CARE ABOUT MURLOUGH ANYMORE?
I KNOW IT SEEMS HARSH, BUT THIS IS THE VAMPIRE WAY. WE CAN DO NO MORE.
...I DO NOT THINK IT PRESSING THAT WE RETURN TO THE CIRQUE DU FREAK IMMEDIATELY.

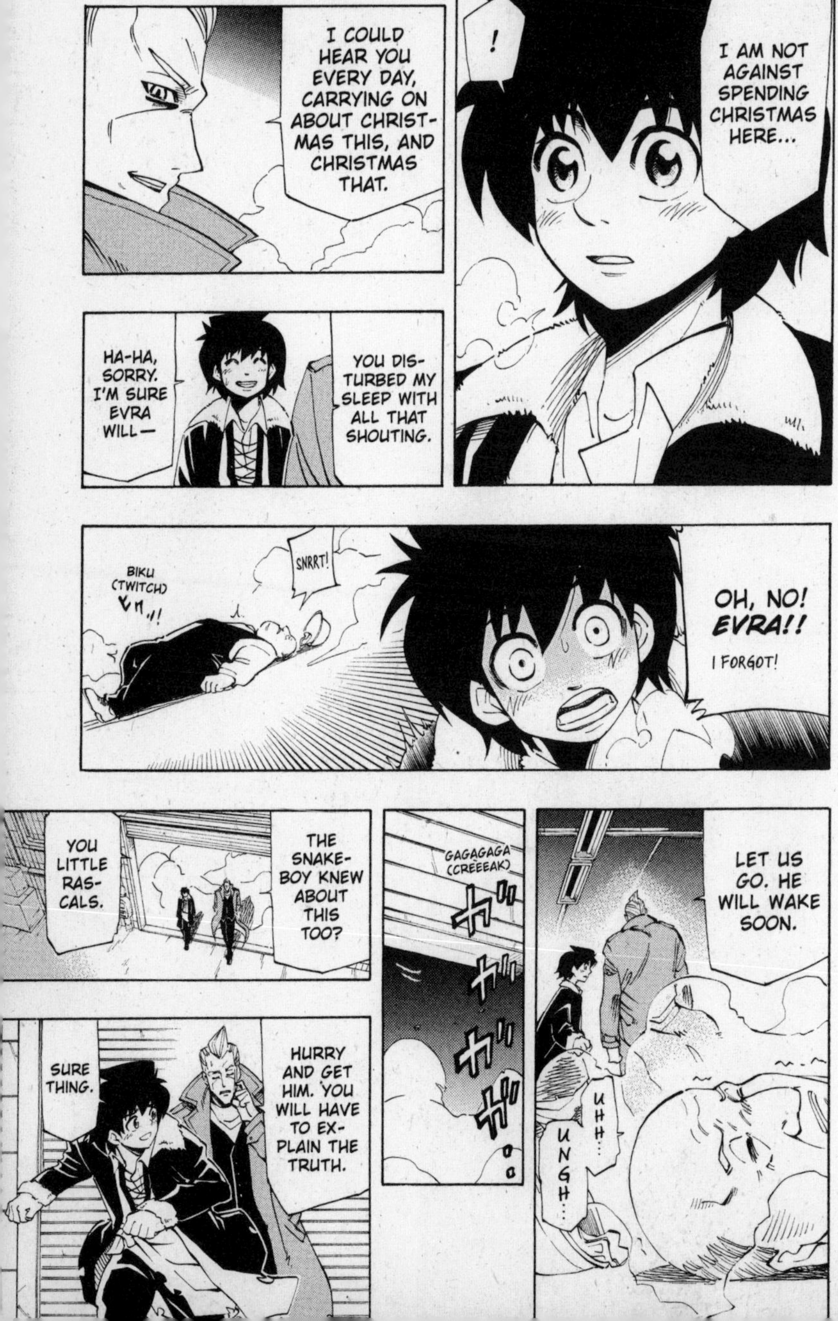
!
I AM NOT AGAINST SPENDING CHRISTMAS HERE...
I COULD HEAR YOU EVERY DAY, CARRYING ON ABOUT CHRISTMAS THIS, AND CHRISTMAS THAT.
YOU DISTURBED MY SLEEP WITH ALL THAT SHOUTING.
HA-HA, SORRY. I'M SURE EVRA WILL—
OH, NO! EVRA!!
I FORGOT!
SNRRT!
BIKU (TWITCH)
LET US GO. HE WILL WAKE SOON.
UHH...
UNGH...
GAGAGAGA (CREEEAK)
THE SNAKE-BOY KNEW ABOUT THIS TOO?
YOU LITTLE RASCALS.
HURRY AND GET HIM. YOU WILL HAVE TO EXPLAIN THE TRUTH.
SURE THING.

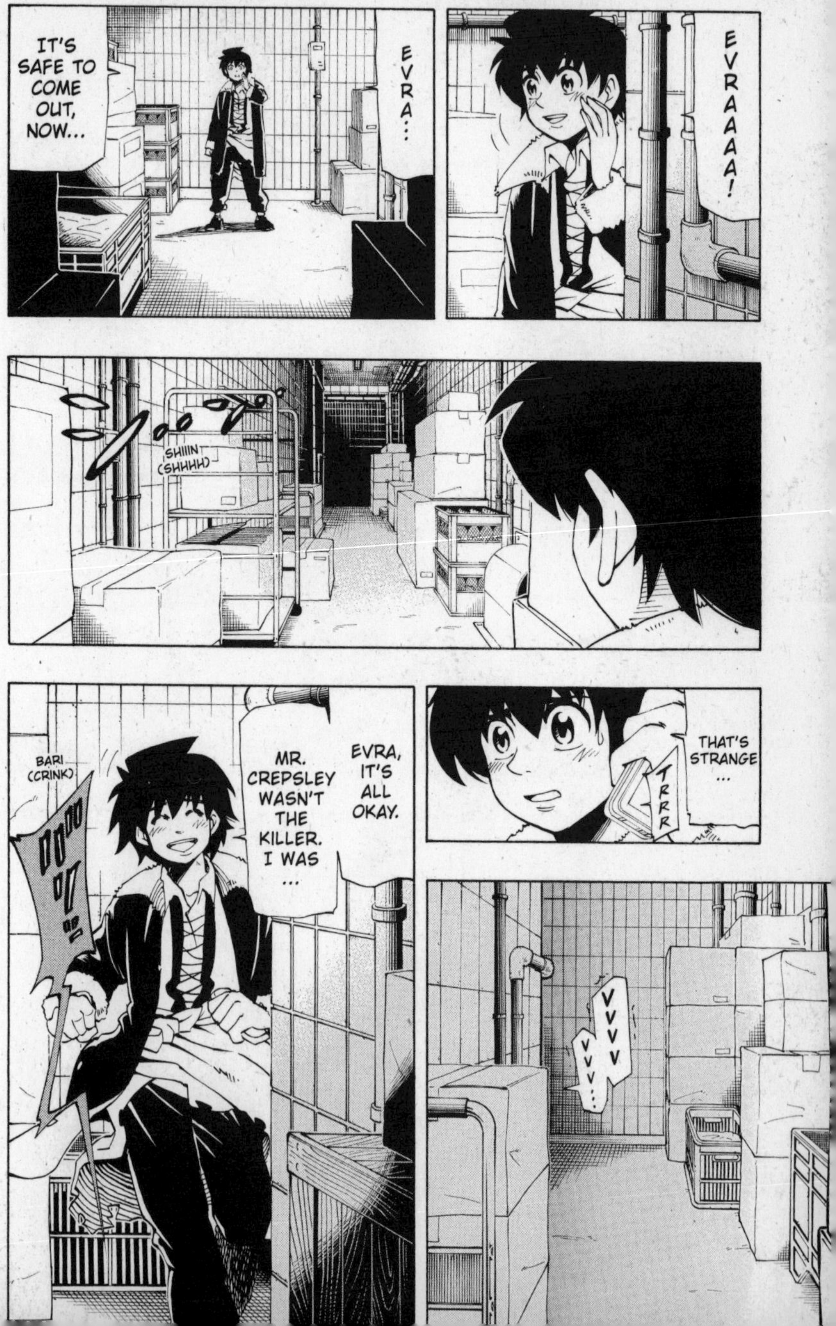
EVRAAAAA!
EVRA...
IT'S SAFE TO COME OUT, NOW...
SHIIIN (SHHHH)
THAT'S STRANGE ...
TRRR
VVVV VVV...
EVRA, IT'S ALL OKAY.
MR. CREPSLEY WASN'T THE KILLER. I WAS ...
BARI (CRINK)

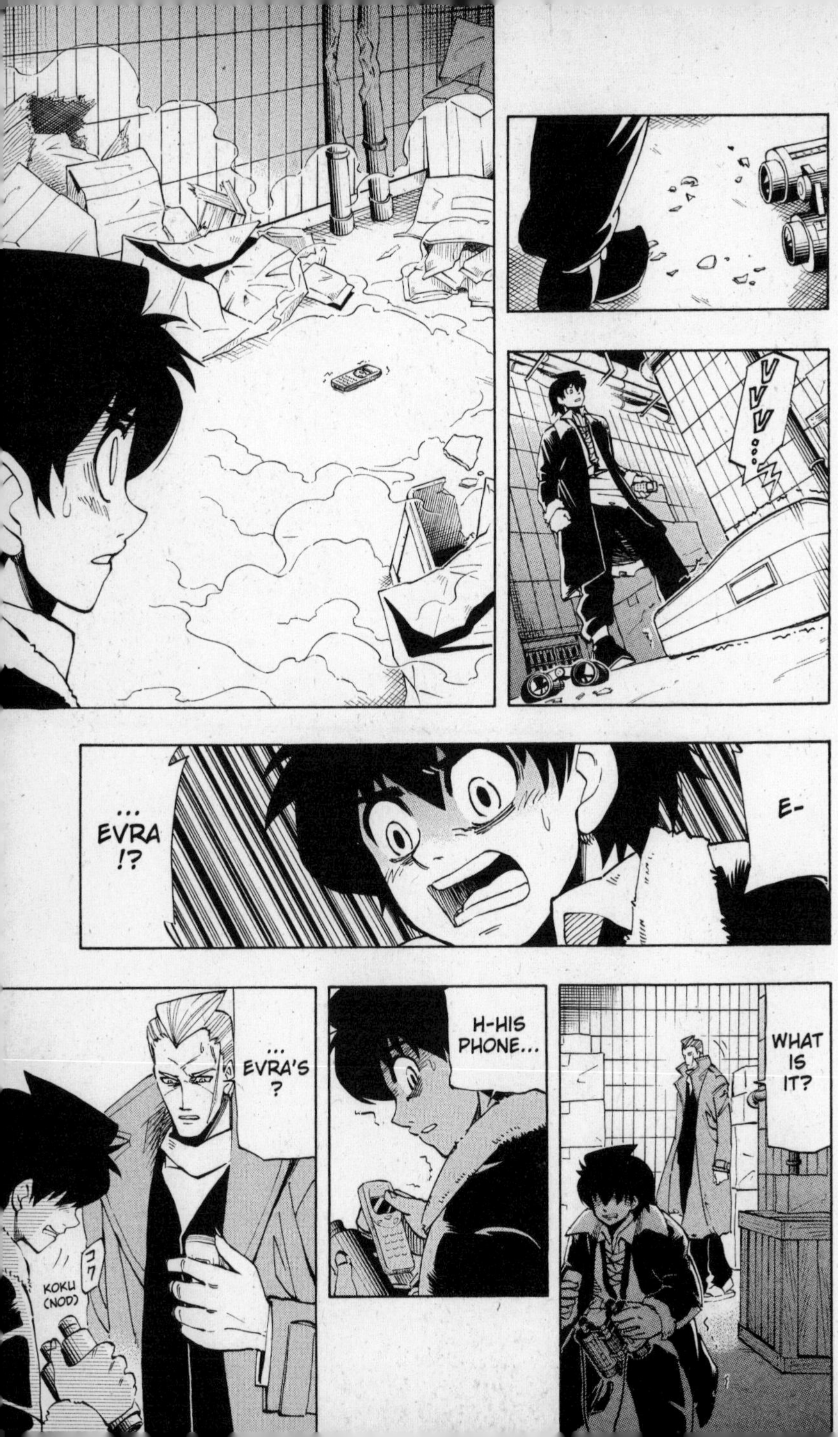
VVV...
E-
... EVRA !?
WHAT IS IT?
H-HIS PHONE...
... EVRA'S ?
コク
KOKU (NOD)

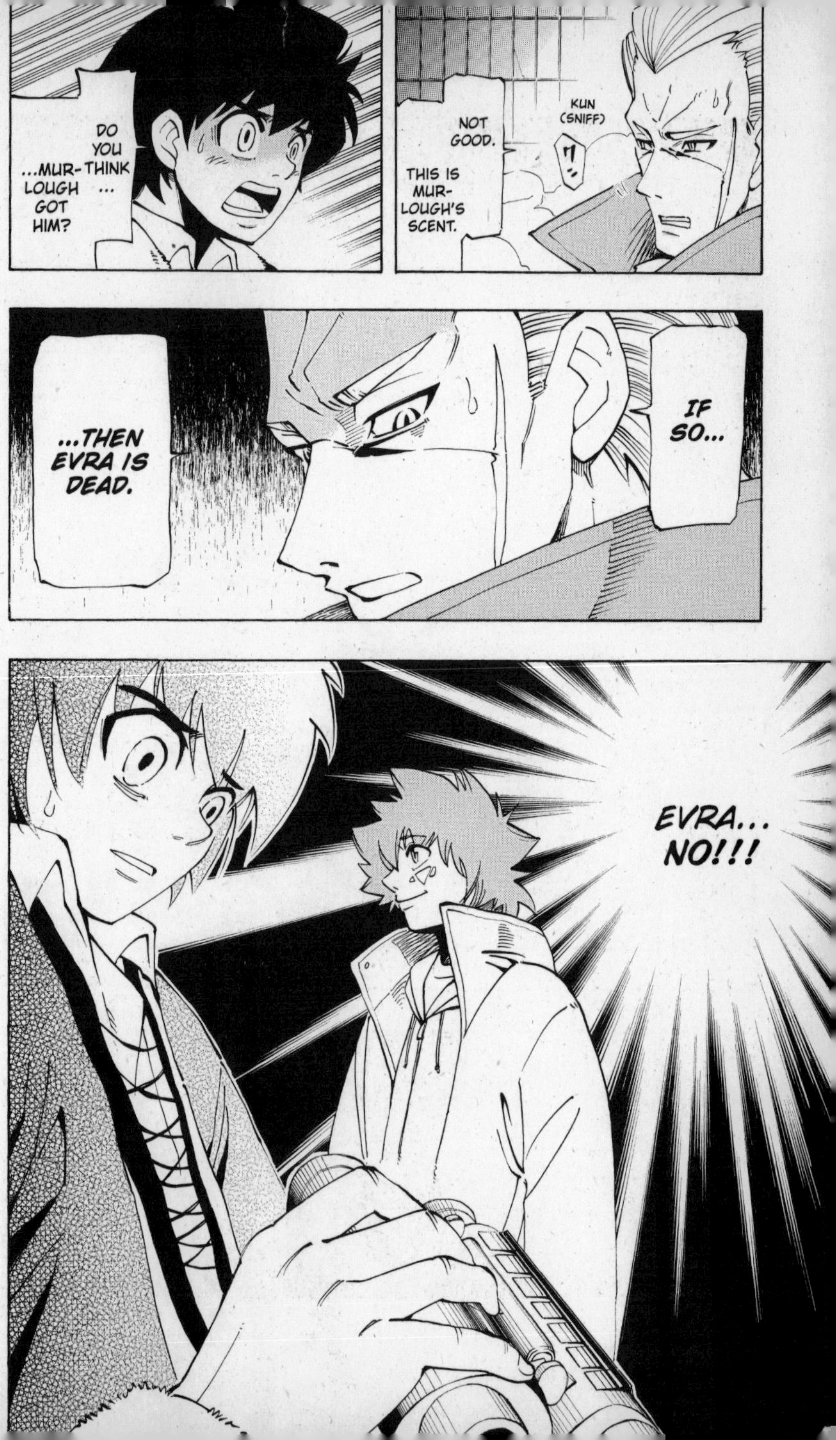
KUN (SNIFF)
NOT GOOD.
THIS IS MUR-LOUGH'S SCENT.
DO YOU THINK ...
...MUR-LOUGH GOT HIM?
IF SO...
...THEN EVRA IS DEAD.
EVRA... NO!!!

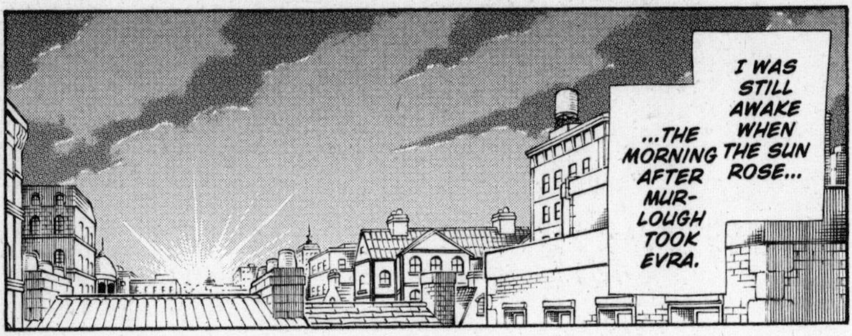
I WAS STILL AWAKE WHEN THE SUN ROSE...
...THE MORNING AFTER MURLOUGH TOOK EVRA.

CHAPTER 21:
THE EVIL BENEATH

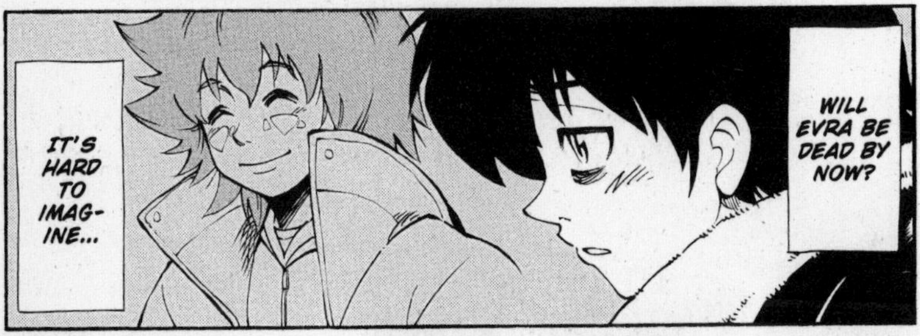
WILL EVRA BE DEAD BY NOW?
IT'S HARD TO IMAGINE...

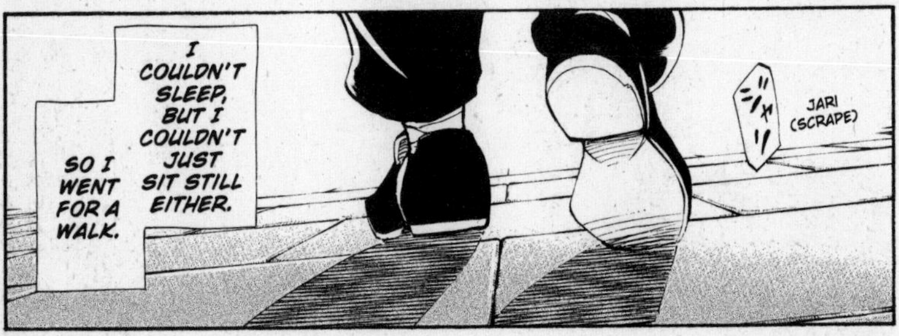
JARI (SCRAPE)
I COULDN'T SLEEP, BUT I COULDN'T JUST SIT STILL EITHER.
SO I WENT FOR A WALK.

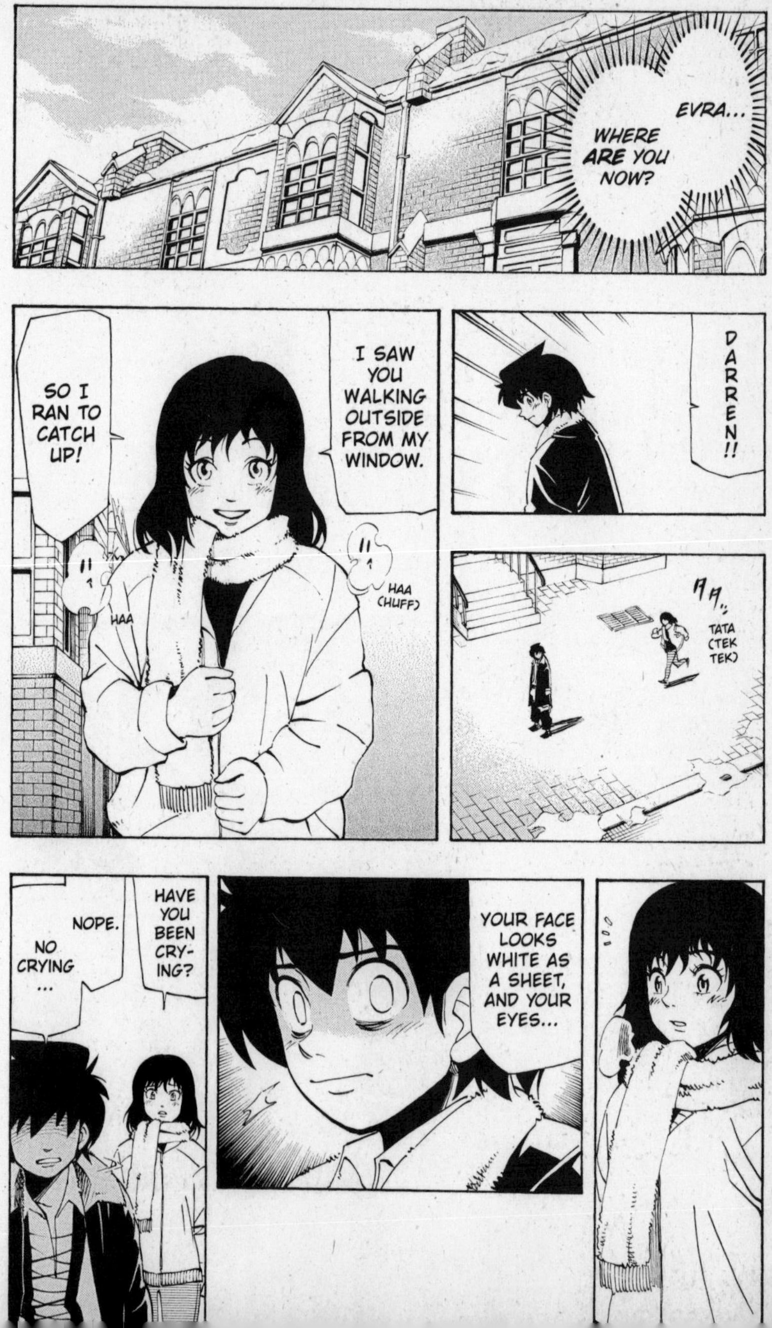
EVRA... WHERE ARE YOU NOW?
DARREN!!
タタ
TATA (TEK TEK)
I SAW YOU WALKING OUTSIDE FROM MY WINDOW.
HAA (HUFF)
SO I RAN TO CATCH UP!
HAA
YOUR FACE LOOKS WHITE AS A SHEET, AND YOUR EYES...
HAVE YOU BEEN CRY-ING?
NOPE.
NO CRYING...

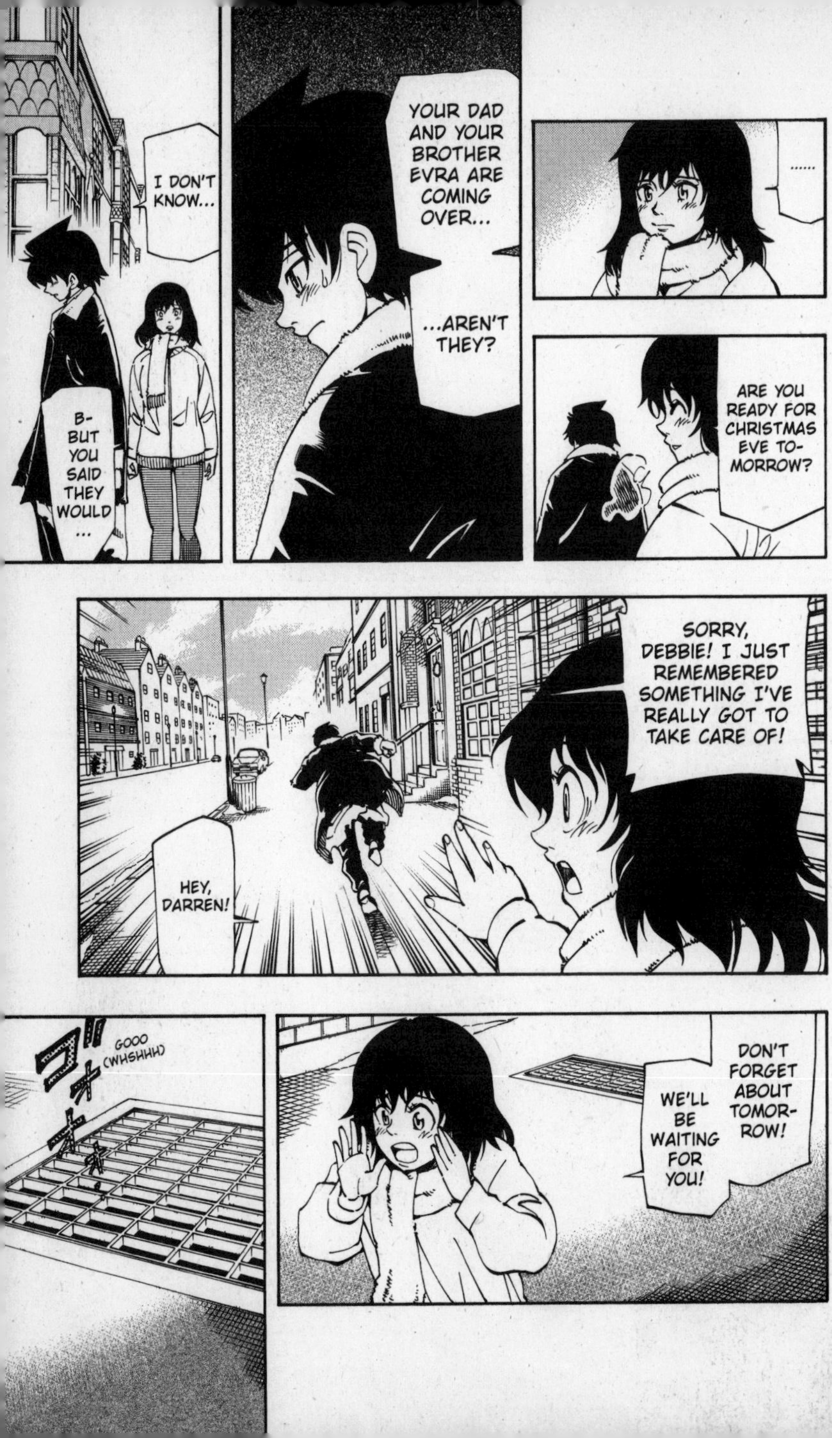
......
ARE YOU READY FOR CHRISTMAS EVE TO-MORROW?
YOUR DAD AND YOUR BROTHER EVRA ARE COMING OVER...
...AREN'T THEY?
I DON'T KNOW...
B-BUT YOU SAID THEY WOULD...
SORRY, DEBBIE! I JUST REMEMBERED SOMETHING I'VE REALLY GOT TO TAKE CARE OF!
HEY, DARREN!
DON'T FORGET ABOUT TOMOR-ROW!
WE'LL BE WAITING FOR YOU!
GOOO (WHSHHH)

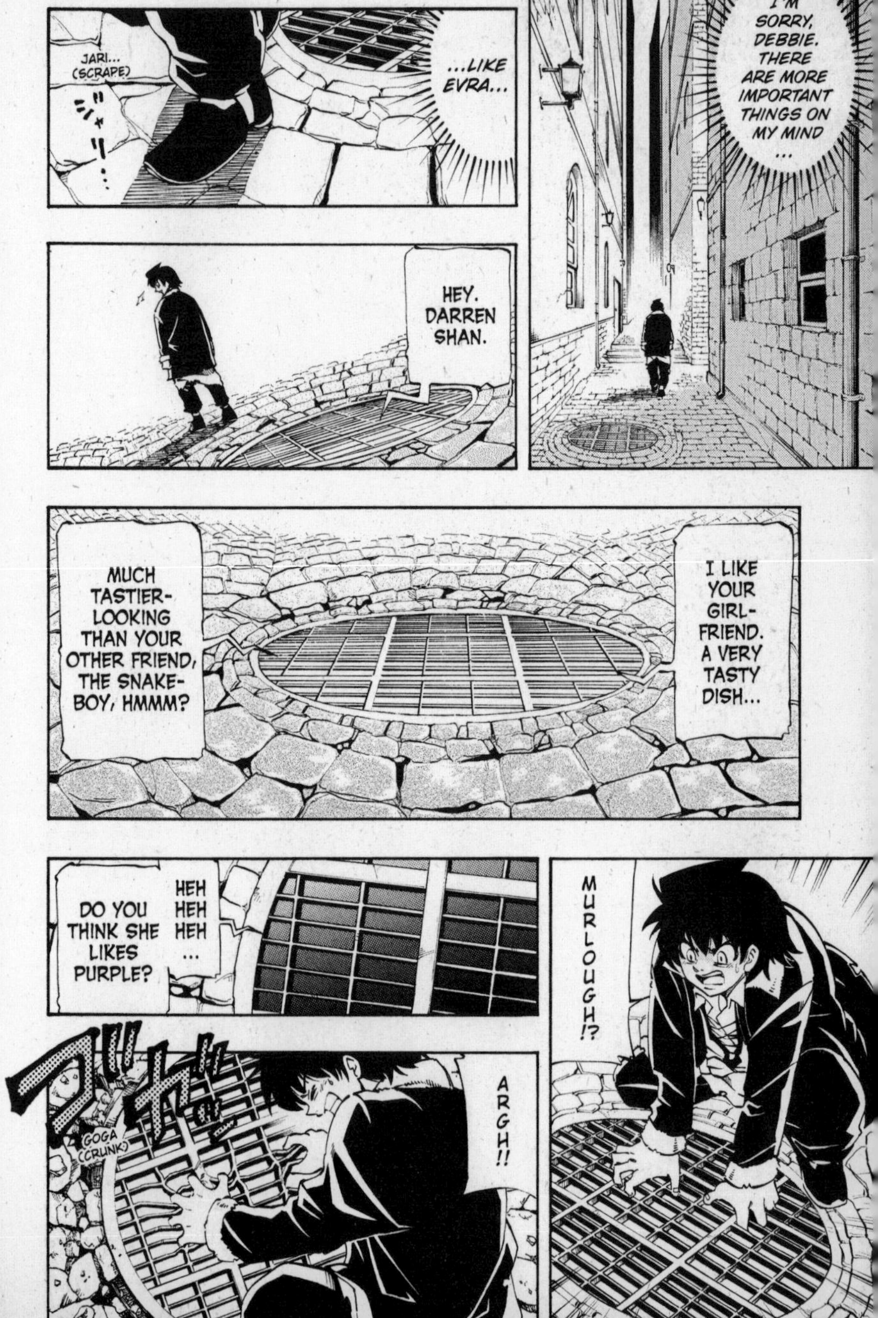
I'M SORRY, DEBBIE. THERE ARE MORE IMPORTANT THINGS ON MY MIND ...
...LIKE EVRA...
JARI... (SCRAPE)
HEY. DARREN SHAN.
I LIKE YOUR GIRL-FRIEND. A VERY TASTY DISH...
MUCH TASTIER-LOOKING THAN YOUR OTHER FRIEND, THE SNAKE-BOY, HMMM?
MURLOUGH!?
HEH HEH HEH ...
DO YOU THINK SHE LIKES PURPLE?
ARGH!!
GOGA (CRUNK)

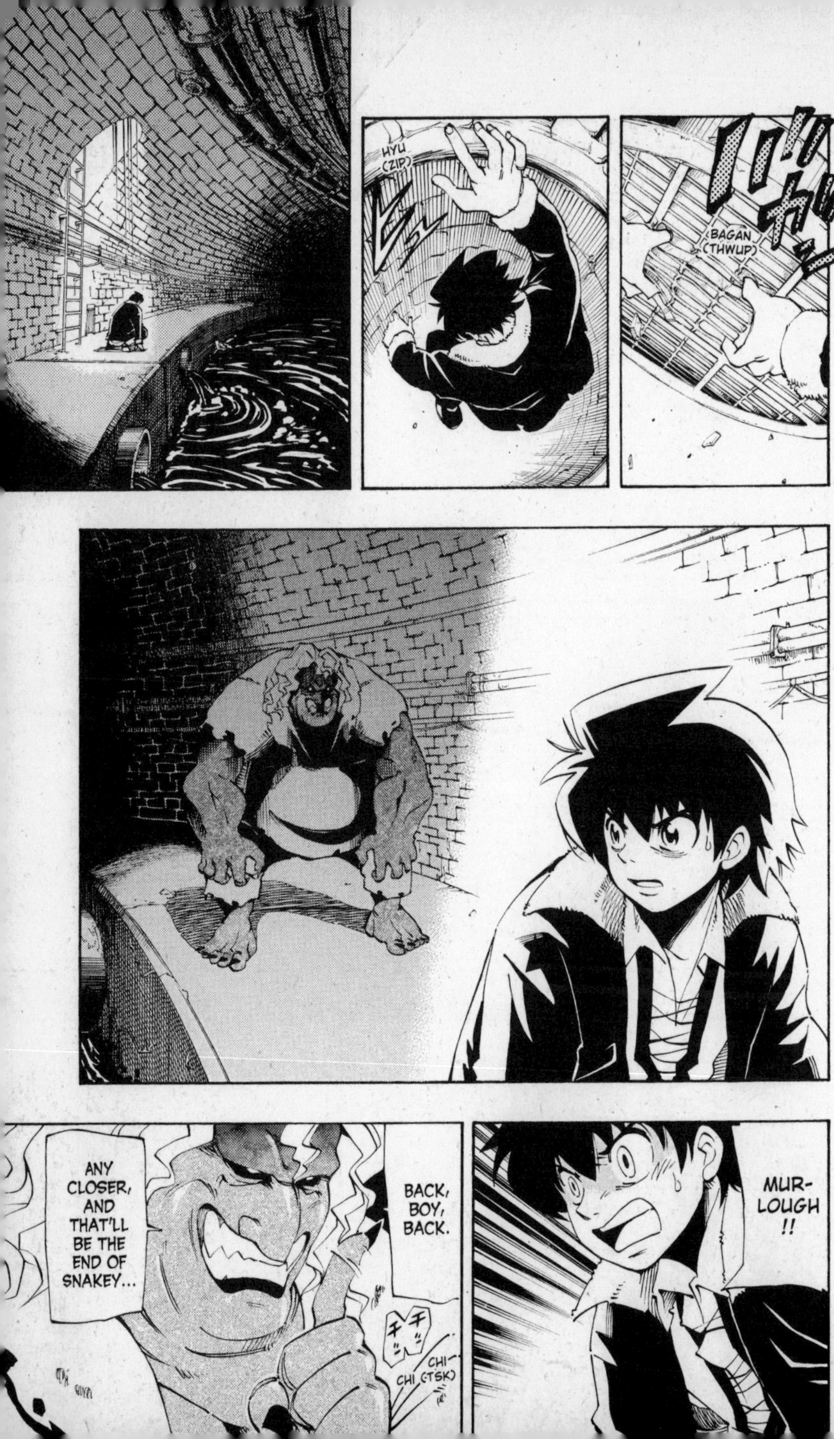
BAGAN (THWUP)
HYU (ZIP)
MUR-LOUGH !!
BACK, BOY, BACK.
ANY CLOSER, AND THAT'LL BE THE END OF SNAKEY...
CHI CHI (TSK)

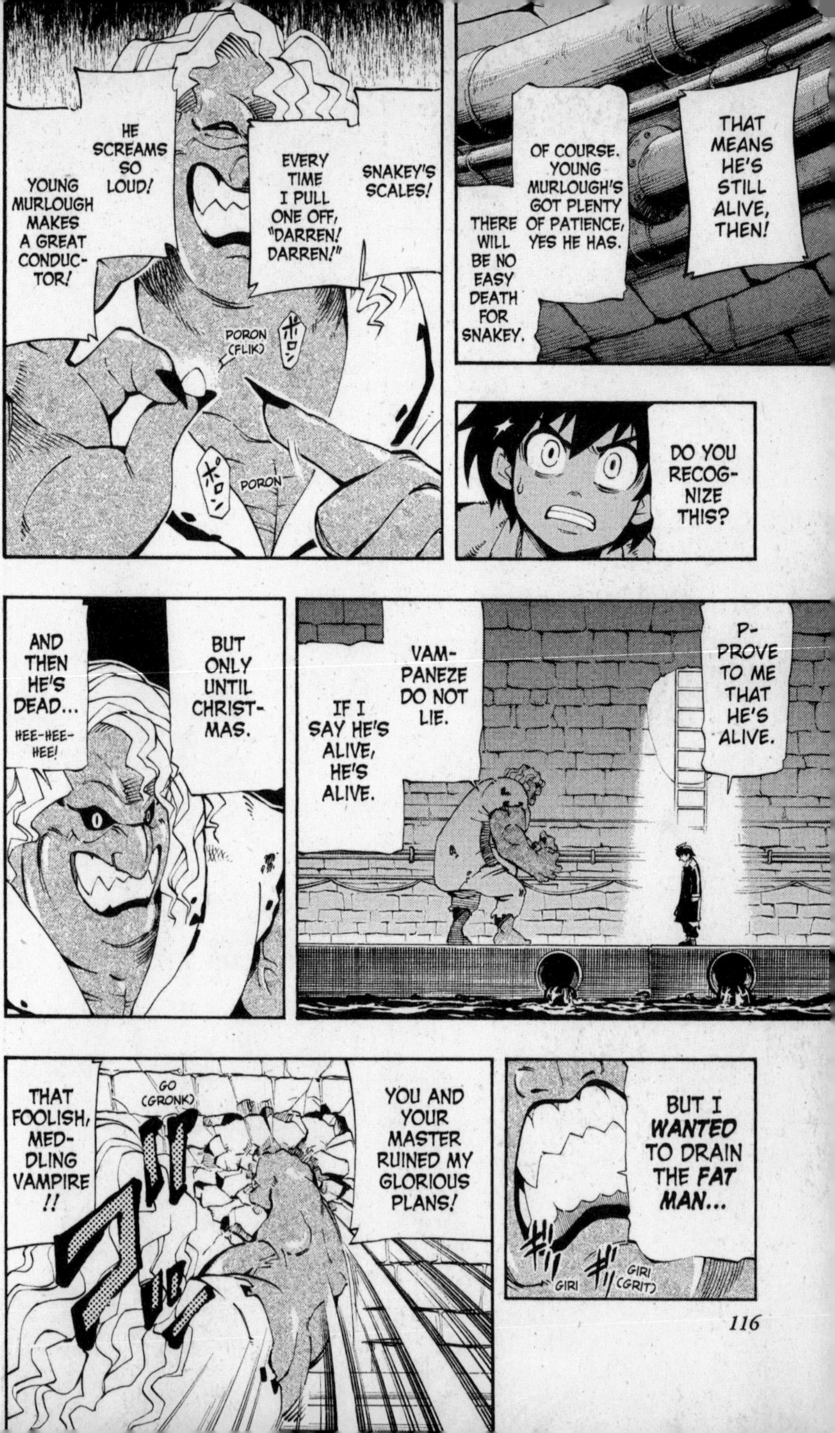
THAT MEANS HE'S STILL ALIVE, THEN!
OF COURSE. YOUNG MURLOUGH'S GOT PLENTY OF PATIENCE, YES HE HAS.
THERE WILL BE NO EASY DEATH FOR SNAKEY.
DO YOU RECOGNIZE THIS?
SNAKEY'S SCALES!
EVERY TIME I PULL ONE OFF, "DARREN! DARREN!"
HE SCREAMS SO LOUD!
YOUNG MURLOUGH MAKES A GREAT CONDUCTOR!
PORON (FLIK)
PORON
P-PROVE TO ME THAT HE'S ALIVE.
VAMPANEZE DO NOT LIE.
IF I SAY HE'S ALIVE, HE'S ALIVE.
BUT ONLY UNTIL CHRISTMAS.
AND THEN HE'S DEAD...
HEE-HEE-HEE!
BUT I *WANTED* TO DRAIN THE *FAT MAN*...
GIRI
GIRI (GRIT)
YOU AND YOUR MASTER RUINED MY GLORIOUS PLANS!
THAT FOOLISH, MEDDLING VAMPIRE!!
GO (GRONK)

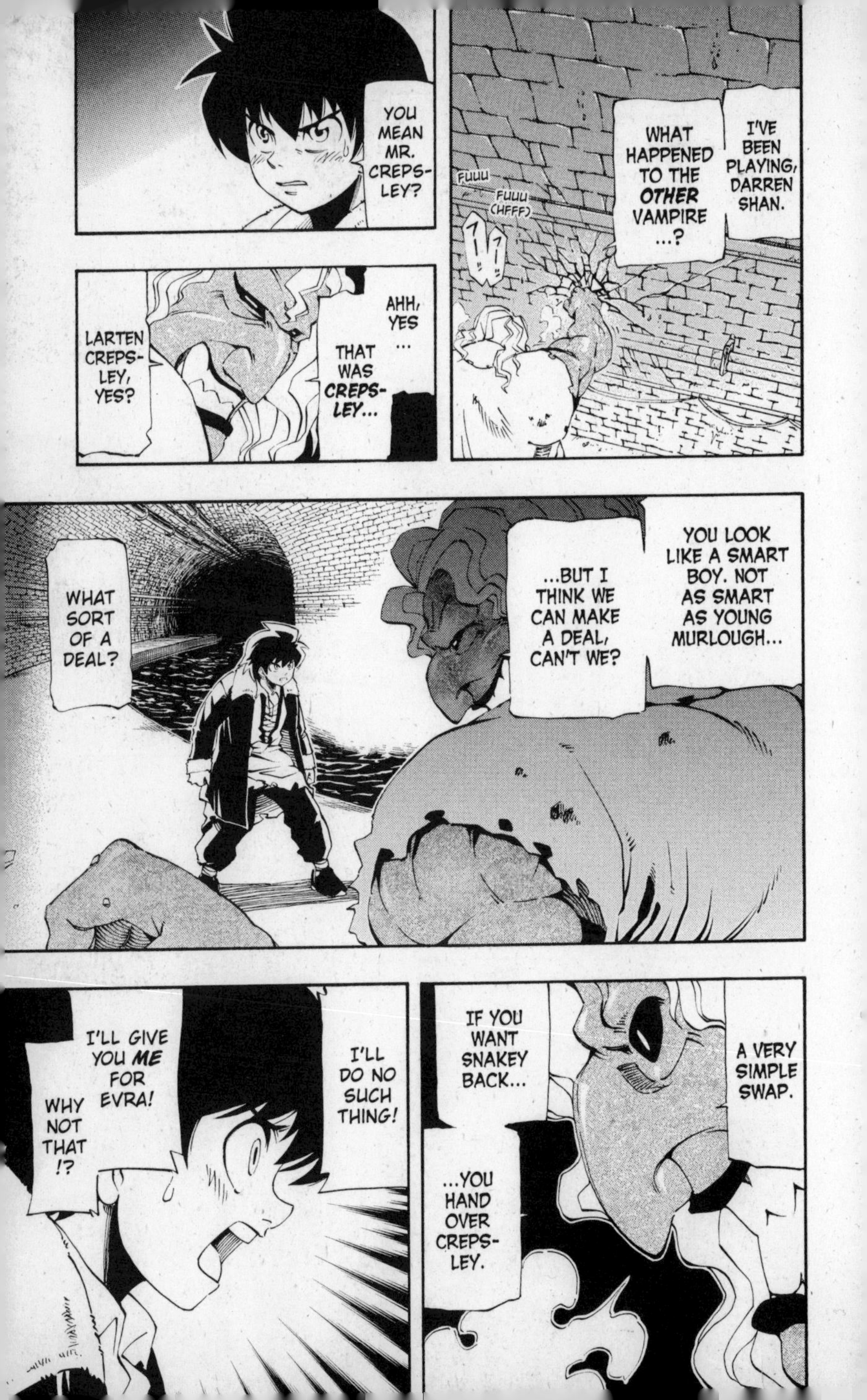
I'VE BEEN PLAYING, DARREN SHAN.
WHAT HAPPENED TO THE OTHER VAMPIRE ...?
FUUU
FUUU (HFFF)
YOU MEAN MR. CREPSLEY?
AHH, YES ...
THAT WAS CREPSLEY...
LARTEN CREPSLEY, YES?
YOU LOOK LIKE A SMART BOY. NOT AS SMART AS YOUNG MURLOUGH...
...BUT I THINK WE CAN MAKE A DEAL, CAN'T WE?
WHAT SORT OF A DEAL?
A VERY SIMPLE SWAP.
IF YOU WANT SNAKEY BACK...
...YOU HAND OVER CREPSLEY.
I'LL DO NO SUCH THING!
I'LL GIVE YOU ME FOR EVRA!
WHY NOT THAT!?

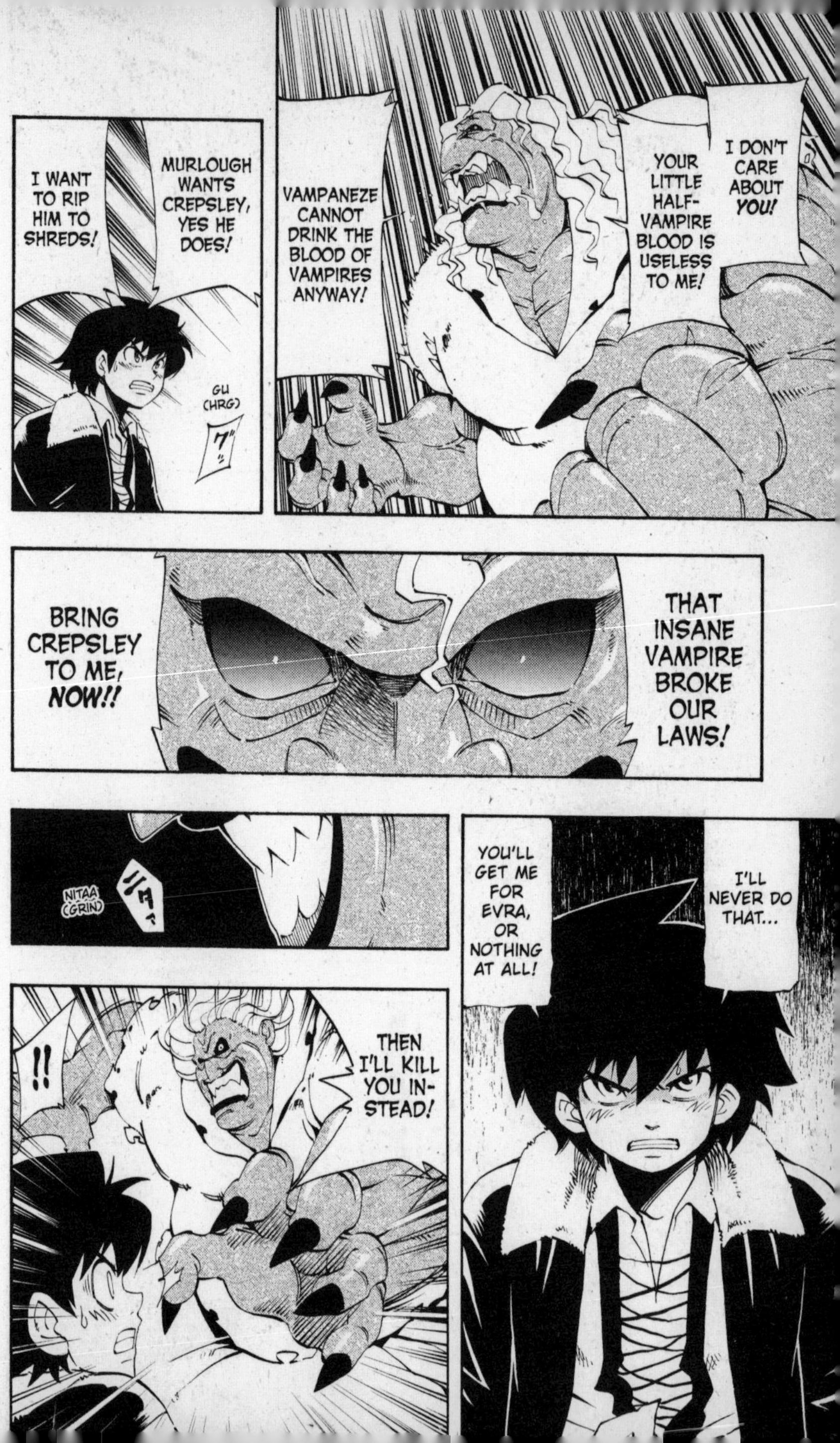
I DON'T CARE ABOUT *YOU!*
YOUR LITTLE HALF-VAMPIRE BLOOD IS USELESS TO ME!
VAMPANEZE CANNOT DRINK THE BLOOD OF VAMPIRES ANYWAY!
MURLOUGH WANTS CREPSLEY, YES HE DOES!
I WANT TO RIP HIM TO SHREDS!
GU (HRG)
THAT INSANE VAMPIRE BROKE OUR LAWS!
BRING CREPSLEY TO ME, *NOW!!*
I'LL NEVER DO THAT...
YOU'LL GET ME FOR EVRA, OR NOTHING AT ALL!
NITAA (GRIN)
THEN I'LL KILL YOU IN-STEAD!
!!

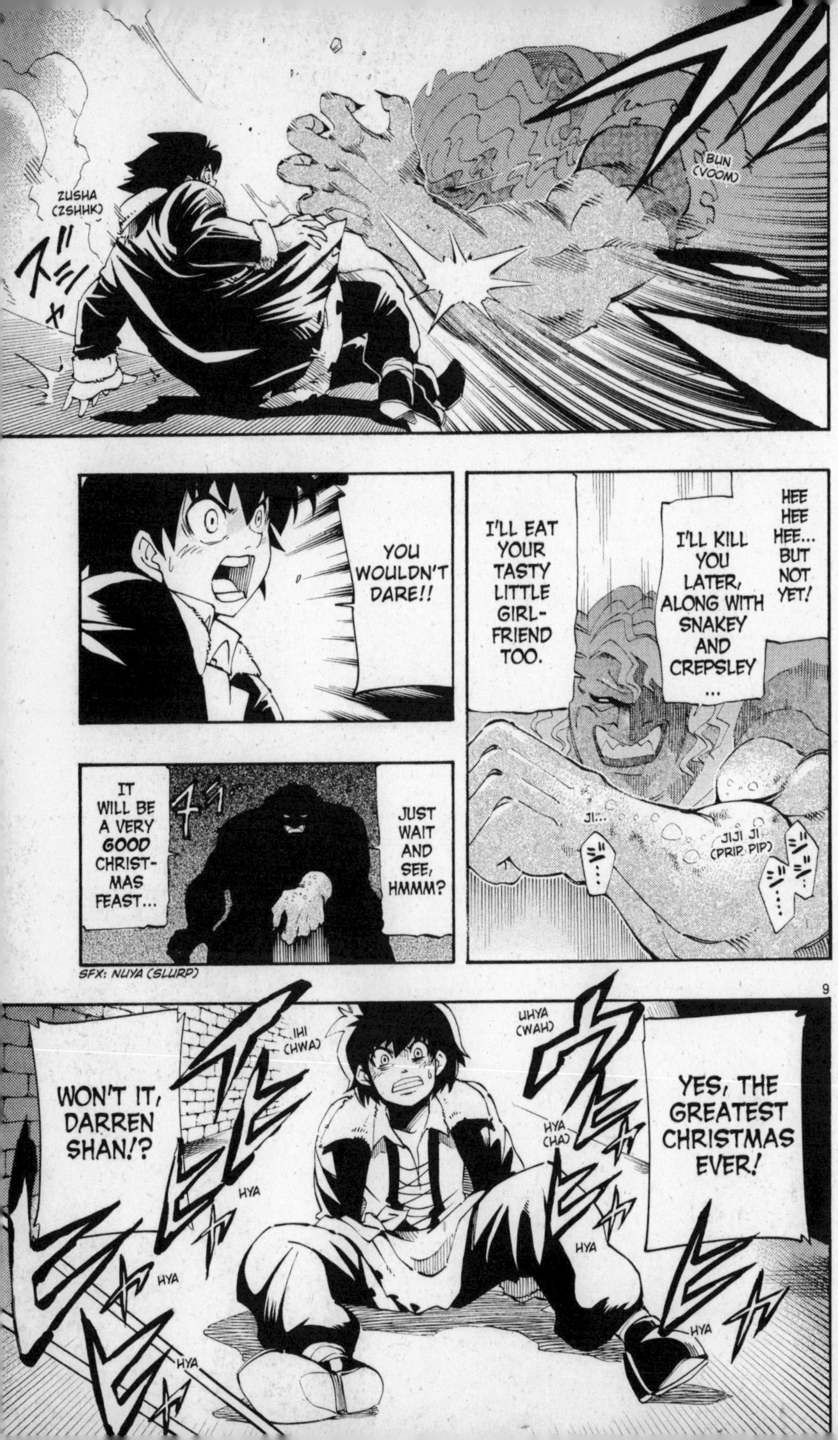
BUN (VOOM)
ZUSHA (ZSHHK)
HEE HEE HEE... BUT NOT YET!
I'LL KILL YOU LATER, ALONG WITH SNAKEY AND CREPSLEY ...
I'LL EAT YOUR TASTY LITTLE GIRL-FRIEND TOO.
JIJI JI (PRIP PIP)
JI...
YOU WOULDN'T DARE!!
JUST WAIT AND SEE, HMMM?
IT WILL BE A VERY GOOD CHRIST-MAS FEAST...
SFX: NUYA (SLURP)
YES, THE GREATEST CHRISTMAS EVER!
UHYA (WAH)
HYA (HA)
IHI (CHWA)
WON'T IT, DARREN SHAN!?
HYA
HYA
HYA
HYA
HYA

MUR-LOUGH! THAT RAT. I DID NOT THINK HE WOULD STILL BE HERE...

YOU KNOW I COULDN'T DO THAT.

WE COULD HAVE LAID A TRAP...

IT IS UNFORTUNATE THAT YOU REFUSED TO SWAP ME FOR EVRA, HOWEVER.

BUT WHY? YOU MUST PREFER EVRA TO ME.

YES, BUT WE SAID WE'D TRUST EACH OTHER, REMEMBER?

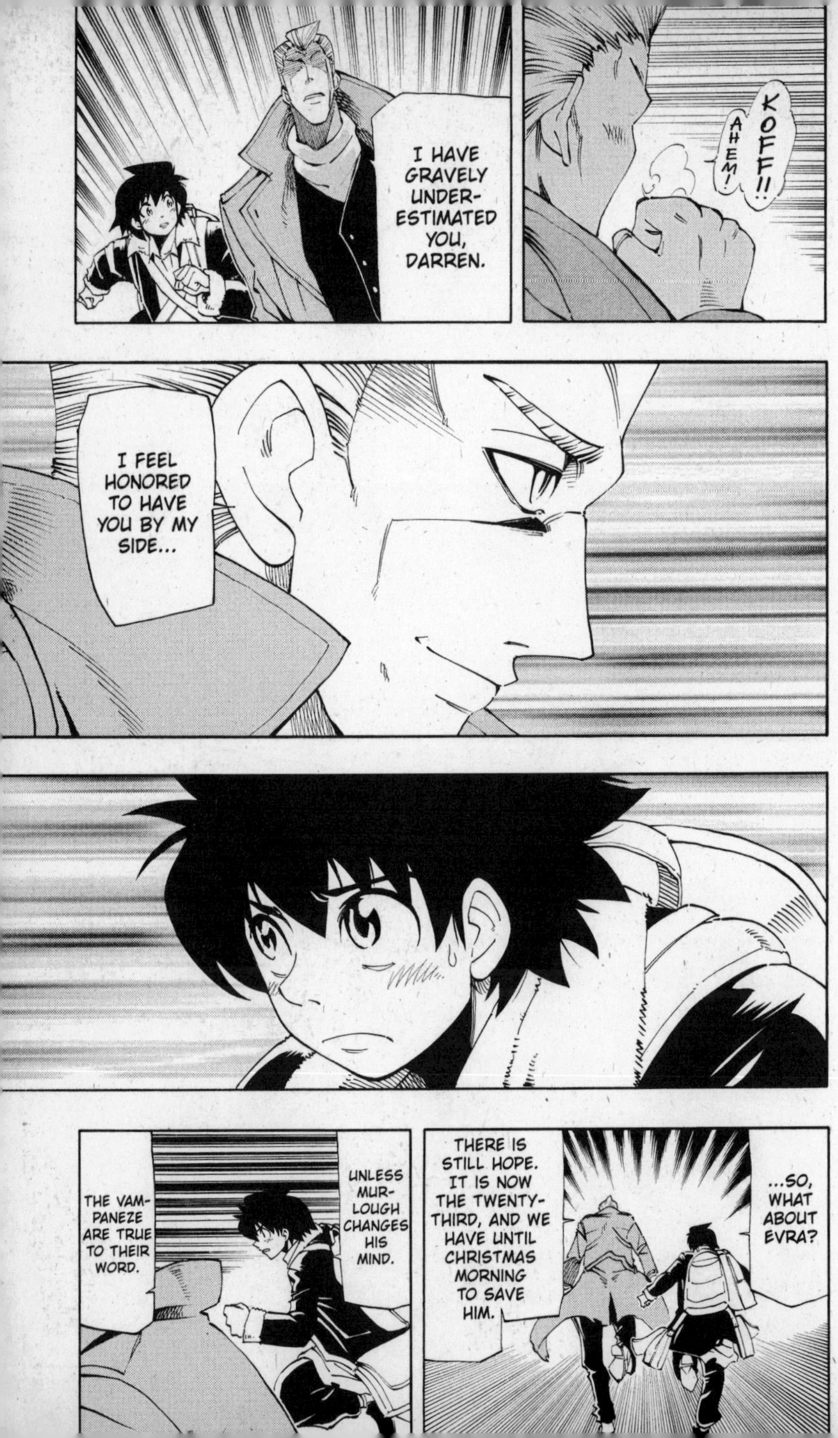
KOFF!!
AHEM!
I HAVE GRAVELY UNDER-ESTIMATED YOU, DARREN.
I FEEL HONORED TO HAVE YOU BY MY SIDE...
...SO, WHAT ABOUT EVRA?
THERE IS STILL HOPE. IT IS NOW THE TWENTY-THIRD, AND WE HAVE UNTIL CHRISTMAS MORNING TO SAVE HIM.
UNLESS MUR-LOUGH CHANGES HIS MIND.
THE VAM-PANEZE ARE TRUE TO THEIR WORD.

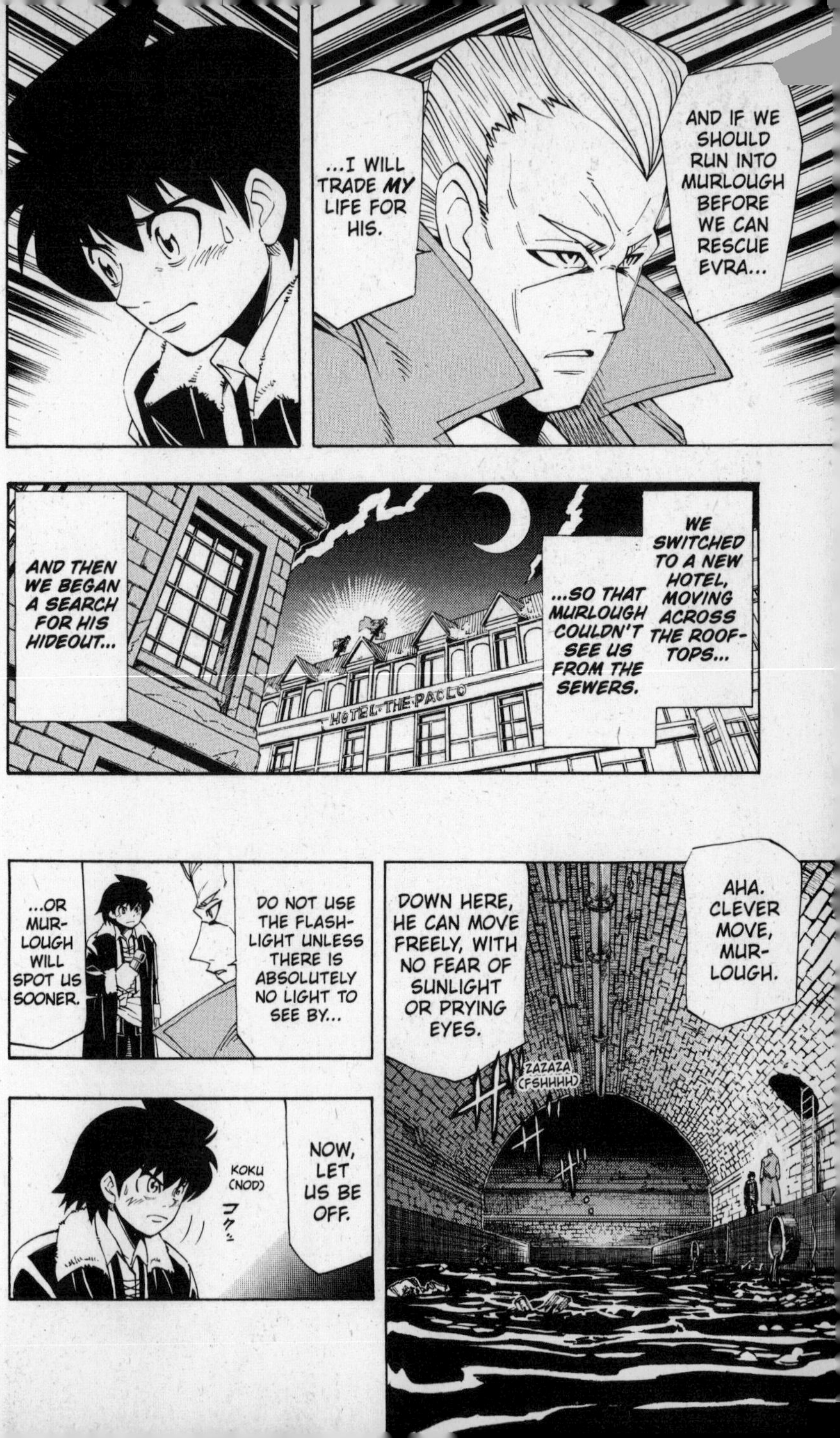
AND IF WE SHOULD RUN INTO MURLOUGH BEFORE WE CAN RESCUE EVRA...
...I WILL TRADE MY LIFE FOR HIS.
WE SWITCHED TO A NEW HOTEL, MOVING ACROSS THE ROOF-TOPS...
...SO THAT MURLOUGH COULDN'T SEE US FROM THE SEWERS.
HOTEL·THE·PACLO
AND THEN WE BEGAN A SEARCH FOR HIS HIDEOUT...
AHA. CLEVER MOVE, MUR-LOUGH.
DOWN HERE, HE CAN MOVE FREELY, WITH NO FEAR OF SUNLIGHT OR PRYING EYES.
ZAZAZA (FSHHHH)
DO NOT USE THE FLASH-LIGHT UNLESS THERE IS ABSOLUTELY NO LIGHT TO SEE BY...
...OR MUR-LOUGH WILL SPOT US SOONER.
NOW, LET US BE OFF.
KOKU (NOD)
コクッ

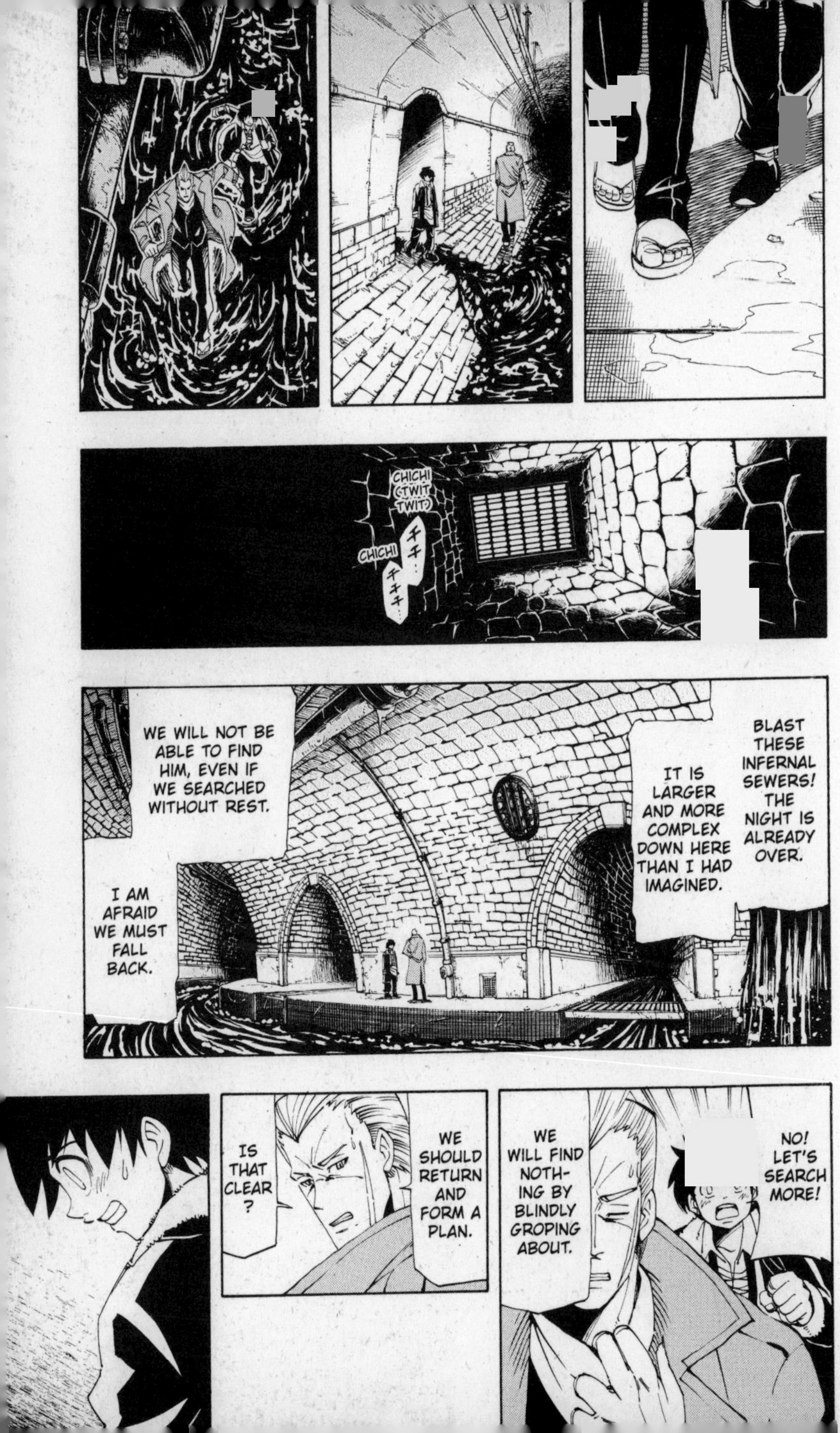
CHICHI (TWIT TWIT)
チチ…
CHICHI
チチチ…
BLAST THESE INFERNAL SEWERS! THE NIGHT IS ALREADY OVER.
IT IS LARGER AND MORE COMPLEX DOWN HERE THAN I HAD IMAGINED.
WE WILL NOT BE ABLE TO FIND HIM, EVEN IF WE SEARCHED WITHOUT REST.
I AM AFRAID WE MUST FALL BACK.
NO! LET'S SEARCH MORE!
WE WILL FIND NOTH-ING BY BLINDLY GROPING ABOUT.
WE SHOULD RETURN AND FORM A PLAN.
IS THAT CLEAR?

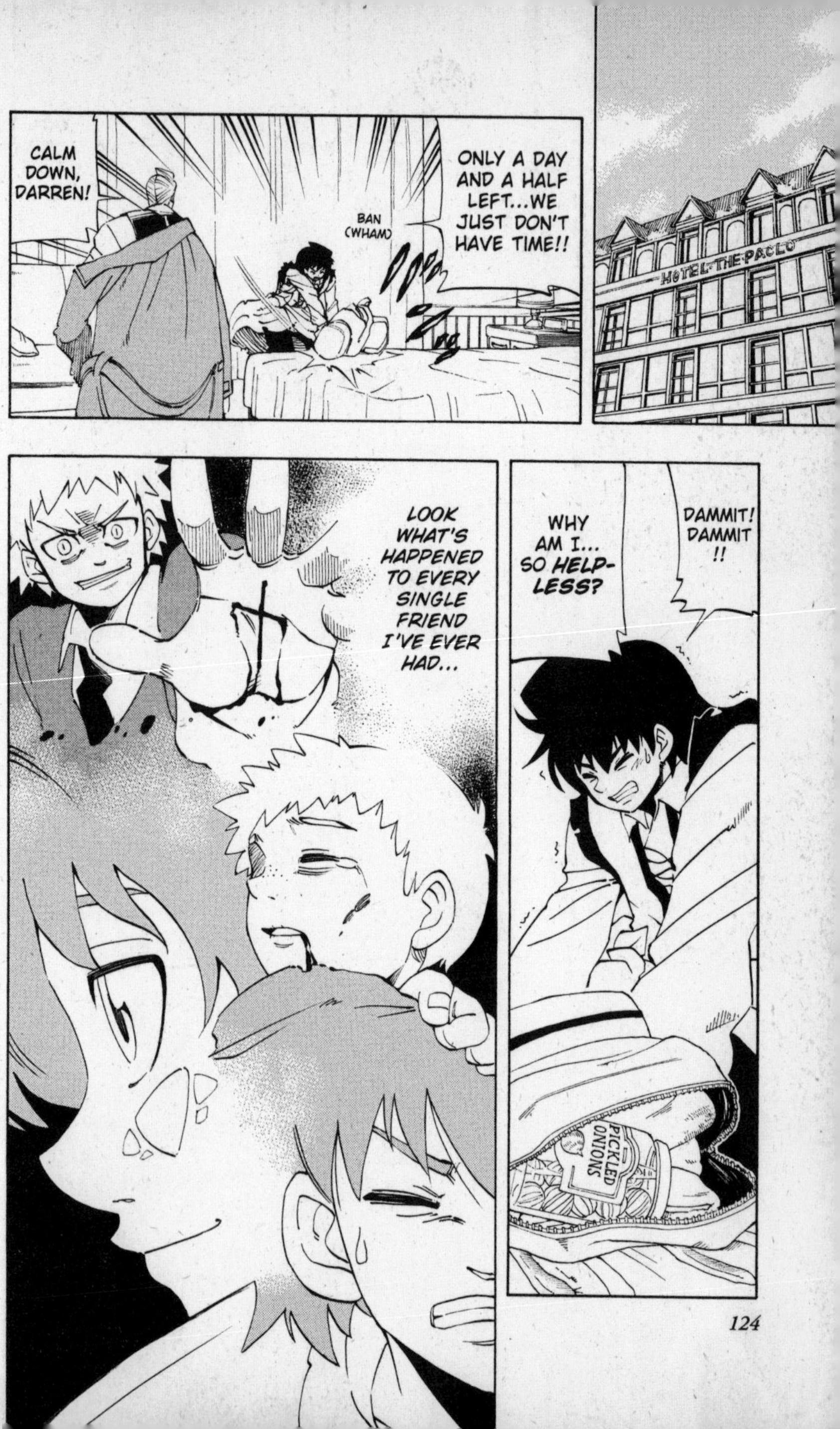
ONLY A DAY AND A HALF LEFT...WE JUST DON'T HAVE TIME!!
BAN (WHAM)
CALM DOWN, DARREN!
DAMMIT! DAMMIT!!
WHY AM I... SO *HELP-LESS?*
PICKLED ONIONS
LOOK WHAT'S HAPPENED TO EVERY SINGLE FRIEND I'VE EVER HAD...

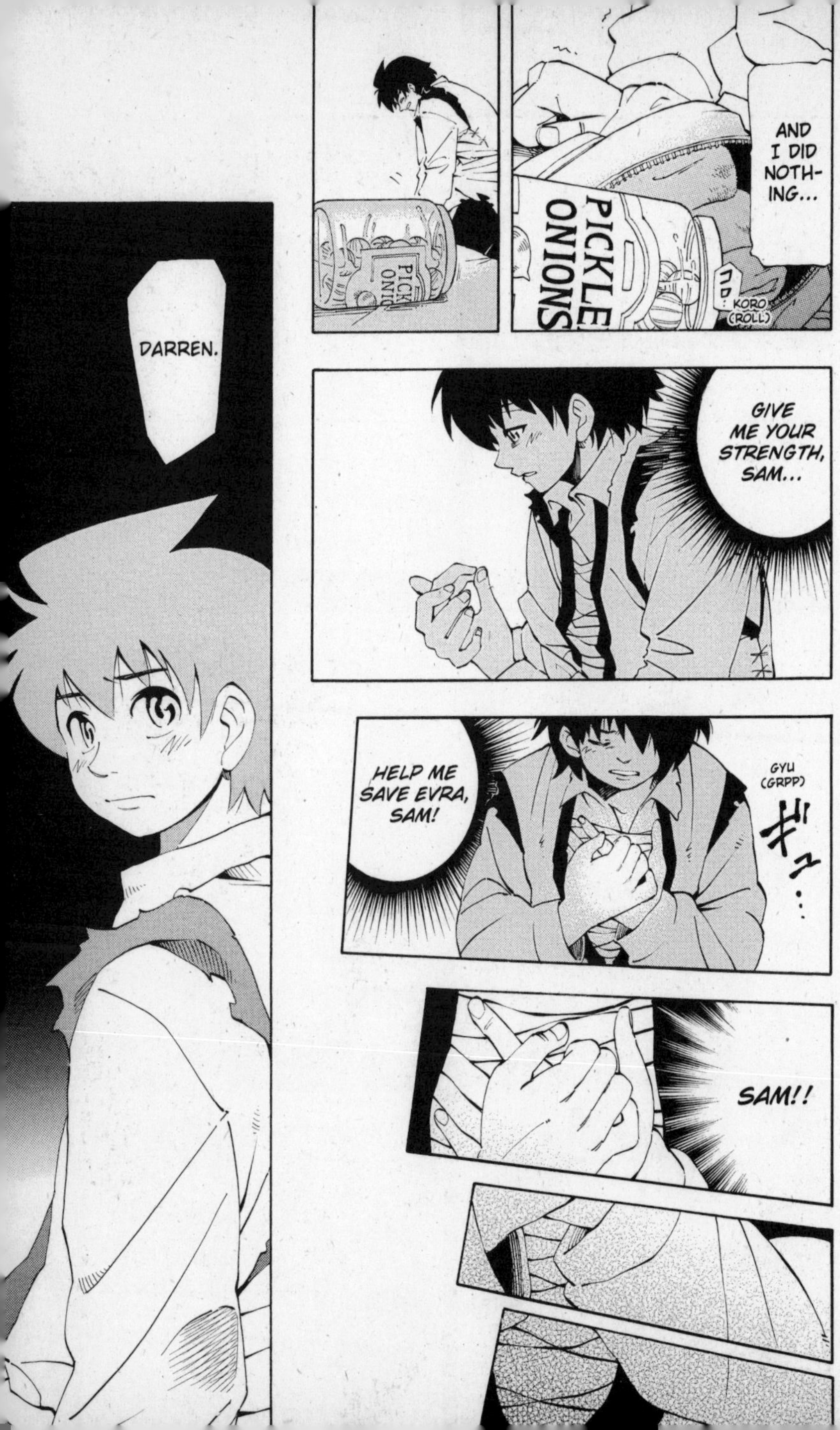
AND I DID NOTHING...
PICKLE ONIONS
KORO (ROLL)
GIVE ME YOUR STRENGTH, SAM...
HELP ME SAVE EVRA, SAM!
GYU (GRPP)
SAM!!
DARREN.

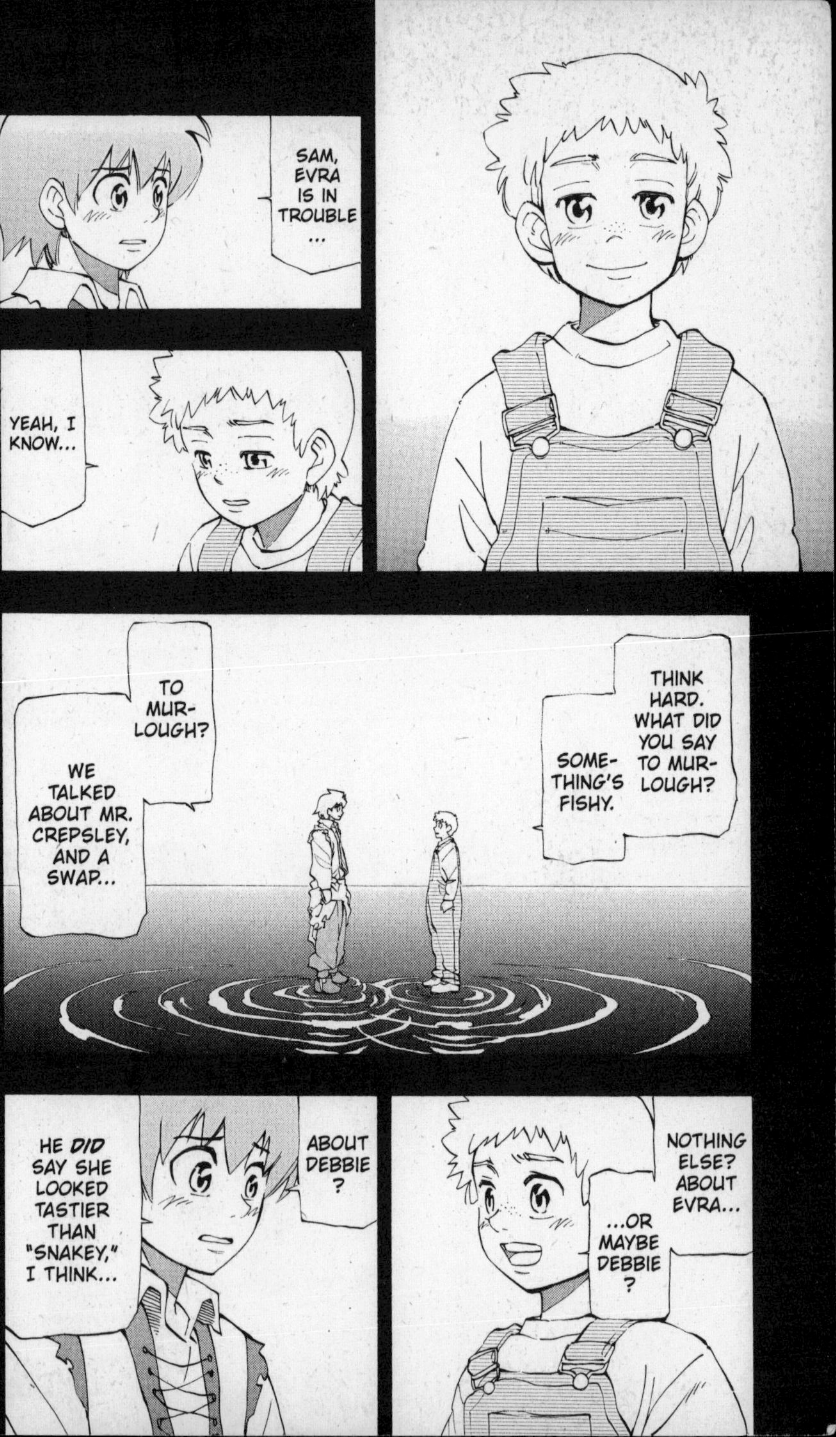
SAM, EVRA IS IN TROUBLE ...
YEAH, I KNOW...
THINK HARD. WHAT DID YOU SAY TO MURLOUGH?
SOMETHING'S FISHY.
TO MURLOUGH?
WE TALKED ABOUT MR. CREPSLEY, AND A SWAP...
NOTHING ELSE? ABOUT EVRA...
...OR MAYBE DEBBIE?
ABOUT DEBBIE?
HE *DID* SAY SHE LOOKED TASTIER THAN "SNAKEY," I THINK...

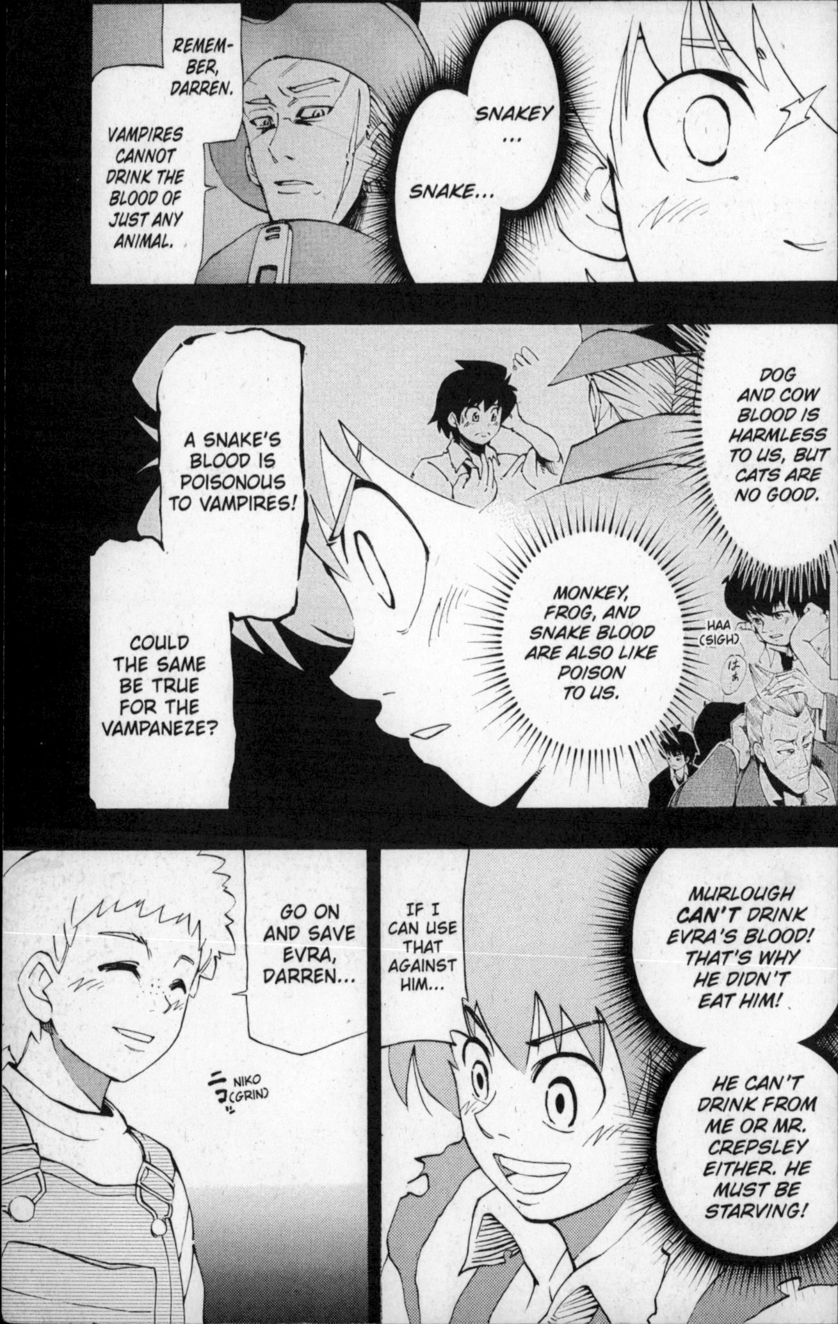

SNAKEY ...
SNAKE...
REMEMBER, DARREN.
VAMPIRES CANNOT DRINK THE BLOOD OF JUST ANY ANIMAL.
DOG AND COW BLOOD IS HARMLESS TO US, BUT CATS ARE NO GOOD.
HAA (SIGH)
MONKEY, FROG, AND SNAKE BLOOD ARE ALSO LIKE POISON TO US.
A SNAKE'S BLOOD IS POISONOUS TO VAMPIRES!
COULD THE SAME BE TRUE FOR THE VAMPANEZE?
MURLOUGH **CAN'T** DRINK EVRA'S BLOOD! THAT'S WHY HE DIDN'T EAT HIM!
HE CAN'T DRINK FROM ME OR MR. CREPSLEY EITHER. HE MUST BE STARVING!
IF I CAN USE THAT AGAINST HIM...
GO ON AND SAVE EVRA, DARREN...
NIKO (GRIN)

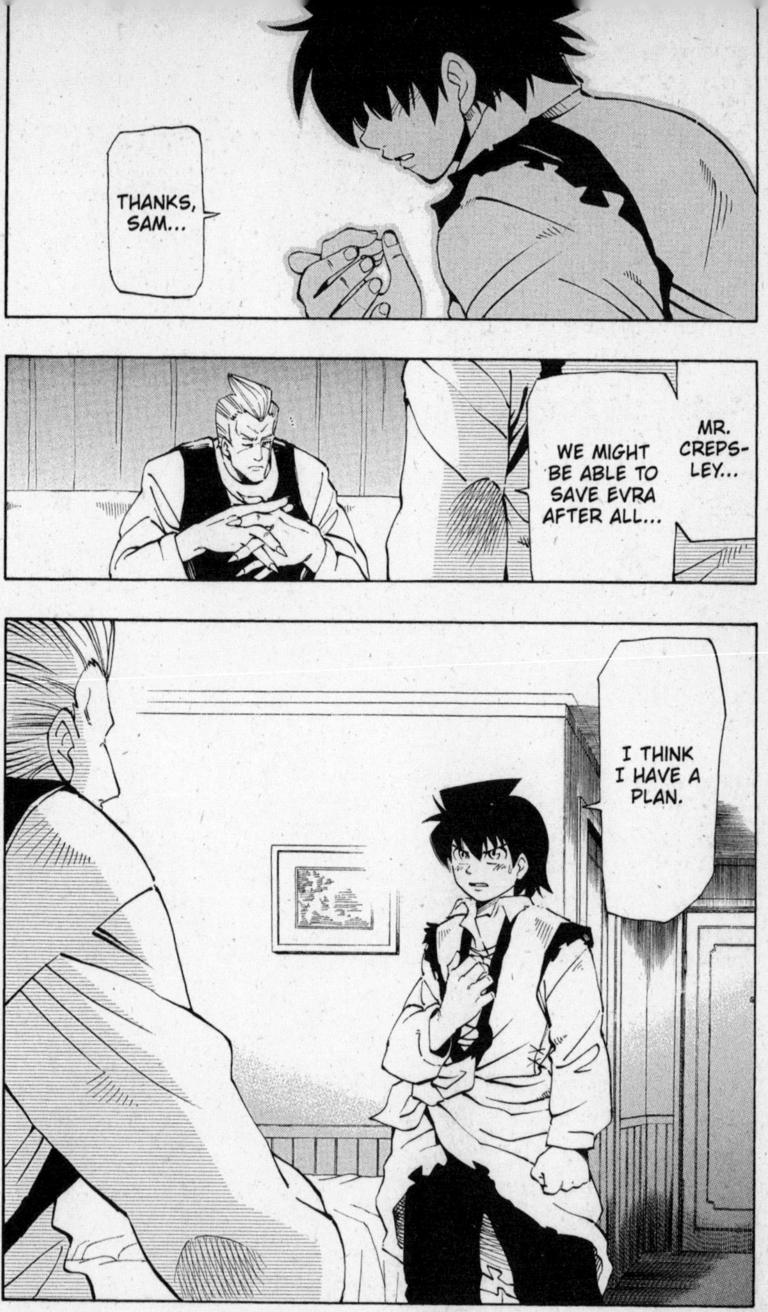
THANKS, SAM...
MR. CREPS-LEY...
WE MIGHT BE ABLE TO SAVE EVRA AFTER ALL...
I THINK I HAVE A PLAN.

CHAPTER 22:
THE ROAD TO EVRA

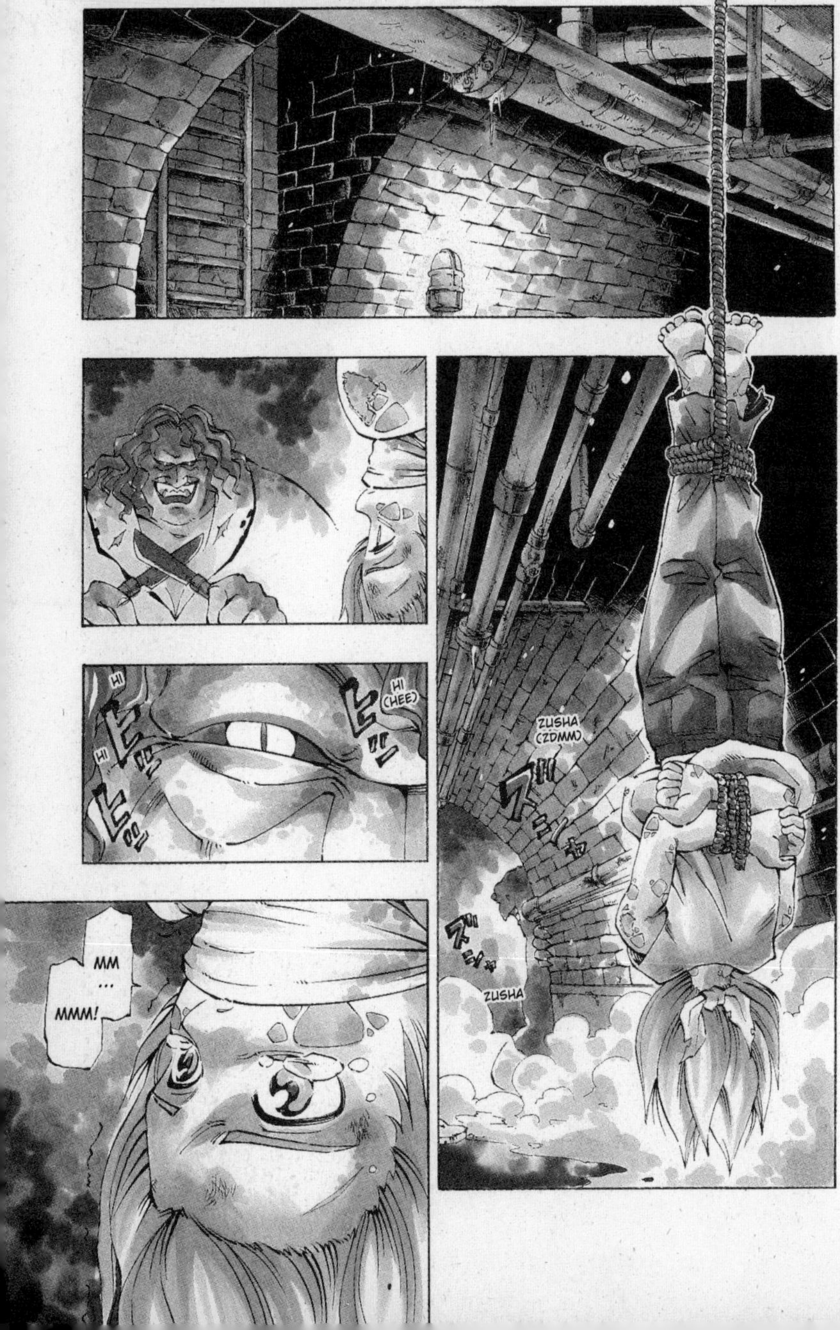
ZUSHA (ZDMM)
ZUSHA
HI (CHEE)
HI
HI
MM ... MMM!

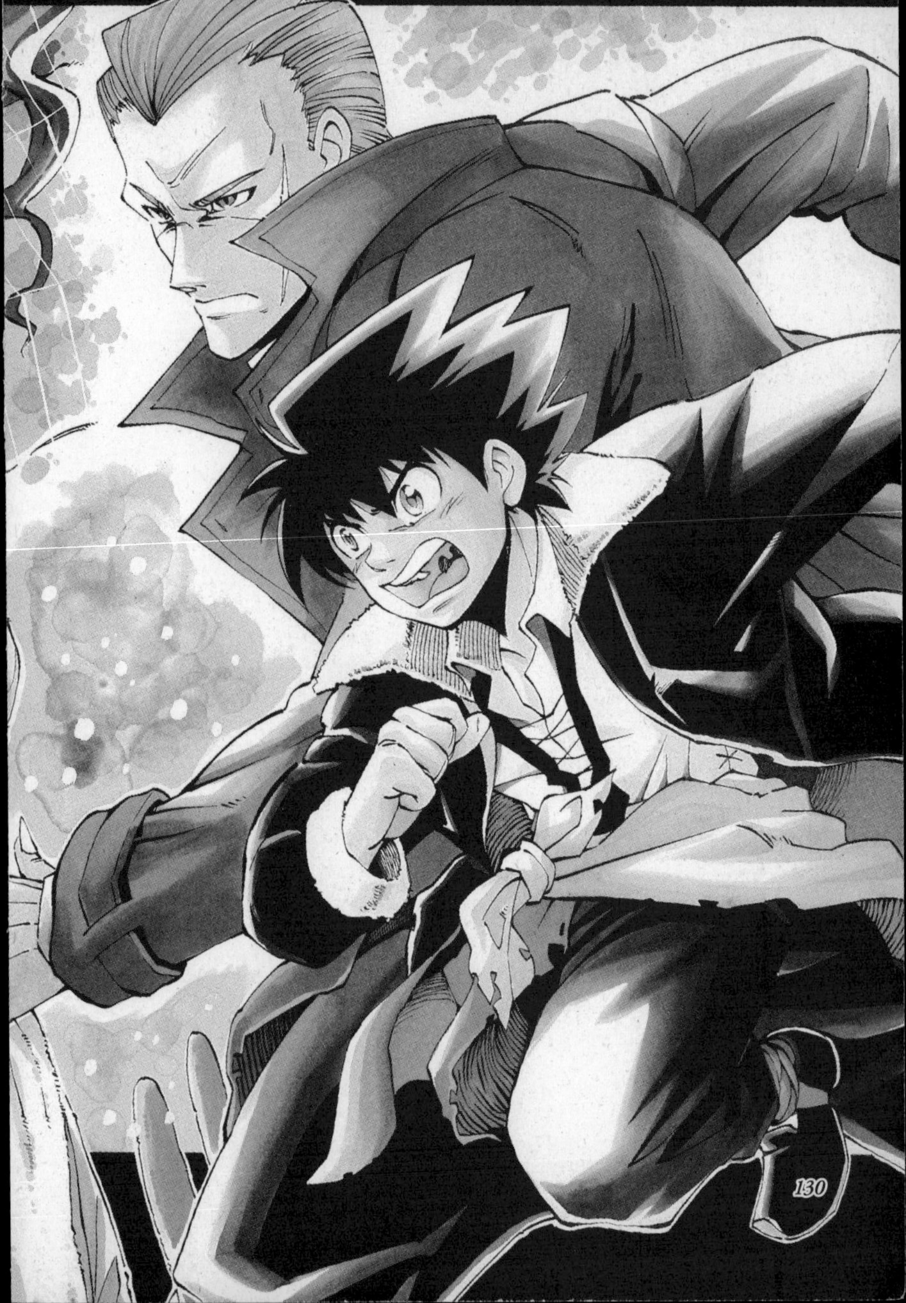

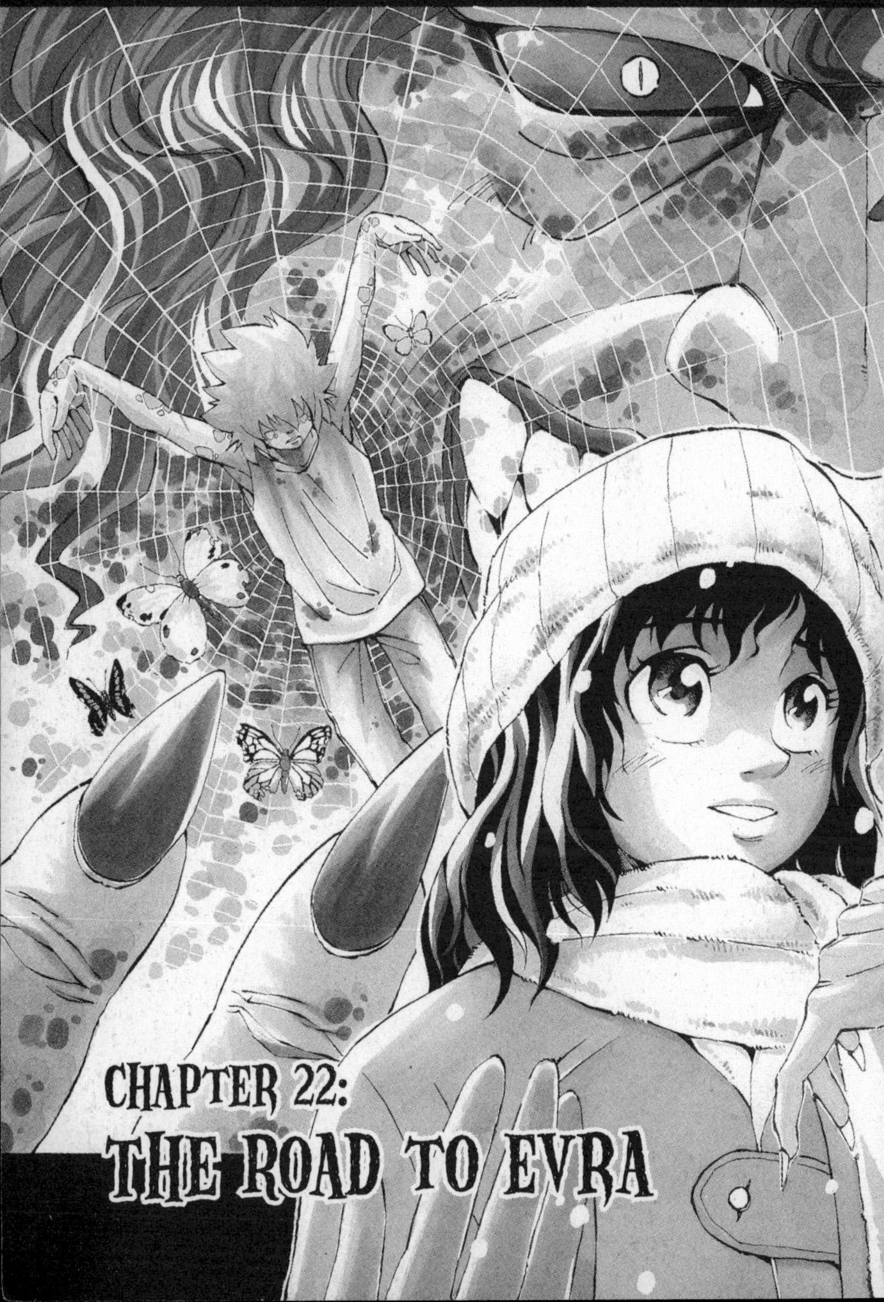
CHAPTER 22:
THE ROAD TO EVRA

HELLO, DEBBIE?

10:00 A.M., DECEMBER 24TH—CHRISTMAS EVE.

...Darren?

SORRY ABOUT YESTERDAY. SAY, IS IT ALL RIGHT IF I COME OVER TODAY AFTER ALL?

You'll come!? Please do! Mom's cooking the dinner already.

Will your brother and dad be there too?

NO, JUST ME.

Oh. That's too bad...

THANKS, DEBBIE. SEE YOU THERE.

I'm glad you're coming, though!

FUU (SIGH)

GACHA (CLICK)

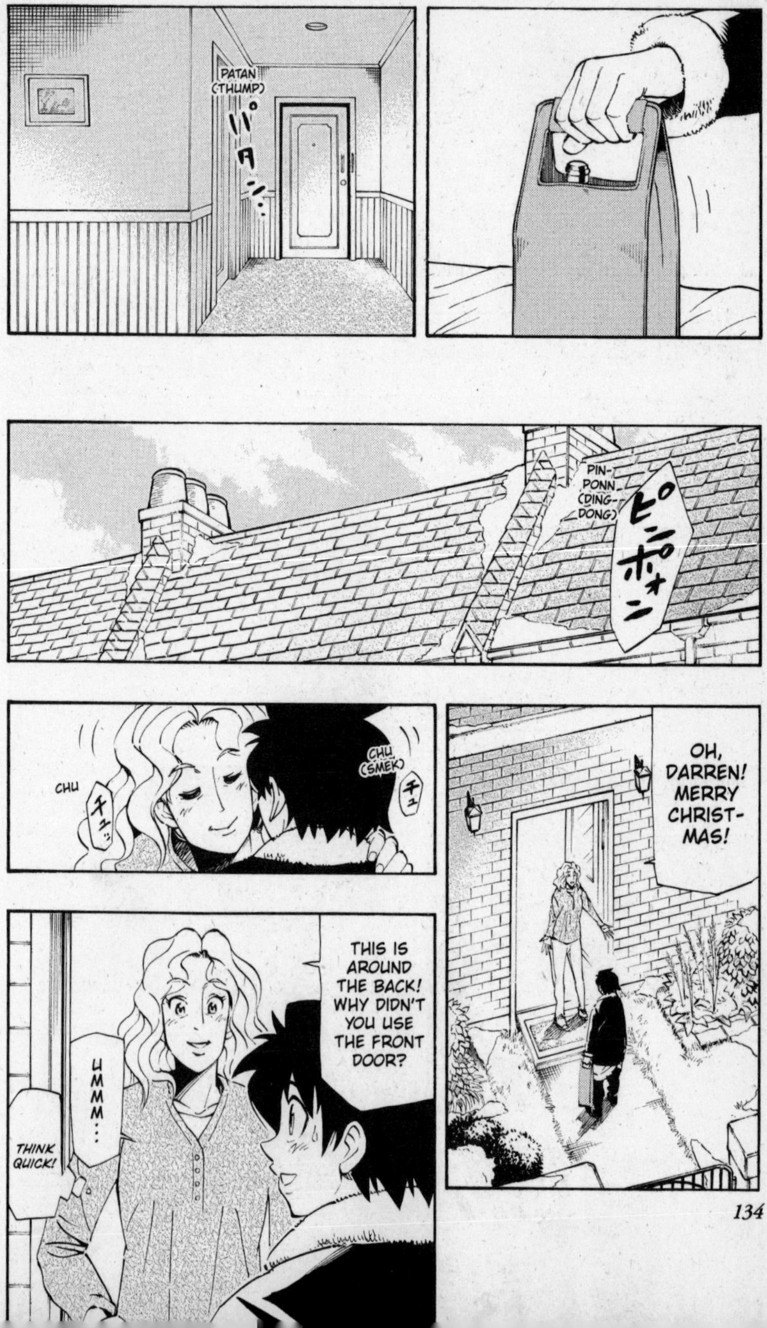
PATAN (THUMP)
パタン…
PIN-PONN (DING-DONG)
ピンポォン
OH, DARREN! MERRY CHRISTMAS!
CHU (SMEK)
チュ
CHU
チュッ
THIS IS AROUND THE BACK! WHY DIDN'T YOU USE THE FRONT DOOR?
UMMM...
THINK QUICK!

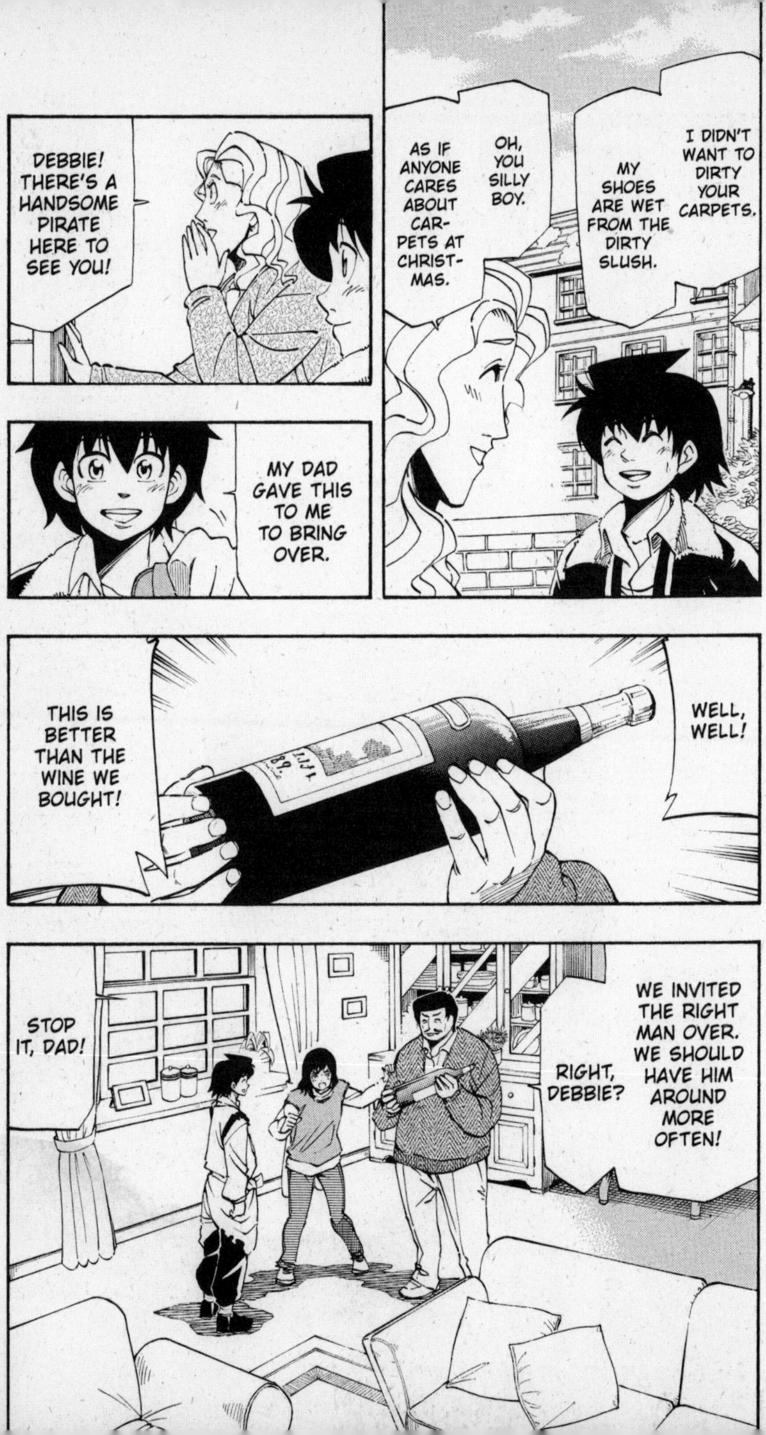
I DIDN'T WANT TO DIRTY YOUR CARPETS.
MY SHOES ARE WET FROM THE DIRTY SLUSH.
OH, YOU SILLY BOY.
AS IF ANYONE CARES ABOUT CAR-PETS AT CHRIST-MAS.
DEBBIE! THERE'S A HANDSOME PIRATE HERE TO SEE YOU!
MY DAD GAVE THIS TO ME TO BRING OVER.
WELL, WELL!
THIS IS BETTER THAN THE WINE WE BOUGHT!
WE INVITED THE RIGHT MAN OVER. WE SHOULD HAVE HIM AROUND MORE OFTEN!
RIGHT, DEBBIE?
STOP IT, DAD!

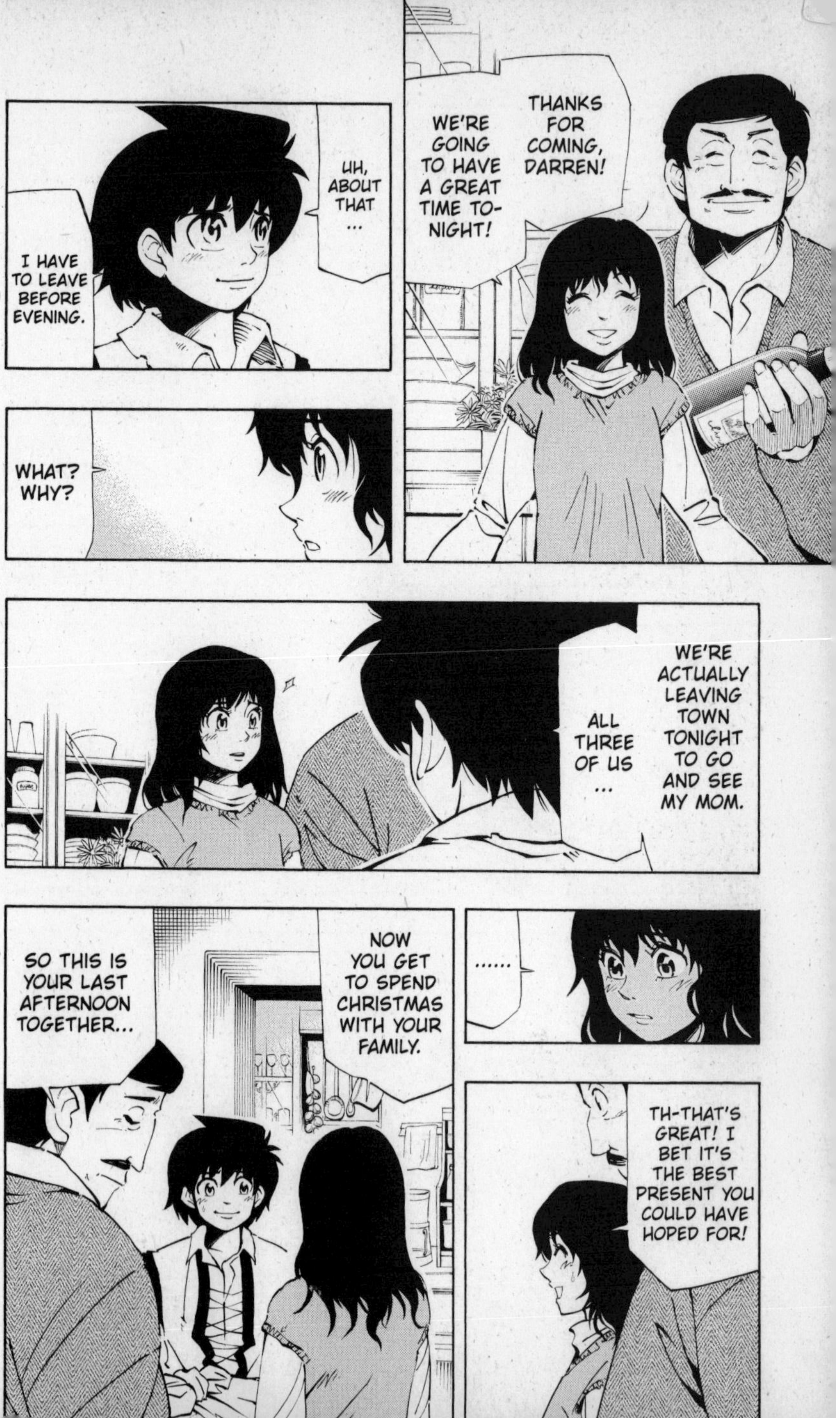
THANKS FOR COMING, DARREN!
WE'RE GOING TO HAVE A GREAT TIME TO-NIGHT!
UH, ABOUT THAT ...
I HAVE TO LEAVE BEFORE EVENING.
WHAT? WHY?
WE'RE ACTUALLY LEAVING TOWN TONIGHT TO GO AND SEE MY MOM.
ALL THREE OF US ...
......
TH-THAT'S GREAT! I BET IT'S THE BEST PRESENT YOU COULD HAVE HOPED FOR!
NOW YOU GET TO SPEND CHRISTMAS WITH YOUR FAMILY.
SO THIS IS YOUR LAST AFTERNOON TOGETHER...

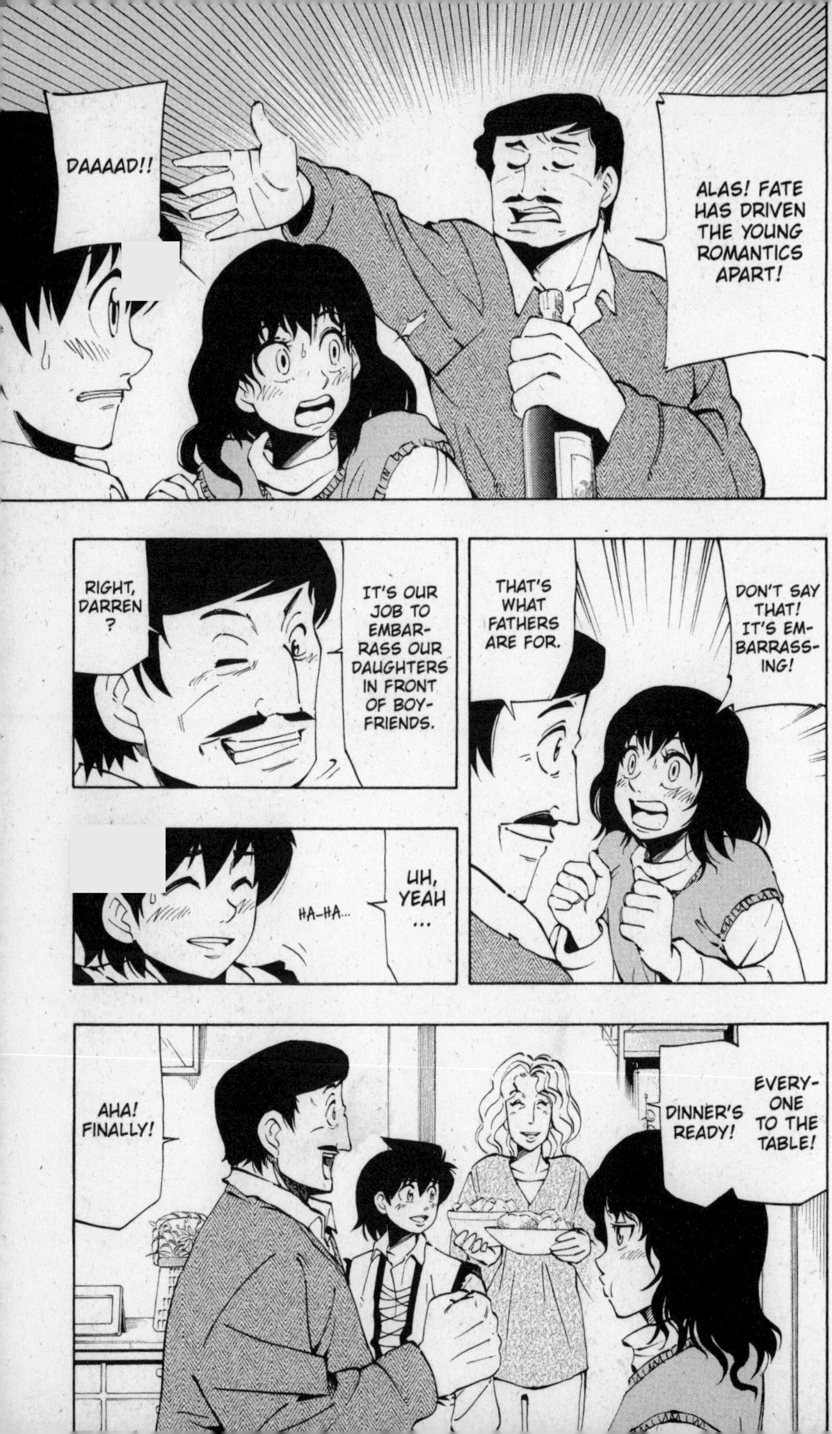
ALAS! FATE HAS DRIVEN THE YOUNG ROMANTICS APART!
DAAAAD!!
DON'T SAY THAT! IT'S EMBARRASSING!
THAT'S WHAT FATHERS ARE FOR.
IT'S OUR JOB TO EMBARRASS OUR DAUGHTERS IN FRONT OF BOYFRIENDS.
RIGHT, DARREN?
UH, YEAH...
HA-HA...
EVERYONE TO THE TABLE!
DINNER'S READY!
AHA! FINALLY!

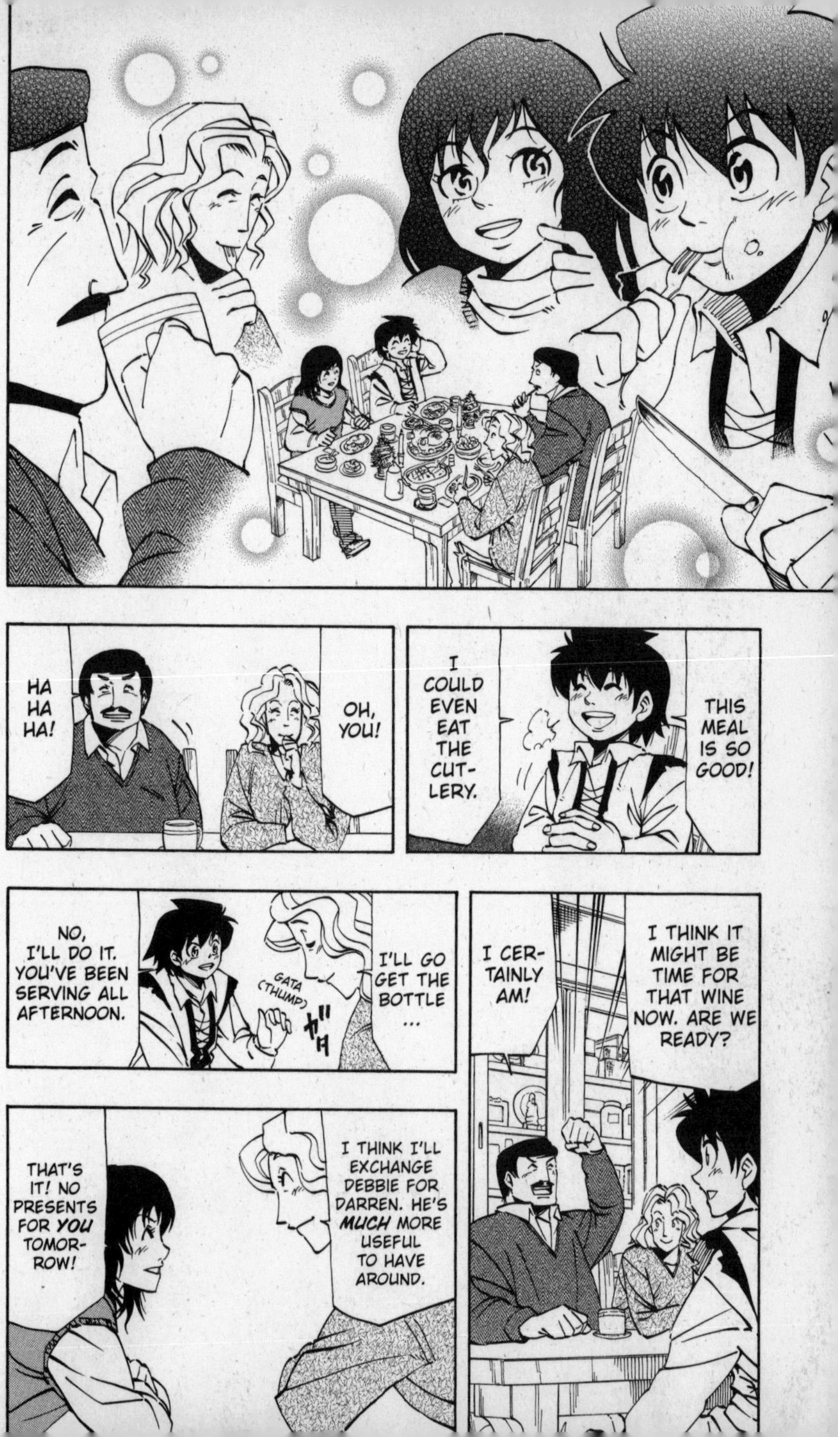
THIS MEAL IS SO GOOD!
I COULD EVEN EAT THE CUT-LERY.
OH, YOU!
HA HA HA!
I THINK IT MIGHT BE TIME FOR THAT WINE NOW. ARE WE READY?
I CER-TAINLY AM!
I'LL GO GET THE BOTTLE ...
GATA (THUMP)
NO, I'LL DO IT. YOU'VE BEEN SERVING ALL AFTERNOON.
I THINK I'LL EXCHANGE DEBBIE FOR DARREN. HE'S *MUCH* MORE USEFUL TO HAVE AROUND.
THAT'S IT! NO PRESENTS FOR *YOU* TOMORROW!

PON
(POP)

GOSO
(RUSTLE)
GOSO

SMELLS
NICE...

YOU
OKAY IN
HERE?

DAR-
REN
...

Y-
YEAH,
OF
COURSE
...

BESIDES,
IT'S NOT
LIKE WE
CAN NEVER
SEE EACH
OTHER
AGAIN.

I'M
JUST
KID-
DING.

SORRY.
IT WAS
ALL SO
SUDDEN
...

I WISH I
COULD HAVE
DECORATED
THE TREE
WITH YOU.

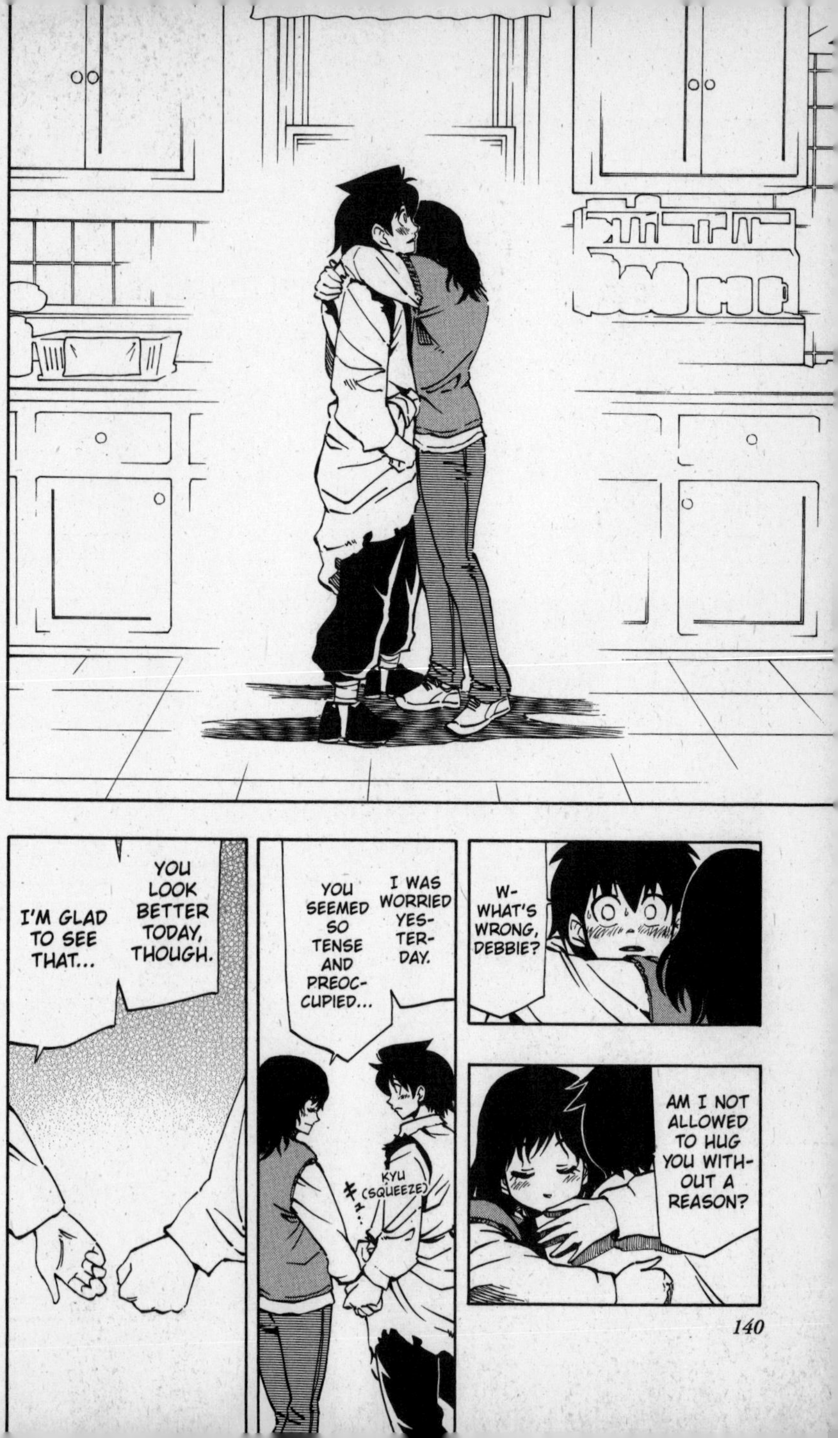
W- WHAT'S WRONG, DEBBIE?
AM I NOT ALLOWED TO HUG YOU WITHOUT A REASON?
I WAS WORRIED YESTERDAY.
YOU SEEMED SO TENSE AND PREOCCUPIED...
キュ…
KYU (SQUEEZE)
YOU LOOK BETTER TODAY, THOUGH.
I'M GLAD TO SEE THAT...

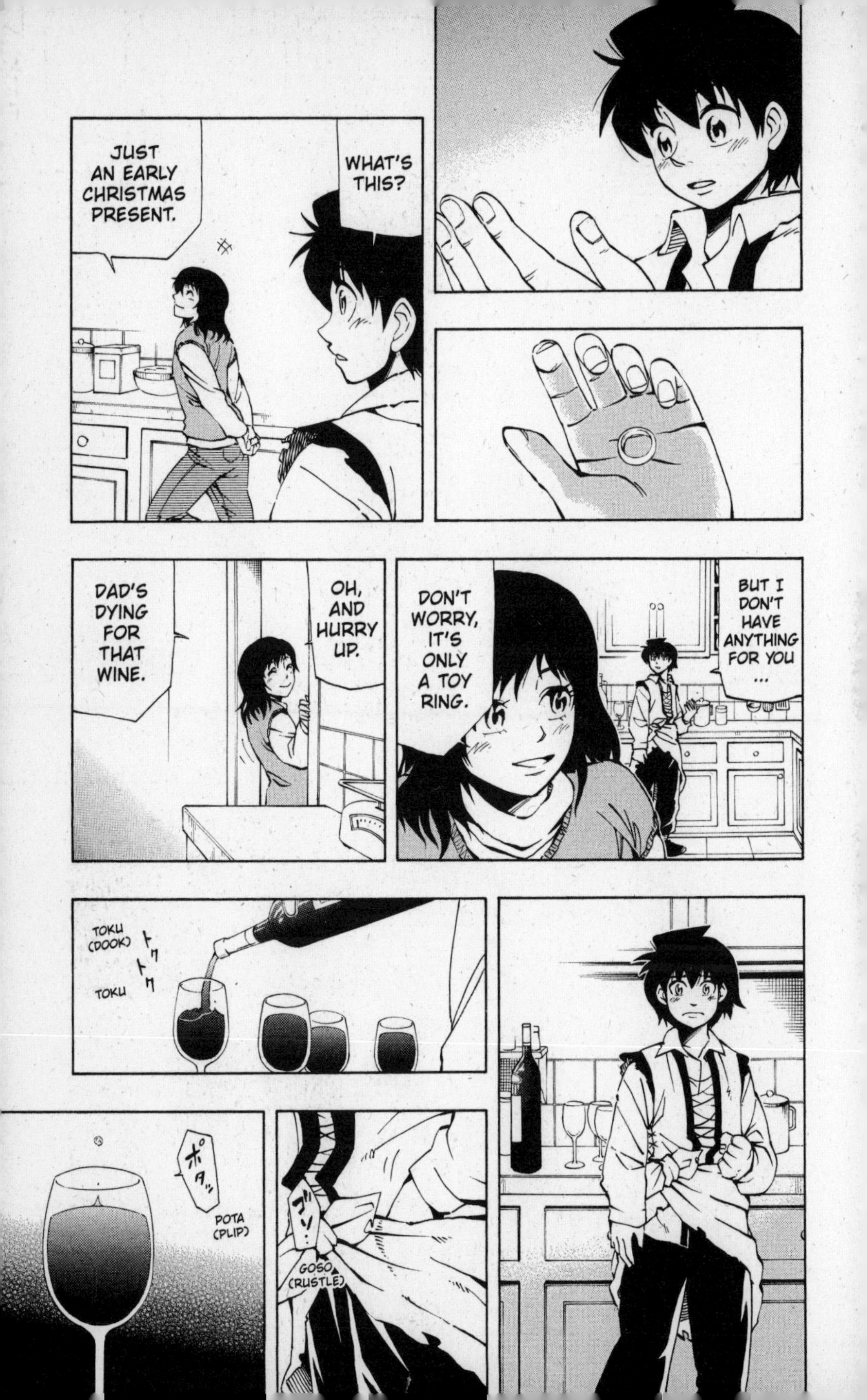
WHAT'S THIS?
JUST AN EARLY CHRISTMAS PRESENT.
BUT I DON'T HAVE ANYTHING FOR YOU ...
DON'T WORRY, IT'S ONLY A TOY RING.
OH, AND HURRY UP.
DAD'S DYING FOR THAT WINE.
TOKU (DOOK)
トクトク
TOKU
ゴソ…
GOSO (RUSTLE)
ポタッ
POTA (PLIP)

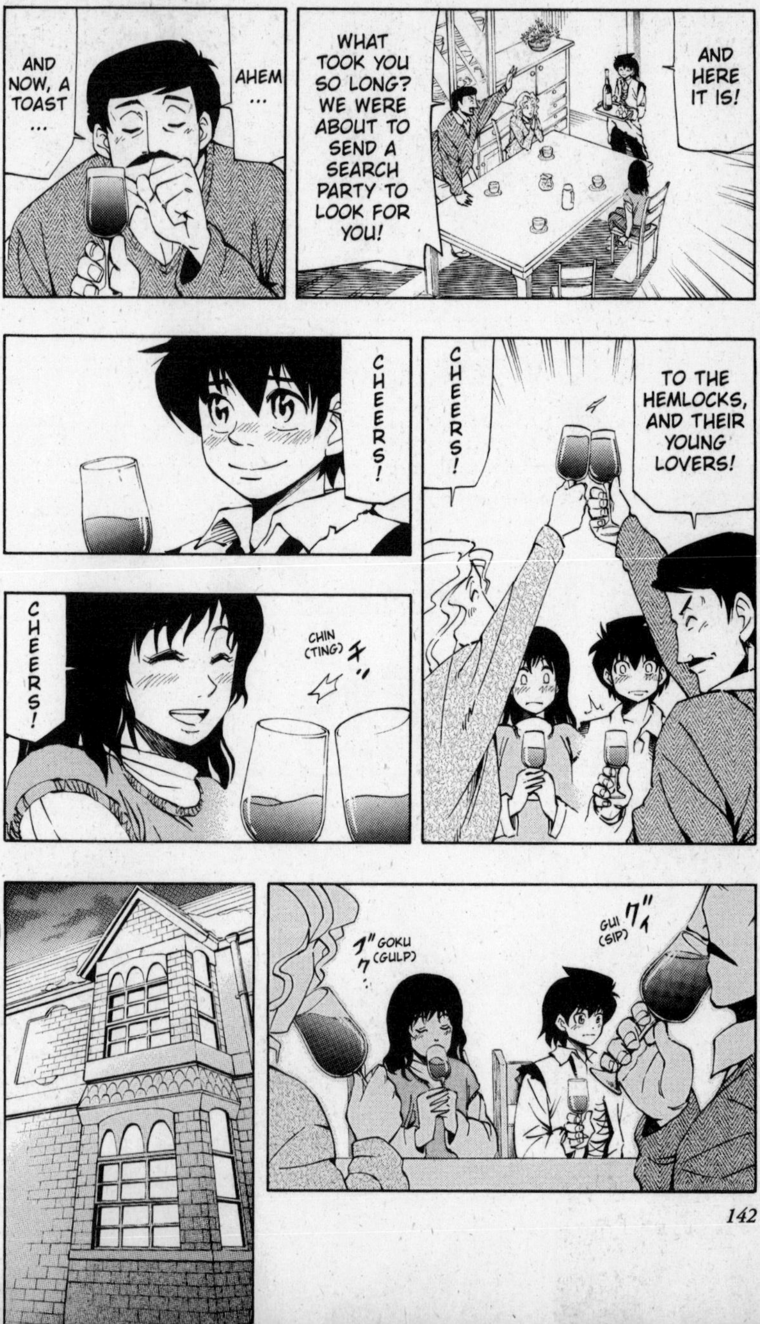
AND HERE IT IS!
WHAT TOOK YOU SO LONG? WE WERE ABOUT TO SEND A SEARCH PARTY TO LOOK FOR YOU!
AHEM ...
AND NOW, A TOAST ...
TO THE HEMLOCKS, AND THEIR YOUNG LOVERS!
CHEERS!
CHEERS!
CHEERS!
CHIN (TING)
GUI (SIP)
グイ
GOKU (GULP)
ゴク

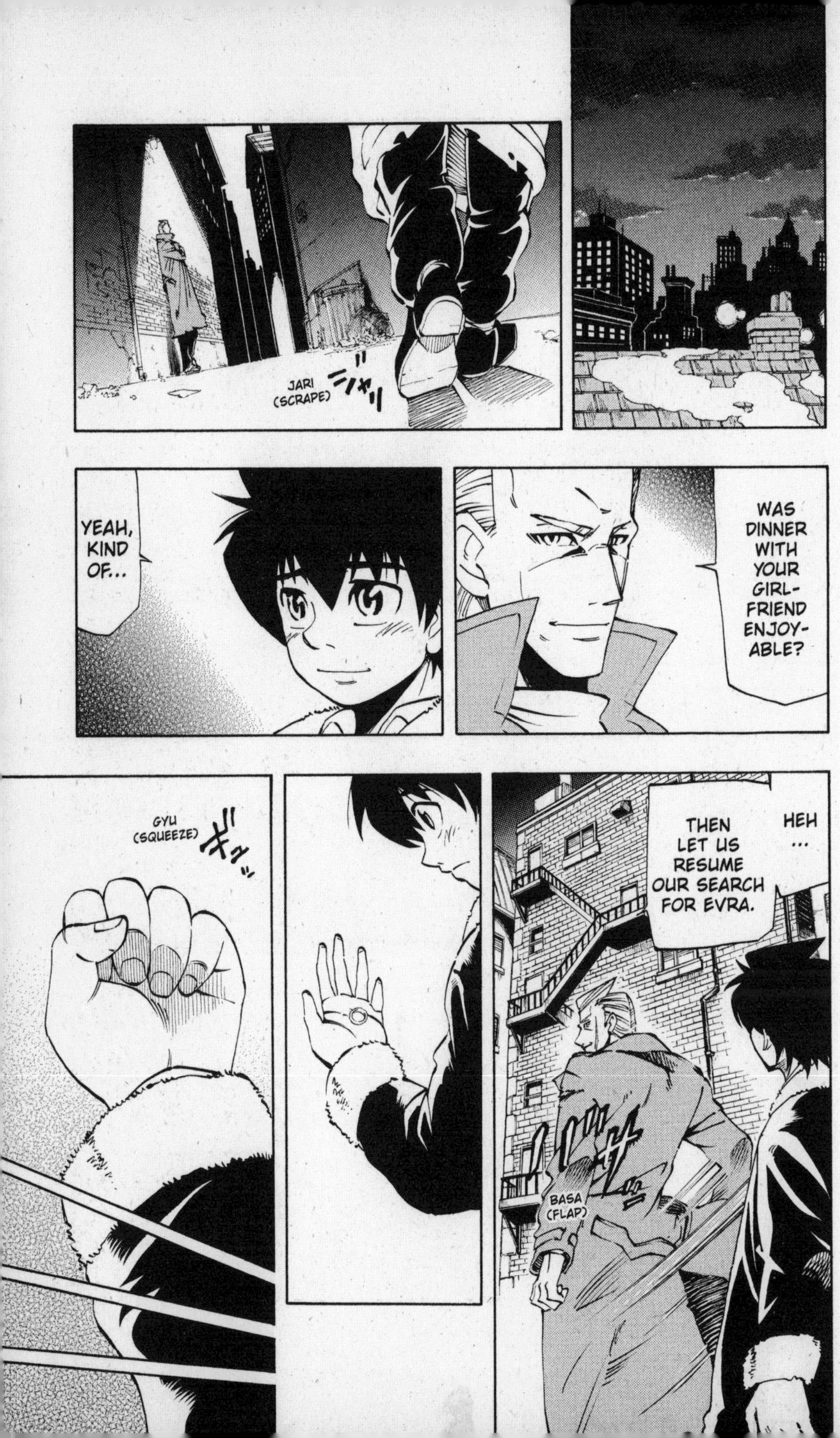
JARI (SCRAPE)
WAS DINNER WITH YOUR GIRL-FRIEND ENJOY-ABLE?
YEAH, KIND OF...
HEH ...
THEN LET US RESUME OUR SEARCH FOR EVRA.
BASA (FLAP)
GYU (SQUEEZE)

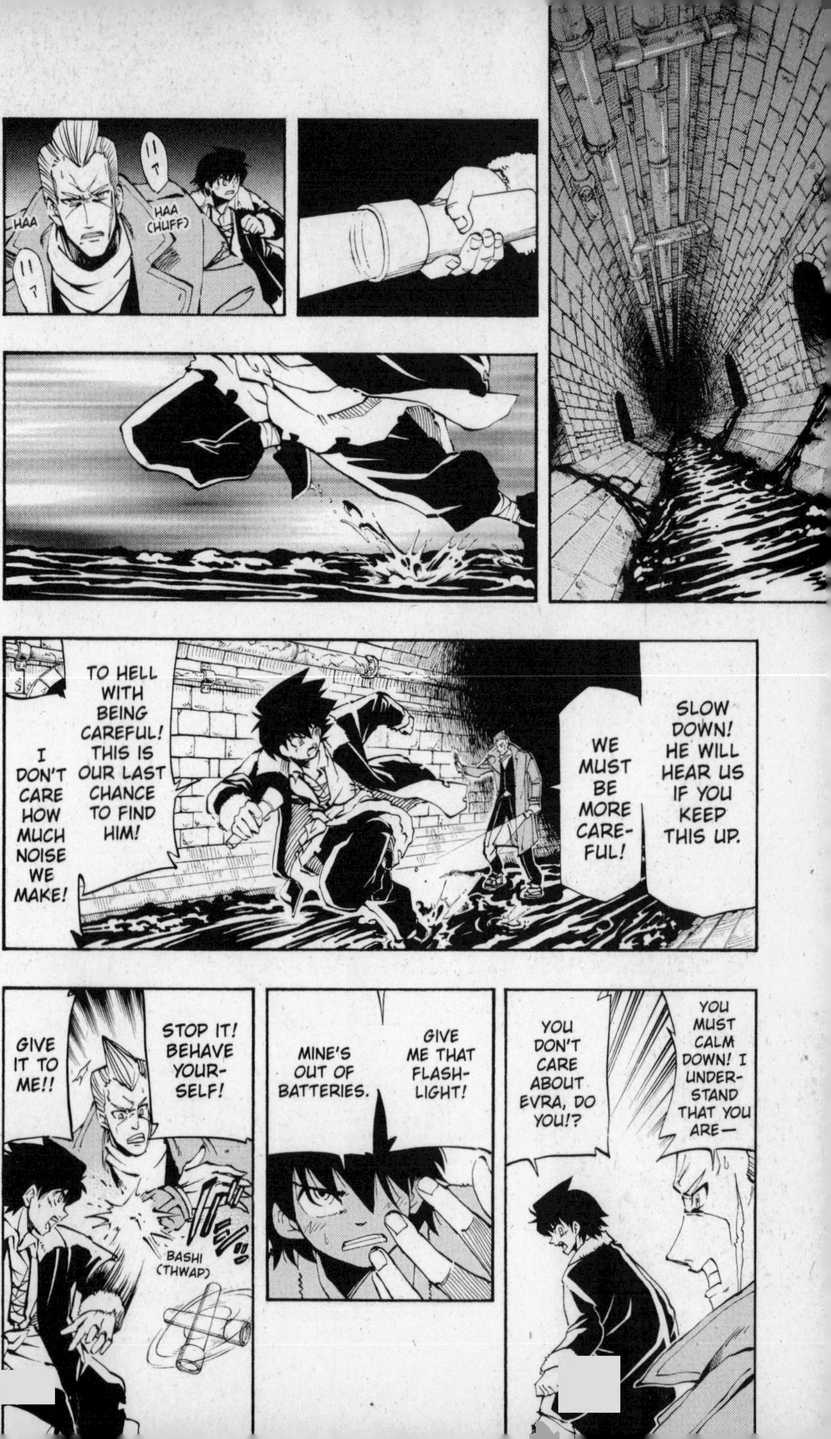
HAA (HUFF)
HAA
SLOW DOWN! HE WILL HEAR US IF YOU KEEP THIS UP.
WE MUST BE MORE CAREFUL!
TO HELL WITH BEING CAREFUL! THIS IS OUR LAST CHANCE TO FIND HIM!
I DON'T CARE HOW MUCH NOISE WE MAKE!
YOU MUST CALM DOWN! I UNDERSTAND THAT YOU ARE—
YOU DON'T CARE ABOUT EVRA, DO YOU!?
GIVE ME THAT FLASHLIGHT!
MINE'S OUT OF BATTERIES.
STOP IT! BEHAVE YOURSELF!
GIVE IT TO ME!!
BASHI (THWAP)

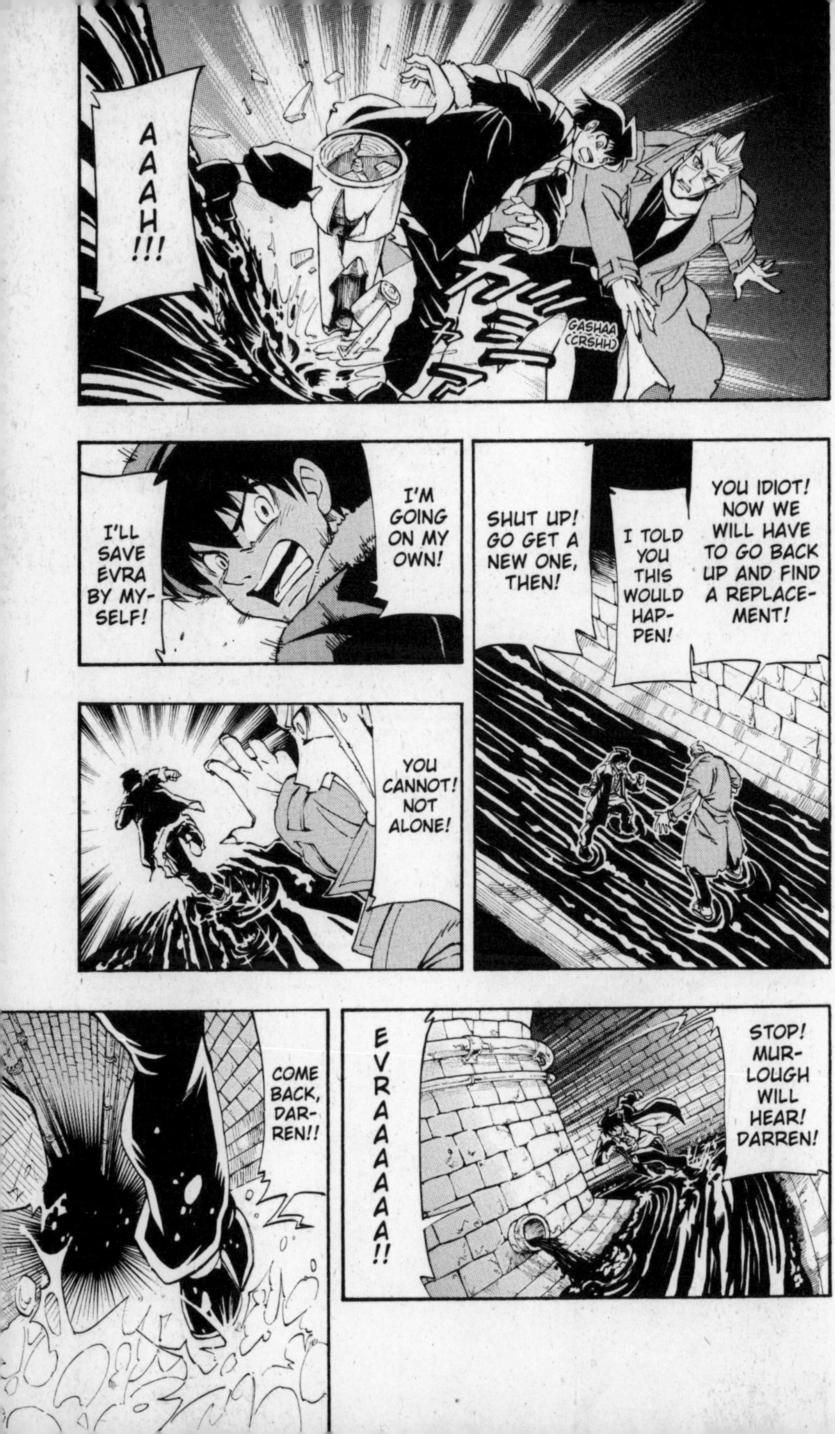
AAAH!!!
GASHAA (CRSHH)
YOU IDIOT! NOW WE WILL HAVE TO GO BACK UP AND FIND A REPLACE-MENT!
I TOLD YOU THIS WOULD HAP-PEN!
SHUT UP! GO GET A NEW ONE, THEN!
I'M GOING ON MY OWN!
I'LL SAVE EVRA BY MY-SELF!
YOU CANNOT! NOT ALONE!
STOP! MUR-LOUGH WILL HEAR! DARREN!
EVRAAAAAAAA!!
COME BACK, DAR-REN!!

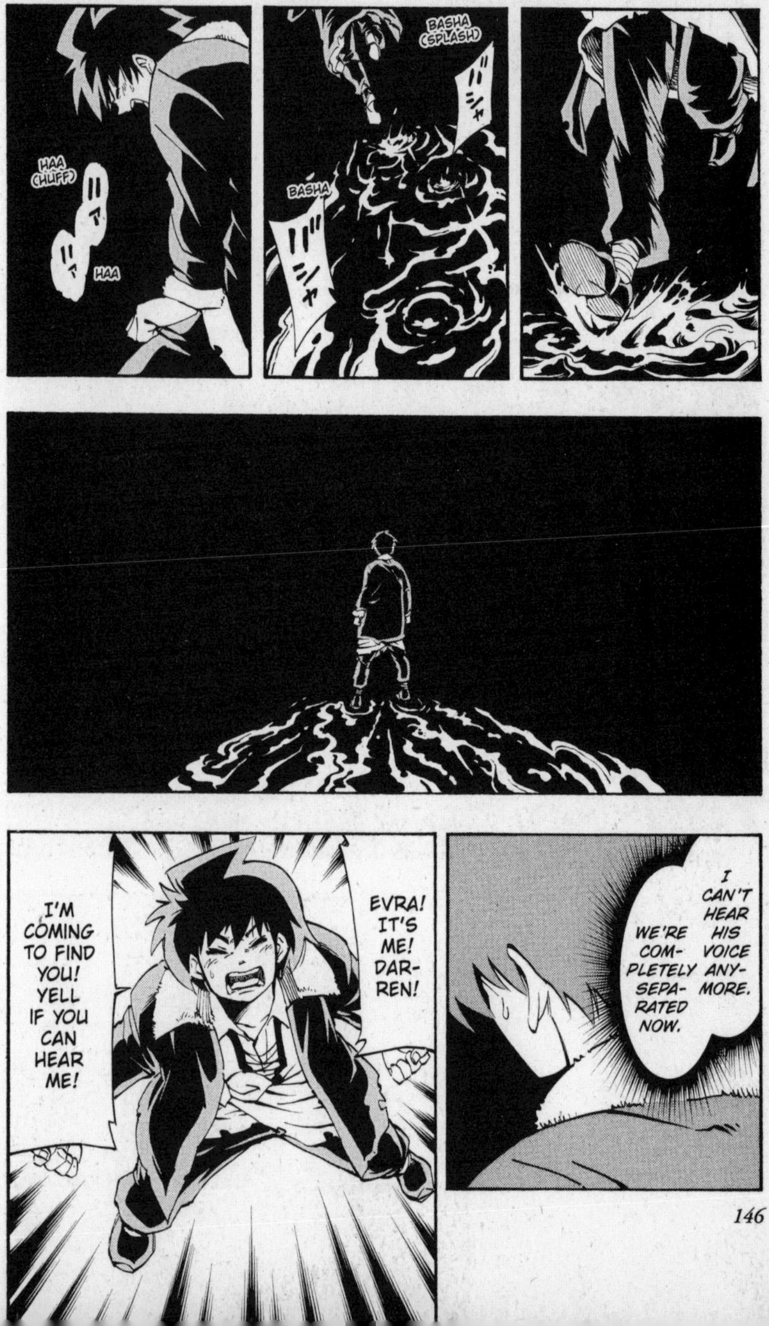
BASHA (SPLASH)
バシャ
BASHA
バシャ
HAA (HUFF)
ハァ
ハァ
HAA
I CAN'T HEAR HIS VOICE ANYMORE.
WE'RE COMPLETELY SEPARATED NOW.
EVRA! IT'S ME! DARREN!
I'M COMING TO FIND YOU! YELL IF YOU CAN HEAR ME!

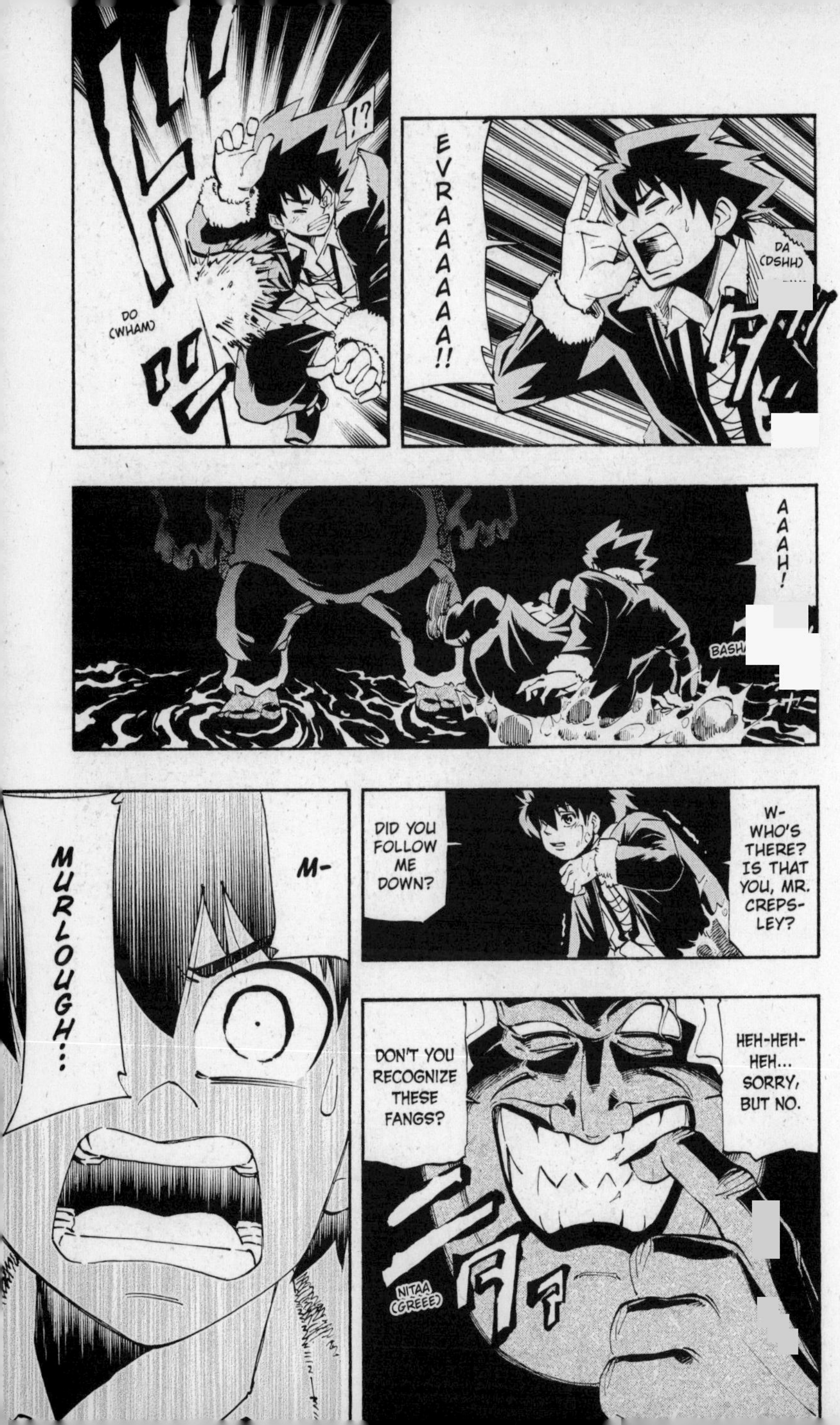
EVRAAAAAAA!!
DA (DSHH)
!?
DO (WHAM)
AAAH!
BASHA
W-WHO'S THERE? IS THAT YOU, MR. CREPS-LEY?
DID YOU FOLLOW ME DOWN?
HEH-HEH-HEH... SORRY, BUT NO.
DON'T YOU RECOGNIZE THESE FANGS?
NITAA (GREEE)
M-
MURLOUGH...

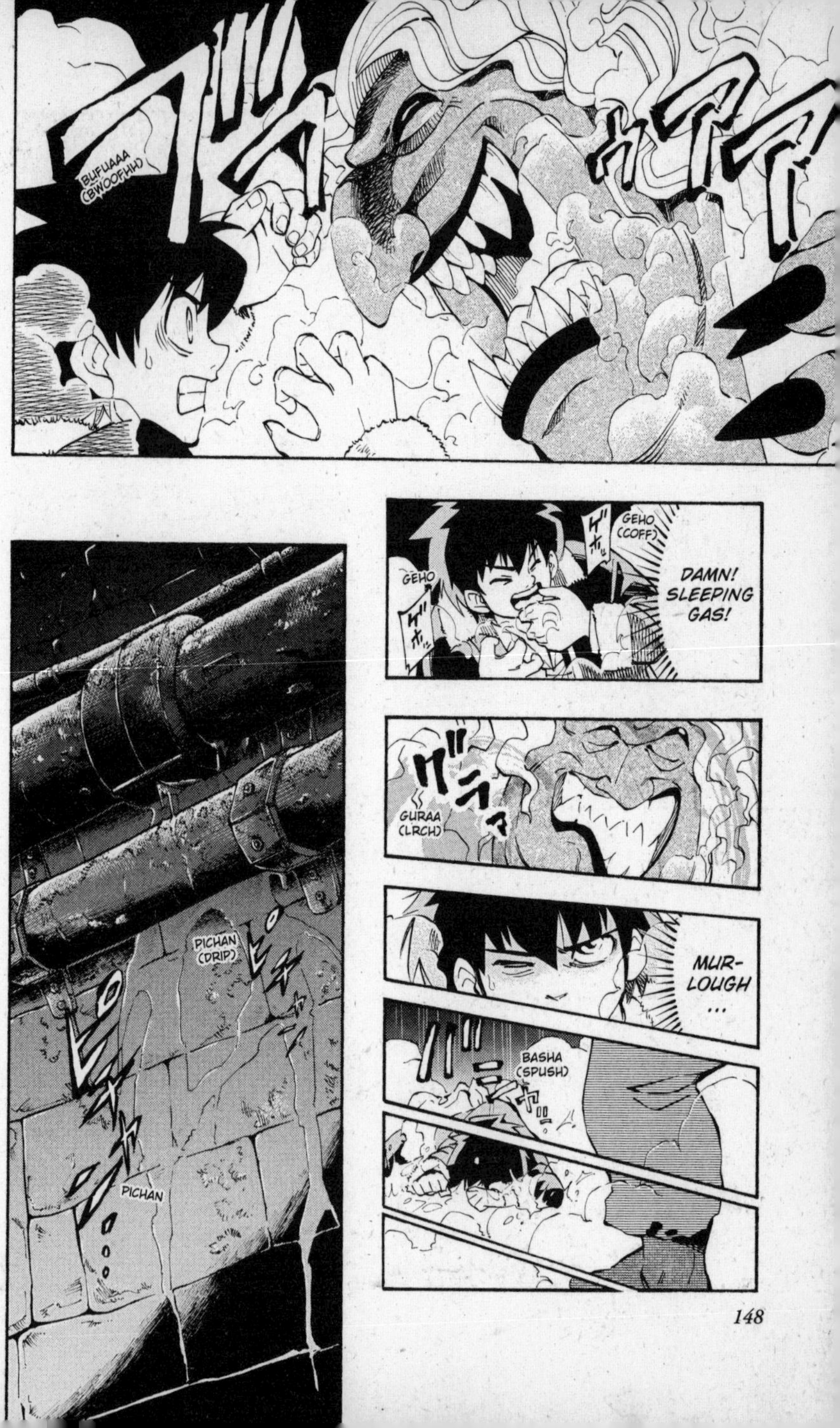
BUFUAAA (BWOOFHH)
GEHO (COFF)
DAMN! SLEEPING GAS!
GEHO
GURAA (LRCH)
MUR-LOUGH ...
BASHA (SPUSH)
PICHAN (DRIP)
PICHAN

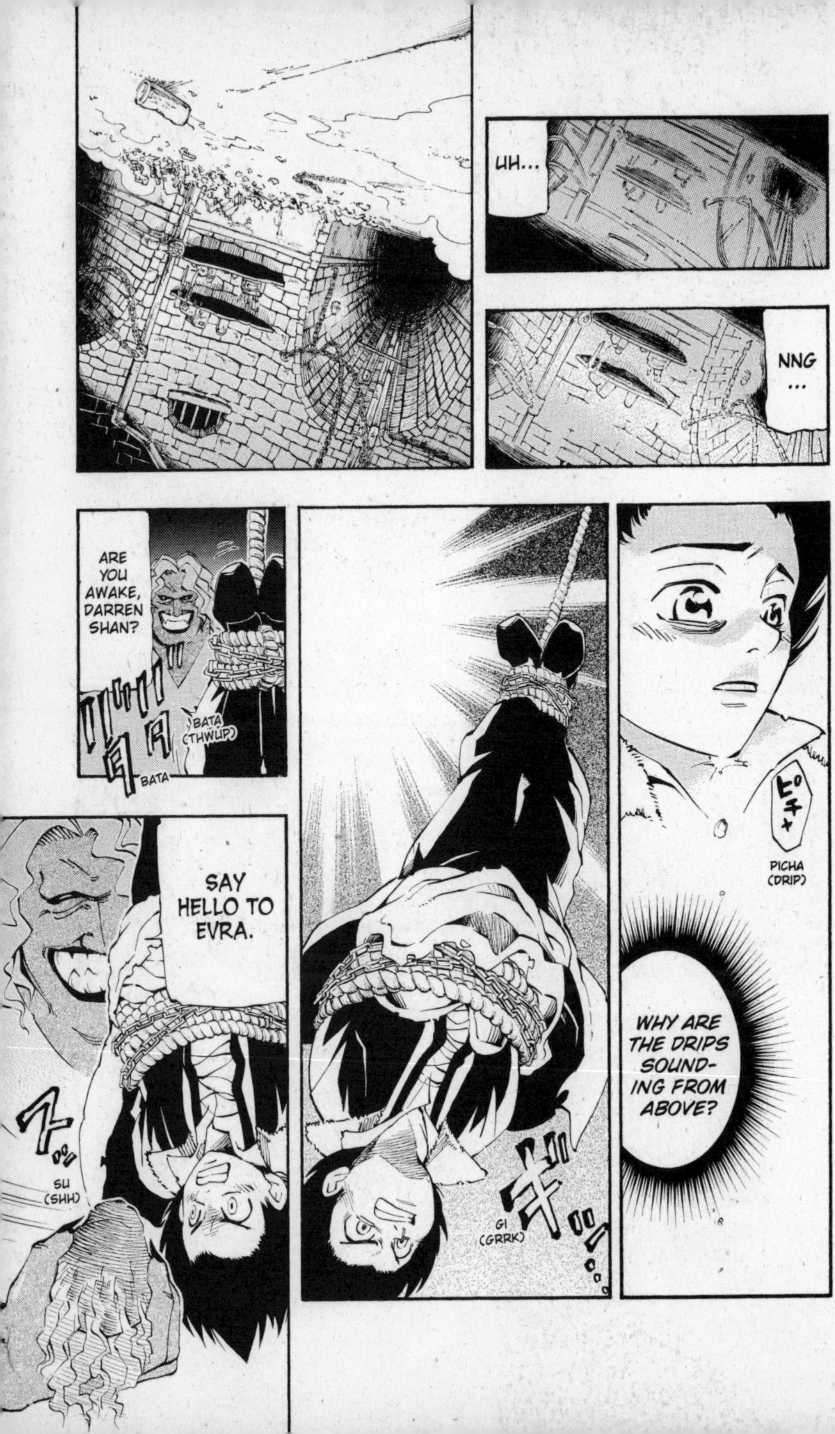
UH...
NNG ...
PICHA (DRIP)
WHY ARE THE DRIPS SOUNDING FROM ABOVE?
GI (GRRK)
ARE YOU AWAKE, DARREN SHAN?
BATA (THWUP)
BATA
SAY HELLO TO EVRA.
SU (SHH)

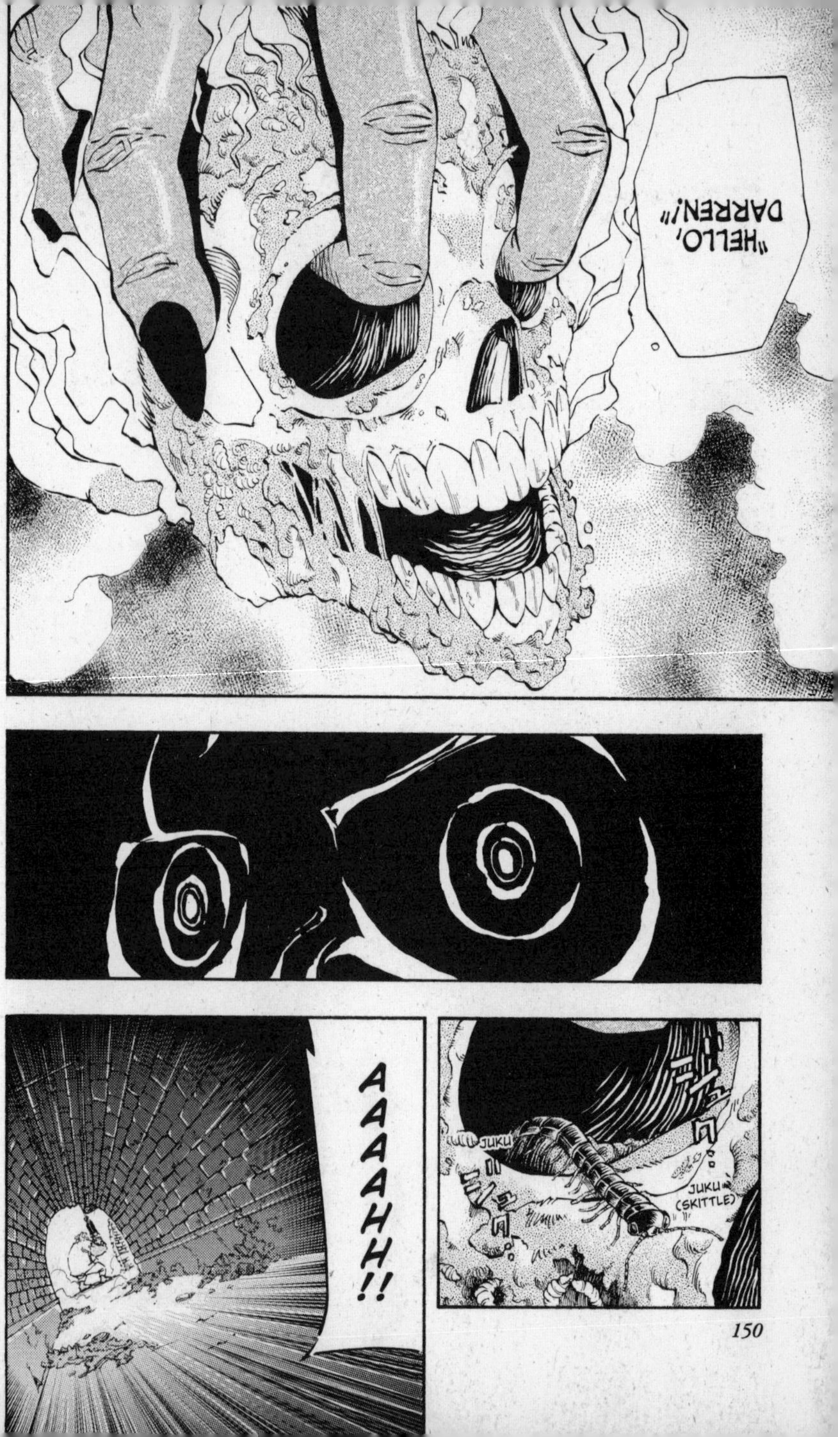
"HELLO, DARREN!"
JUKU
JUKU (SKITTLE)
AAAAAHH!!

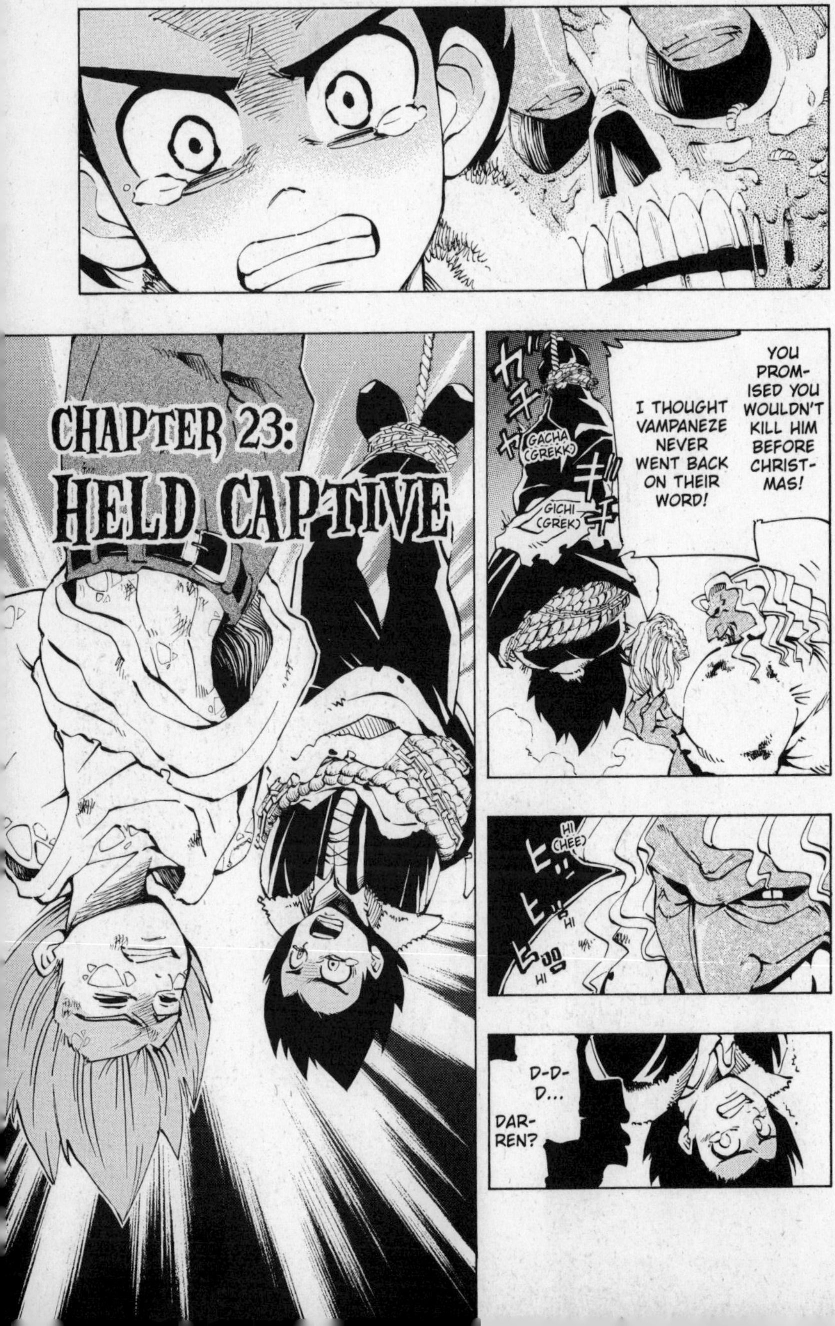
GACHA (GREKK)
GICHI (GREK)
YOU PROMISED YOU WOULDN'T KILL HIM BEFORE CHRISTMAS!
I THOUGHT VAMPANEZE NEVER WENT BACK ON THEIR WORD!
HI (HEE)
HI
HI
D-D-D... DARREN?
CHAPTER 23: HELD CAPTIVE

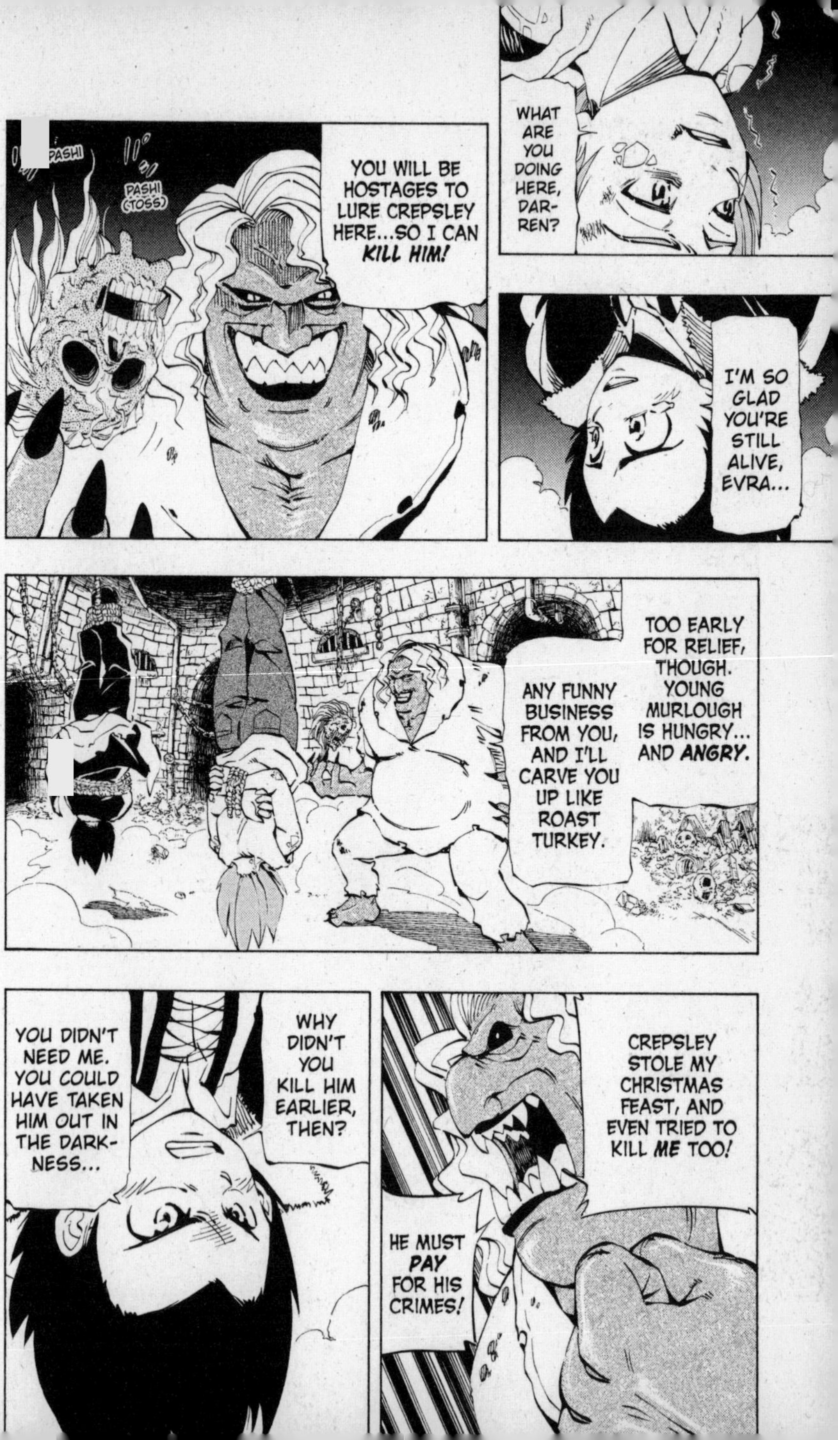
WHAT ARE YOU DOING HERE, DAR-REN?
I'M SO GLAD YOU'RE STILL ALIVE, EVRA...
YOU WILL BE HOSTAGES TO LURE CREPSLEY HERE...SO I CAN *KILL HIM!*
PASHI
PASHI (TOSS)
TOO EARLY FOR RELIEF, THOUGH. YOUNG MURLOUGH IS HUNGRY... AND **ANGRY**.
ANY FUNNY BUSINESS FROM YOU, AND I'LL CARVE YOU UP LIKE ROAST TURKEY.
CREPSLEY STOLE MY CHRISTMAS FEAST, AND EVEN TRIED TO KILL *ME* TOO!
HE MUST *PAY* FOR HIS CRIMES!
WHY DIDN'T YOU KILL HIM EARLIER, THEN?
YOU DIDN'T NEED ME. YOU COULD HAVE TAKEN HIM OUT IN THE DARK-NESS...

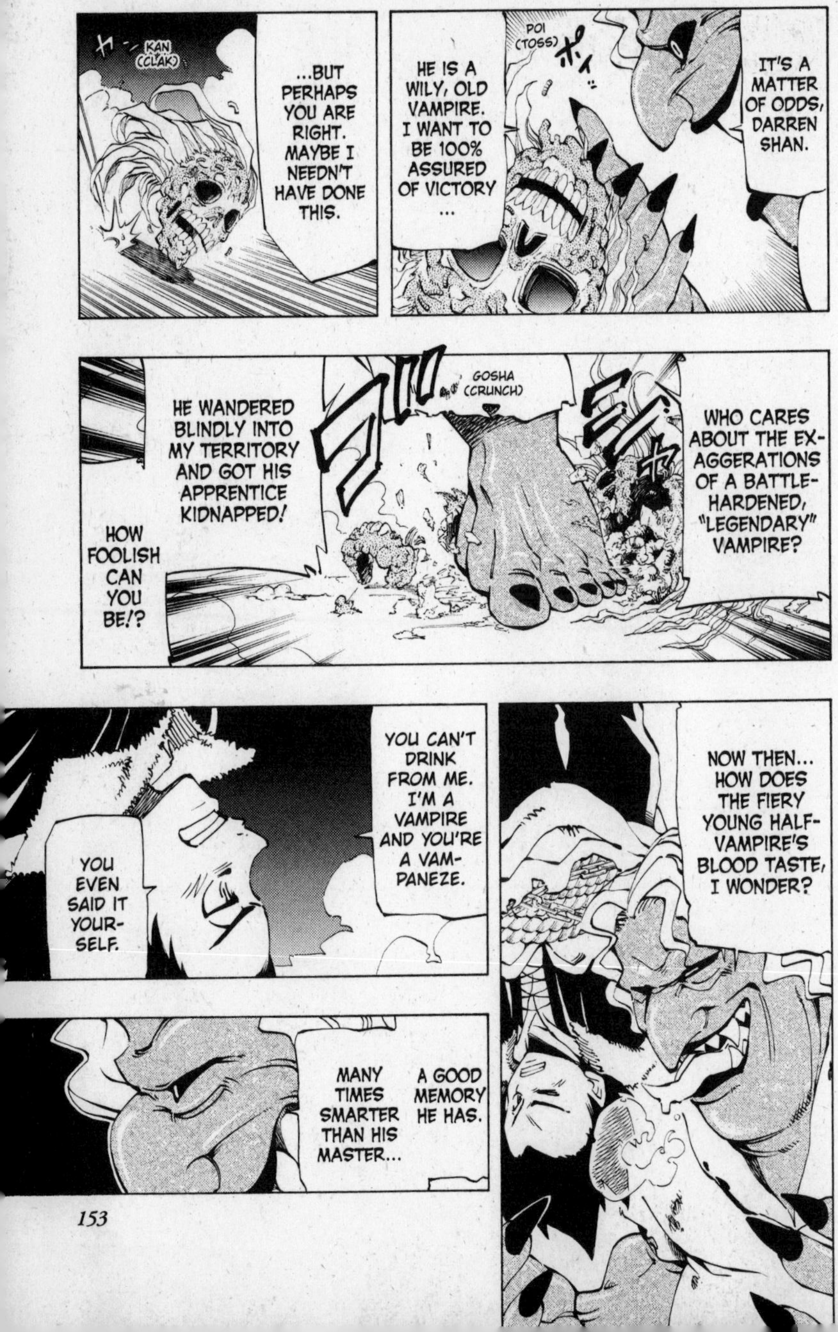
IT'S A MATTER OF ODDS, DARREN SHAN.
POI (TOSS)
HE IS A WILY, OLD VAMPIRE. I WANT TO BE 100% ASSURED OF VICTORY ...
KAN (CLAK)
...BUT PERHAPS YOU ARE RIGHT. MAYBE I NEEDN'T HAVE DONE THIS.
WHO CARES ABOUT THE EXAGGERATIONS OF A BATTLE-HARDENED, "LEGENDARY" VAMPIRE?
GOSHA (CRUNCH)
HE WANDERED BLINDLY INTO MY TERRITORY AND GOT HIS APPRENTICE KIDNAPPED!
HOW FOOLISH CAN YOU BE!?
NOW THEN... HOW DOES THE FIERY YOUNG HALF-VAMPIRE'S BLOOD TASTE, I WONDER?
YOU CAN'T DRINK FROM ME. I'M A VAMPIRE AND YOU'RE A VAMPANEZE.
YOU EVEN SAID IT YOURSELF.
A GOOD MEMORY HE HAS.
MANY TIMES SMARTER THAN HIS MASTER...

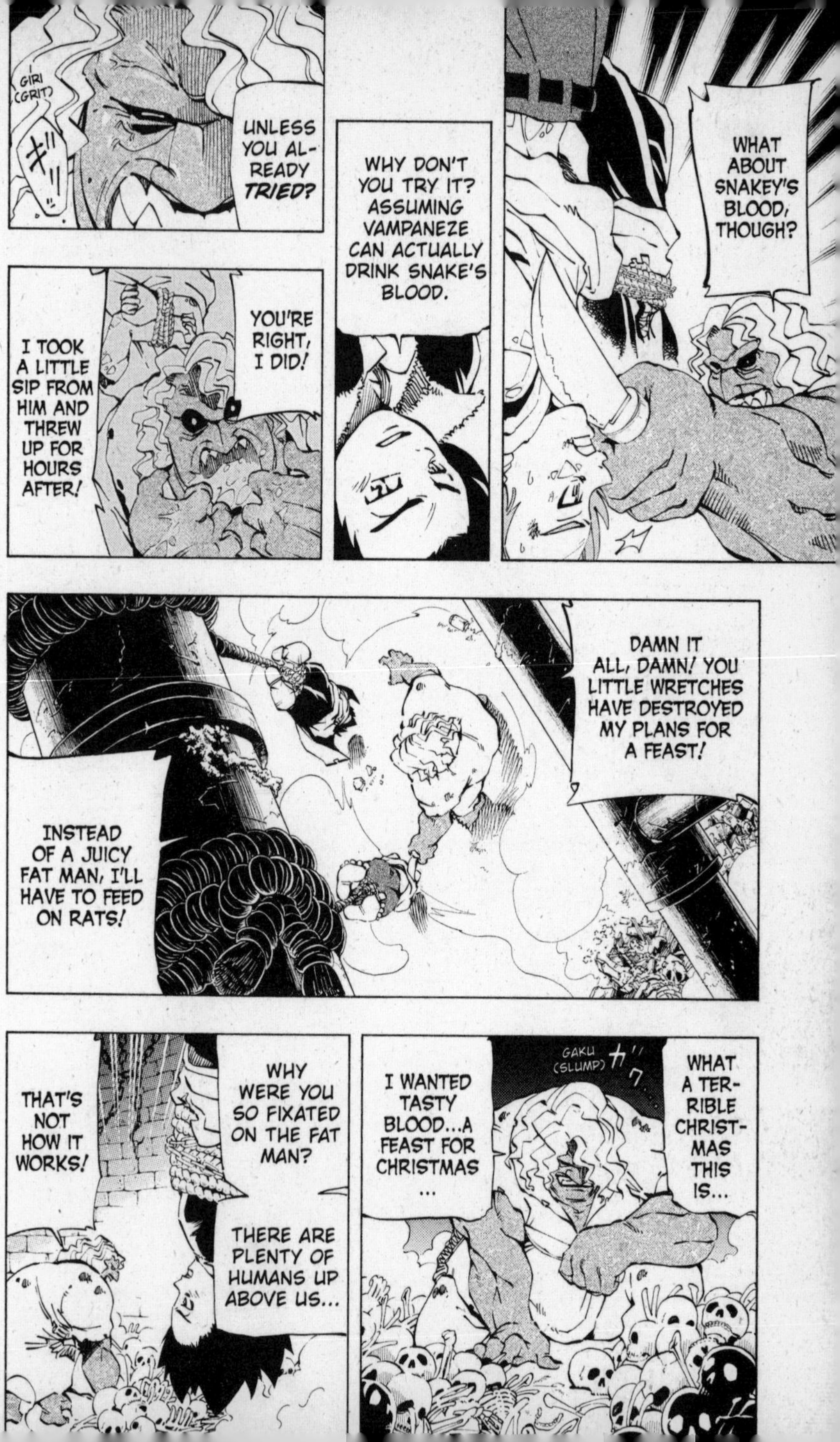
WHAT ABOUT SNAKEY'S BLOOD, THOUGH?
WHY DON'T YOU TRY IT? ASSUMING VAMPANEZE CAN ACTUALLY DRINK SNAKE'S BLOOD.
UNLESS YOU AL-READY *TRIED?*
GIRI (GRIT)
ギリ
YOU'RE RIGHT, I DID!
I TOOK A LITTLE SIP FROM HIM AND THREW UP FOR HOURS AFTER!
DAMN IT ALL, DAMN! YOU LITTLE WRETCHES HAVE DESTROYED MY PLANS FOR A FEAST!
INSTEAD OF A JUICY FAT MAN, I'LL HAVE TO FEED ON RATS!
WHAT A TER-RIBLE CHRIST-MAS THIS IS...
GAKU (SLUMP)
ガク
I WANTED TASTY BLOOD...A FEAST FOR CHRISTMAS ...
WHY WERE YOU SO FIXATED ON THE FAT MAN?
THERE ARE PLENTY OF HUMANS UP ABOVE US...
THAT'S NOT HOW IT WORKS!

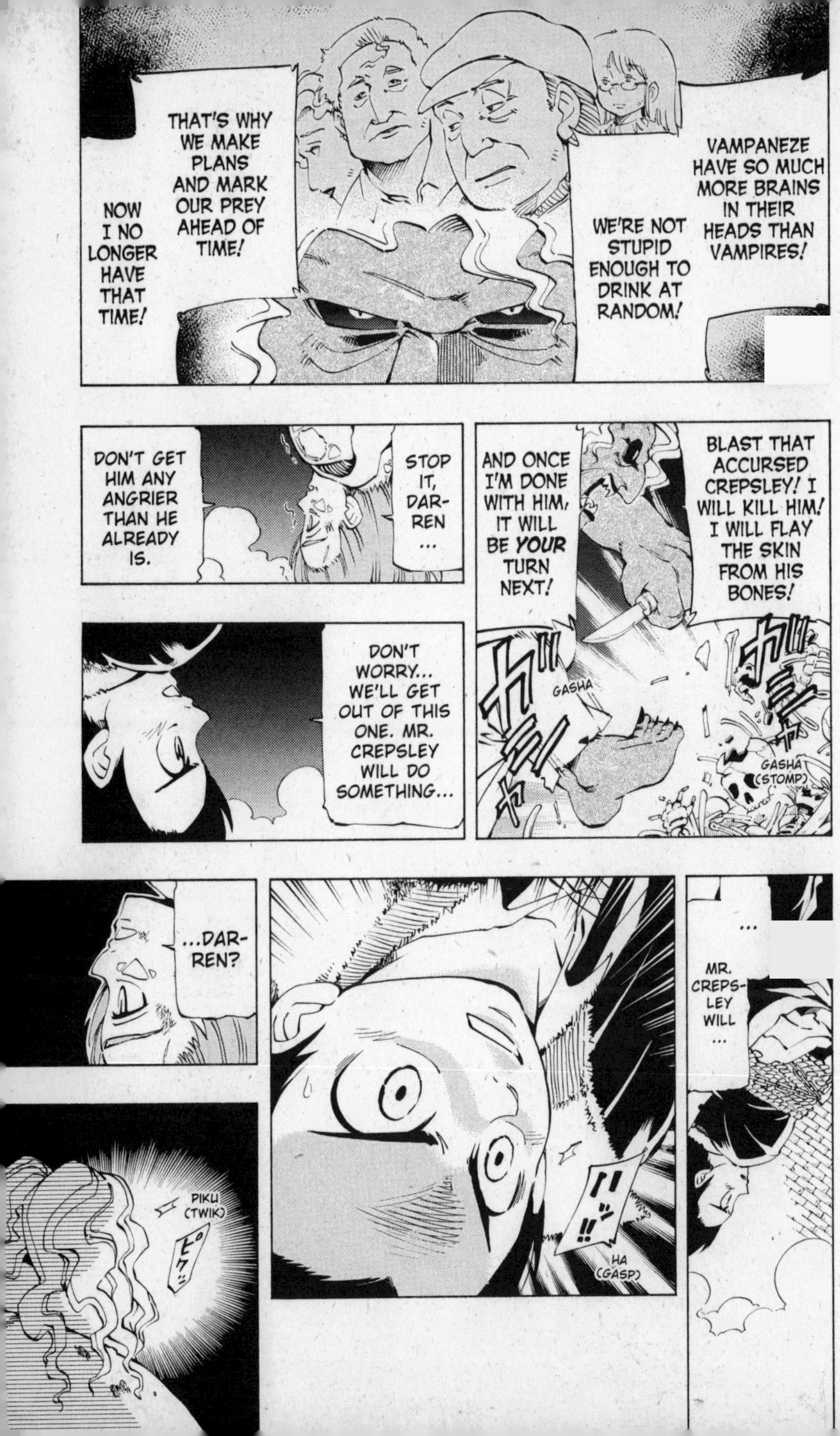
VAMPANEZE HAVE SO MUCH MORE BRAINS IN THEIR HEADS THAN VAMPIRES!
WE'RE NOT STUPID ENOUGH TO DRINK AT RANDOM!
THAT'S WHY WE MAKE PLANS AND MARK OUR PREY AHEAD OF TIME!
NOW I NO LONGER HAVE THAT TIME!
BLAST THAT ACCURSED CREPSLEY! I WILL KILL HIM! I WILL FLAY THE SKIN FROM HIS BONES!
AND ONCE I'M DONE WITH HIM, IT WILL BE *YOUR* TURN NEXT!
GASHA (STOMP)
GASHA
STOP IT, DAR-REN ...
DON'T GET HIM ANY ANGRIER THAN HE ALREADY IS.
DON'T WORRY... WE'LL GET OUT OF THIS ONE. MR. CREPSLEY WILL DO SOMETHING...
...
MR. CREPS-LEY WILL ...
HA (GASP)
...DAR-REN?
PIKU (TWIK)

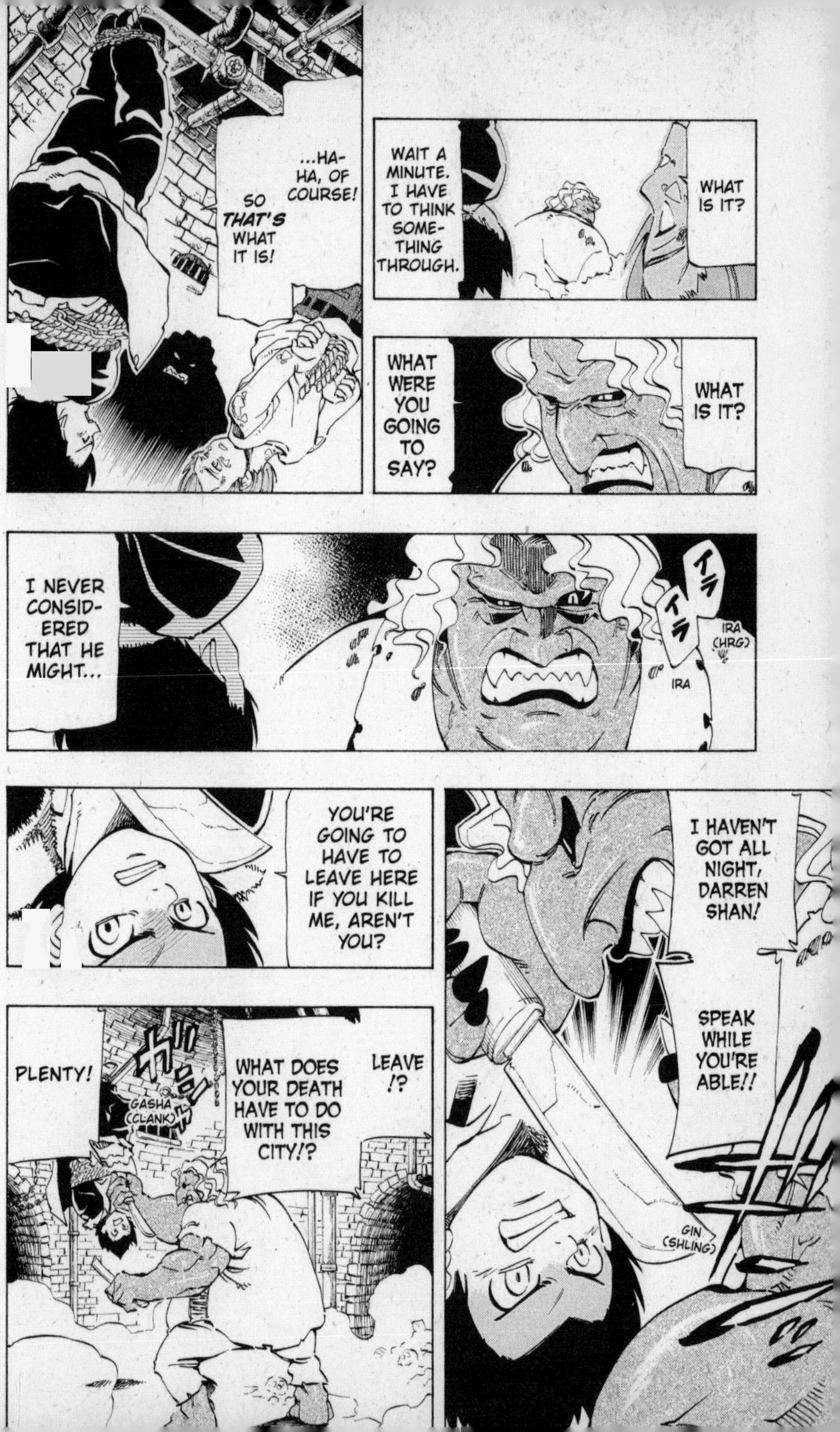
WHAT IS IT?
WAIT A MINUTE. I HAVE TO THINK SOME-THING THROUGH.
WHAT IS IT?
WHAT WERE YOU GOING TO SAY?
...HA-HA, OF COURSE!
SO *THAT'S* WHAT IT IS!
イラ イラ
IRA (HRG)
IRA
I NEVER CONSID-ERED THAT HE MIGHT...
I HAVEN'T GOT ALL NIGHT, DARREN SHAN!
SPEAK WHILE YOU'RE ABLE!!
GIN (SHLING)
YOU'RE GOING TO HAVE TO LEAVE HERE IF YOU KILL ME, AREN'T YOU?
LEAVE!?
WHAT DOES YOUR DEATH HAVE TO DO WITH THIS CITY!?
GASHA (CLANK)
PLENTY!

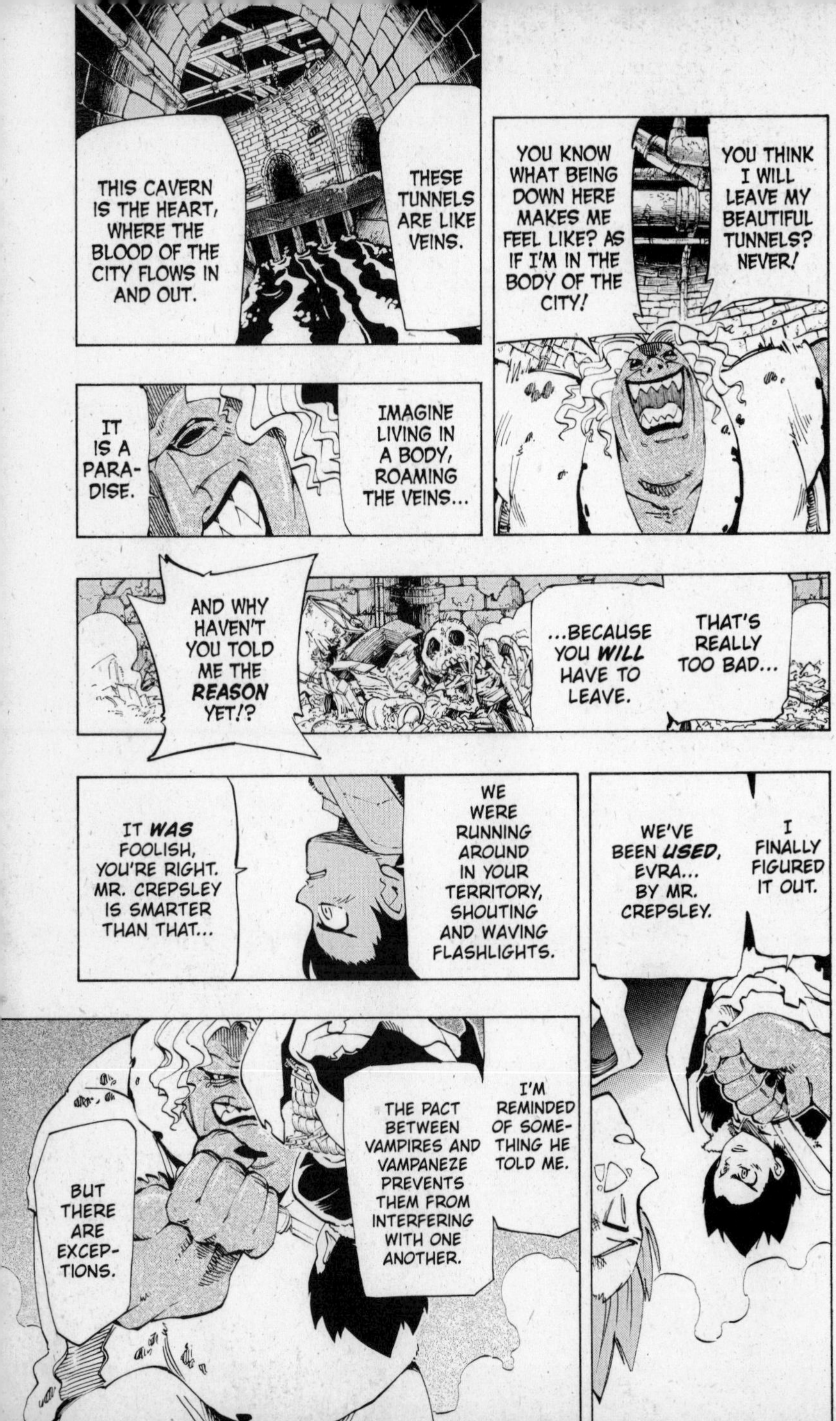
YOU THINK I WILL LEAVE MY BEAUTIFUL TUNNELS? NEVER!
YOU KNOW WHAT BEING DOWN HERE MAKES ME FEEL LIKE? AS IF I'M IN THE BODY OF THE CITY!
THESE TUNNELS ARE LIKE VEINS.
THIS CAVERN IS THE HEART, WHERE THE BLOOD OF THE CITY FLOWS IN AND OUT.
IMAGINE LIVING IN A BODY, ROAMING THE VEINS...
IT IS A PARA-DISE.
THAT'S REALLY TOO BAD...
...BECAUSE YOU ***WILL*** HAVE TO LEAVE.
AND WHY HAVEN'T YOU TOLD ME THE ***REASON*** YET!?
I FINALLY FIGURED IT OUT.
WE'VE BEEN ***USED***, EVRA... BY MR. CREPSLEY.
WE WERE RUNNING AROUND IN YOUR TERRITORY, SHOUTING AND WAVING FLASHLIGHTS.
IT ***WAS*** FOOLISH, YOU'RE RIGHT. MR. CREPSLEY IS SMARTER THAN THAT...
I'M REMINDED OF SOME-THING HE TOLD ME.
THE PACT BETWEEN VAMPIRES AND VAMPANEZE PREVENTS THEM FROM INTERFERING WITH ONE ANOTHER.
BUT THERE ARE EXCEP-TIONS.

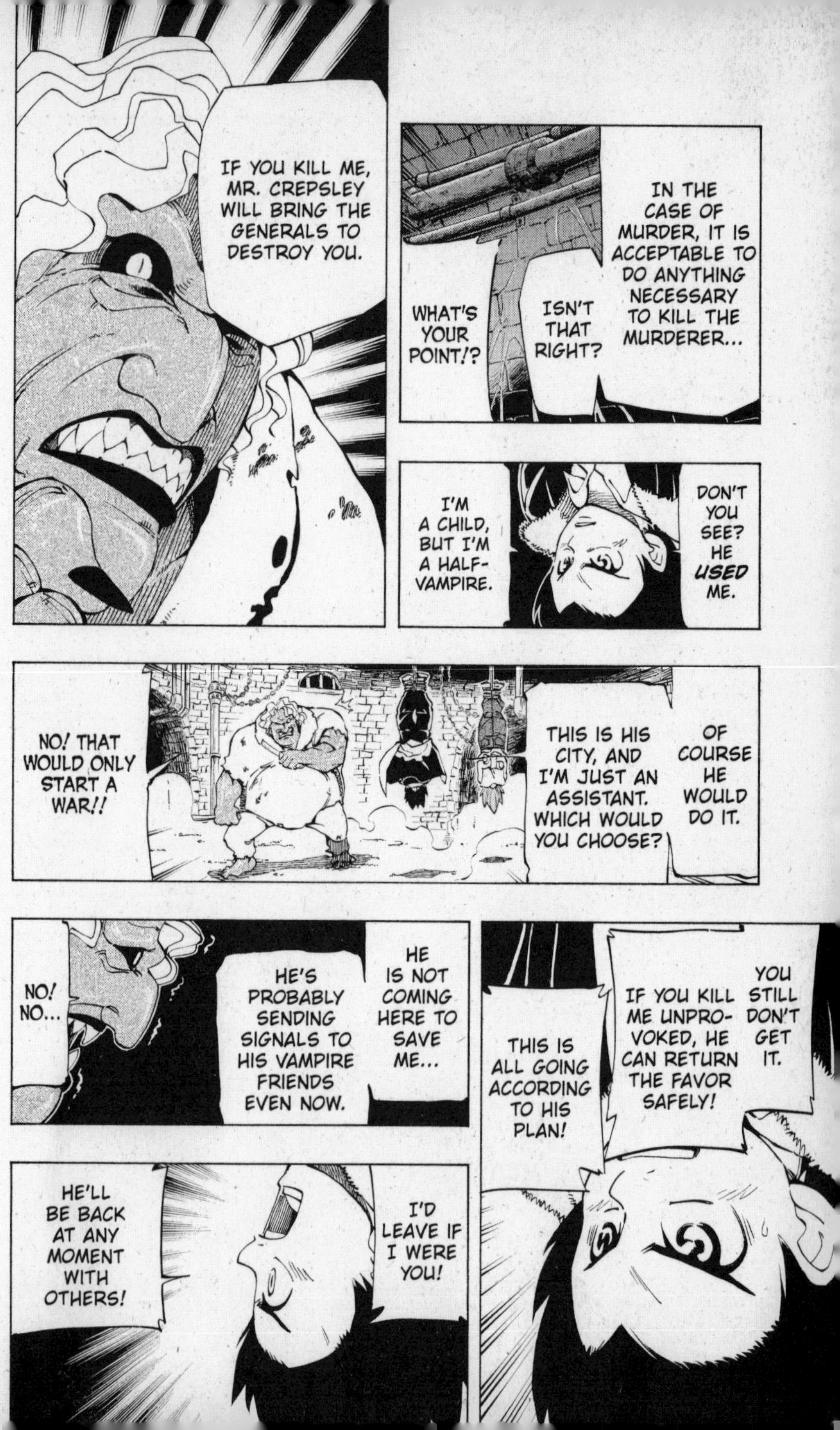
IN THE CASE OF MURDER, IT IS ACCEPTABLE TO DO ANYTHING NECESSARY TO KILL THE MURDERER...
ISN'T THAT RIGHT?
WHAT'S YOUR POINT!?
DON'T YOU SEE? HE *USED* ME.
I'M A CHILD, BUT I'M A HALF-VAMPIRE.
IF YOU KILL ME, MR. CREPSLEY WILL BRING THE GENERALS TO DESTROY YOU.
OF COURSE HE WOULD DO IT.
THIS IS HIS CITY, AND I'M JUST AN ASSISTANT. WHICH WOULD YOU CHOOSE?
NO! THAT WOULD ONLY START A WAR!!
YOU STILL DON'T GET IT.
IF YOU KILL ME UNPRO-VOKED, HE CAN RETURN THE FAVOR SAFELY!
THIS IS ALL GOING ACCORDING TO HIS PLAN!
HE IS NOT COMING HERE TO SAVE ME...
HE'S PROBABLY SENDING SIGNALS TO HIS VAMPIRE FRIENDS EVEN NOW.
NO! NO...
I'D LEAVE IF I WERE YOU!
HE'LL BE BACK AT ANY MOMENT WITH OTHERS!

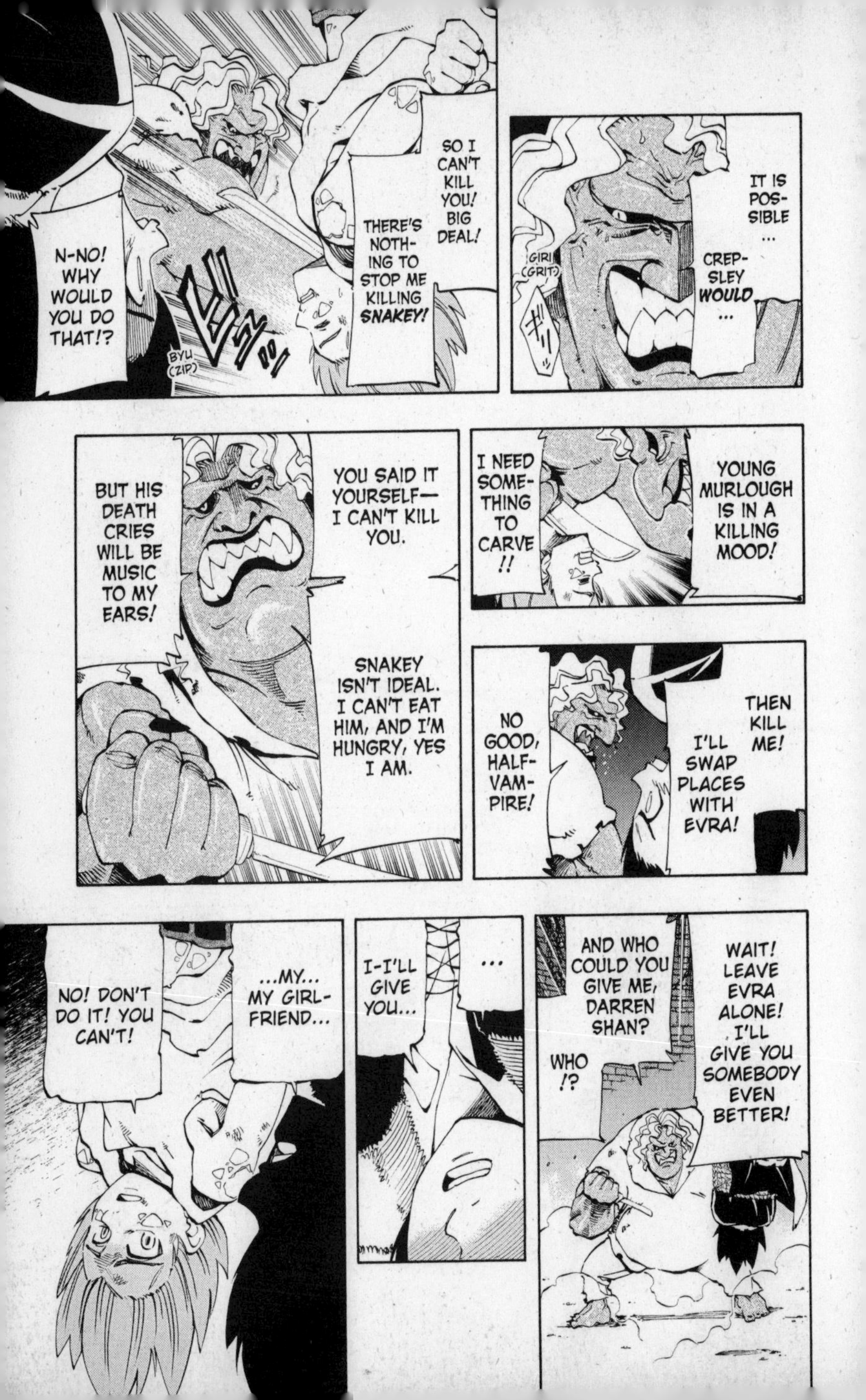
IT IS POS-SIBLE ... CREPSLEY WOULD ...
GIRI (GRIT)
SO I CAN'T KILL YOU! BIG DEAL!
THERE'S NOTHING TO STOP ME KILLING SNAKEY!
N-NO! WHY WOULD YOU DO THAT!?
BYU (ZIP)
YOUNG MURLOUGH IS IN A KILLING MOOD!
I NEED SOMETHING TO CARVE!!
THEN KILL ME!
I'LL SWAP PLACES WITH EVRA!
NO GOOD, HALF-VAMPIRE!
YOU SAID IT YOURSELF— I CAN'T KILL YOU.
BUT HIS DEATH CRIES WILL BE MUSIC TO MY EARS!
SNAKEY ISN'T IDEAL. I CAN'T EAT HIM, AND I'M HUNGRY, YES I AM.
WAIT! LEAVE EVRA ALONE! I'LL GIVE YOU SOMEBODY EVEN BETTER!
AND WHO COULD YOU GIVE ME, DARREN SHAN?
WHO !?
...
I-I'LL GIVE YOU...
...MY... MY GIRLFRIEND...
NO! DON'T DO IT! YOU CAN'T!

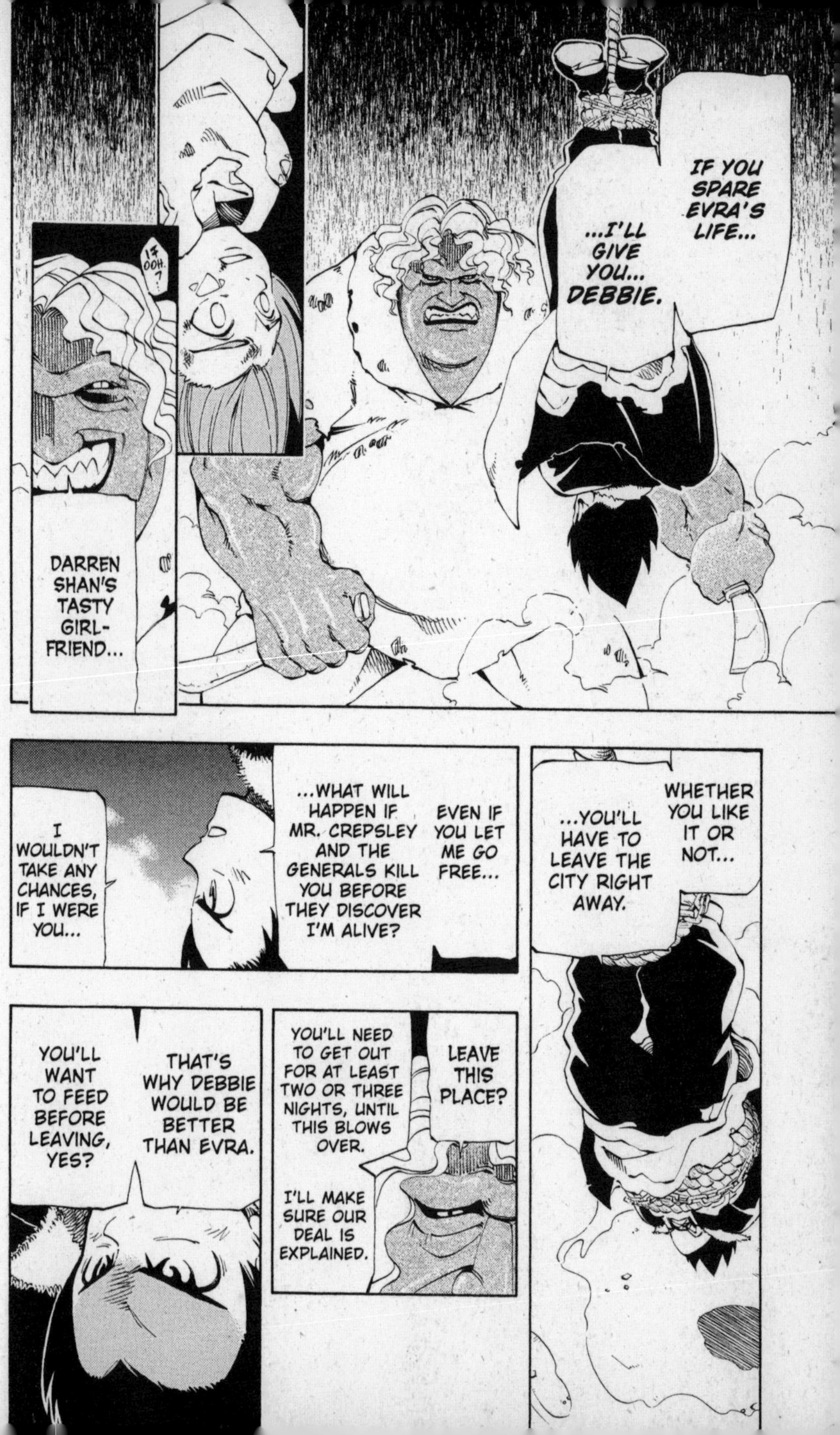
IF YOU SPARE EVRA'S LIFE...
...I'LL GIVE YOU... DEBBIE.
OOH.?
DARREN SHAN'S TASTY GIRL-FRIEND...
WHETHER YOU LIKE IT OR NOT...
...YOU'LL HAVE TO LEAVE THE CITY RIGHT AWAY.
EVEN IF YOU LET ME GO FREE...
...WHAT WILL HAPPEN IF MR. CREPSLEY AND THE GENERALS KILL YOU BEFORE THEY DISCOVER I'M ALIVE?
I WOULDN'T TAKE ANY CHANCES, IF I WERE YOU...
LEAVE THIS PLACE?
YOU'LL NEED TO GET OUT FOR AT LEAST TWO OR THREE NIGHTS, UNTIL THIS BLOWS OVER.
I'LL MAKE SURE OUR DEAL IS EXPLAINED.
THAT'S WHY DEBBIE WOULD BE BETTER THAN EVRA.
YOU'LL WANT TO FEED BEFORE LEAVING, YES?

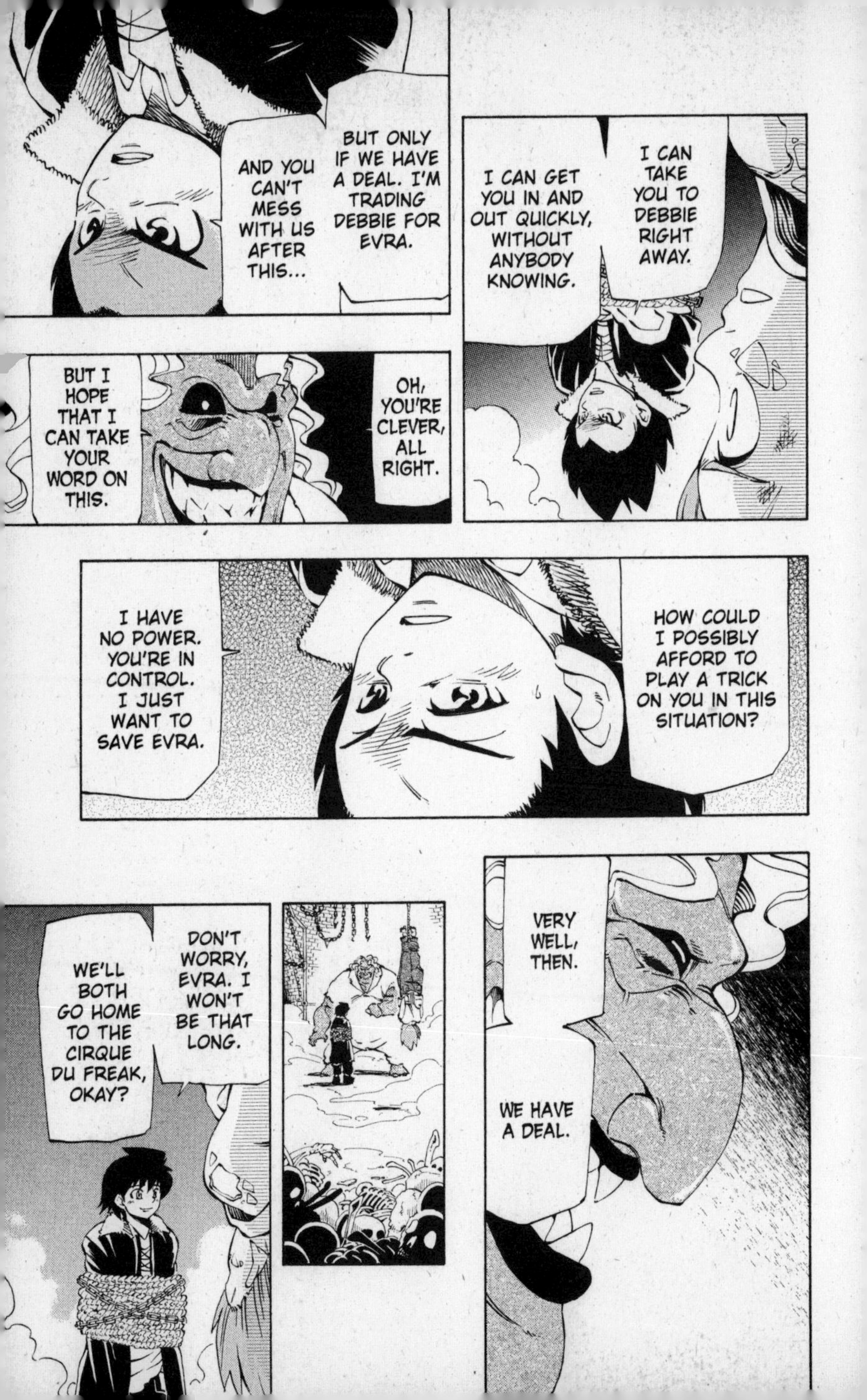
I CAN TAKE YOU TO DEBBIE RIGHT AWAY.
I CAN GET YOU IN AND OUT QUICKLY, WITHOUT ANYBODY KNOWING.
BUT ONLY IF WE HAVE A DEAL. I'M TRADING DEBBIE FOR EVRA.
AND YOU CAN'T MESS WITH US AFTER THIS...
OH, YOU'RE CLEVER, ALL RIGHT.
BUT I HOPE THAT I CAN TAKE YOUR WORD ON THIS.
HOW COULD I POSSIBLY AFFORD TO PLAY A TRICK ON YOU IN THIS SITUATION?
I HAVE NO POWER. YOU'RE IN CONTROL. I JUST WANT TO SAVE EVRA.
VERY WELL, THEN.
WE HAVE A DEAL.
DON'T WORRY, EVRA. I WON'T BE THAT LONG.
WE'LL BOTH GO HOME TO THE CIRQUE DU FREAK, OKAY?

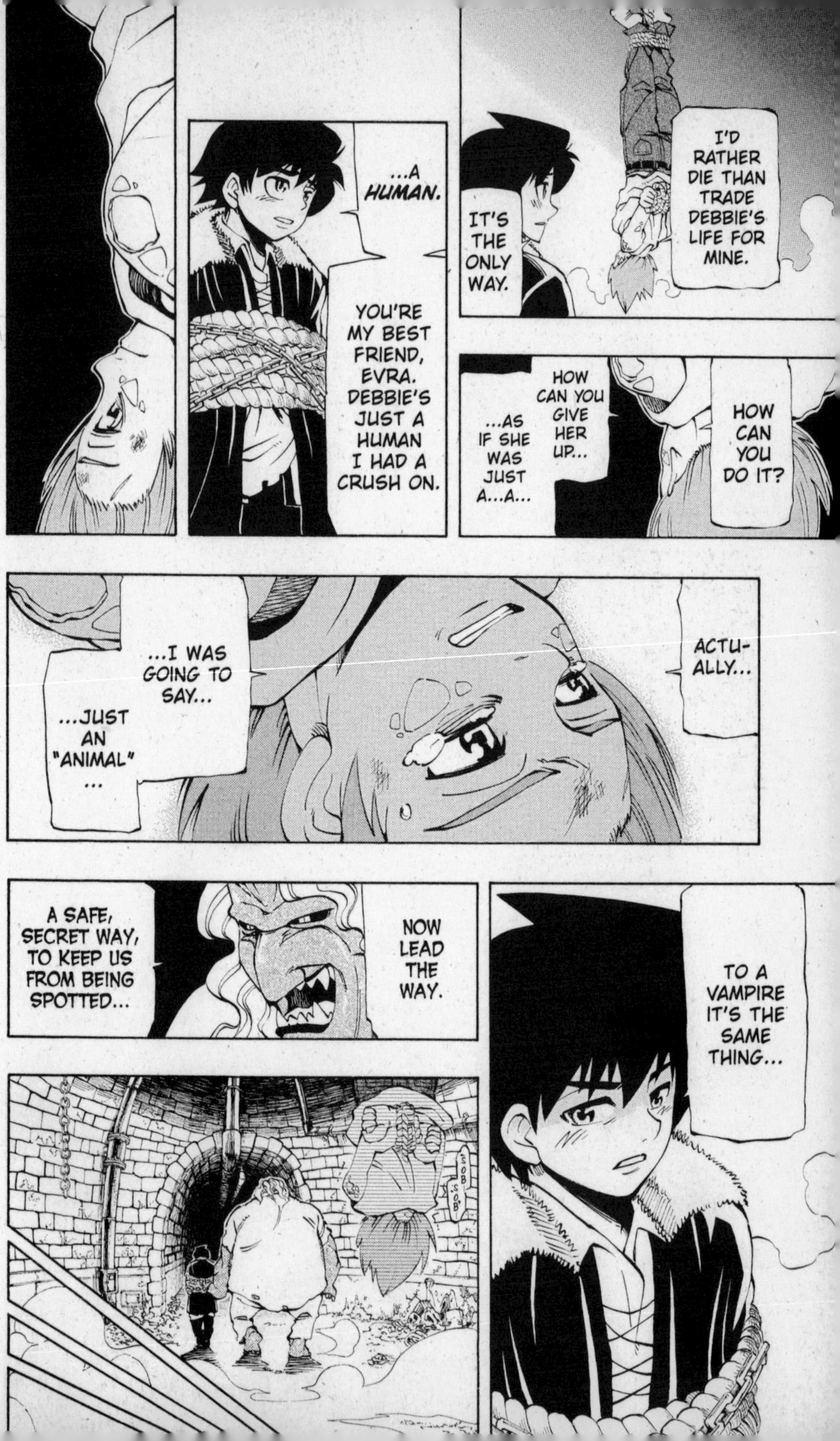
I'D RATHER DIE THAN TRADE DEBBIE'S LIFE FOR MINE.
IT'S THE ONLY WAY.
HOW CAN YOU DO IT?
HOW CAN YOU GIVE HER UP...
...AS IF SHE WAS JUST A...A...
...A HUMAN.
YOU'RE MY BEST FRIEND, EVRA. DEBBIE'S JUST A HUMAN I HAD A CRUSH ON.
ACTU-ALLY...
...I WAS GOING TO SAY...
...JUST AN "ANIMAL" ...
TO A VAMPIRE IT'S THE SAME THING...
NOW LEAD THE WAY.
A SAFE, SECRET WAY, TO KEEP US FROM BEING SPOTTED...
SOB... SOB...

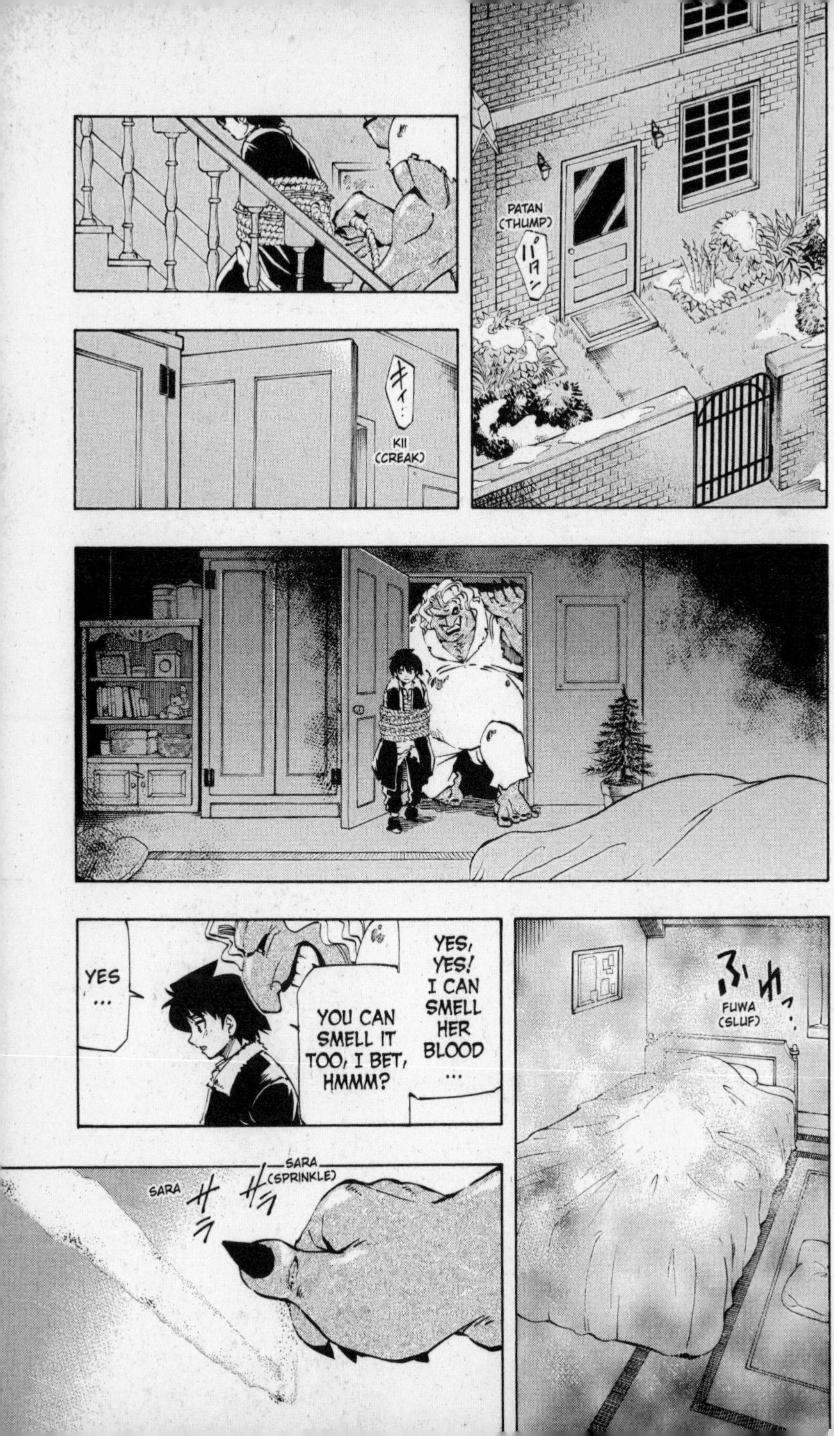
パタン
PATAN (THUMP)
キィ
KII (CREAK)
ふわっ
FUWA (SLUF)
YES, YES! I CAN SMELL HER BLOOD ...
YOU CAN SMELL IT TOO, I BET, HMMM?
YES ...
サラ
SARA (SPRINKLE)
サラ
SARA

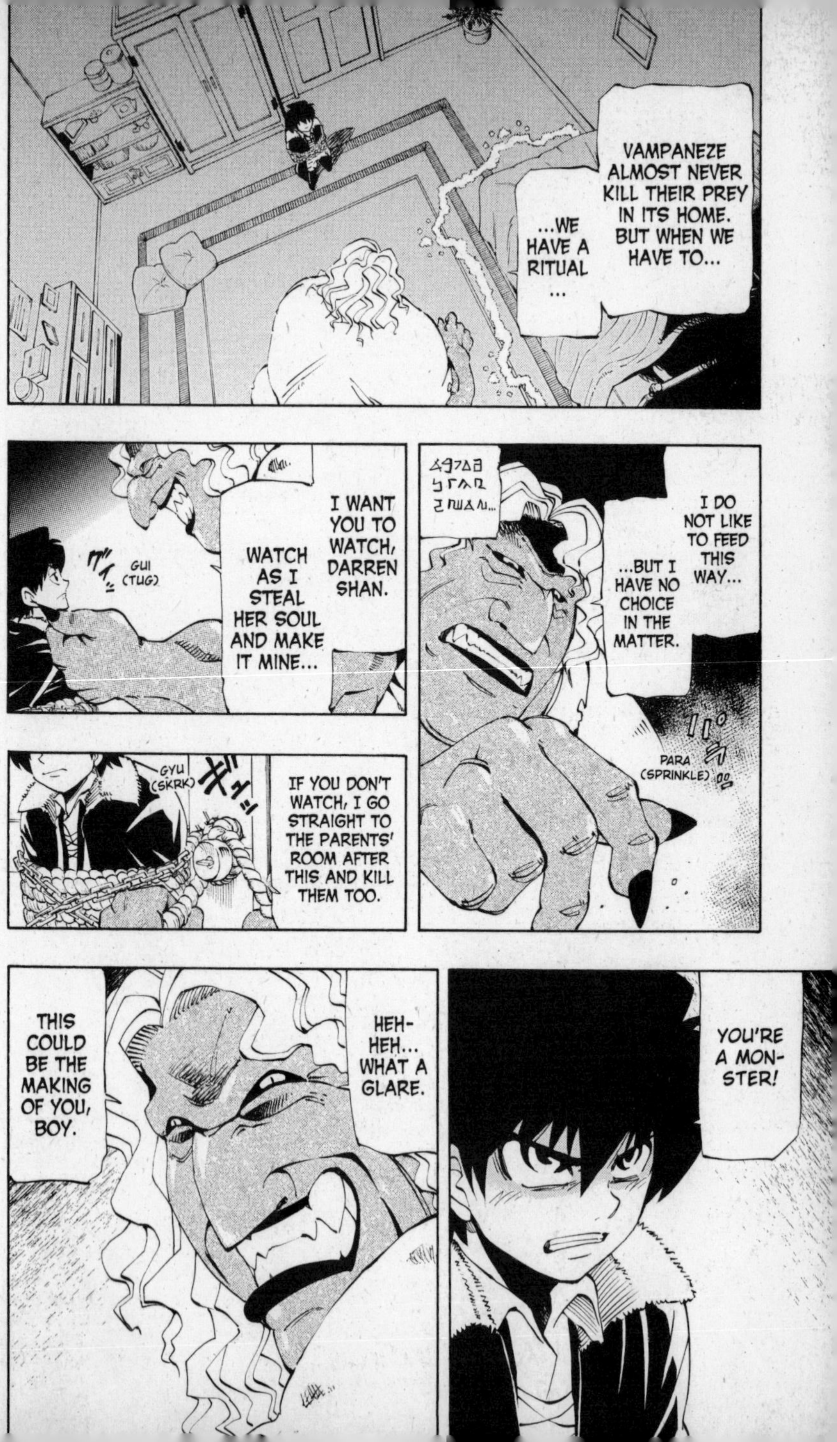
VAMPANEZE ALMOST NEVER KILL THEIR PREY IN ITS HOME. BUT WHEN WE HAVE TO...
...WE HAVE A RITUAL ...
I DO NOT LIKE TO FEED THIS WAY...
...BUT I HAVE NO CHOICE IN THE MATTER.
PARA (SPRINKLE)
I WANT YOU TO WATCH, DARREN SHAN.
WATCH AS I STEAL HER SOUL AND MAKE IT MINE...
GUI (TUG)
IF YOU DON'T WATCH, I GO STRAIGHT TO THE PARENTS' ROOM AFTER THIS AND KILL THEM TOO.
GYU (SKRK)
YOU'RE A MON-STER!
HEH-HEH... WHAT A GLARE.
THIS COULD BE THE MAKING OF YOU, BOY.

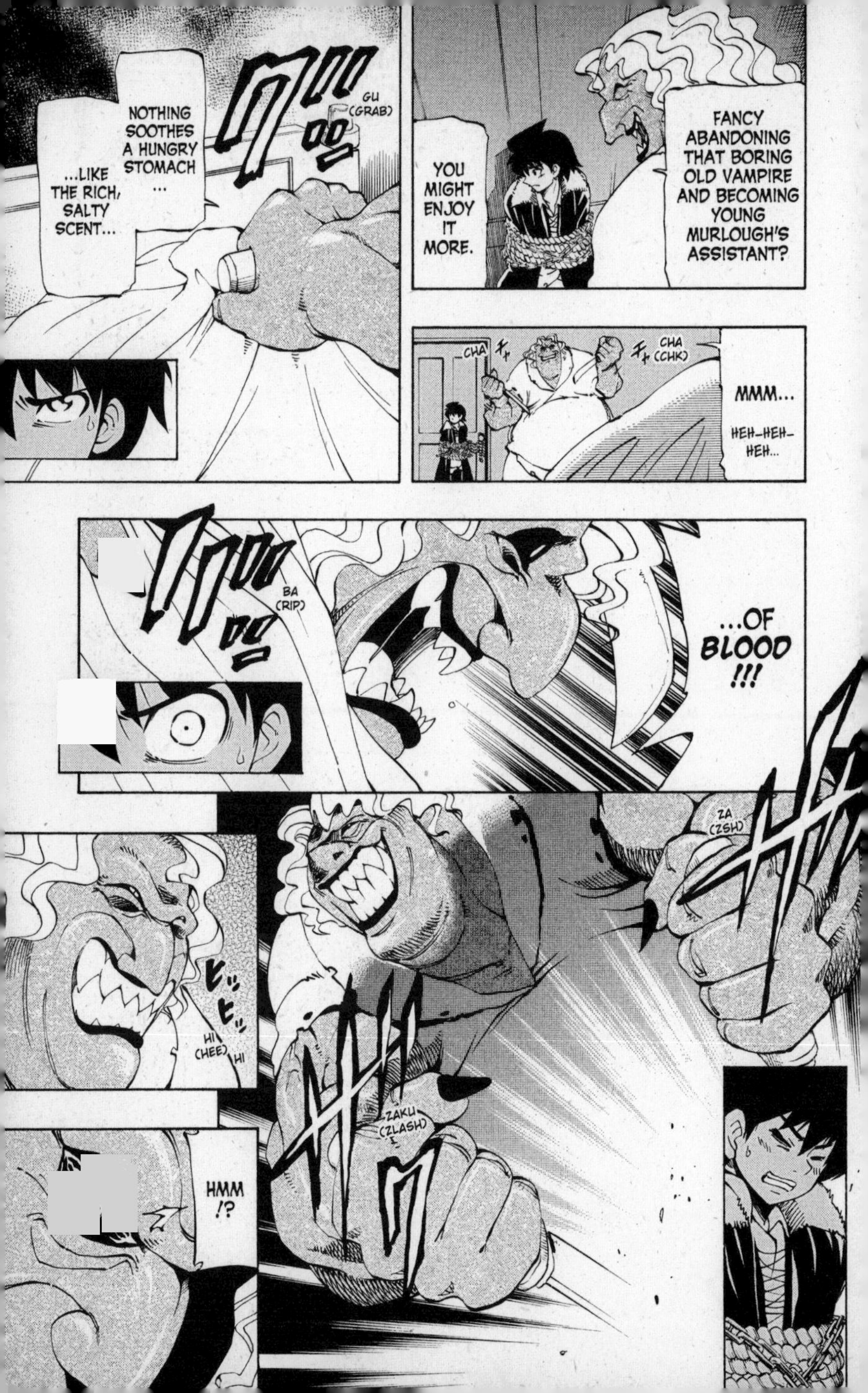
FANCY ABANDONING THAT BORING OLD VAMPIRE AND BECOMING YOUNG MURLOUGH'S ASSISTANT?
YOU MIGHT ENJOY IT MORE.
CHA (CHK)
CHA
MMM...
HEH-HEH-HEH...
GU (GRAB)
NOTHING SOOTHES A HUNGRY STOMACH ...
...LIKE THE RICH, SALTY SCENT...
...OF BLOOD !!!
BA (RIP)
ZA (ZSH)
ZAKU (ZLASH)
HI (CHEE) HI
HMM !?

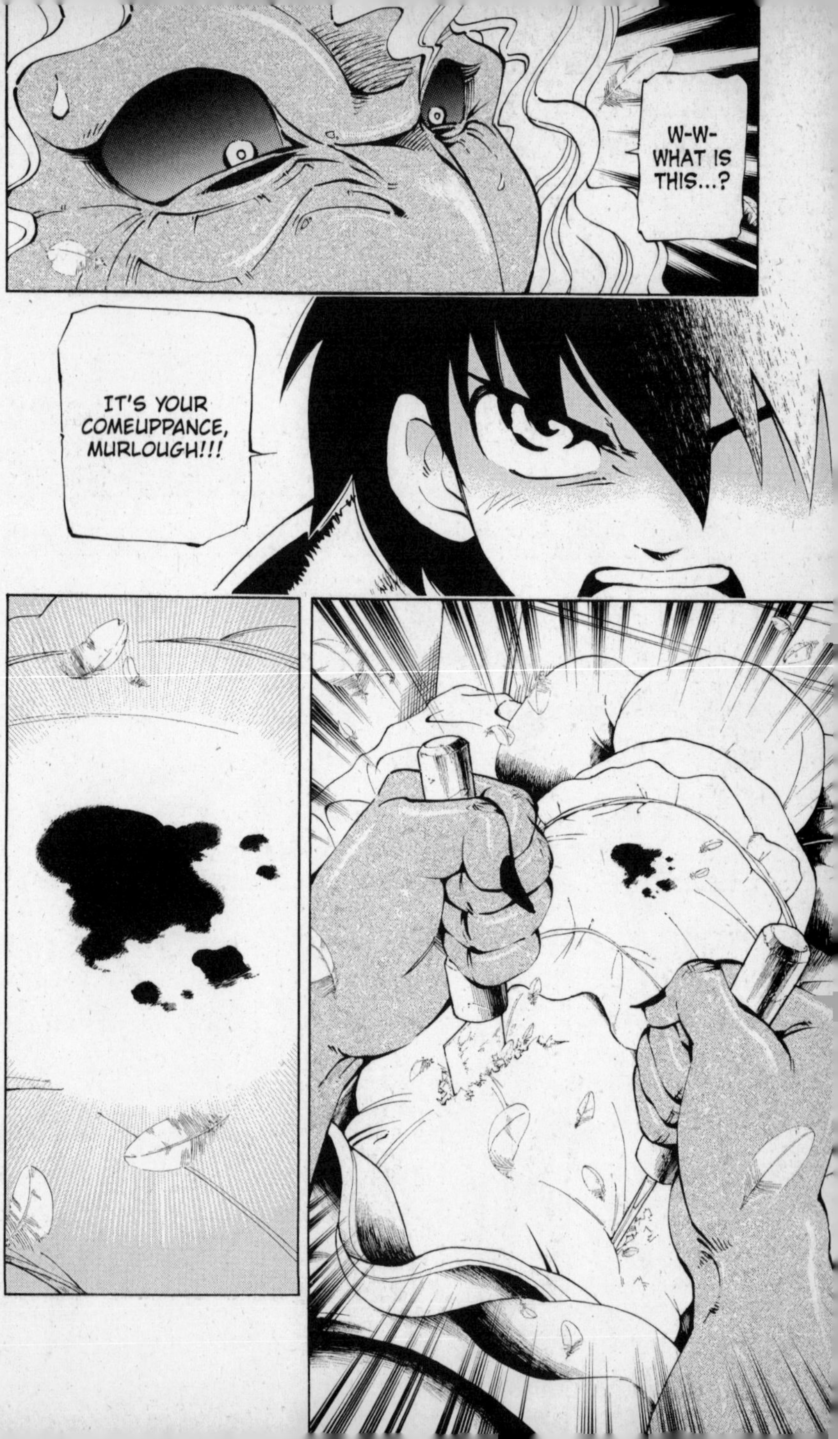
W-W-WHAT IS THIS...?
IT'S YOUR COMEUPPANCE, MURLOUGH!!!

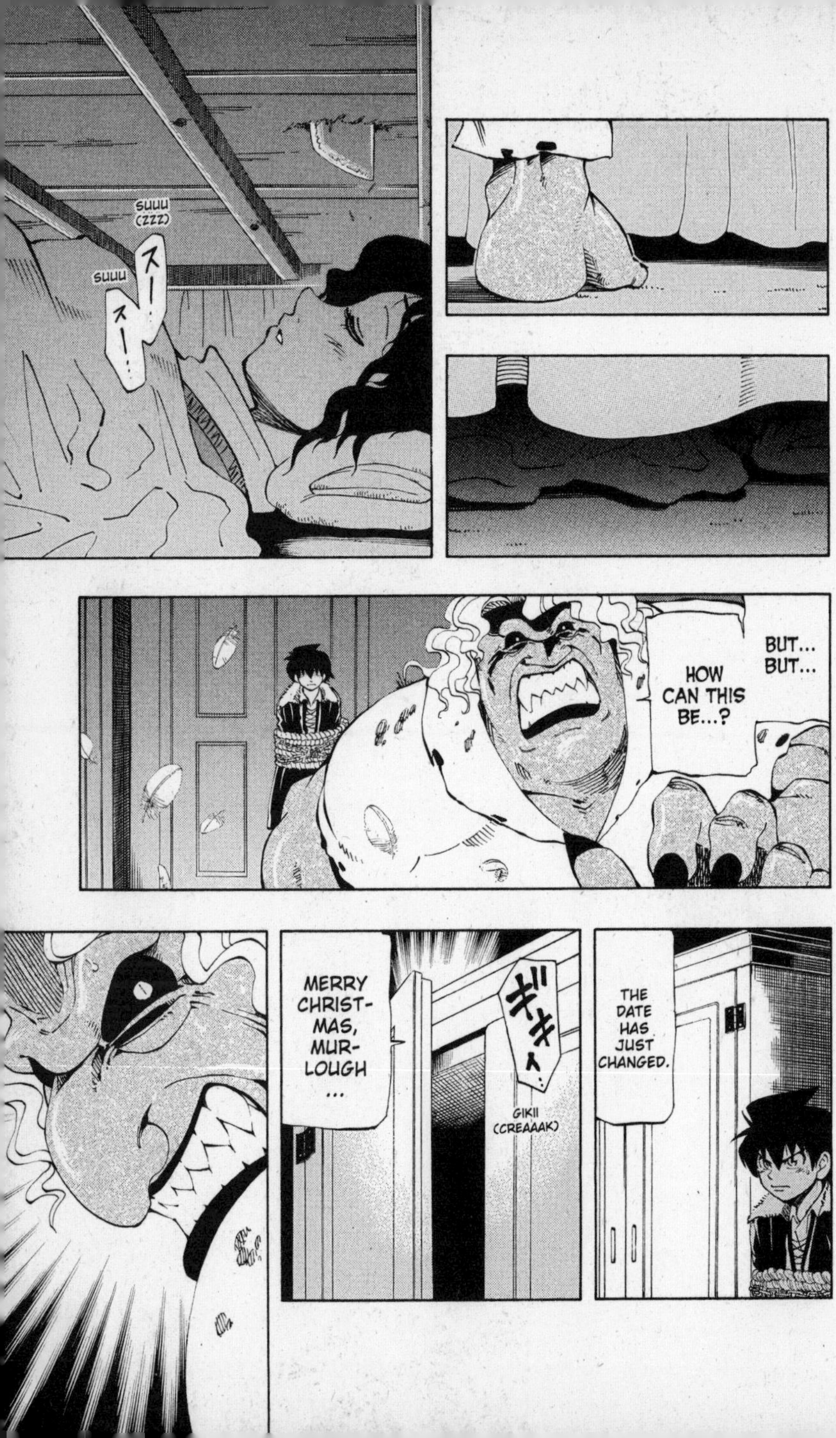
スー…
SUUU (ZZZ)
スー…
SUUU
BUT... BUT...
HOW CAN THIS BE...?
THE DATE HAS JUST CHANGED.
ギキィ…
GIKII (CREAAAK)
MERRY CHRIST-MAS, MUR-LOUGH ...

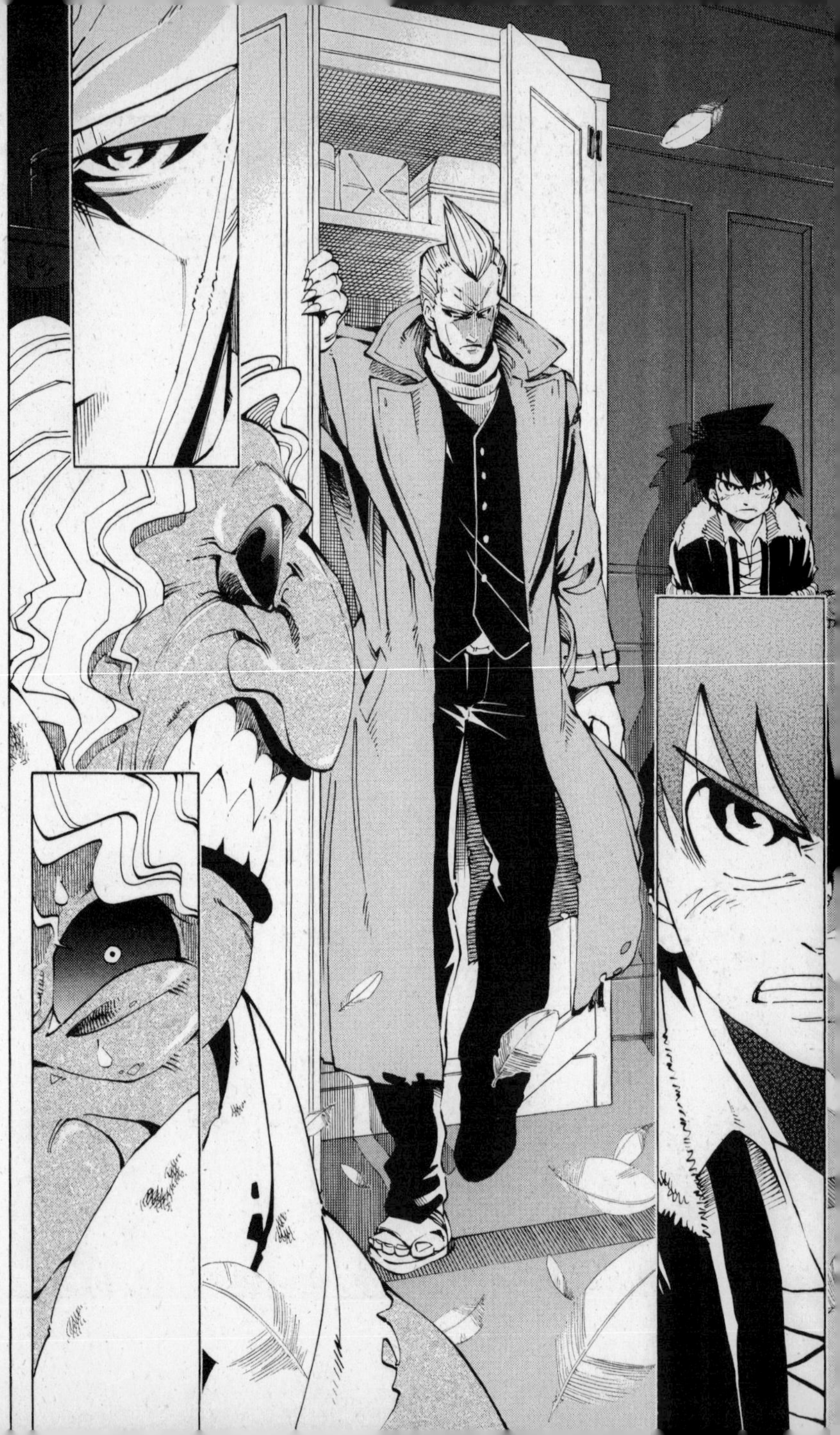

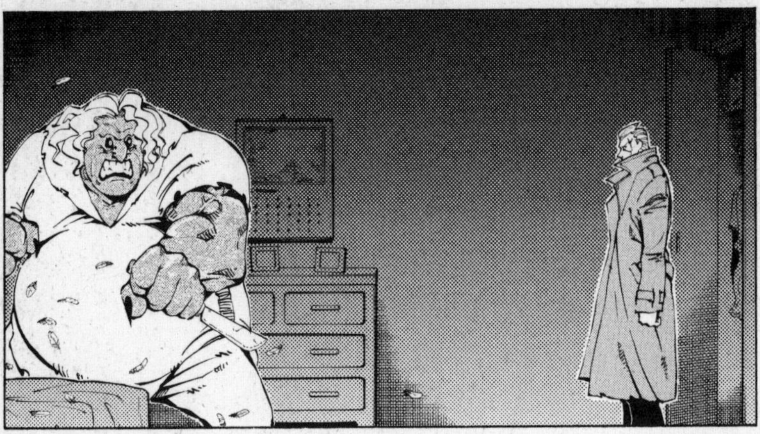

CHAPTER 24: BATTLE TO THE DEATH

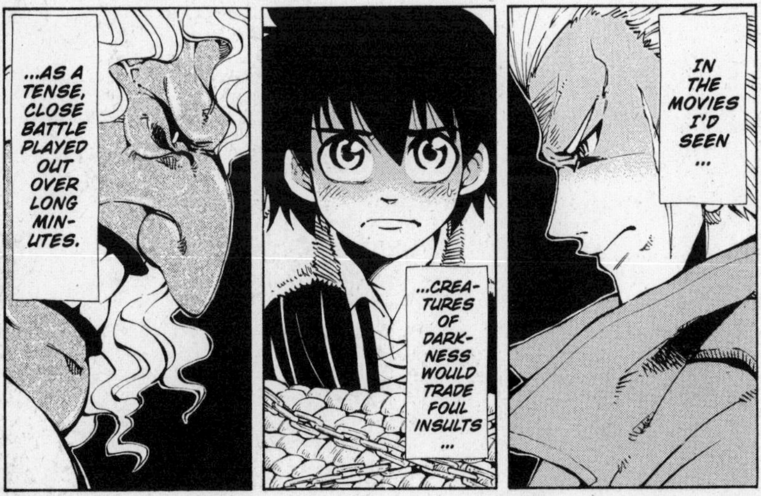
IN THE MOVIES I'D SEEN ...
...CREATURES OF DARKNESS WOULD TRADE FOUL INSULTS ...
...AS A TENSE, CLOSE BATTLE PLAYED OUT OVER LONG MINUTES.

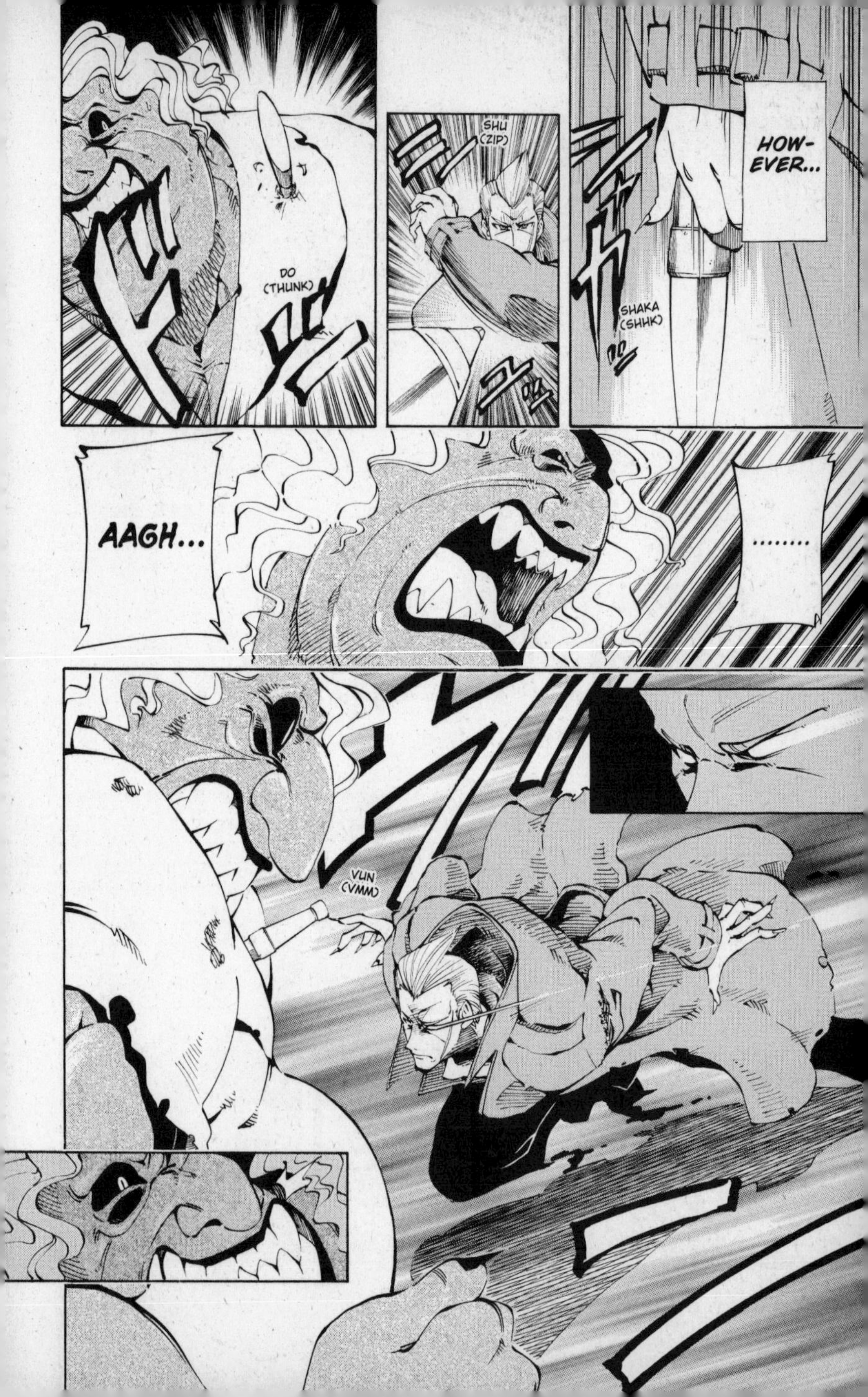
HOW-EVER...
SHAKA (SHHK)
SHU (ZIP)
DO (THUNK)
....
AAGH...
VUN (VMM)

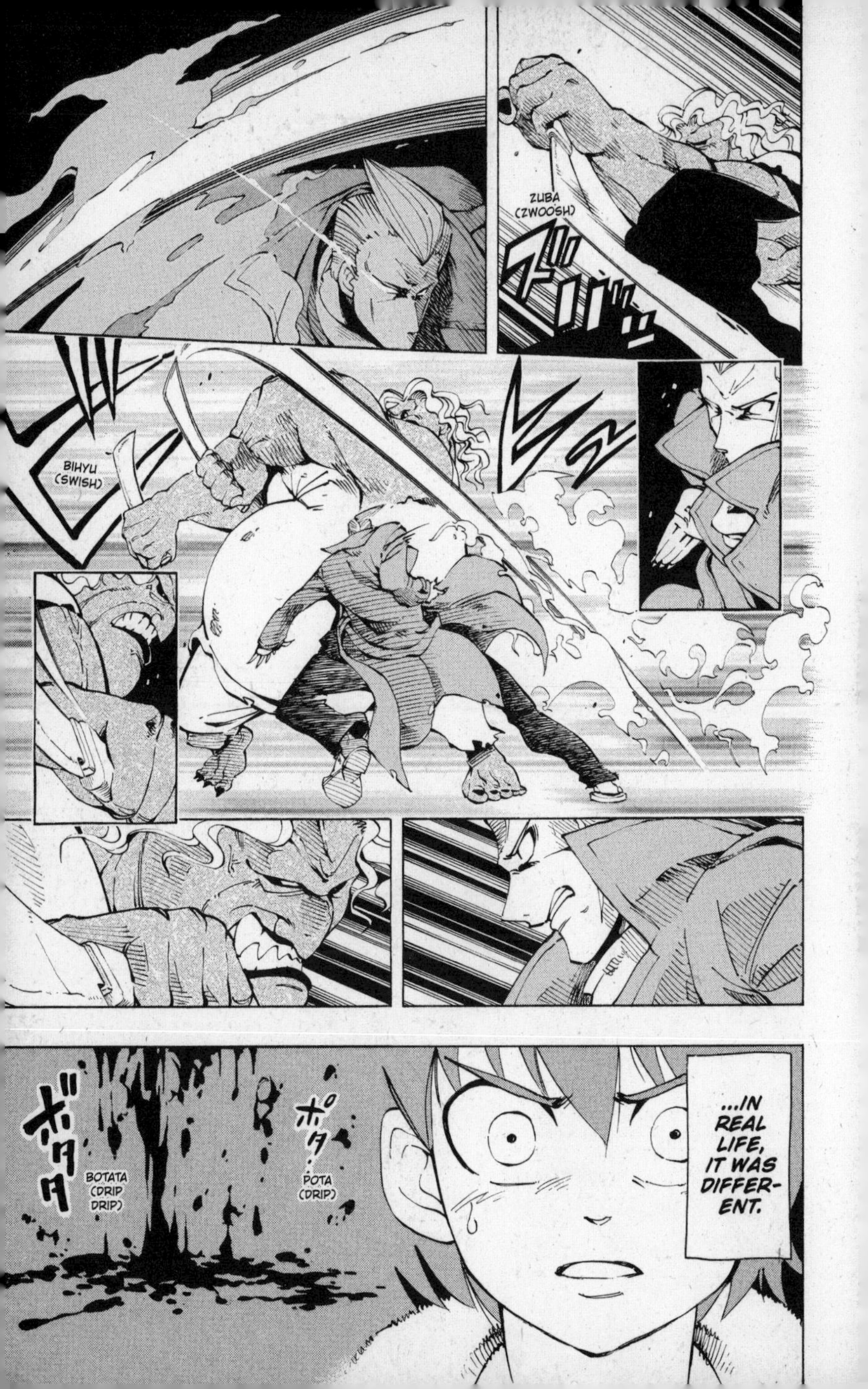
ZUBA
(ZWOOSH)
BIHYU
(SWISH)
...IN REAL LIFE, IT WAS DIFFERENT.
ポタ
POTA
(DRIP)
ボタタ
BOTATA
(DRIP DRIP)

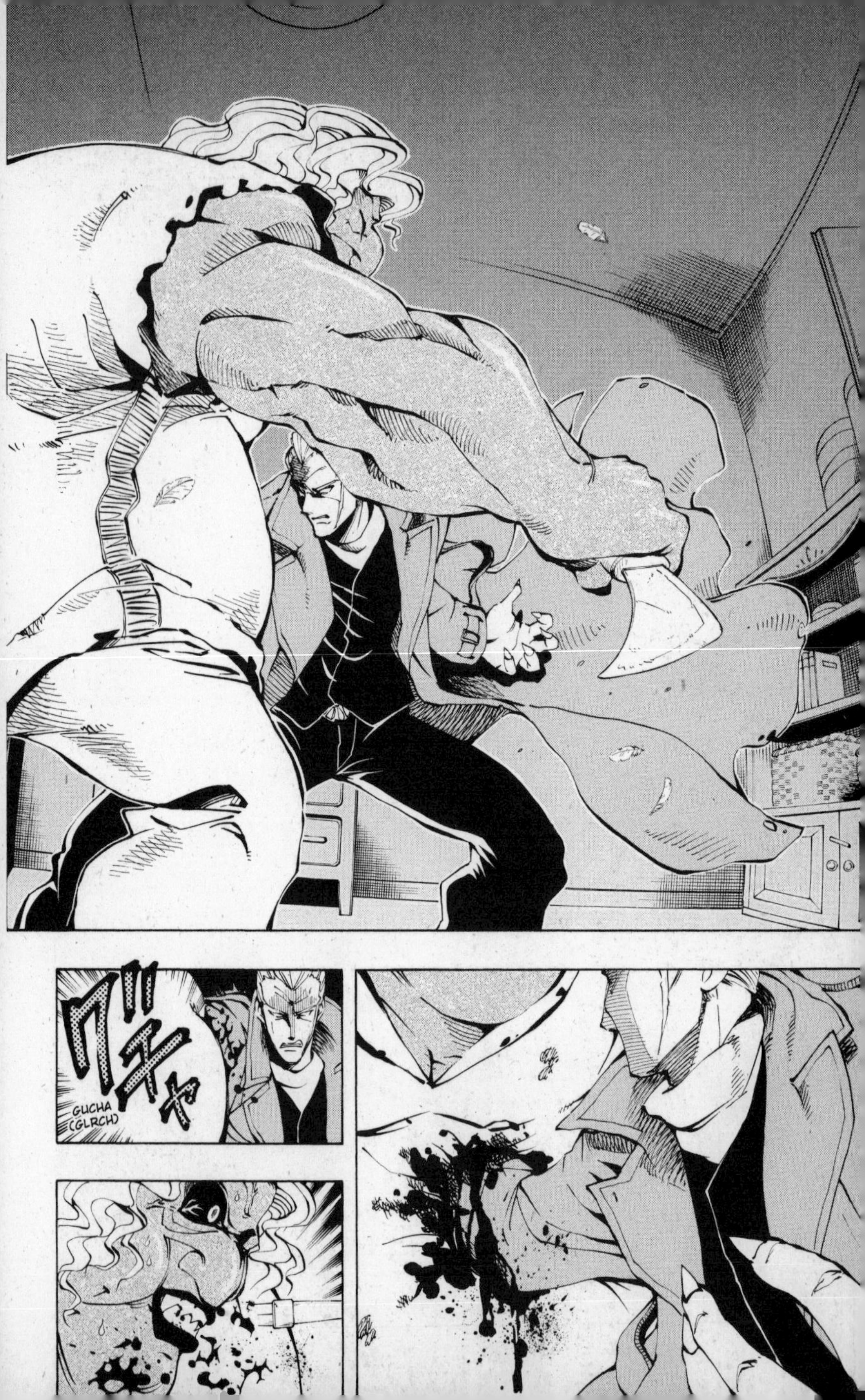
グチャ
GUCHA
(GLRCH)

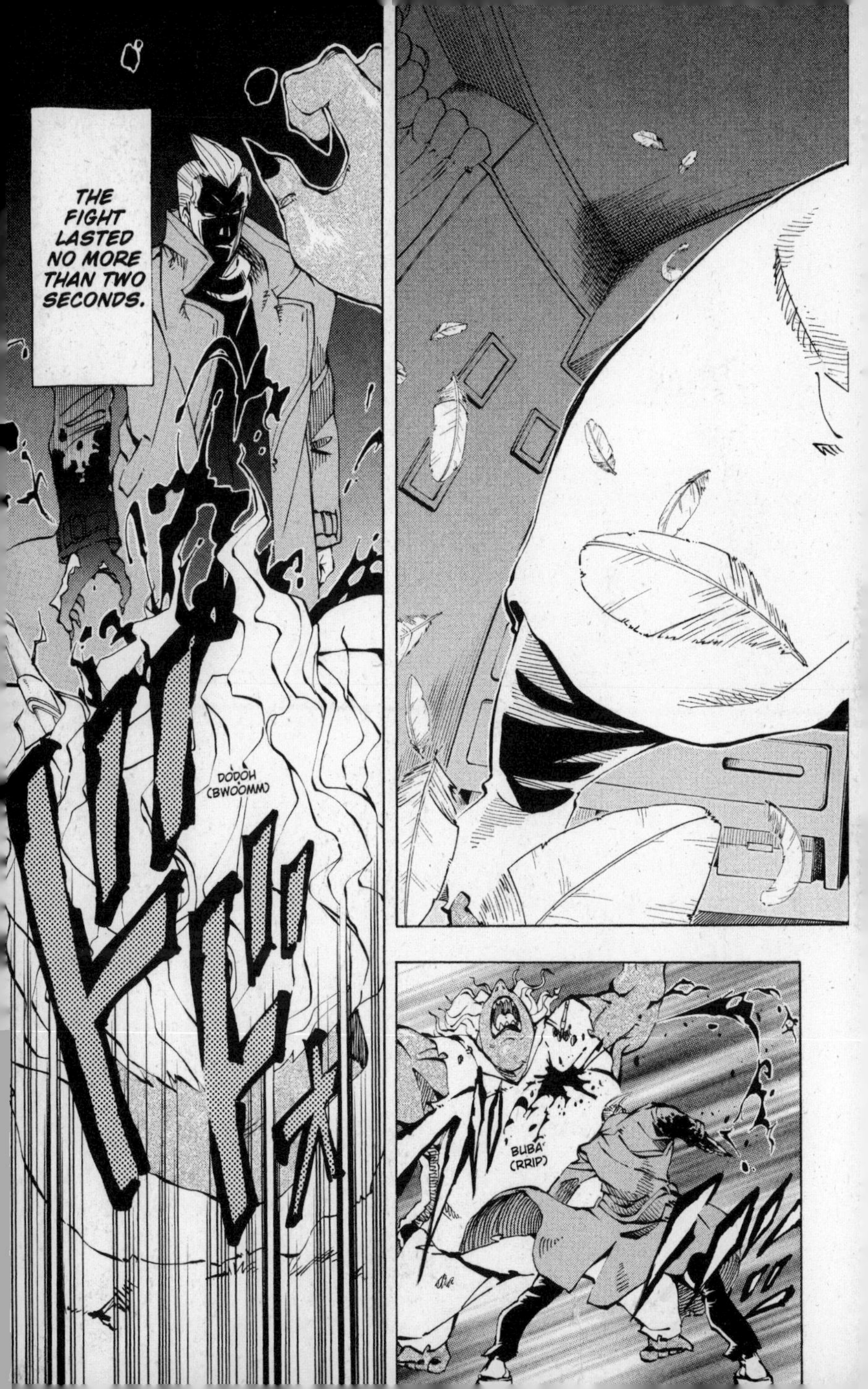
BUBA (RRIP)
THE FIGHT LASTED NO MORE THAN TWO SECONDS.
DODOH (BWOOMM)

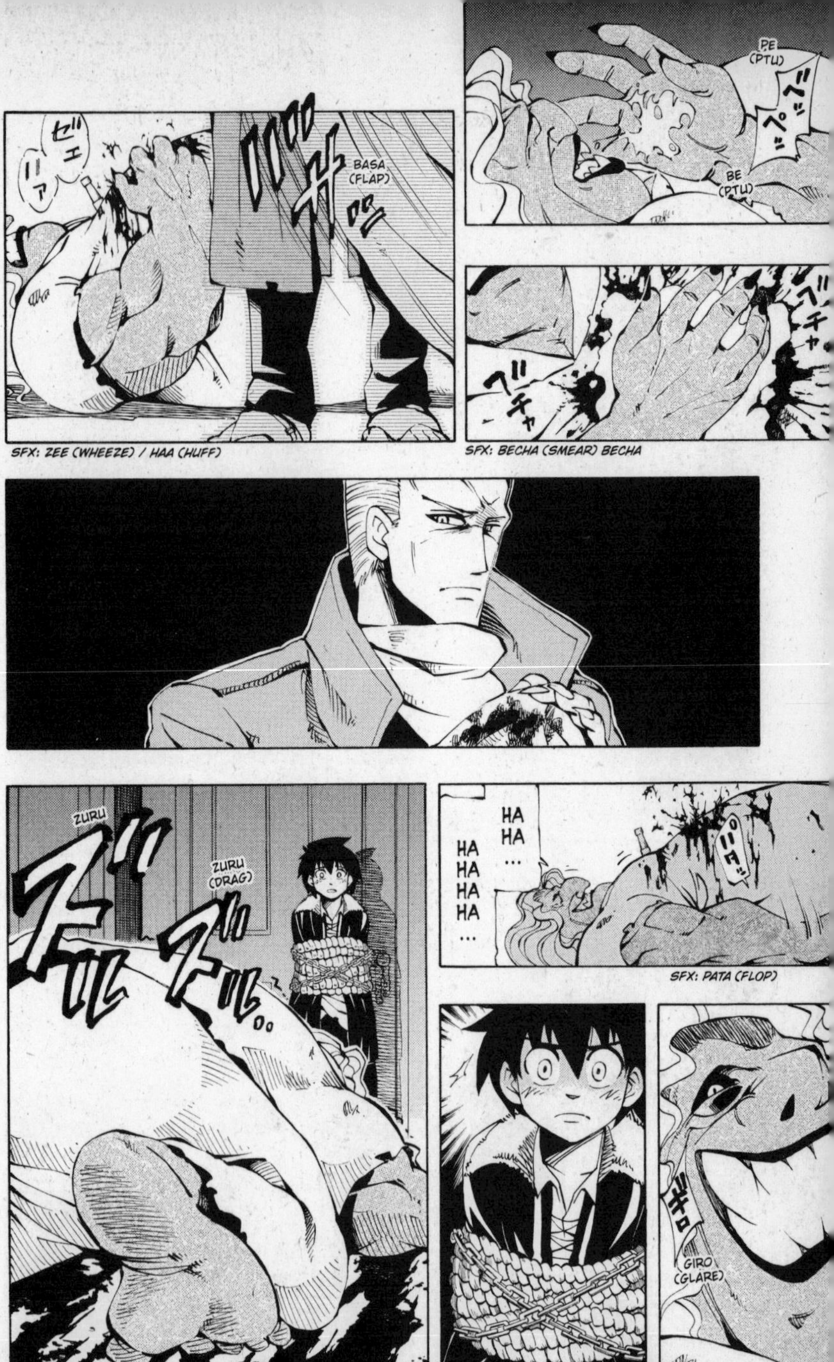
PE
(PTU)
BE
(PTU)
SFX: BECHA (SMEAR) BECHA
BASA
(FLAP)
SFX: ZEE (WHEEZE) / HAA (HUFF)
HA
HA
...
HA
HA
HA
HA
...
SFX: PATA (FLOP)
GIRO
(GLARE)
ZURU
ZURU
(DRAG)

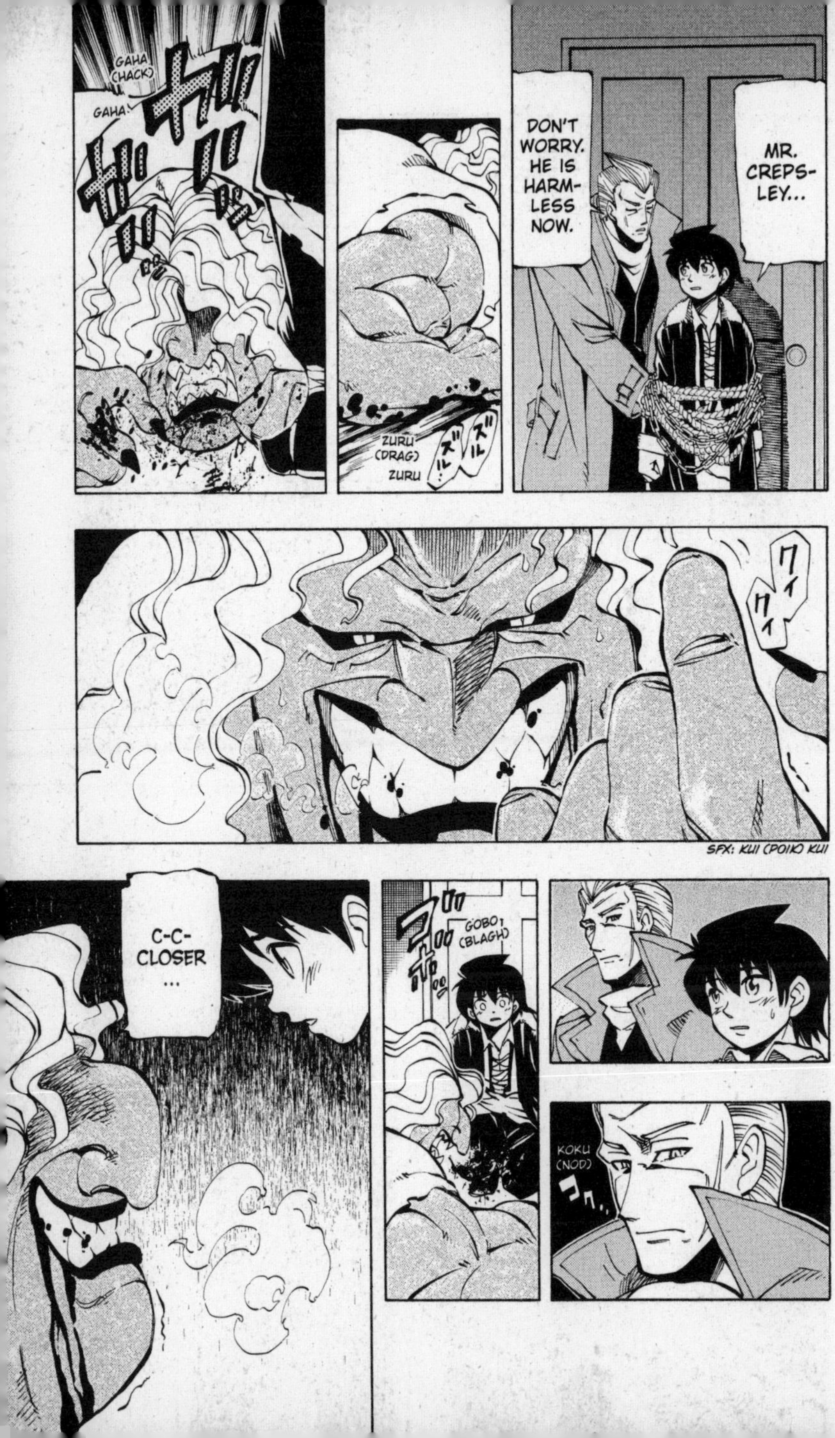
MR. CREPS-LEY...
DON'T WORRY. HE IS HARM-LESS NOW.
ZURU (DRAG) ZURU
GAHA (HACK) GAHA
SFX: KUI (POIK) KUI
KOKU (NOD)
GOBO (BLAGH)
C-C-CLOSER ...

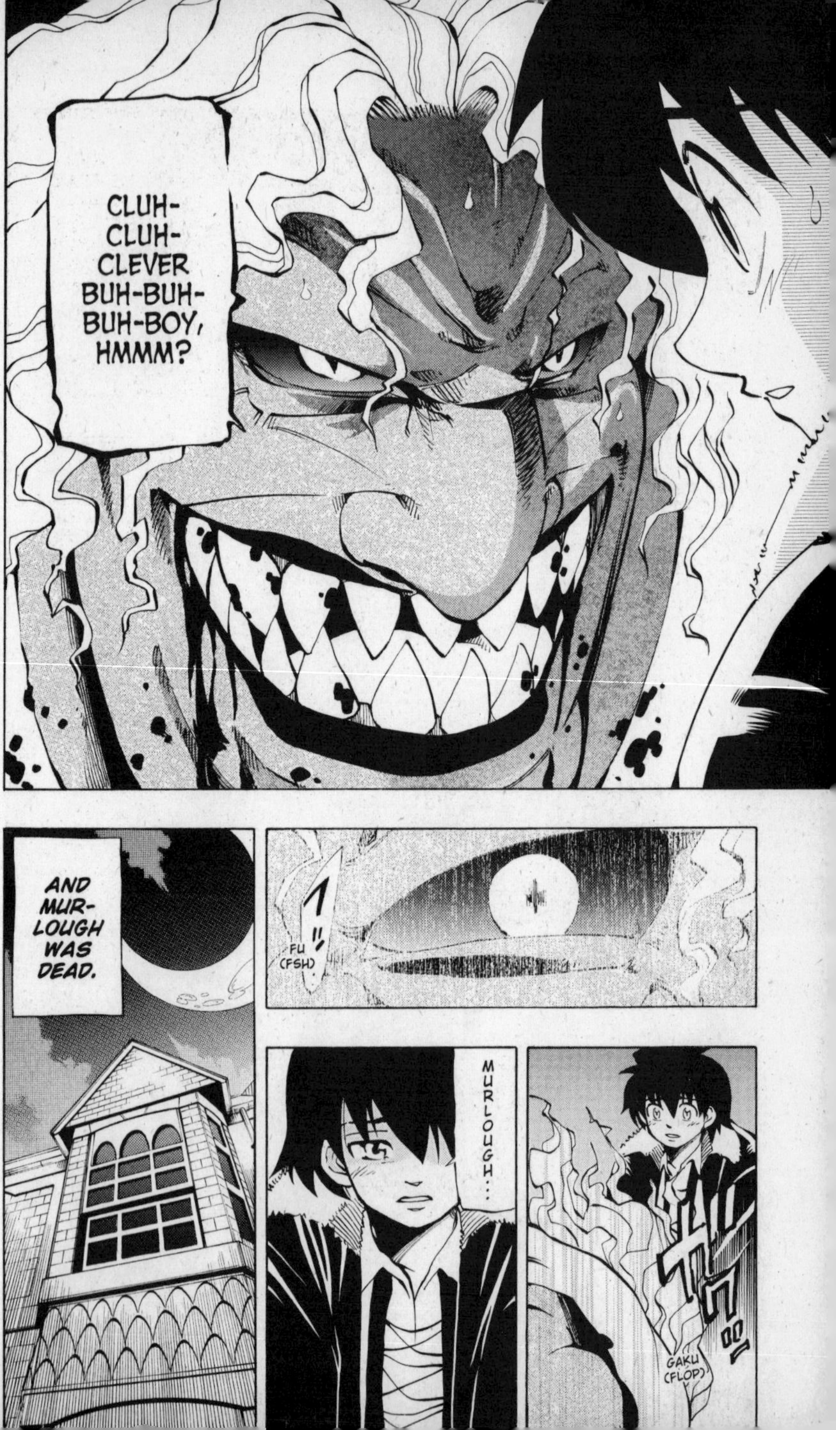
CLUH-CLUH-CLEVER BUH-BUH-BUH-BOY, HMMM?
FU (FSH)
GAKU (FLOP)
MURLOUGH...
AND MURLOUGH WAS DEAD.

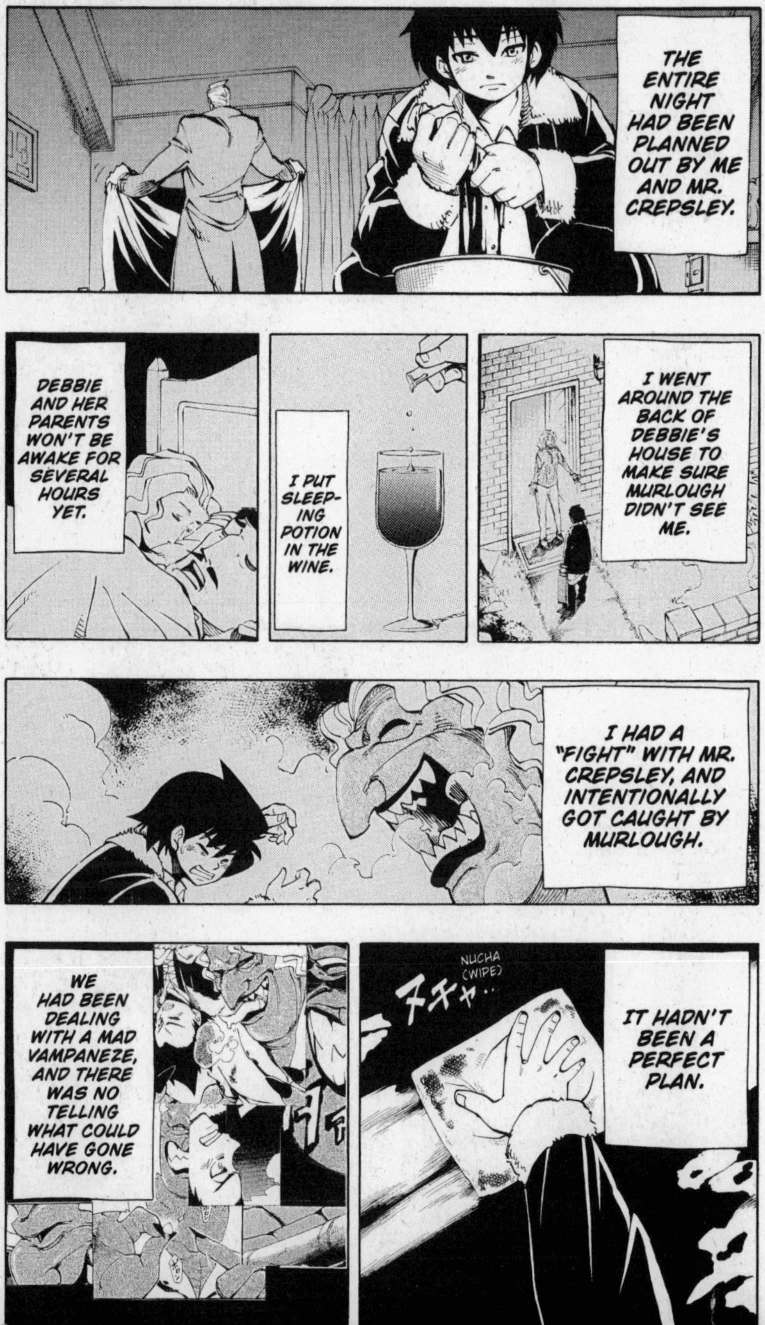
THE ENTIRE NIGHT HAD BEEN PLANNED OUT BY ME AND MR. CREPSLEY.
I WENT AROUND THE BACK OF DEBBIE'S HOUSE TO MAKE SURE MURLOUGH DIDN'T SEE ME.
I PUT SLEEP-ING POTION IN THE WINE.
DEBBIE AND HER PARENTS WON'T BE AWAKE FOR SEVERAL HOURS YET.
I HAD A "FIGHT" WITH MR. CREPSLEY, AND INTENTIONALLY GOT CAUGHT BY MURLOUGH.
IT HADN'T BEEN A PERFECT PLAN.
NUCHA (WIPE)
ヌチャ..
WE HAD BEEN DEALING WITH A MAD VAMPANEZE, AND THERE WAS NO TELLING WHAT COULD HAVE GONE WRONG.

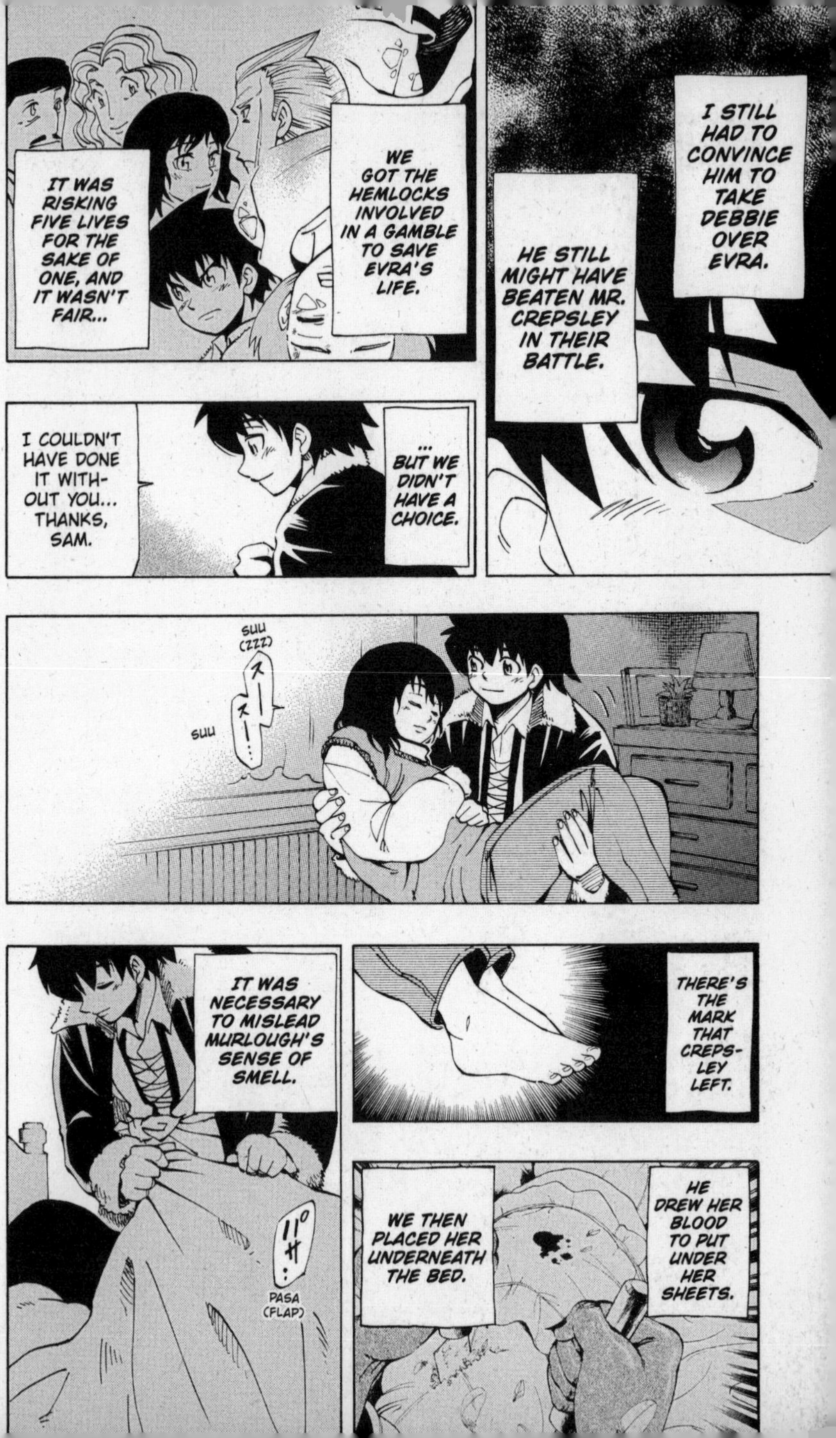
I STILL HAD TO CONVINCE HIM TO TAKE DEBBIE OVER EVRA.
HE STILL MIGHT HAVE BEATEN MR. CREPSLEY IN THEIR BATTLE.
WE GOT THE HEMLOCKS INVOLVED IN A GAMBLE TO SAVE EVRA'S LIFE.
IT WAS RISKING FIVE LIVES FOR THE SAKE OF ONE, AND IT WASN'T FAIR...
... BUT WE DIDN'T HAVE A CHOICE.
I COULDN'T HAVE DONE IT WITH-OUT YOU... THANKS, SAM.
SUU (ZZZ)
スー スー…
SUU
THERE'S THE MARK THAT CREPS-LEY LEFT.
HE DREW HER BLOOD TO PUT UNDER HER SHEETS.
WE THEN PLACED HER UNDERNEATH THE BED.
IT WAS NECESSARY TO MISLEAD MURLOUGH'S SENSE OF SMELL.
パサ…
PASA (FLAP)

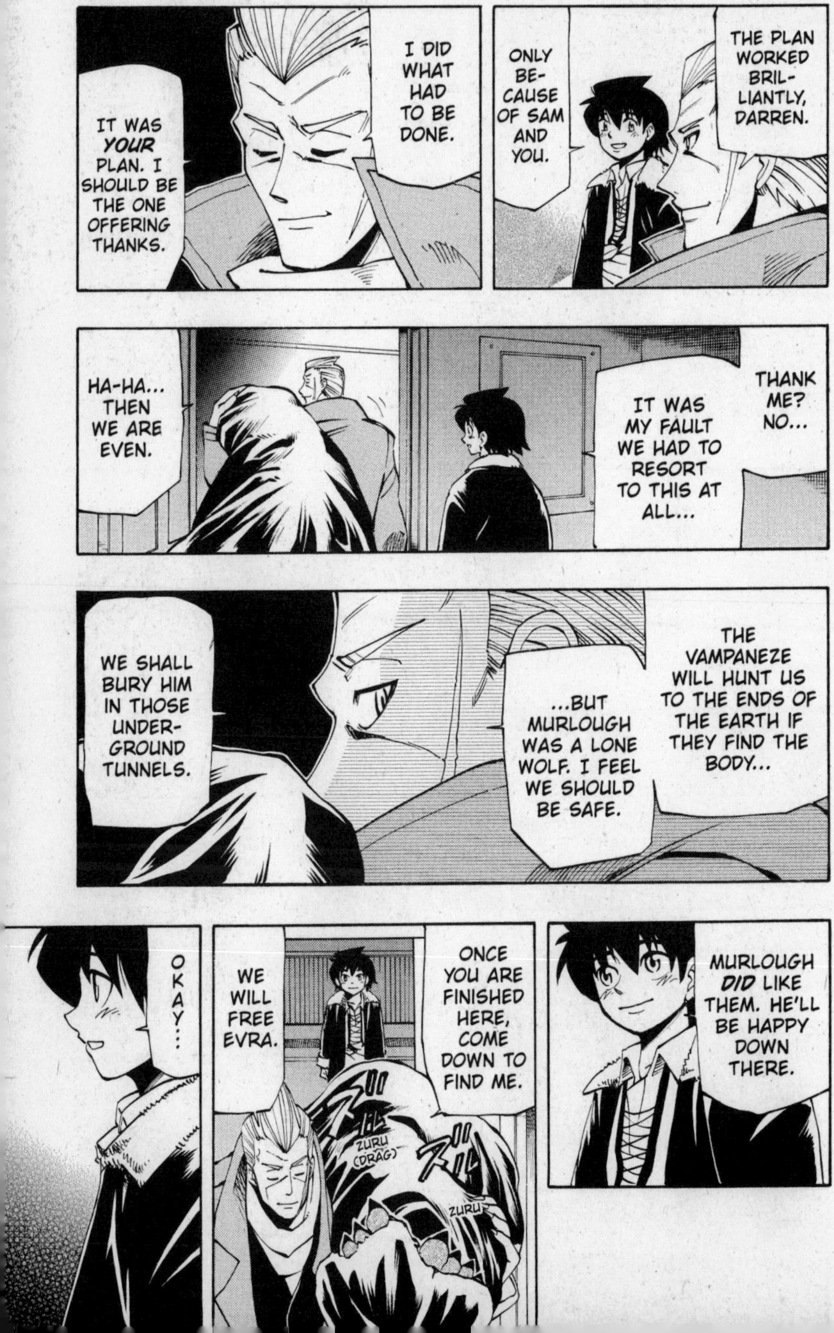
THE PLAN WORKED BRILLIANTLY, DARREN.
ONLY BECAUSE OF SAM AND YOU.
I DID WHAT HAD TO BE DONE.
IT WAS *YOUR* PLAN. I SHOULD BE THE ONE OFFERING THANKS.
THANK ME? NO...
IT WAS MY FAULT WE HAD TO RESORT TO THIS AT ALL...
HA-HA... THEN WE ARE EVEN.
THE VAMPANEZE WILL HUNT US TO THE ENDS OF THE EARTH IF THEY FIND THE BODY...
...BUT MURLOUGH WAS A LONE WOLF. I FEEL WE SHOULD BE SAFE.
WE SHALL BURY HIM IN THOSE UNDERGROUND TUNNELS.
MURLOUGH *DID* LIKE THEM. HE'LL BE HAPPY DOWN THERE.
ONCE YOU ARE FINISHED HERE, COME DOWN TO FIND ME.
WE WILL FREE EVRA.
ZURU (DRAG)
ZURU
OKAY...

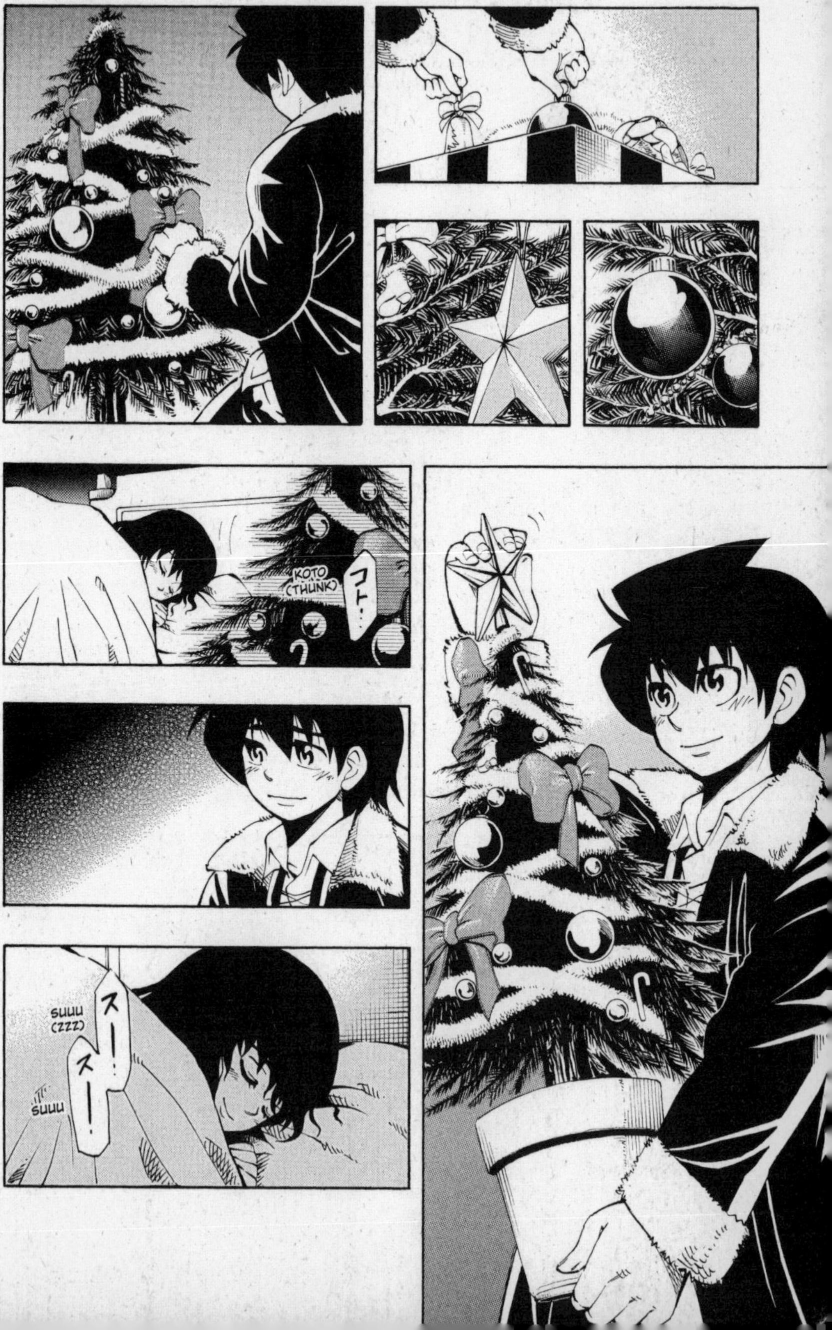
KOTO (THUNK)
コト…
SUUU (ZZZ)
スー!
SUUU
スー!

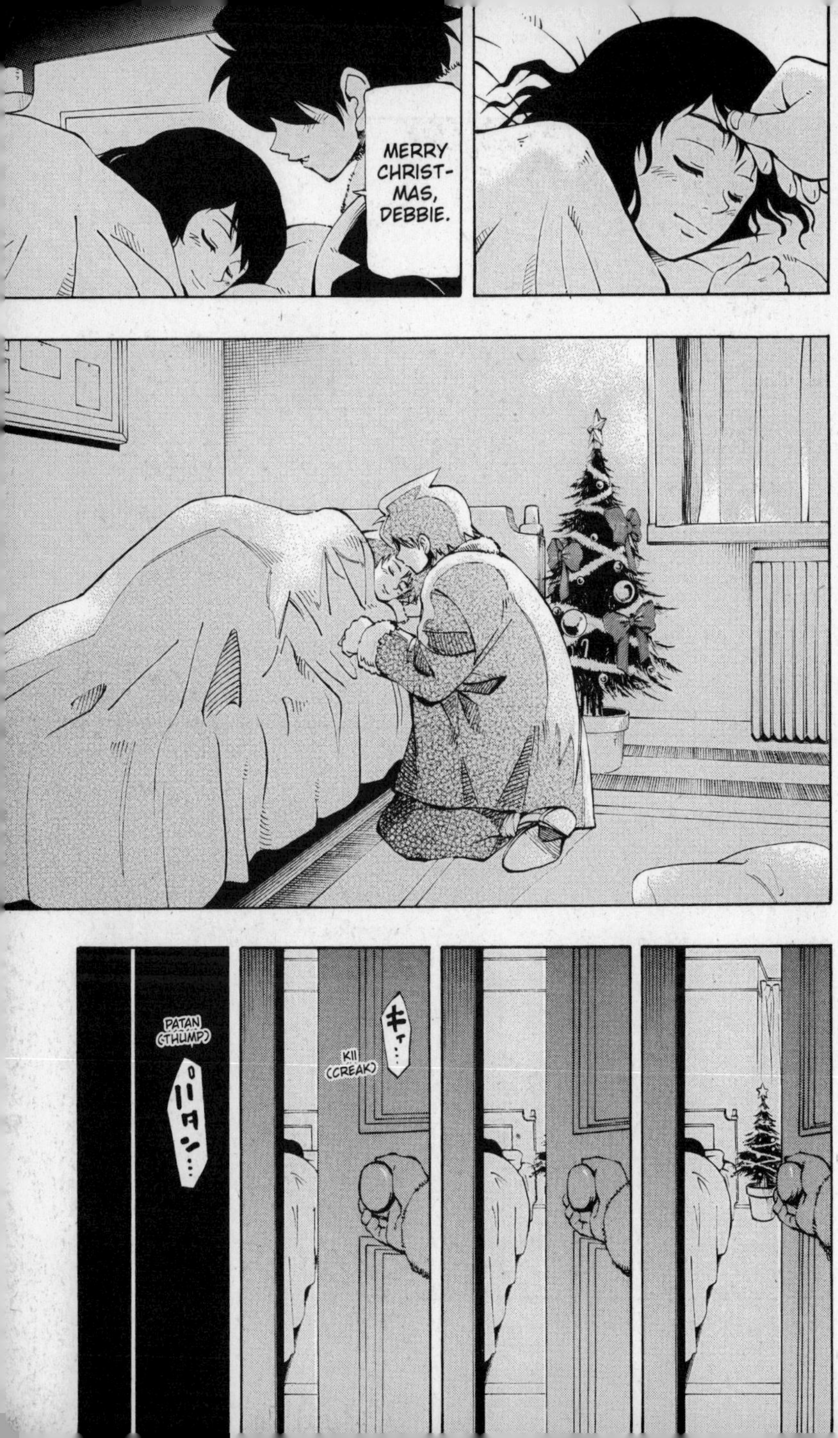
MERRY CHRIST-MAS, DEBBIE.
キィ…
KII (CREAK)
パタン…
PATAN (THUMP)

IT WASN'T RIGHT OF ME TO PUT YOU THROUGH THAT...

I'M SORRY, EVRA, I REALLY AM.

ムス
MUSU
(CHRMP)

GOTON
(TONK)

GATAN
(TANK)

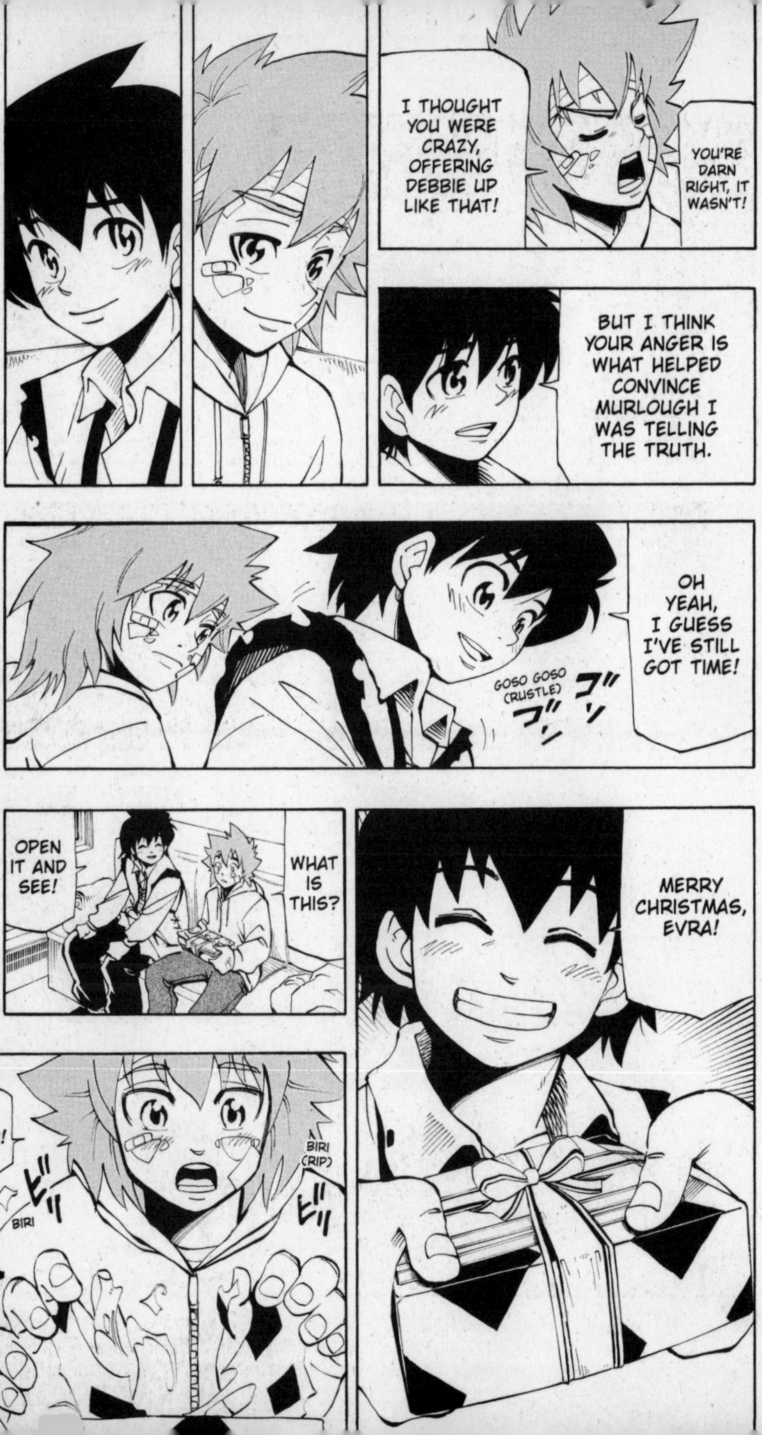
YOU'RE DARN RIGHT, IT WASN'T!
I THOUGHT YOU WERE CRAZY, OFFERING DEBBIE UP LIKE THAT!
BUT I THINK YOUR ANGER IS WHAT HELPED CONVINCE MURLOUGH I WAS TELLING THE TRUTH.
OH YEAH, I GUESS I'VE STILL GOT TIME!
ゴソゴソ
GOSO GOSO (RUSTLE)
MERRY CHRISTMAS, EVRA!
WHAT IS THIS?
OPEN IT AND SEE!
ビリ
BIRI (RIP)
OH!
ビリ
BIRI

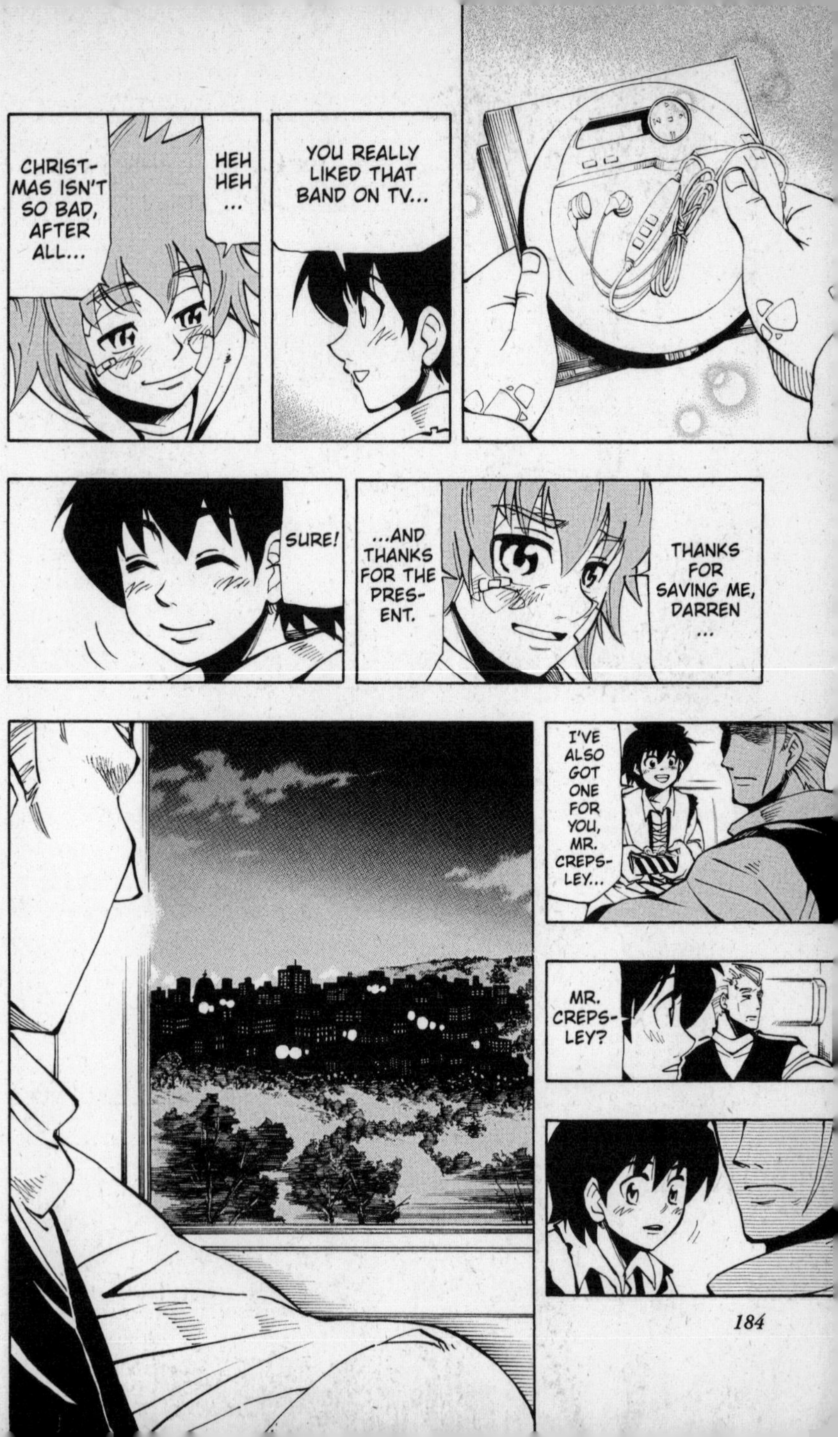
YOU REALLY LIKED THAT BAND ON TV...
HEH HEH ...
CHRISTMAS ISN'T SO BAD, AFTER ALL...
THANKS FOR SAVING ME, DARREN ...
...AND THANKS FOR THE PRESENT.
SURE!
I'VE ALSO GOT ONE FOR YOU, MR. CREPSLEY...
MR. CREPSLEY?

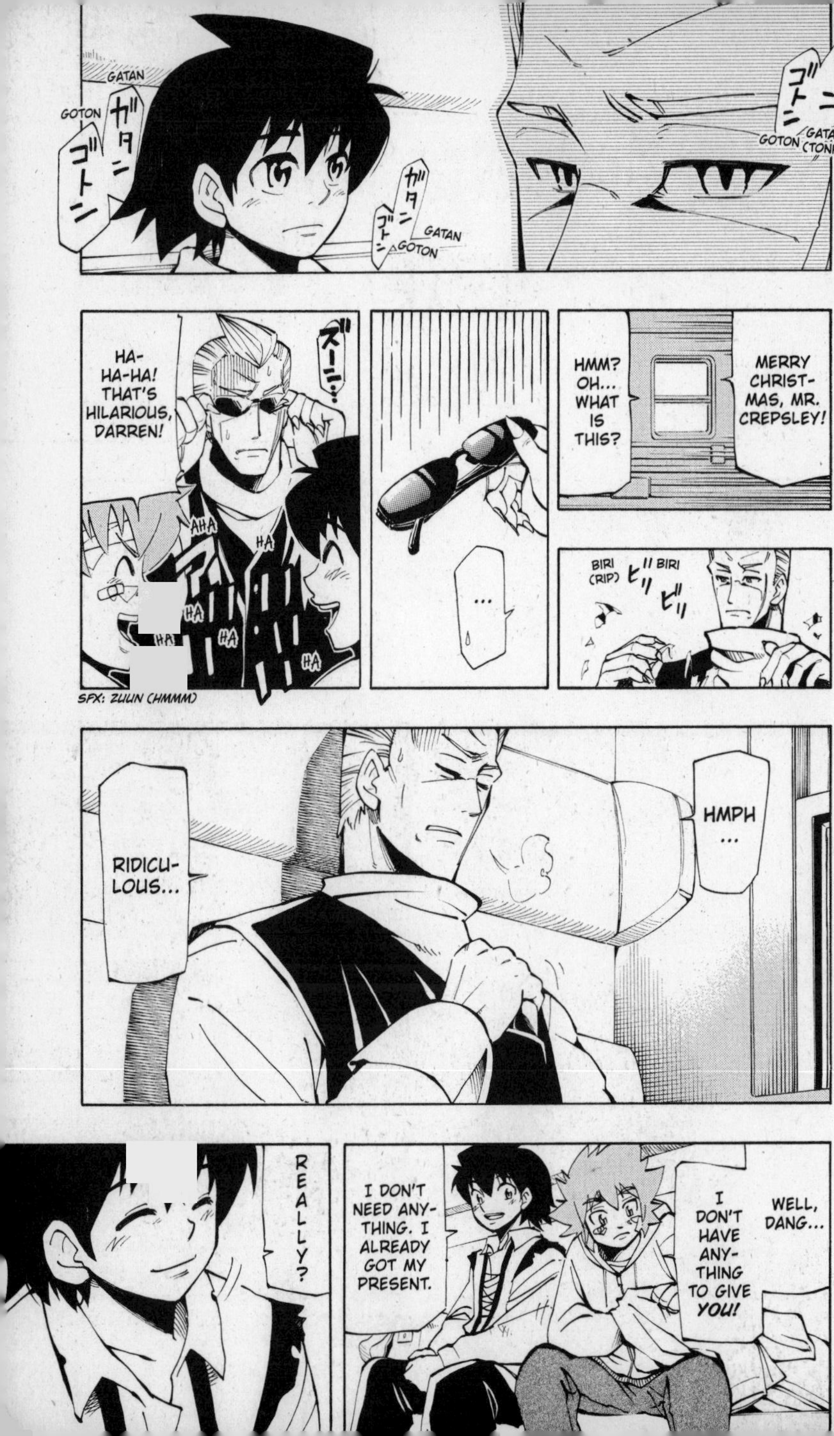
ガタンゴトン
GATAN
GOTON (TONK)
GATAN
GOTON
ガタンゴトン
ガタンゴトン
GATAN
GOTON
MERRY CHRISTMAS, MR. CREPSLEY!
HMM? OH... WHAT IS THIS?
BIRI (RIP) ビリ
ビリ BIRI
...
ズーン
HA-HA-HA! THAT'S HILARIOUS, DARREN!
AHA HA HA HA HA HA
SFX: ZUUN (HMMM)
HMPH...
RIDICULOUS...
WELL, DANG...
I DON'T HAVE ANYTHING TO GIVE *YOU!*
I DON'T NEED ANYTHING. I ALREADY GOT MY PRESENT.
REALLY?

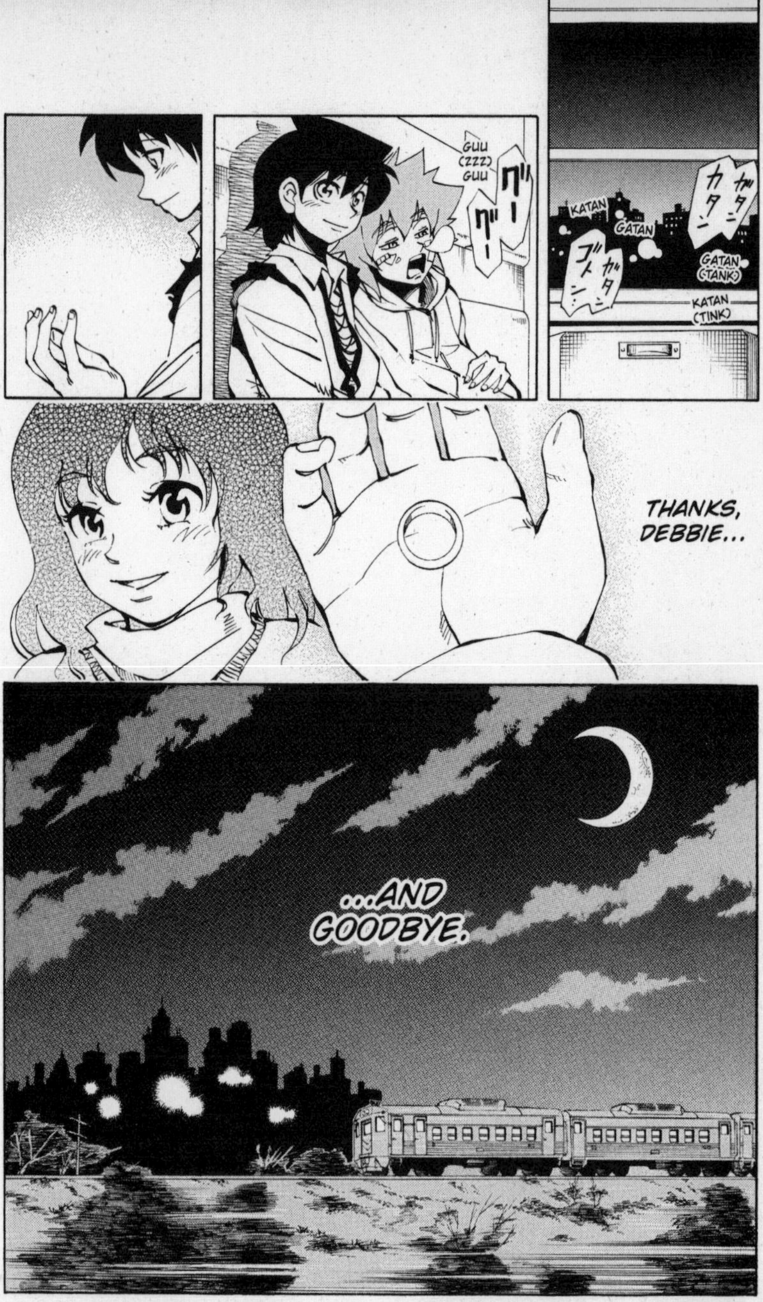
GATAN (TANK)
KATAN (TINK)
KATAN
GATAN
GUU (ZZZ) GUU
THANKS, DEBBIE...
...AND GOODBYE.

CIRQUE DU FREAK 3 - END

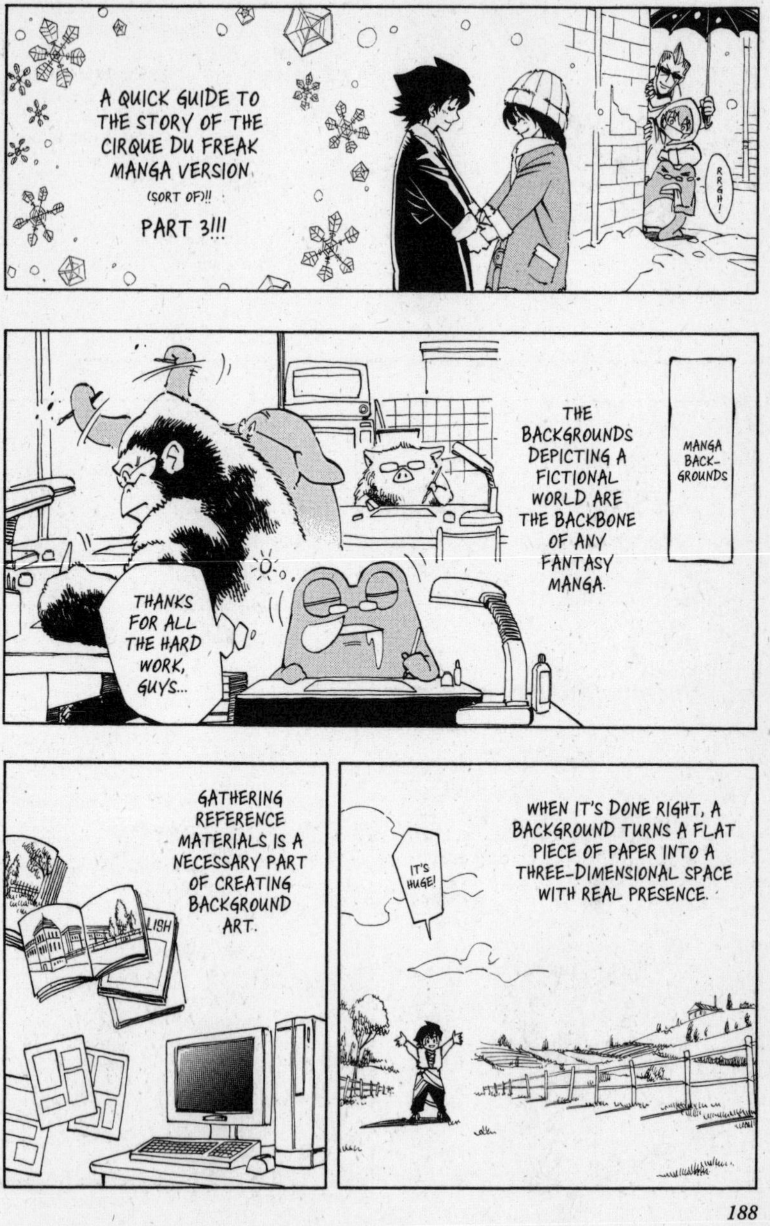
A QUICK GUIDE TO THE STORY OF THE CIRQUE DU FREAK MANGA VERSION
(SORT OF)!!
PART 3!!!
RRGH!
MANGA BACKGROUNDS
THE BACKGROUNDS DEPICTING A FICTIONAL WORLD ARE THE BACKBONE OF ANY FANTASY MANGA.
THANKS FOR ALL THE HARD WORK, GUYS...
WHEN IT'S DONE RIGHT, A BACKGROUND TURNS A FLAT PIECE OF PAPER INTO A THREE-DIMENSIONAL SPACE WITH REAL PRESENCE.
IT'S HUGE!
GATHERING REFERENCE MATERIALS IS A NECESSARY PART OF CREATING BACKGROUND ART.

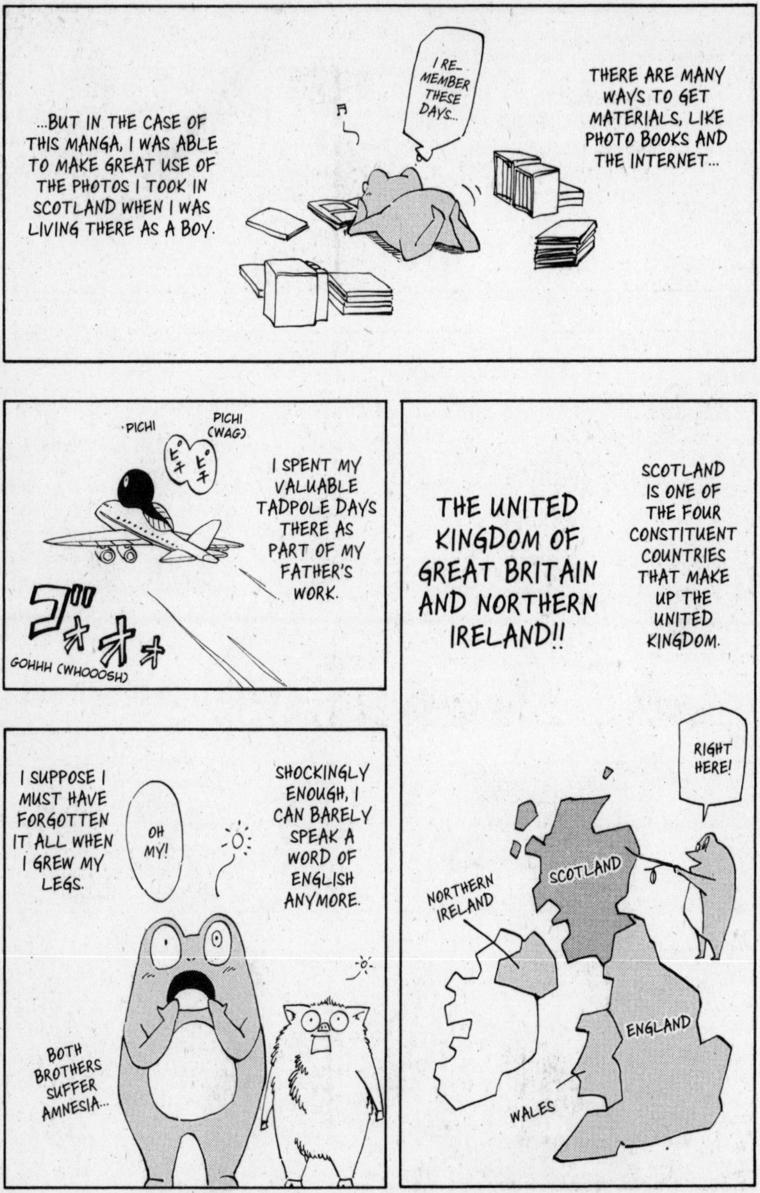
THERE ARE MANY WAYS TO GET MATERIALS, LIKE PHOTO BOOKS AND THE INTERNET...
I RE-MEMBER THESE DAYS...
...BUT IN THE CASE OF THIS MANGA, I WAS ABLE TO MAKE GREAT USE OF THE PHOTOS I TOOK IN SCOTLAND WHEN I WAS LIVING THERE AS A BOY.
SCOTLAND IS ONE OF THE FOUR CONSTITUENT COUNTRIES THAT MAKE UP THE UNITED KINGDOM.
THE UNITED KINGDOM OF GREAT BRITAIN AND NORTHERN IRELAND!!
RIGHT HERE!
SCOTLAND
NORTHERN IRELAND
ENGLAND
WALES
I SPENT MY VALUABLE TADPOLE DAYS THERE AS PART OF MY FATHER'S WORK.
PICHI (WAG)
ピチ ピチ
PICHI
GOHHH (WHOOOSH)
SHOCKINGLY ENOUGH, I CAN BARELY SPEAK A WORD OF ENGLISH ANYMORE.
OH MY!
I SUPPOSE I MUST HAVE FORGOTTEN IT ALL WHEN I GREW MY LEGS.
BOTH BROTHERS SUFFER AMNESIA...

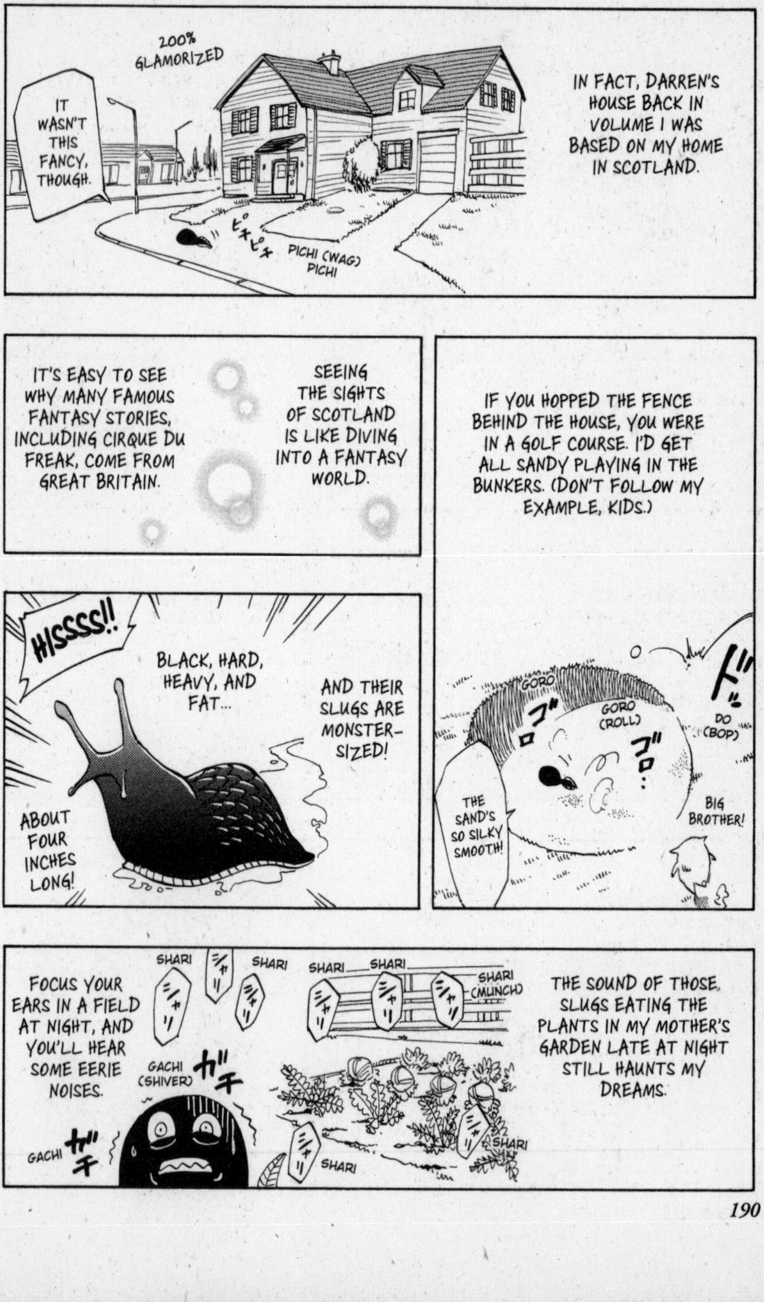
IN FACT, DARREN'S HOUSE BACK IN VOLUME 1 WAS BASED ON MY HOME IN SCOTLAND.
200% GLAMORIZED
IT WASN'T THIS FANCY, THOUGH.
ピチピチ
PICHI (WAG) PICHI
IF YOU HOPPED THE FENCE BEHIND THE HOUSE, YOU WERE IN A GOLF COURSE. I'D GET ALL SANDY PLAYING IN THE BUNKERS. (DON'T FOLLOW MY EXAMPLE, KIDS.)
DO (BOP)
GORO
GORO (ROLL)
BIG BROTHER!
THE SAND'S SO SILKY SMOOTH!
SEEING THE SIGHTS OF SCOTLAND IS LIKE DIVING INTO A FANTASY WORLD.
IT'S EASY TO SEE WHY MANY FAMOUS FANTASY STORIES, INCLUDING CIRQUE DU FREAK, COME FROM GREAT BRITAIN.
AND THEIR SLUGS ARE MONSTER-SIZED!
BLACK, HARD, HEAVY, AND FAT...
HISSSS!!
ABOUT FOUR INCHES LONG!
THE SOUND OF THOSE SLUGS EATING THE PLANTS IN MY MOTHER'S GARDEN LATE AT NIGHT STILL HAUNTS MY DREAMS.
SHARI (MUNCH)
SHARI
SHARI
SHARI
SHARI
SHARI
SHARI
FOCUS YOUR EARS IN A FIELD AT NIGHT, AND YOU'LL HEAR SOME EERIE NOISES.
GACHI (SHIVER)
GACHI

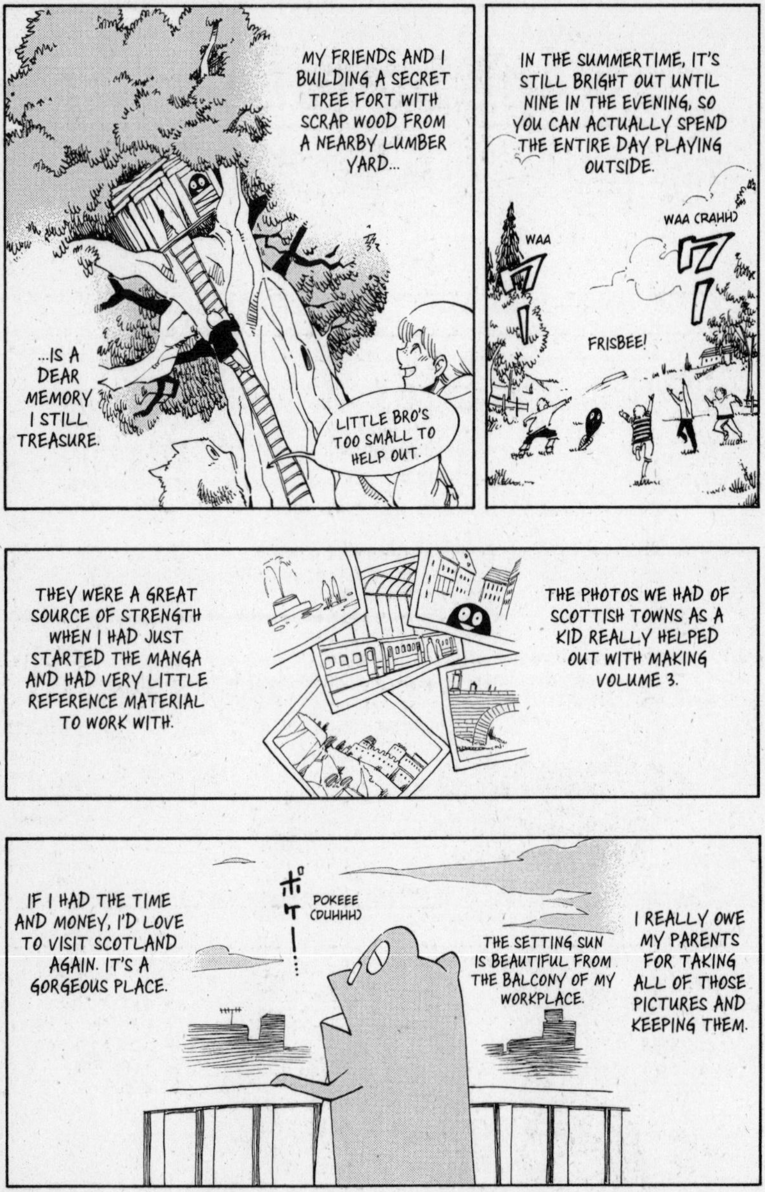

IN THE SUMMERTIME, IT'S STILL BRIGHT OUT UNTIL NINE IN THE EVENING, SO YOU CAN ACTUALLY SPEND THE ENTIRE DAY PLAYING OUTSIDE.
ワー
WAA (RAHH)
ワー
WAA
FRISBEE!
MY FRIENDS AND I BUILDING A SECRET TREE FORT WITH SCRAP WOOD FROM A NEARBY LUMBER YARD...
...IS A DEAR MEMORY I STILL TREASURE.
LITTLE BRO'S TOO SMALL TO HELP OUT.
THE PHOTOS WE HAD OF SCOTTISH TOWNS AS A KID REALLY HELPED OUT WITH MAKING VOLUME 3.
THEY WERE A GREAT SOURCE OF STRENGTH WHEN I HAD JUST STARTED THE MANGA AND HAD VERY LITTLE REFERENCE MATERIAL TO WORK WITH.
I REALLY OWE MY PARENTS FOR TAKING ALL OF THOSE PICTURES AND KEEPING THEM.
THE SETTING SUN IS BEAUTIFUL FROM THE BALCONY OF MY WORKPLACE.
ポケー…
POKEEE (DUHHH)
IF I HAD THE TIME AND MONEY, I'D LOVE TO VISIT SCOTLAND AGAIN. IT'S A GORGEOUS PLACE.

The End

CIRQUE DU FREAK ③

DARREN SHAN
TAKAHIRO ARAI

Translation: Stephen Paul　　•　　Lettering: AndWorld Design
Original Cover Design: Hitoshi SHIRAYAMA + Bay Bridge Studio

Yen Press
Hachette Book Group
237 Park Avenue, New York, NY 10017

Visit our websites at www.HachetteBookGroup.com and www.YenPress.com.

Yen Press is an imprint of Hachette Book Group, Inc. The Yen Press name and logo are trademarks of Hachette Book Group, Inc.

First Yen Press Edition: October 2009

ISBN: 978-0-7595-3043-0

10 9 8 7 6 5 4 3

BVG

Printed in the United States of America